DICTIONARY OF MIXED TELUGU

DICTIONARY
OF
MIXED TELUGU

ALSO AN

EXPLANATION OF THE TELUGU ALPHABET.

CHARLES PHILIP BROWN

GYAN

Published by

Gyan Publishing House
5, Ansari Road
Daryaganj, New Delhi-110002
Phone: 011-47034999, 9811692060
E-mail: books@gyanbooks.com

Distribution Network
gyanbooks.com
India, USA, Canada, UK, Australia, France

ISBN : 978-81-212-4295-0 (PB)
First Published, 1854

2nd Impression 2020

Printed at: Gyan Press, Delhi.

బ్రౌణ్య

మిశ్రభాషా

నిఘంటు

DICTIONARY

OF MIXED TELUGU.

ALSO AN

EXPLANATION OF THE TELUGU ALPHABET.

MADRAS:

PRINTED AT THE CHRISTIAN KNOWLEDGE SOCIETY'S PRESS,

CHURCH STREET, VEPERY.

1854.

WORKS PUBLISHED BY MR. BROWN.

A Grammar of the Telugu Language. First edition, 1840.

English-Telugu Dictionary.

Telugu-English Dictionary.

Dictionary of Mixed Telugu, and the language used in business.

Telugu Reader : being a first book in the language : with English Translation, Grammatical Analysis, and Little Lexicon.

English Irregular Verbs explained in Telugu.

Telugu and English Dialogues, with Grammatical Analysis. These have also been printed in Tamil : and in Kannadi.

The Vakyāvali, or Exercises in Idioms : English and Telugu. This has also been translated into Hindustani.

Wars of the Rajas, in Telugu and English.

Telugu Disputations on village business : with an English translation.

NOTE—*The above books are all that the learner requires.*

The Verses of Vemana : with an English Version. printed in 1829.

Essay on Telugu Literature.

Zillah Dictionary ; a Glossary in the English Character.

The proverbs of Solomon and the Book of Psalms : in Sanscrit metre : reprinted in the Telugu character from the Calcutta edition.

Three Treatises on Mirasi Right, by Ellis, Blackburne and Munro.

The Tale of Nala : and the Adventures of Harischandra : in Telugu metre.

The Tales of Nala and of Savitri in Sanscrit : from the Mahabharat.

Cyclic Tables of Hindu and Musulman Chronology.

An Ephemeris, shewing the corresponding dates according to the English, Hindu (Telugu, Tamil, and Malayalam) and Mahomedan Calendars from A. D. 1751 until 1850, with Table of events : and explanatory Preface, 600 pages royal octavo.

Memoirs of Hyder Ali Bahadar, and his son Tippoo Sultan, translated from Marata into English.

PREPARING FOR PUBLICATION.

A Second edition of the Telugu Grammar.

A Treatise on Hindu rites and ceremonies translated from the French, with emendations.

Telugu Histories and Tales, with a Translation : being a continuation of the Reader.

A Telugu Translation of the Holy Bible.

The Book of Common Prayer, in Telugu.

Shāsan' A'nus'āsanīcamu ; శాసనానుశాసనీకము ; Chronological Tables, of Indian History : in Telugu.

The Hitopadesa, in Sanscrit, with explanatory notes in Telugu.

Popular Telugu Tales.

Various volumes for the School Book Society.

A DICTIONARY

OF THE

MIXED DIALECTS AND FOREIGN WORDS

USED IN

TELUGU.

WITH AN

EXPLANATION OF THE TELUGU ALPHABET.

BY

CHARLES PHILIP BROWN,

AUTHOR OF A DICTIONARY AND GRAMMAR OF THE TELUGU LANGUAGE, &c. &c.

MADRAS:

PRINTED AT THE CHRISTIAN KNOWLEDGE SOCIETY'S PRESS,
CHURCH STREET, VEPERY.
1854.

PREFACE.

Government business in Southern India is chiefly transacted in the language of the Hindus, either Tamil, Telugu, Kannadi, Malayalam or Marata ; while the Musulmans still speak Hindustani (as well as the local native tongue) but Hindustani is seldom written.

The long continued dominion of the Musulmans introduced many foreign words into the various Hindu languages. Thus the modern Telugu contains a variety of Persian and Arabic expressions. In later years, some English words have crept into use. The present vocabulary of the Mixed dialects therefore forms a requisite supplement to a Dictionary of the Telugu language : and it contains only those phrases which are current among the natives.

This dialect is convenient: resembling Law-Latin on which Judge Blackstone has pronounced an eulogium. See his Commentaries, Vol. 3, p. 318—323 and 149. And the Gentleman's Magazine, 1813, part 2, page 643. It deviates from Telugu nearly as much as Law-French deviated from the language of Parisians : for instance (Coke upon Littleton, t. 2, p. 1.) "En ce tierce liver, ascun chose sera dict a toy mon fitz, de parceners, de joint tenantz," &c.

Indeed the business dialect may be considered another language, often deviating both in words and Syntax from correct Telugu. The following is an instance; clearly intelligible to any native who is acquainted with business.

యీనంబరులో డిఫెండంటు సమ్మను చూచి సైను (or దస్ఖత్) చేసి వాయిదా చొప్పున కోర్టులో హాజరు ఐ ఆన్సరు ఇయ్యక పోయినందున యిందులో ఎక్సుపార్టి దర్యాఫ్తు చేయవలెనని ప్లెంటిఫ్ ప్లీడరు మోషను చేసినాడు గనుక ఆ మోషను రికార్డులో దాఖలు (or ఫయిలు) చేసి అందులో దర్ఖాస్తు చేసిన చొప్పున నడిపించే లాగున ప్రొసీడింగులలో ఆర్డరు ఎంటరు చేయడం అయినది.

Which might be thus expressed in the English character: the foreign words being marked in Italics.

I' *number* ló, *defendant*, *summons* çūchi, *sign* (or *dastkhat*) chési, *wāida* çoppuna *Court* lō hāzir ai, *answer* iyyaca-pōinanduna, indulō *ex-parte daryāft* chēya valen' ani, *plaintiff pleader motion chesināḍu* ganuca, ā *motion record* lō *dākhil* (or file) chēsi, andu-lō *darkhast* chēsina çoppuna nadipinchē lāguna, *proceedings* ló *order enter* cheyadam ayinadi.

This in English would run thus :—

'The Defendant in this case, having seen the summons, and having signed it, has failed to appear in Court at the fixed time to present his answer. The plaintiff's pleader thereupon made a motion wherein he prayed that an *exparte* trial may be made; that motion was therefore filed in the record, and an order was entered in the proceedings that this shoud be done according to his desire.'

The diary of any court of justice in the Telugu country will furnish specimens of this useful though inelegant dialect. The instance now given is copied from the journal of the Court at Masulipatam.

The language used in familiar intercourse is often of the same description : and those who wish for specimens may turn to my Telugu Reader ; for instance page 138, where is given an account of Baillie's defeat in the year 1778.

The grammar and syntax of the mixed dialect are far from complete : and as it is generally written with celerity, the style is in many places obscure. Yet it is easier to translate than the correct and grammatical Telugu found in the familiar writings of educated natives.

The Hindus are unable to enunciate several of the sounds which occur in the English and the Persian alphabets. Foreign words are therefore often erroneously spelt. "Collector" becomes కల్కటరు Kalcaṭar, "assistant" అశిస్టాంటు "ashistaunt" Gholām, gulāb ; wāqif, wākhab, and wākhoob : dārōgha, dērōgh. Jawāb, an answer, has been changed into *Zābu*, which now means an epistle.

In copying foreign phrases they sometimes leave the syntax unaltered, though contrary to the Telugu idiom—Thus instead of *Kadapa Desam* (the Cuddapa country,) they often use the Persian phraseology *Tālūk-i-Karpa*. But not understanding the genitive sign ("i") which connects the words, they dispense with it.

The Hindustani dialect is used in some modern Telugu poems : particularly in the రాధామాధవసంవాదము, బలరామచరిత్ర, భల్లాణచరిత్ర, and in many శతకములు. Even some poems of eminent merit such as the దశావతారచరిత్ర and the కళాపూర్ణోదయము written by పింగళిసూరన్న admit some Hindustani phrases. Thus in the days of Dryden, Addison, and Pope, many English compositions admitted French or Dutch expressions.

To each word in this vocabulary I have appended a Telugu synonyme. This will aid those who wish to get rid of these foreign words. Perhaps one word in twenty may merit preservation. But in talking and writing Telugu we ought to avoid this mixed dialect.

Some years after preparing this glossary I perused two manuscript collections which gave me much aid. One of these is a series of Telugu Letters collected by me in eight volumes. The other is a set of "Local Records" including all the modern historical documents in the Mackenzie Library ; which are slightly noticed in Professor Wilson's Descriptive Catalogue.

The Local Records (transcribed under my orders, and at my expense) fill sixty-two volumes : which (with the Telugu Letters) I bestowed on the Library of the Madras College : wherein are also lodged the original records, collected by Mackenzie. Many of his volumes are perishing : being written with English ink (which soon fades) on country paper which the worms rapidly destroy. But the copies made under my directions, and at my cost, are written on English paper with country ink : which being made with lampblack does not fade.

The same library now contains my own ample collection of Telugu and Sanscrit manuscripts.

Some passages in this vocabulary allude to privileges, fines, dues, rights, fees or gratuities which, (like the *corvées* and arbitrary exactions legalized in France under the *ancien regime*) no longer exist.

An explanation of Telugu orthography is placed in this volume.

This Dictionary is printed at the expense of the Society for Promoting Christian Knowledge. I desire to tender my hearty acknowledgments to that Venerable body for thus producing a work which otherwise might not perhaps have been printed.

C. P. BROWN.

EXPLANATION OF SOME REFERENCES.

"Fifth Report," on the affairs of the East India Company. London 1812, folio.

Selections from the Records at the East India House, relating to Revenue, Police, Civil and Criminal Justice, 4 Vols. folio, 1820.

"MM." Molesworth's Marata Dictionary.

Wilks—Colonel Wilks's History of Mysore, 3 Vol. 4to.

ML. S. J. (or) Lit. Soc. Jour.—The Journal of the Madras Literary Society.

Prinsep—The Journal of the Asiatic Society : edited by the learned Prinsep.

Sullivan's British India Analyzed, 3 Vols.

"Treaties"—"A collection of Treaties and engagements with the Native Princes, &c." Printed for the Hon'ble E. I. Company, London 1812.

Local—A collection of "Local Records," Manuscript, in 48 Volumes : chiefly in Sanscrit, Canadi, and Telugu.

"Fr. Bu. Ha."—Dr. Francis Buchanan's "Mysore"—He afterwards took the name "Hamilton." His work on Eastern India was published by Mr. Montgomery Martin; who leaves the reader to believe the work was written by himself.

"Elphinstone." Report on the Territories conquered from the Paishwah, 1819.

Malcolm's Memoir on (Malwah) Central India.

Steele (Arthur) on Hindu castes, laws and Customs. Fol Bombay, 1827.

"Qanun-i-Islam." Herklots on the Mahomedans.

Lres Ed. "Letters Edifiantes at Curieuses."

Transactions of the Bombay Literary Society.

In the year 1824 various Catalogues of Revenue Expressions were compiled in the different Zillas, at the desire of the Board of Revenue. The lists are referred to as "Bel." "Cud," "Nell," &c. &c. denoting the lists prepared at Bellary, Cuddapa, Nelloor, or elsewhere.

WORKS PUBLISHED BY MR. BROWN.

A Grammar of the Telugu Language. First edition, 1840.
English-Telugu Dictionary.
Telugu-English Dictionary.
Dictionary of Mixed Telugu, and the language used in business.
Telugu Reader: being a first book in the language: with English Translation, Grammatical Analysis, and Little Lexicon.
English Irregular Verbs explained in Telugu.
Telugu and English Dialogues, with Grammatical Analysis. These have also been printed in Tamil: and in Kannadi.
The Vakyāvali, or Exercises in Idioms: English and Telugu. This has also been translated into Hindustani.

NOTE.—*The above books are all that the learner requires. The volume of Histories must be added, when complete.*

The Verses of Vemana: with an English version. Printed in 1829.
Essay on Telugu Literature.
Zillah Dictionary; a glossary in the English character.
The Proverbs of Solomon and the Book of Psalms: in Sanscrit metre: reprinted in the Telugu character from the Calcutta edition.
Three Treatises on Mirasi Right, by Ellis, Blackburne and Munro.
The Tale of Nala: and the Adventures of Harischandra: in Telugu metre.
The Tales of Nala and of Savitri in Sanscrit: from the Mahabharat.
Cyclic Tables of Hindu and Musulman Chronology.
An Ephemeris, shewing the corresponding dates according to the English, Hindu (Telugu, Tamil, and Malayalam) and Mahomedan Calendars from A. D. 1751 until 1850, with Table of events: and explanatory Preface, 600 pages royal octavo.
Memoirs of Hyder Ali Bahadar, and his son Tippoo Sultan, translated from Marata into English.

PREPARING FOR PUBLICATION.

A second edition of the Telugu Grammar.
A Treatise on Hindu rites and ceremonies translated from the French, with emendations.
Telugu Histories and Tales, with a Translation: being a continuation of the Reader.
A Telugu Translation of the Holy Bible.
The Book of Common Prayer, in Telugu.
Shāsan' A'nus'āsanīcam; శాసనానుశాసనీకం Chronological Tables, of Indian History: in Telugu.
The Hitopadesa, in Sanscrit, with explanatory notes in Telugu.
Various volumes for the School Book Society.
Popular Telugu Tales.

EXPLANATION

OF THE

TELUGU ALPHABET.

[BEING THE FIRST BOOK OF THE TELUGU GRAMMAR.]

THE TELUGU language is written from left to right, like English: and the best writing is upright: or sloping a little, (unlike English) towards the left. The words are in general pronounced, (as in Greek) precisely as they are spelt: thus the ear is a sufficient guide in orthography. In the round hand used in books every letter stands separate as in printing. In running hand the letters are shaped differently, and are combined, as in English; the words not being divided from each other. To render the alphabet easy it will be requisite first to explain the principles on which it proceeds.

Many letters have two forms: one appears in the alphabet as a capital or primary, and the other is secondary. Thus అ, ఇ, ఉ, are the alphabetical or capital forms of the vowels A, I, U, which are respectively called అకారం, ఇకారం, ఉకారం, Acāram, Icāram, and Ucāram: because cāram is equivalent to 'letter.'

Thus the consonants క, గ, చ, are Ka, Ga, Cha; the mark ✓ above each being the Talacaṭṭu or sign of A. కి, గి, చి, are Ki, Gi, and Chi: and కు, గు, చు, are Ku, Gu, Chu. With this last vowel ు, the ✓ talacaṭṭu is retained, though it is not pronounced.

The letters క, గ, చ, have as secondary shapes, ్క, ్గ, and ్చ, which are written under the line. Thus అక్క akka, అగ్గ agga, and అచ్చ açça; which last is pronounced atsa, or as azza would be sounded in Italian.

The talacaṭṭu, or A, is thus attached to most letters. Thus ర Ra, డ da, త ta; but some letters write ✓ talacaṭṭu and ి gudi, separately. Thus స sa, సి si, ప pa, పి pi.

Ten consonants never use the sign talacaṭṭu: for it is sounded though not written. These are ఖ kha, ఙ gna, జ ja, ౙ za, ఞ jna, ట ta, ణ ṇa, బ ba, ల la, ఱ ra. Excepting these, it is not the custom to write any letter, even in the alphabet, without the talacaṭṭu. In modern printing, the Kannadi (or "Cannarese") types ప, స are used; which remove all doubt.

The mark | called జడ jada, or ఒత్తు ottu, or వొత్తు vottu, is a breathing, and being placed under some letters, makes them aspirates. Thus బి Bi, డి Di, బు Bu, డు Du, are not aspirated. But భి Bhi, ధి Dhi, భు Bhu, ధు Dhu, have the aspirate sound.

A circle, ం, is in some places used for N or M. Thus అంత is anta, అంబ is amba, పంపుట is pamputa 'to send.' The circle (called సున్న sunna) is usually formed like the English letter o. Thus అంగం is angam; but, for the sake of clearness, the form ం is frequently used in this grammar.

As certain consonants have the vowel A "inherent" so the consonant య ya-(of which ్య is the second form) has the vowel I, inherent. For if written without ✓ the letter య is i or yi. Thus పోయి is pō-yi (pronounced pō-i) 'having gone.' వెయ్యి veyyi (ve-i) 'a thousand.' చెయ్యి cheyyi (chē-i) 'the hand.'

The mark ా is called దీర్ఘం dīrgham; and is the common name for broad ā. Thus కకారదీర్ఘం kakāra-dīrgham signifies (కా kā) the consonant k with ā added.

As I is inherent in y, యీ is yī; sounded as ī in machine, or ee in seen.

The *letter* ă అ is called అకారం acāram or 'letter A' as in Amelia; but the *sign* ✓ ă is called తలకట్టు talacaṭṭu or crest. The *letter* ఇ I is called ఇకారం i-cāram: but the *sign* ి ĭ, is called గుడి gudi 'a whirl.' The *letter* ఉ U is called ఉకారం Ucāram: but the *sign* ు is called కొమ్ము commu 'a horn.'

Instead of కారం cāram, the word త్వం twam (a word like *ness* as దిట్టత్వం stoutness, గురుత్వం heaviness) is sometimes used. Thus these three vowels are at pleasure called అత్వం, ఇత్వం, ఉత్వం, atwam, itwam, and utwam.

If two consonants meet, one is written without a vowel, under the other. Thus నక్క

a a
n c, *nacca* 'a fox.' కుక్క ku k, *kukka* 'a dog.'
c k

బల్లెము b l mu, *ballemu* 'a spear.' గుర్రము
(e above l, l beneath)

gu r mu *gurramu* 'a horse.' Here we see
(a above r, r beneath)

that B బ is written without the vowel a; and GU గు has the vowel a written above it, but not pronounced.

In గుర్రము the mark ్ర is R and comes between gu and ram. This mark shaped ్ర or ‿ or ౢ is called క్రారావడి crā-rāvadi. That is "The syllable crā, (and) (rā-vadi) R written beneath." Here the name 'Rāvadi,' would suffice, without prefixing the syllable క్రా Crā.

The letter ‿ is used in writing: but in printing it is more convenient to use the ancient forms ్ర or ౢ thus క్ర or క్ర kra. This form is used in inscriptions on some ancient temples; and is retained in many manuscripts, both Telugu and Cannadi.

The letter that stands on the line is pronounced first; then the one, or two, under it. Then the vowel above. Thus ప్ర is pra: and

స్త్రీ s, t, r, ī, strī, a woman, also written స్త్రీ; that is, సీ sī with ్త t and ్ర r beneath.

Thus also శాస్త్రి s ā s t r i that is, Sāstri, 'a learned man.'

Sometimes a consonant is marked as "silent;" no vowel being attached to it. The silent mark called పొల్లు pollu is ్ or ౕ added to the top of the letter instead of a vowel. Thus పృథక్ pridhac (*i. e.* separately, apart.) Here the mark written above k shows that it is silent. Thus also ల is the letter La; but by adding this sign it becomes ల్ as in the word హల్ hal; meaning a consonant. So అచ్ ach (*i. e.* a vowel.) Thus త ta becomes త్ as in the word అవశాత్ avasāt 'unexpectedly.' The letter స sa becomes స్ as in the word తేజస్ tējas 'lustre.' Thus ప or pa becomes ప్ as అప్ ap *i. e.* water. These are Sanscrit words and rarely occur in the free dialect.

The letter న Na when *silent*, assumes the form ౝ as in the word ఇంటన్ intan 'in the house;' లోపలన్ lopalan 'within.'

This mark is called నకారపొల్లు nacāra-pollu.

The letter ర R when followed by another consonant adds it beneath, as in the word ar-

a
ca అర్చ ar or sometimes changes places with
c

a
it and assumes the form ౯ thus అచ౯ acr.

a a
So ధర్మం Dh r m, *dharmam*, may also be writ-
m

a a a a
ten ధమ౯ం dh m r m. So కర్త c r *carta* 'a
t

a a
lord' may be written కత౯ c t r. Thus పూ

a
ర్వం p r m *pūrvam* 'formerly' may be written
ū v

a
పూవ౯ం, p v r m. Either way the pronunci-
ū

ation is the same.

This mark ౯ is called గిలక gilaca (literally a rattle, from a fancied resemblance in shape) or more usually వలపలగిలక valapala gilaka, which means, "the gilaca on the right hand," *i. e.* placed beyond the letter.

The letters of the alphabet appear very numerous, but the reason is that a separate character is used for each sound, instead of using the same letter with two or three different sounds, as happens in English.

The consonants also are multiplied and have such a variety of forms, because they use a separate shape for each variety of sound. T has one form and Th another; K has one form and Kh another. And this happens also in the Greek alphabet.

This spelling is easy; as the letters when correctly pronounced, never deviate from the sound given in the alphabet.

C. P. Brown's Mixed Dictionary.

But a difficulty (felt by those who have advanced far) arises from the liberty of spelling the same word in various ways.

The student should provide himself with the edition, lately printed in the Telugu character, of the Sanscrit Bhagavad Gītā. This will furnish a good key to the character if he already knows the Sanscrit alphabet.

When we have occasion to write Hindu or Mahomedan names in English letters, too great precision would be pedantic. It is usual to write Bramin for Brahman, or Bramhan; and Rajahmundry for Rājamahēndravaram.

When a letter is written under the line it is usually larger than if written on the line.

It is not the custom to separate the words. Thus a paragraph looks as if it was all one word. But in printing it will be found easy to separate words, as is done in English.

The mark | is used as a comma; and || is used for a period. The comma is used at the end of each line in poetry except the last; which is marked with the period.

In some Telugu printing, the English comma, semicolon, period and other stops have been introduced with good effect.

A letter is called అక్షరము axaram. An aspirated letter is called ఒత్తక్షరము or ఒత్తక్షర ము likewise means a syllable. Thus స్త్రీ strī 'a woman' is considered to be ఏకాక్షరము ēc āxaram, a monosyllable: lit. one letter.

Unless thoroughly acquainted with the principles of spelling and the variations therein allowed, we shall not be able to find words in the dictionary. The reader must therefore pardon what he may consider a tedious degree of preciseness regarding orthography.

The vowels cannot be correctly pronounced without opening the mouth wide, looking up, and using a loud tone. Natives complain that the English mumble their words.*

The learner should write the letters on a slate, in a large flourishing style: this is the easiest method of attaining fluency in writing.

THE ALPHABET.

Vowels.

అ ă ఆ ā ఇ ĭ ఈ ī ఉ ŭ (or అఆ ŭ) ఊ ū (or అఆ-ఽ ū) ఋ rŭ ౠ rū ఌ or లు lŭ ఎ ĕ ఏ ē ఐ ai ఒ ŏ ఓ ō ఔ au.

Consonants; (in five classes.)

Class					
1.	క ca	ఖ kha	గ ga	ఘ gha	ఙ gna.
2.	చ cha	ఛ chha	జ ja	ఝ jha	ఞ jna.
3.	ట ṭa	ఠ ṭha	డ ḍa	ఢ ḍha	ణ ṇa
4.	త ta	థ tha	ద da	ధ dha	న na
5.	ప pa	ఫ pha	బ ba	భ bha	మ ma

Miscellaneous.

య ya ర ra ల la ళ ḷa వ va.
శ ṣa ష sha స sa హ ha క్ష xa.

The dots placed under the letters ṭ ṭh ḍ ḍh ṇ ḷ and ṣ denote that these letters are sounded hard. They are sometimes marked with accents, as t′, t′h, d′, d′h, n′, l′, and s′.

Numerals.

౧	౨	౩	౪	౫	౬	౭	౮	౯,	౯ or ౯,	౧౦,
1	2	3	4	5	6	7	8	9	9,	10

౧౮౫౦.

1850.

The numerals ౩ three and ౭ seven are frequently confounded in manuscript.

The first 25 consonants are arranged in *classes* or sets (called వర్గము vargamu) having five letters in each: and on arranging these in five lines, we shall observe that the first and third letter in each line, are simple: but the second and fourth are aspirated. For the sake of distinction the consonants that stand in the first column, being క, చ, ట, త, ప, &c., are called పరుష hard: and గ, జ, డ, ద, బ, &c. in the third column are called సరళ soft. Thus Ga is the soft sound of ka: and P is the hard sound of B.

In some places a hard initial is softened: that is, T changes into D; or P into B, &c. Thus తమ్ముడు Tammudu 'a younger brother changes into దమ్ముడు dammudu, పోవుట pōvuta 'to go' becomes బోవుట bōvuta, పడుట 'to fall' becomes బడుట baduta, and కలుగుట caluguta 'to be' becomes గలుగుట galuguta. But a soft letter is never changed into a hard one.

The expressions dentals, palatals, labials, &c., which are used in Sanscrit Grammar are needless here: or belong only to the rules regarding Sanscrit words.

In expressing the sounds in English letters, the spelling used in the works of Colebrooke, Jones, Wilson, and Wilkins is the most convenient.

The rules for spelling, which native grammarians inculcate, are tediously minute, and widely different from those used in ordinary writing; which they consider beneath their notice; giving rules for the poetical dialect alone. Hence their rules are of little use to a foreigner; and my object being to assist the foreigner, the present grammar is so constructed as to meet his wants: the rules for the poetical dialect are therefore removed from the beginning to the end of the grammar. Indeed, we need notice no rules of permutation but those requisite for finding words in the dictionary.

* The native tutors also complain that English pupils touch their mouths with their hands: and then defile books with hands thus dirtied. Hindus hold spittle in abomination. We should respect their prejudices, and treat them kindly.

The alphabet exhibits the capitals or first forms. The secondary form of అ ă being ✓ this is added to the consonants. In some grammars all the consonants are exhibited without vowels attached: but it seems useless to give forms that are not in use.

Six consonants ఘు, పు, ఫు, షు, సు, హు, gha, pa, pha, sha, sa, ha, use this sign, as here shewn, above the letter; but written without touching it. If they were joined, the letter itself would change; thus, పస are pa, sa; but వన are va, na.

In common writing, the letters often take other shapes. Thus over the letters క, త, కి, తి, ka, ta, ki, ti, we often see the vowel written without touching the consonant.

The nasals are placed at the ends of those classes in the alphabet to which they belong.

All the nasal letters may be changed into ౦ sunna (the sign or contraction for N or M) either when they are followed by a consonant or when they are final. Thus గ్రంథం grandham 'a book' would according to Sanscrit rule be written గ్రన్థమ్; and అంగం angam 'the body' would be written అఙ్గమ్.

Regarding Telugu words also, instead of కిన్ద kinda, the spelling in use is కింద. The sound remains unaltered.

In the Dēvanāgari alphabet, as exhibited in Wilson's Sanscrit Dictionary, the appropriate nasal is retained; but in Telugu, as in common Dēvanágari or Bangāli writing, the dot or circlet is substituted. Thus అలఙ్కారమ్ alancāram (ornament) is written అలంకారం which form alone is intelligible. This occasionally alters the place of a word in the dictionary.

ON SPELLING.

If a word borrowed from Sanscrit ends in a long vowel, this is generally shortened. కలీ calī becomes కలి cală; and దేవీ Dēvī becomes దేవి Dēvĭ. Monosyllables, as శ్రీ srī and స్త్రీ strī retain the long vowel.

The sound of అ A is that used in ăbout, ăround. Thus the name అలకనంద is pronounced Alacananda. నల Nala, the name of a certain prince, is sounded like the Latin Nulla. హరి Hari, a name of Vishnu, is pronounced like the English word hurry. అమరకోశ Amara cōsha (the title of a Dictionary) is written Ummuru Koshu by those who prefer that mode of spelling.*

The long (or broad) ā ఆ is sounded as in the English words half, hard, laugh. తాత tāta, 'grandfather' is sounded as the English pronounce Tārtar. మాట māta 'a word' like the English 'Martyr.' In ఆంధ్రం A'ndhra (the learned name for Telugu) the first vowel is long, as though written ārn. The second shape of ā is ా as in తాత tāta 'grandfather.' This ా is called దీర్ఘం (long) and is, added to the letters thus.

కా kā ఖా khā గా gā ఘా ghā
చా chā ఛా chhā జా jā ఝా jhā
టా ṭā ఠా ṭhā డా ḍā ఢా ḍhā ణా or
ణ్ ṇā తా tā థా thā దా dā ధా dhā
నా nā పా pā ఫా phā బా bā భా bhā
మా mā యా yā రా rā ఱా ṛā లా lā
ళా ḷā వా vā శా śā షా shā సా or
సా sā హా hā క్షా xā.

The vowel ఇ is short I as in 'India.' Thus ఇఱ్ఱి irri 'a fawn' ఇల్లు illu 'a house' ఇచ్చి içci 'having given.' The word English is written ఇంగ్లీషు *Inglishu* and England is ఇం

---

* The short vowel A is written in eight ways in English: with five vowels and three dipthongs: thus (A) Ashore, Amelia, Victoria, Woman, (E) writer, flower, other, (I) stir, Cheshire, (O) London, son, mother, Hertford, (U) gun, cup, until, (IE) soldier, (OU) neighbour, (IO) fiction, occasion. The Sanscrit asti and santi, become in Latin est and sunt; the a changing into e, and into u. Many Sanscrit words are identical with Latin. సంతి santi *sunt*, ప్రవహంతి pravahanti *provehunt*. These instances shew, that the Sanscrit vowel A is convertible into E, I, O, and U.

గ్లండు Inglandu. The ఇ is called ఇత్వం it-wam : (త్వం twăm is the name given to the vowels only; while cāram as అకారం Acāram, చకారం cacāram is common to both vowels and consonants :) the long sound is named ఈత్వం ītwam. The secondary shape ి is called గుడి gudi (like goody) and the long sound is ీ గుడిదీర్ఘం gudi-dīrgham. It is sounded ī or ēē like ī in machine, ravine, Louisa. Thus స్త్రీ (a woman) is strī, or strēē. లీల Līla (a comedy) is sounded Leeler. The sign for dīrgham or the longer sound is often omitted in writing; it is the accent written above. Thus తి కి సి are ti, ki, si (short) but తీ, కీ, సీ tī, kī, sī are long.

Added to various consonants this somewhat changes their shapes. Thus

కి ki కీ kī ఖి khi ఖీ khī గి gi గీ gī ఘి ghi ఘీ ghī or ఘీ ghī.

In *ghī* we see that instead of adding the accent above, they add the sign ా dīrgham at the end.

చి chi చీ chī జి ji జీ jī ఝి jhi ఝీ jhī or ఝీ jhī టి ṭi టి ṭi టీ ṭī or టీ ṭī ఠి ṭhi ఠీ ṭhī డి ḍi డీ ḍī ఢి ḍhi ఢీ ḍhī ణి ṇi ణీ ṇī or ణీ ṇī ణీ ṇī తి ti తీ tī or తి ti తీ tī థి thi థీ thī ది di దీ dī ధి dhi ధీ dhī ని ni నీ nī పి pi పీ pī ఫి phi ఫీ phī బి bi బీ bī భి bhi భీ bhī [*in common writing* ఛి chi ఛి chhi and బి bi భి bhi *are shaped alike*] మి mi మీ mī or మీ mī యి yi యీ yī (*This consonant having the vowel inherent*) రి ri రీ rī లి li లీ lī ళి ḷi ళీ ḷī వి vi వీ vī శి ṣi శీ ṣī షి shi షీ shī or షీ shī సి si సీ or సీ sī హి hi హీ హీ hī హి hi హీ hī క్షి xi క్షీ xī.

It will be observed that some of these letters have two or three forms just as happens in English. In common writing లి li and వి vi are shaped alike.

Instead of the initial (or capital forms) ఇ ĭ ఈ ī they use యి yĭ and యీ yī which however are pronounced simply ĭ and ī. Thus యిక్కడ iccada (here) యీడు īdu (age) are written instead of ఇక్కడ and ఈడు. The initial forms ఇ, ఈ are seldom used unless in poems and dictionaries.

It will be observed that the six consonants ఘ gha, ప pa, ఫ pha, ష sha, స sa, హ ha, which have the vowel 'a' written separate from them, likewise have the vowel ి (i) written in the same manner separately.

ఉ or ఒ the short vowel U as in *Superb*, or ŏŏ in book. Thus ఉప్పు uppu 'salt' పులి puli 'a tiger.' And ఊ or ఒూ is the same vowel long, as ū in Lucy, chuse, choose or oo in root, shoot. Thus ఊగుట ūguta 'to swing.'

In common business this is best represented by ŏŏ; thus Ramoodoo for Ramudu : for in the affairs of ordinary life more precision in spelling would be pedantic.*

The form ఒ is constantly used for this vowel, thus ఉత్తరువు uttaravu 'an answer,' is written ఒత్తరువు; but grammarians assert that this form belongs to R, as will be stated in a future page.

The second forms are ు and ూ with which ✓ (the sign of ă) is used : excepting as regards the ten letters that never use ✓. These are ఖ ఛ జ ఝ ట ణ బ ల ఒ which are written ఖు, ఛు, జు, ఝు, టు, ణు, బు, లు, ఒు. The rest use it as follows :

కు ku ఖు khu గు gu ఘు ghu చు chu ఛు chhu జు ju ఝు jhu టు ṭu ఠు ṭhu డు ḍu ఢు ḍhu ణు ṇu తు tu థు thu దు du ధు dhu ను nu పు pu ఫు phu బు bu భు bhu ము mu యు yu రు ru లు lu ళు ḷu వు vu శు ṣu షు shu సు su హు hu క్షు xu. కూ, చూ are kū, chū, formed by adding the ా to ు.

Here it will be observed that the letters ప pa ఫ pha and వ va add the vowel ు in a

* See on this subject Prinsep's remarks in Journal of Asiatic Society, June 1834, page 281.

peculiar manner. This is done to distinguish them from ఘు gha and ము ma. But in common hasty writing these distinctions are sometimes confounded.

In like manner న 'N' is often written for స S; and వ V is often written for ప P. But over S and P, when thus written, a little upright dash is often placed to shew the difference, and to denote that the vowel ought to be separated from the consonant.

Instead of the initial forms ఉ and ఊ the consonants వు vu and వూ vū are generally used. Thus the words ఉప్పు uppu 'salt' ఉడుత uduta 'a squirrel' are in the dictionary spelt ఉప్పు and ఉడుత; but in common life వుప్పు vuppu, and వుడుత vuduta. But the V or W is not sounded and accordingly the sounds are uppu, uduta, or ooppoo, oodoota.

The short ŭ when it is final is written indeed, but is very often (like the silent e in hare, ride) dropped in pronunciation. Thus చేను chēnu 'a field' is always called చేన్ chēn; బాతు bātu 'a duck' is pronounced బాత్ bāt; తాళుతాళు stop! stop! is pronounced తాళ్ తాళ్ Tarl! Tarl! or Tāl Tāl! దున్నపోతు 'a he buffalo' in like manner is called దున్నపోత్ dunnapōt. Words that end in ము mu as బేరము, bēramu 'merchandize' కారము cāramu 'acrid' are always pronounced బేరం bēram కారం cāram. In such words the final U is necessary only in poetry: for in Telugu as in French verse each syllable is enunciated. In the words borrowed from Hindustani, English or other languages (and which have a final silent consonant) as fir-yād (a complaint) vakīl (a pleader) *book*, *major*, *line*, *number*, (the English words) the Telugus do indeed add a final u, thus ఫిర్యాదు, వకీలు, బుక్కు, మేజరు, లైను, నంబరు; they write the vowel U, but do not pronounce it.

At the end of a verse in poetry, the syllables లు, ని, ను, often drop their vowels and are contracted into ల్, న్. Thus వనులు becomes వనుల్, అతనికిని and వాండ్లకును become అతనికిన్, వాండ్లకున్. But vulgar copyists instead of dropping the vowel, lengthen it; thus వనులూ, అతనికినీ, వాండ్లకునూ.

Many Telugu words use the vowels A and U in the second syllable at pleasure; thus వాలగ vālaga, or వాలుగ vāluga, బుడములు or బుడుములు, మెరగు or మెరుగు, తరము or తరుము, అటక ataca, or అటుక atuca. The same happens in verbs, thus పరచుట paraçuta, పొగలుట, పలకరించుట may at pleasure be spelt పరుచుట paruçuta, పొగులుట, పలుకరించుట, or dropping both vowels పర్చుట parçuta, పల్కరించుట palkarinçuta. Accordingly if we do not find one form in the Dictionary we must look for the other.

The short vowel ఋ is rĭ or rŏŏ as in the words rig, rich, trick, rŏŏk, brŏŏk. Thus ఋషి rishi 'a prophet' ఋతువు rutuvu 'a season' ఋణము debt. The second form is ృ as in తృప్తి tripti 'satisfaction' కృప cripa 'favor' సంస్కృతము Sanscrit.

In common writing, the letters ఝు zu and ఝూ zū are often shaped exactly like the vowels ఋ ri and ౠ rū. And instead of the capital ఋ they use రు. Thus ఋణము is written రుణము. But this is wrong.

The vowel ~ is also written (but not pronounced) along with ఋ. Thus కృ crĭ గృ grĭ పృ prĭ శృ srĭ, &c. But తృప్తి tripti is generally, though not correctly spelt త్రుప్తి trupti and గృహం griham (a house) is wrongly written గ్రుహము; while కృష్ణ krushna or krishna, (a certain name) is vulgarly written క్రుష్ణ and వైకృతి vaicriti is written వైక్రుతి.

The vowel ఌ Lŭ as in *will run, shall read,* is rarely used, and the learner may safely neglect it. Indeed లు (that is, the consonant L) is generally substituted. Thus clripta క్లృప్త (short) is written క్లుప్త and pronounced clupta. The word ప్లృత pluta 'extension' is written ప్లుత. Plava ప్లవ the name of a year is pronounced like the English word Plover. In fact ఌ is peculiar to a few Sanscrit words, and ought to be pronounced lri as in bell-ringer. But no one gives it that sound.

The short vowel ఎ is E short, as in Bella, Betty, periphery. Thus ఎనుము enumu 'a she buffalo' తెలుగు Telugu or తెనుగు Tenugu* (the name of this language) చెన్నపట్నము Chenna-Patnam, the original name (still in use) of Madras. వ్రాసె vrāsĕ 'he wrote' పలికె pălīkĕ 'he spoke.' If such words are written in English characters the addition of h (vrāseh, palikeh) will conveniently shew that the ĕ is to be sounded as a syllable: not being silent. Thus in Latin bonĕ, talĕ, malĕ.

The long vowel ఏ is ē long as in the French words mēme, blēme and the Persian words shēkh, shēr, dēr; different from the sound given in English to the vowel a in name, or same. Thus ఏమి ēmi 'what' ఏనుగ ēnuga 'an elephant' తేనె tēnĕ 'honey' లేడి lēdi 'an antelope' లేళ్లు leḷḷu 'antelopes.'

The short vowel a is vulgarly changed into e in a few words. Thus గడ్డి gaddi 'grass' is pronounced గెడ్డి geddi, గంధకం, గెంధకం. The word వేళ vēḷa 'time' is written and pronounced వ్యాళ vyāḷa. These are mere vulgarisms and should be avoided. So నేదరి nēdari 'lout' లేక lēka 'without' లేత lēta 'soft' become న్యాదరి n-yādari, ల్యాక l-yāca, ల్యాత l-yāta; while వేట vēṭa 'venison' (the common word also for a sheep) becomes వ్యాట and యాట v-yāta and yāta.

By a similar error, which is universal, the words beginning with చే or తే, &c., are perpetually written చా and త్యా; thus చేయుట *to do* is almost invariably written చాయుట; and చేరుట (to arrive) చారుట; చేత chēta (by) చేప chēpa (a fish) are usually written చాత, చాప chāta, chāpa: because the illiterate spell by the ear alone. బట్టమేక batta-mēka 'a bustard' is pronounced vulgarly butter-maker. పేట a suburb becomes ప్యాట p-yāta, తేట téta 'clear' becomes త్యాట t-yāta. So పేరు a name (instead of pēru) becomes ప్యారు p-yāru. And (as vulgarism is capricious) the contrary happens: thus శరీరం sarīram 'the body' is always written శెరీరం serīram.

This must be remedied in searching for a word in the dictionary. The correct spelling is uniform: the vulgar forms are devoid of rule; and various people use various spellings. They often know and acknowledge these deviations to be wrong, and entirely approve the more correct mode of spelling. Among ourselves orthography has only in late years become fixed: our ancestors cared little for the spelling even of proper names.

The final short ă is sometimes written ĕ. Thus అల్లిక, పెంటిక, allică, pentică are written అల్లికె, పెంటికె allikĕ, pentikĕ.

The second forms are ె ĕ and ే ē. Thus కె kĕ కే kē ఖె khĕ ఖే khē గె gĕ గే gē ఘె ghĕ ఘే ghē, &c.

The long vowel differs from the short only by adding the ˆ mark above called పొల్లు pollu; which in ordinary writing is omitted. Thus the long and short vowels are written alike. Sanscrit writing never uses the pollu; but the sound is invariably long.

In the copies of the Telugu Poems which have been transcribed for me (now amounting to some hundred volumes) the spelling has been left as it was in the original. To rectify the vulgar errors would have been an endless task: the spelling has been rectified only in those volumes which have been prepared for printing.

The shapes ె ే are drawn from right to left, (backwards) and ా the sign of ā is drawn (forwards) the opposite way. Thus కా is kā, but కె is kĕ, and కే is kē. Accordingly we have these forms ఖె khĕ, గె gĕ, ఘె ghĕ, ఙె gnĕ, చె chĕ, ఛె chhĕ, ఞె jnĕ, జె jĕ, ఝె jhĕ, టె ṭĕ, ఠె thĕ

* It is high time to abolish the absurd name Gentoo which was introduced by the Portugueze, and is ignorantly used by some persons for the name 'Telugu.'

డె ḍĕ, ఢె ḍhĕ, ణె ṇĕ, తె tĕ, థె thĕ, దె dĕ, ధె dhĕ, నె nĕ, పె pĕ, ఫె phĕ, బె bĕ, భె bhĕ, మె mĕ, యె yĕ, రె rĕ, ఱె ṛĕ, లె lĕ, ళె ḷĕ, వె vĕ, శె śĕ, షె shĕ, సె sĕ, హె hĕ, క్షె xĕ. And if the accent is added, thus కే kē, ఖే khē, గే gē, ఘే ghē, &c. the vowel becomes long.

Instead of the initial form of ఎ ĕ (which is confined to poems and dictionaries,) యె yĕ is in use. Thus for ఎవడు evadu 'who' ఎక్కడ eccada 'where' ఎనిమిది enimidi 'eight' ఎందుకు enduku 'why' we write and pronounce యెవడు yevaḍu, యెక్కడ yeccaḍa, యెనిమిది, yenimidi, యెందుకు yenduku. And the long vowels as ఏతాం, ఏల, ఏగాణి are always changed into యాతాం or యేతాం, &c.

The letter Y though thus written (the learned say) ought not affect the pronunciation.

The vowels A and E are in vulgar writing used for one another: chiefly in initial syllables. Thus యెనిమిది enimidi 'eight' is written యనిమిది yanimidi; యెక్కడ is spelt యక్కడ; యెవ్వరు evvaru becomes యవ్వరు yavvaru.

It will be observed that the six letters over which the vowel ి i is written without touching them, likewise have ĕ and ē written in the same manner.

ఐ ai; ఐశ్వర్యం ais-war-yam, (prosperity) ఐక్యం aik-yam 'unitedness.' This is sounded as the English sounds of sky, like, heights.

Words beginning with this vowel use the shape ఐ in the dictionary, (See rules for finding words in the dictionary) but in common use this is laid aside, and అయి ăyi is substituted. Thus ఐనాను I became is written అయినాను ayinānu. Under the vowel ఇ it has been shewn that యి yi is used for i, and in fact does not retain the sound y (which is reckoned as a consonant) thus a-yi-nā-nu is pronounced ai-nānu. The second form is ై: thus కై Kai, ఖై Khai, గై gai, &c.

The forms therefore are as follows:

కై ఖై గై ఘై చై ఛై జై ఝై టై ఠై డై ఢై ణై &c.

This vowel must always be expressed by AI in English—never by Y. Thus నైరృతి is nairruti, not nyruti; పైకము is paicam, not py-cum; సైన్యము is sain-yam, not synyam. If it is written Y, this leads to uncertainty, as will be seen in the remarks on the consonant Y. For the letter Y is, in Sanscrit and in Telugu, always a consonant; and య cannot be used without a vowel following it.

The vowel ఒ is ŏ as in Sŏphia, Pŏlice, prŏduced, Mŏravia, pŏtential, Lŏcated. Or the French words folle, monnoie, montagne. The longer sound ఓ is that which occurs in the Persian words shōr, tōp, mōr, or in the French words lorgner, monde, fosse.

These initial forms are found in the dictionary, but are laid aside in common use. వొ vŏ and వో vō being substituted.*

But the consonant V if followed by U or O is not pronounced.

Thus వొ is simple ŏ and వో is long ō.

ఒప్పు ŏppu 'right' is usually written వొప్పు.

ఒకటి ŏcati 'one' is written వొకటి or even వకటి.

ఒత్తుట ŏttuṭa 'to press' is written వొత్తుట.

ఓగు ōgu 'wicked' is written వోగు.

ఓపిక ōpica 'patience' is written వోపిక.

ఓమము ōmamu 'bishop's weed,' is written వోమము.

Elsewhere the long vowel is changed into వా; thus the word for a boat or ship is always written and pronounced వాడ vāda; unless in poems, where it is written ఓడ ōda.

* The alphabet is called ఓనమాలు ónamálu from the words ఓంనమశ్శివాయసిద్ధంనమః which is to Hindus what the Bismillah is to Musulmans.

The short ŏ has two forms, viz. కొ co, గొ go, ఖొ kho, &c. and the second form is ఘొ ghŏ, ఝొ jhŏ, మొ mŏ, యొ yŏ, పొ pŏ వొ vŏ, &c. The second form is compounded of ె ĕ and ు the sign of u.

This compound form is used by all consonants: but all do not use the simple form. The simple forms are these;

కొ ఖొ గొ చొ ఛొ జొ టొ ఠొ ṭho డొ ḍo ఢొ ḍho తొ థొ దొ ధొ బొ bo భొ bho రొ ro లొ lo. Four letters have a peculiar shape పొ po ఫొ pho షొ sho సొ so.

All these may be made long by adding the accent, thus కో cō, గో gō, &c.

Some are elongated by adding ా (dirgham) to the second form, as కో cō, ఖో khō, &c. పో pō, వో vō, నో nō.

Thus ĕ and ū compounded (like eau in French) become ō. But four letters omit the sign ు when the vowel is long. ఘో ghō, ఝో jhō, మో mō, యో yō. Thus one commu is omitted: but uneducated persons often use two.

It is a very common error to write the long ō, instead of the short ŏ. Thus కొంత, కొంద రు are written కోంత, కోందరు. This does not affect the pronunciation: which remains short.

The vowel ఔ au or ow, as in cow, out, mount; but it is compounded of A and U; and accordingly in common writing the initial shape ఔ is never used; అవు avu or awu, being substituted; and the V or W being silent as already shewn, this is pronounced aw or au. Thus అవుట awṭa or avuṭa (to become) which in the dictionary is ఔట auṭa: pronounced like the English word outer. Thus ఔదార్యం audāryam 'generosity' ఔన్నత్యం aunnatyam 'loftiness' are commonly written అవుదార్యం, అవున్నత్యం, but the pronunciation remains unaltered. In these Sanscrit words this change is not approved.

Few of the Telugus are able to pronounce the short vowel o in the English words lost, hot, horse, top, God, law, lord, order, which they make లాస్టు, హాటు హార్సు, టాపు, గాడు, లా, లాడు, ఆర్డరు. thus born becomes barn, God, guard, and former, farmer. In the Telugu newspapers Hong Kong is spelt హాంగు కాంగు Hangu-Kangu. In English neither sound is used unless in some districts as Derbyshire where honey and more are pronounced in the ancient manner: the sounds are quite different from those of rod and rode.

The sign ౕ is (very needlessly) retained in combination with au as regards some letters. Thus మౌ mau, యౌ yau, హౌ hau.

The following are the shapes used,

కౌ ఖౌ గౌ ఘౌ చౌ ఛౌ జౌ
ఝౌ టౌ ఠౌ డౌ ఢౌ ణౌ తౌ
థౌ దౌ ధౌ నౌ పౌ ఫౌ బౌ
భౌ మౌ యౌ రౌ లౌ ళౌ శౌ
షౌ సౌ హౌ క్షౌ

Throughout the grammar I have used the common forms of the initial vowels. For the sake of uniformity *in the dictionary*, however, monosyllabic forms of ai and au are used. Thus for the words పయిట payita (a woman's veil) and కవుజు cavuzu (a partridge) we must use the spelling పైట and కౌజు. Sanscrit words invariably use the monosyllabic forms. Telugu words use these or the dissyllabic forms at pleasure. Poets adopt whichever form suits the metre; thus కౌగిలి cau-gi-li (an embrace) is a dactyl formed of a long syllable and two shorts. But this may be written కవుగిలి căvŭgĭlĭ (four shorts) or by inserting ం (that is N,) poets write కవుంగిలి căvŭngĭlĭ whereby the second syllable becomes long.

Thus, besides the forms exhibited in the alphabet the vowels take the following forms; both in poems and in every day business.

అ	a becomes	య	ya
ఆ	ā	యా	yā
ఇ	i	యి	yi
ఈ	ī	యీ	yī
ఉ	u	వు	vu (but sounded u or ŏŏ)
ఊ	ū	వూ	vū (sounded ū or ōō)
ఋ	ri	రు	rŭ or రి ri
ఎ	ĕ	యె	yĕ (or *wrongly*, య ya)
ఏ	ē	యే	yē (or *wrongly*, యా yā)
ఐ	ai	అయి	a-yi
ఒ	o	వొ	vo, wo, or యొ yo
ఓ	ō	వో	vō, wō, or యో yō
ఔ	au	అవు	a-vu, awu.

ౠ rū and ఌ lu are not in use.

A short vowel is called హ్రస్వము hraswamu, హ్రస్వాక్షరం hraswāxaram, or లఘువు laghuvu : each of which words literally means (levis) light; as opposed to గురువు guruvu 'heavy' which is the same as దీర్ఘం dīrgham 'long.' A vowel which is long by nature as ఆ, ఈ, ā, ī, &c., is called దీర్ఘం dīrgham : but it is called *guru* if long either by nature or *position :* that is by being followed by two consonants. Thus in the words అంత anta 'all' అన్న anna 'elder brother' తమ్ముడు tammudu 'younger brother' &c. &c., the first vowel is short ; but is *guru* because followed by two consonants. The word *guru* is only used in prosody.

In the Rambler, No. 90, Johnson uses the preferable expressions ***strong*** and ***weak*** syllables. These words are referred to in various parts of Telugu Grammar and therefore are here noticed. They are also used regarding the గణప్రస్తారం or Table of (గణము లు) Prosodial feet : wherein the sign | (a short upright line) is used for ***short***, and ◡ (our mark for short) denotes ***long***. As the quantity of every syllable is evident to the eye, scanning is perfectly easy, and the marks | and ◡ are rarely used. We may therefore without any inconvenience use the marks found in Latin and Greek. In reading verse, the natives use particular chanting tones which to our ear are far from agreeable. It is such as the Romans used, according to Ovid, (Art. 3, 345) Vel tibi compositâ cantetur epistola voce. This passage should have been noticed in Monk's Life of Bentley, Vol. II.' p. 324. See Smollet's remarks (Humphrey Clinker, letter of 13th July,) "Every language has it's peculiar recitative" &c. Natives are accustomed to read in a very loud voice : whenever we find this disagreeable, we merely need remark యెందుకు అరిచేది? మెల్లగా చదవండి. The student will find it useful to read the first two sections of the chapter on Telugu Prosody.

On the Consonants.

The first 25 consonants, as shewn in the alphabet, stand in five lines, each of which contains four letters besides a nasal.

The four letters which thus form one line are often looked upon as equivalent. This particularly happens as regards initials changed by grammatical rule ; which will be explained elsewhere. The "Primary" letters క చ ట త ప ka, cha, ṭa, ta, pa, are changed into "Secondaries" and respectively become గ జ డ ద బ ga, ja, ḍa, da, ba, or గ స డ ద వ ga, sa, ḍa, da, va.

The sounds of many consonants require no explanation. Thus, క ka గ ga చ cha జ ja న na ప pa బ ba మ ma య ya ర ra ల la వ va స sa హ ha are usually pronounced like the corresponding English letters as sounded in Kate, Gate, chase, jackal, no, put, be, me, you, row, low, vale, sale, hale. The letter గ is always hard, (as in gorge,) thus గిన్నె *ginneh* 'a cup' and గెలుచు *geluçu* 'to conquer ;' but it is never pronounced soft as in *George.*

The aspirates are the following.

ఖ kha as in 'park-house ;' 'buck-horn ;' ఘ gha as in 'log-house,' 'stag-horn ;' ఛ chha as in 'coach-horse ;' ఝ as in 'hedgehog ;' ఠ ṭha as in 'cart-horse ;' ఢ Dh, as in 'bid him ;' థ ṭha as in 'but-him ;' 'not-here ;' ధ tha as in 'ad-here ;' ఫ pha as in 'up-here ;' భ bha as in 'club-house.'

The learned affirm that aspirates are peculiar to Sanscrit, and never should be used in native Telugu words. Thus they wish us to write these words without the aspirates: దొర dora 'a master' గాలి gāli 'wind' గట్టి gaṭṭi 'strong' కొబ్బెర kobbera 'cocoanut kernel' దుముకుట dŭmŭkŭṭă 'to leap,' జంకుట zankuṭa 'to fear,' దట్టి daṭṭi 'a girdle:' but in this they are not countenanced by general use, which gives the aspirate to these words; viz. ధొర dhora, ఘాలి ghāli, ఘట్టి ghaṭṭi, ఖొబ్బెర khobbera, ధుముకుట dhumukuta, ఝంకించుట jhankinçuta (HD. 2. 901) also ఝంకుట jhancuta, and ధట్టి dhaṭṭi.

The capital shapes of the consonants are given in the alphabet. But some of them take another form, without Talacattu, when written beneath the line. Thus క is the capital form and ్క is the second form of ka; in the words లెక్క lecca (an account) పల్కు palcu (a word.) Thus మ is ma; but the second shape is ్మ as in the name మన్మథుడు Manmathuḍu (Cupid) or మర్మం marmam 'a secret.'

The following are the letters with their second shapes. Some of which (as బ Ba) are nearly the same as the capital shapes.

క్క kka గ్గ gga ద్ఘ dgha చ్చ chcha or çça చ్ఛ chchha జ్జ jja or zza జ్ఝ jjha ట్ట ṭṭa ట్ఠ ṭṭha డ్డ ḍḍa డ్ఢ ḍḍha ణ్ణ ṇṇa త్త tta త్థ ttha ద్ద dda ద్ధ ddha న్న nna ప్ప ppa ప్ఫ ppha బ్బ bba ద్భ dbha మ్మ mma య్య yya ర్ర or ఱ్ర rra (also ఱ్ఱ rra) ల్ల lla ళ్ళ ḷḷa వ్వ vva శ్శ ṣṣa ష్ష shsha స్స ssa.

In some of these combinations the upper letter is different from the lower as (జ్ఝ) because the other combinations (as ఝ్ఝ) are wrong; though they sometimes occur in writing. Native tutors would teach us about a hundred more combinations, though well aware that they are never used.

The pronunciation of some consonants is peculiar. Thus చ cha and జ ja are sometimes softened into ça (or tsa, as in *hot-sun*, *Betsy*) and z or ds (as in *swordsman*.) The softer sounds ça and za are peculiar to Telugu, and the harder sounds cha, ja, originate in Sanscrit: no Sanscrit word can use the soft sounds.

The letters చ and జ take the hard sound with (I, I′, E, E′ AI,) ఇ ఈ ఎ ఏ ఐ. Thus చిప్ప chippa 'a plate' చీమ chīma 'an ant' చెప్పుట chepputa 'to say' జెర్రి jerri 'a centipede' జెర్రిపోతు jerri-pōtu 'a cobra de capello' చేను chēnu 'a field' జేన jēna 'a span' చైత్రము chaitramu 'the name of a month' and జైమిని Jaimini 'a certain name.' All these take the hard sound. And చంద్రుడు chandrudu 'the moon' చాకచక్యము chacachakyamu 'brilliancy' చోరుడు chōrudu 'a thief' being words of Sanscrit origin give the hard sound of ch. And జలము jalamu 'water' జాలము jālamu 'a net' జీవము jīvamu, 'life' give the hard sound of J.

The following words being Telugu, give the soft sounds; చలము çalamu 'anger' చాచుట çāçuṭa 'to extend' చోటు çōṭu 'a place' వచ్చుట vaççuṭa 'to come' చొచ్చుచున్నారు çoççuçunnāru 'they enter' which might be spelt in English letters tsalam, tsātsuṭa, tsōṭu, vatsuṭa, sossusunnāru.

This is the German sound of C; for in the names of the letters in the German Alphabet the letter C is called Tsay, and Z is called Tsett.

And the soft sound (dz) of జ is perceived in the Telugu words జబ్బు zabbu '*slow*' బెజ్జము bezzamu 'a hole or bore' జోడు zōḍu 'a pair' which might be written dzabbu, bedzamu, dzōḍu. In common writing the letter జ is wrongly shaped like బు bu.

Instances wherein the consonant is doubled: పిచ్చి piççi or pichchi (foolish) is pronounced like the English word *pitchy*: and వచ్చె vaççeh (he came) is pronounced like vat-cheh. మజ్జిగ mazziga 'butter-milk' is pronounced madjiga; and గజ్జెలు gazzelu (anclets) would according to English ear be written gud-jelloo.

In some grammars and in some recent editions of poems, the numerals ౧ and ౨

(1 and 2) have been placed over these letters: one denoting the soft, the other the hard sound. But the principle is so easily understood that marks (which indeed few understand) are superfluous.

The mutation of ça, into sta is obvious in the verb: where the participle చేయుచు chē-yu-tsu is at pleasure spelt చేస్తు chēstu: thus the sounds of S and T change places.

In the rustic or ancient pronunciation, the Telugus use the soft sounds alone. Thus we frequently hear the words చిన్న chinna, చెప్పు cheppu, జిలుగు jilugu, జెముడు jemuḍu pronounced çinna, çeppu, zilugu, zemuḍu.

They in like manner mispronounce Sanscrit words.

The soft sounds are common in Irish, where true, dry &c., are pronounced thrue, dhry, &c.

The nasal sound ఙ gna or ng of the first varga or class is like *nio* in the word *mignionette* or in *opinion*. It occurs in the common words వాఙ్మూలము vāng-mū-lamu 'a recorded deposition or statement.' Like all other nasals, it is usually changed into ం as in the word అంగం angam 'the body.'

The nasal of the second *varga* or class is ఞ and never appears alone: being always written under the letter జ j, as in the word జ్ఞాపకము jnāpacamu 'recollection' and జ్ఞానము jnānamu 'knowledge' సంజ్ఞ san-jna, 'a sign.' These words are usually though not correctly pronounced గ్యాపకము gyāpa-camu, గ్యానము gyā-namu, సౌగ్య saugya.

In teaching Sanscrit or Telugu the teacher is obliged continually to make his pupils pronounce louder and harder than they fancy requisite.

The letters ట Ṭa, డ Ḍa, and ణ Ṇa, are harder, and the letters త Ta, ద Da, and న Na are softer, than the sound they have in English.

The soft D and the soft T are used in modern Greek: as is shewn in Dallaway's Constantinople.

The hard D is often pronounced nearly like R, thus బెజవాడ Bezavāḍa becomes Bezoara.

The distinction between the hard and soft T is perceived in these words.

పోటు	a stab	పోతు	a beast
కోట	a fort	కోత	cutting
పాట	a song	పాత	old
తాట	the bark of a tree	తాత	a grandfather
వింట	on a bow	వింత	strange
చెట్ట	evil	చెత్త	rubbish
మట్టు	limit	మత్తు	intoxication,
మూట	a bundle	మూత	a cover
కోటి	ten millions	కోతి	a monkey
చేటులు, చేట్లు	evils	చేతులు	hands
పొట్టు	husk	పొత్తు	friendship
పొట్టి	short, not tall	పొత్తి	a rag
వట్టి	mere, only	వత్తి	a wick
తిట్టి	reviling	తిత్తి	a bag
పట్టి	holding, a list	పత్తి	silk
కట్టి	binding	కత్తి	a sword.

The distinction between the hard and soft D is important.

పొడ	a speck	పొద	a bush
పొడి	powder	పొది	a pouch
పాడు	waste	పాదు	bed of a tree
నిండ	(adv.) fully	నింద	blame
గడ్డ	a boil	గద్ద	a vulture
దిడ్డి	a door	దిద్ది	correcting
గుడ్డు	an egg	గుద్దు	a blow
బుడ్డి	a bottle	బుద్ధి	sense
పొడుగు	length	పొదుగు	the udder
మండ	a bough	మంద	a flock
వాడు	he	వాదు	battle, quarrel
ఊడుట	to slip out	ఊదుట	to blow
పడి	having fallen	పది	ten
పడ్డ	fallen	పద్ద	a bit
పండి	having fruited	పంది	a pig.

In the negative verbs some masculines end in the hard sound, and some feminines or neuters in the soft sound. Thus,

కాడు	he becomes not	కాదు	she becomes not
లేడు	he lives not	లేదు	she lives not
రాడు	he comes not	రాదు	she comes not

ఉండడు	he will not stay	ఉండదు	she will not not
పలుకడు	he speaks not	పలుకదు	she speaks not
వినడు	he hears not	వినదు	she hears not.

This aorist form is used in all verbs. The following call for particular attention ;

వాడు వ్రాయలేడు	he cannot write
వ్రాయలేదు	he did not write
వాడు చదవలేడు	he cannot read
చదవలేదు	he did not read.

The difference between the following words is equally important,

శోణము	crimson	జోన	a waterfall;

And between soft and hard L.

పేలు	lice	పేళ్లు	names
రాలు	to flow	రాళ్లు	stones
కాలు	a leg	కాళ్లు	legs.

The hard sound of ణ is exemplified in the words కణితి kaṇiti, 'an elk' and కణుజు caṇuzu 'a partridge.'

The letters P Ph B Bh M call for no remarks in addition to what is stated already regarding aspirates.

The letter Y is always a consonant, and requires the addition of a vowel. Thus చేయుట chē-yu-ṭa 'to do' చెయ్యి che-yyi 'the hand' కొయ్య co-yya 'wood' బియ్యము bi-yya-mu 'rice' అయ్యా a-yy-ā 'sir.' Likewise in Sanscrit words as పద్యము pad-ya-mu 'stanza' న్యాయము nya-ya-mu 'justice' కన్య can-ya 'a virgin' సూర్యుడు sūr-yu-ḍu 'the sun.' When yy occurs in a name we may conveniently express it by ii. Thus వెంకయ్య Venk-ayya and సూరయ్య Su-rayya (certain names) may be written Venkiia and Suriia.

The letter య 'y' is denominated కొయ్య or కొయ్యాకది.

The letter R is a fruitful source of idle disputation among the learned: some of whom assert that in certain words, as మరియు, మరలి, కర్ర, &c., we ought to use the obsolete form మఱియు, మఱలి, కఱ్ఱ. It is sufficient to point out that the shape ఱ is obsolete, and good authors neglect it. In ancient times the two letters varied so far in sound that they were not allowed to rhyme together: and the excellent poet who wrote the Telugu vèrsion of the Srī Bhāgavat is blamed by pedants for neglecting this refinement. The letter ర is called మండిరేఫ and the letter ఱ is called బండిరేఫ.

The obsolete ఱ R and ౘ the semi-circle have crept even into some of the books printed under my directions. These letters ought to be set aside and not allowed a place at the compositor's table. In the language of Burma the letter R ◡ (crara vadi) is written under the letter, and shaped thus. The Burmese letter G is also shaped like the form ∩. The letter H is also similar. Some other characters also are evidently cognate.

When R is connected with a consonant, with no vowel between, it may be written thus; కర్త carta 'Lord' కర్మము carmamu, 'act' మర్మము marmamu a 'secret.' Or the mark ౖ called వలపలగిలక is placed beyond: thus కర్త, కర్మము, మర్మము.

The letter R in such places must always be clearly pronounced as in the practice of the Scotch and of the Germans. The English are apt to *slur* or omit the sound.

In some printed books the silent ర R is shaped ర్. This is chiefly used in foreign words; as గవర్నర్ Governor, సీనియర్ senior, జూనియర్ junior.

Many pure Telugu words have a liberty of adding R to the initial consonant: thus తోవ, త్రోవ, దోవ, ద్రోవ tova, trōva, dōva, drōva, all mean 'a road' కొత్త cotta (new) may be spelt క్రొత్త crotta: and కింద kinda (under) may be spelt క్రింద krinda: thus in English there are words that resemble others in the initial, as cave, crave, gave, grave; tie, try, die, dry; cape, crape, gape, grape; pay, bay, pray, bray; couch, or crouch, babble, or brabble, petty, or pretty. Chaucer writes droil for toil, prin for pin, grin for gin (a trap) and brids for birds. Spenser writes thrust for thirst (F. Q. 3. 7. 50.) A similar liberty is found in all languages of the Celtic family. In English these are separate words, but in Telugu they are often only various spellings of the same word. For this reason, in the dictionary I have mingled these four classes. While the consonants were classed separately, in the Telugu dictionary, this uncertainty regarding the initial often rendered it requisite to search for a word in three or four places before it came to light. By mingling the initials, and excluding the optional R, all the various modes of spelling usually appear in the same page. This arrangement diminishes the size of the dictionary; as formerly two or more forms were inserted; and were explained separately, or referred to another page.

By "pure Telugu words" (అచ్చ తెలుగు) or "Radical Telugu" grammarians intend such as are not derived from Sanscrit. The principles of Telugu and Sanscrit spelling are widely different: but as it is requisite to explain both, the reader will observe that such rules as mention one of these languages apply to it alone.

The expediency of the present arrangement of the dictionary will be hourly felt in reading: when asked whether we are to look for the word in question, under the primary initial K or the secondary G; under Ch or J (చెట్ట, జెట్ట and సెట్ట *chetta*, *jetta*, and *setta* are all the same word,) under T or D: under P or B; under స s or శ ṣ, a native tutor is very apt to reply that either spelling is equally good.

The letter ల is L as in తెలుగు Telugu. The letter ళ is the same pronounced harshly turning the tongue upwards: thus పేళ్లు pēḷḷu 'names' కోళ్లు cōḷḷu 'birds.' Certain Sanscrit words always use ల and others always use ళ.

The letter వ V or W; this is generally sounded V; thus, వాడు vāḍu 'that man, వీడు vīḍu 'this man' ఎవడు evaḍu 'who.' In Sanscrit words it ought to be pronounced V as వయసు va-yasu 'age' వీణ vīṇa 'a lute;' but in many Telugu words the sound is more like W, thus వట్టి vaṭṭi 'mere' is usually sounded waṭṭi. The learned prefer the sound V, the illiterate often use the sound W. In English words the Telugus find V hard to pronounce; usually changing it into W. When it is doubled, as in పువ్వు puvvu 'a flower' కొవ్వు covvu 'fat' దవ్వున davvuna 'afar' it is usually pronounced as W, thus pu-wu, co-wu, da-wuna. In common talking the V is often dropt: thus వేట vēṭa (hunting, the chase, venison, a goat) is generally changed into యేట yēṭa and యాట yāṭa. Elsewhere V changes into O. Thus వచ్చె vaççe 'he came,' is pronounced by rusticks ఒచ్చె oççĕ.

The three letters శ ṣa ష sha and స sa are as different in sound as the English words sharp, action, soul. They are exemplified in the names శనివారము, లక్ష్మీవారము, సోమవారము Sanivaramu 'Saturday' Laxmivāramu 'Thursday' Sōmavāramu 'Monday.' As distinct names are convenient, some call these శాంతిశకారము ṣanti ṣacāramu, కష్టషకారము cashṭa-shacāramu, సులభసకారము sulabha-sacāramu: others use the words దశమి, షష్ఠి, సప్తమి. The commonest phrases are, విష్ణుషకారము, శివశకారము, వ్యాసునిసకారము, because the names Vishnu, Siva, and Vyāsa exemplify the three sounds. Any three words in a similar order are more easily remembered than the grammatical phrases ఓష్ఠ్యము 'labial, దంత్యము dental, and తాలవ్యము palatal.'

The learned state that శ Sānti-Sacāramu, belongs solely to words of Sanscrit origin: and wish us to exclude it from all Telugu words. Thus they think కలిశనది 'must' ought to be written కలిసినది: and చేశి, వేశి, వ్రాశి should be చేసి, వేసి, వ్రాసి. But the voice of the nation is against them: and common usage is the best guide in this matter.

The word శ్రీ, or శ్రీ "blest, happy, auspicious" is superstitiously placed at the beginning of papers and books; but in government business at Calcutta this is forbidden: and books printed at Madras omit it at pleasure.

The consonant హ H takes peculiar forms with the various vowels; thus హ ha హా hā హి or హి hi హీ or హీ hī హు హూ hū హృ hri హె hĕ హే hē హై hai హొ ho హో hō or హో hō హౌ hau.

The interjection ఆహా āhā denotes yes.

The letter హ H is sometimes pronounced as F. Thus జిహ్వ Jihva, pronounced jifva, (ignorantly written జింహ్వ Jimha) is the Sanscrit name for the tongue. ఆహ్లాదం āhlādam (āfiādam) delight. It sometimes changes places, in pronunciation, with the letter under it. Thus the name బ్రహ్మ Bramha (a name of God) is written Brahma. And the name for a bramin is written బ్రాహ్మణుడు brāhmanudu but pronounced brāmhanudu.

Thus in Danish Hval is the name for *a whale*. In Swedish Hvad is *what* and Hvar is *where*. See Rae Wilson' Norway and Sweden 1826, Page [60] Appendix.

When the letter H is silent, as in Rāmah it is expressed by two dots ః thus రామః and దుఃఖము duh-khamu.

The letter క్ష csha, more conveniently expressed by X, is a compound of క ka and ష sha; and is sounded like cti in action, direction, section. Thus అక్షి axi 'the eye' పరీక్ష parīxa 'examination' అక్షరము axaramu 'a letter of the alphabet.'

The letter X is in Spanish pronounced like ch. Thus Texiera and Xeres are sounded Tesshira and Sheres, or Sherry.

The letter X is placed by the native authors at the end of the alphabet. In Wilson's Sanscrit Lexicon it is placed with the letter k.

The Telugus are as negligent in spelling as the English were before the days of Johnson. The words borrowed from Sanscrit are often misspelt. Thus స్త్రీ strī 'a woman' is often written శ్రీ Srī 'fortune' and vice versâ. The word అన్నం annam 'food' is constantly written and pronounced వణ్ణం. The word బ్రాహ్మణుడు Brāmhanuḍu is frequently mispronounced బ్యామనుడు Biāmanuḍu.

On the Sunna and Half Sunna.

It has already been stated that the circle or cipher ○ called sunna is used as a substitute for a nasal letter. But it is wrong, though customary, to place it in conjunction with న N or మ M. When N or M occurs double, as అన్న, అమ్మ the vulgar write అంన, అంమ or even అంన్న, and అంమ్మ.

The following observations regarding the circle and semi-circle need not be read by beginners. They can only be understood by those who have made some progress in the language.

When sunna is followed by a consonant of the first four classes (varga) it is N; but the remaining letters (pa, pha, ba, bha, ma, ya, ra, la, va, ṣa, sha, sa, ha, xa,) sound it as M; and it likewise is M whenever it stands at the end of a word. Thus the word Sanscrit సంస్కృతం is pronounced sams-cru-tam. The Sanscrit words సంవాదం conversation, సంశయం doubt, are pronounced sam-vādam, samṣayam. When followed by Y, the sunna is pronounced, nasally: thus సంయమి say-yami, 'a hermit,' సంయోగము say-yōgamu, 'juncture:' here the nasal sound of n is used, as in some French words, bien, sien, chien, requin. Thus sunna is *written* full but only half *pronounced*.

These words are Sanscrit; but in some Telugu words the letter ఁ called the half sunna or semi-circle is used by some grammarians* but in common use the circle alone is used: though it sometimes is pronounced full N, as in the English words song, long.

The learned declare that the semicircle is peculiar to verse, and that to use it in prose is absurd.†

The spelling used in ordinary writing deviates from that approved by the learned. Thus అతండు atandu is pronounced అతఁడు atŭdu.

In some particular words the sunna is inserted *after a short syllable*. Thus తమ్ముడు tammuḍu may become తమ్ముండు tammunḍu; అల్లుడు becomes అల్లుండు a son-in-law; తోడ బుట్టువు, తోడఁబుట్టువు. M. 17. 1. 55. ఏనుగు or ఏనుంగు an elephant. తెలుగు or తెలుంగు.

---

* It is analogous to the sign used in old Latin printing for m or n. Thus gemitu, indignata sub umbras became 'gēitu, īdignata sub ūbras.' In some ancient Latin words the letter N was optional; thus toties or totiens; quoties or quotiens. In his life of Numa, Plutarch mentions Pontifex as written Potifex.

† The printers of many recent publications seem to be unaware of this rule. In a Telugu version of the Arabian Nights we even find (p. 582) such odd forms as కుంభ్ళంబాఁడి; and similar refinements may be seen in most pages of that book.

The sunna thus inserted is called ఆగమసున్న or *optional N*. Thus అరటి becomes అరంటి. వెదక or వెదంక ; పైట, కయుట or కయుంట ; తొల్లిటి or తొల్లింటి ; కడక, కడంక. తెలుగు Telugu or తెలుంగు Telungu also spelt తెనుగు Tenugu (See M. Virat. 1. 6.) or తెనుంగు Tenungu, and even త్రెనుగు Trenugu or త్రెనుంగు Trenungu.

It is inserted before గా when that adverbial affix is added to the *Root in A*. Thus రాగా or రాంగా ; ఎరుకగా or ఎరుకంగా.

And after words of colour. Thus ఎఱ్ఱగా or ఎఱ్ఱంగా redly. నల్లగా or నల్లంగా blackly.

It is sometimes inserted in the verb, in the third person singular masculine of the negative voice. Thus కడడు or కడండు ; ఉండడు or ఉండండు. Thus (Līla XI. 83.) మెచ్చండు for మెచ్చడు 'he disapproves :' పుండండు for పుండడు. This spelling is rustic ; and is used in verse merely to lengthen the preceding short vowel.* Also in other parts of the verb, as తలచుట, తలంచుట ; తొలగక, తొలంగక ; కలగుట 'to grieve' may become కలంగుట. It seems to be prefixed to the letters K. G. D. and B alone.

It is even inserted in pronouns, ఎవ్వడు becomes ఎవ్వండు (M. XII. 6. 615. here ĕvāḍŭ becomes ĕvvanḍu.) And ఎప్పటి, ఎప్పంటి the genitive of ఎప్పుడు.†

In such places the N is used or dropt at pleasure : like U in honour or favour. Practice alone can determine where we must use it.

In the ancient pronunciation of Telugu, (which the rustic classes still retain) the nasal sound was very prevalent : but the educated classes have laid aside this disagreeable accent. In England the rustic pronunciation, particularly in Derbyshire, is more antique and nasal than that of the higher ranks.

The nasal (following a *long syllable*) is preserved among the illiterate in many Telugu words : as వాడు vāḍu 'he' వేట vēṭa 'hunting' the chase' వీక vīka 'strength' తోక tōka 'a tail' కాక kāka 'heat' జాడ zāḍa 'trace,' లేడు, కాడు he is not : which the rustic classes write వాండు, వేంట, వీంక, తోంక, కాంక, జాండ, లేండు, కాండు. The verb కాచుట is written కాంచుట which properly is another verb. ఆడుట is the spelling in the dictionary, but ఆండుట in ordinary writing, though condemned. ఆడది ; is written ఆండది ; పోతాడు, పోంతాడు; రాండు for రాడు. The learned have attempted to reconcile this discrepancy by using ఁ the semicircle ; they wish such words to be written thus వాఁడు, వీఁక, తోఁక, కాఁక. In like manner the forms చేయగా *chāyogā*, పోవగా *pōvagā* రాగా rāgā (doing, going, coming) are commonly written and pronounced చేయంగా *chēyanga ;* పోవంగా *pōvangā ;* రాంగా rāngā. This is the older spelling, now disused by the learned. The slightly nasal sound answers to the indistinct N used in French or in the Hindustani language.

This semi-circle is occasionally used in poetry (when written on palm leaves) as a hyphen at the end of a line.

The vulgar often write the long vowel short and substitute the circle for ardha sunna. Thus వీక vīca 'force' is written వింక vīnca, రోఁజుట is written రోంజుట and జోంతిగ is written for జోఁతిగ. పోక pōca 'a nut' is written పోంక pŏnca, గోకు becomes గోంకు, తోంచగా for తోఁచగా. తెంగె for తెఁగె tĕgeh. పింట for పీట. Rasica. 1. 52. Though written wrong these words are pronounced right. This error often occurs both in poems and in ordinary letters : and must be observed by the student who otherwise may be misled in the dictionary. On the other hand, sunna is omitted with equal carelessness : thus ఇంగువ is written, ఇగ్గువ, ఇంగిలము, ఇగ్గిలము, కుంకుమ, కుక్కుమ

* It is sometimes omitted to suit the metre. గుదించి becomes గుదిచి, పేరంటాలు becomes పేరటాలు. In M. 4. 2. 169. we find ఎరిగి, ఎఱింగి erigi, eringi, here the same word is used twice ; with and without sunna, to suit the metre. See quotations in the dictionary.

† The poets (like Homer) sometimes alter the spelling of words to suit the metre. Thus ఎప్పుడు eppudu "when" is —◡◡ a dactyl : but may change into ఎపుడు epudu [a tribrach ◡◡◡] or even ఎపూడు epūdu ◡—◡ 'an amphibrach' or ఎప్డు epdu, —◡ a trochee.

సంగతి, సఙ్గతి, పొండి (go ye) పొండి, కాంచి Kanchi (a certain town) is written కాచి, ఒంగోలు the town of Ongole is written ఒఙ్గోలు and yet no one pronounces the words in the wrong way. Thus in hasty English writing, letter, teller, litter, tiller, tetter, titter, may easily be understood, though written wrongly.

The semi-circle has never come into general use among the people, and it will be hard to prove the expedience of a refinement like this: which is discountenanced by most manuscripts of the poets and it is unprofitable.

Experience and the advice of sound scholars among the natives has shown me it's futility; but some bramins of ordinary learning uphold this character. They acknowledge that in practice it is laid aside, and that there is no rule in any grammar to vindicate the various ways in which the ardha bindu is inserted.

They insist upon an English pupil acquiring the practice of using the semi-circle; as well as the obsolete R; and leave him to find out, by experience, that both these are unknown to all but pedants. Yet as few students continue the study after acquiring a smattering of Telugu, the emptiness of these instructions generally remains undetected.

The ordinary teachers are apt to speak to students on some learned subjects which are ill suited to beginners. The tutor should on such occasions be desired to read the following caution. ఇంగిలీషువారుఆంధ్రముచదవనారంభించేటప్పుడు కేవలంసంస్కారదూరులైయున్నారుగనుకశబ్దపరిచ్ఛేదం,క్రియాపరిచ్ఛేదం,సూత్రముతోలుతనేర్చుకోవలసినదేగానికళ-ద్రుతం-సంధి-సరళాదేశం-తద్భవం-తత్సమం-దేశ్యం-యిత్యాదిప్రమేయములనుగురించిప్రస్తుతంతలపెట్టకనేలేదు - యీచోటువల్లనే యీప్రమేయములు యీవ్యాకరణములో ఆదిభాగములోవ్రాయక అంత్యభాగములో వ్రాయడమైనది - పైగాఆరంభములో పద్యాలుచదవడముఅన్నివిధాలానిష్ఫలముగనకతొలుతఅజ్ఝలు-జాబులు-వాక్యాలములుగాక మరియేదిన్ని చదవనగత్యములేదు. In reading any manuscript with a learned Bramin, we shall find him object to the spelling in almost every line: asserting that the ignorance of the transcribers has vitiated the book. But our business is to study the language as it is: to take it as we find it: and errors that do not injure the sense or the metre may safely be left unaltered. Much that is pressed upon our notice as highly momentous, is in truth mere learned trifling.

Some modern pedants among the Telugus have attempted (in imitation of some Dēvanagari printing to abolish the ○: thus instead of అందము, and ఆంధ్రము they affect to write అన్దము, and ఆన్ధ్రము. This idle whim appears in some recent publications both Sanscrit and Telugu. It is an empty innovation and is not likely to become popular.

From what has been stated the reader will observe that there are (as in some other languages) two or even three modes of spelling: one in daily use and indispensable; this alone is used in the present grammar; the second mode is poetical, and uses particular forms of certain initial and final letters, as ఒప్పదము for (in common spelling) ఒప్పదము, and వానికిన్ for వానికి; and a third, which is pedantic, using the obsolete R and the obsolete semi-nasal.

In poetry a word may sometimes stand part in one line, and part in the next: thus Nala Dwip. 2. 831. తదను+వగి and in 2, 166, the word అయితి+వి 'thou becamest' is thus divided.

It will be seen in the chapter on Elision that the final M is often dropped in Sanscrit words. Thus గ్రంథం+ఆరంభం grandham—ārambham becomes గ్రంథారంభం grandh'ā-rambham: the Elision being the same as occurs in Latin. But with Telugu words the rule is different; thus బోగము an actress, ఆట play, may form బోగమాట bōgam-āta 'the actress's play' never బోగాట. And కరణము అన్న caranamu-anna 'the clerk's brother' may become కరణమన్న *caranam anna* but cannot become కరణాన్న *caran'anna.* In Sanscrit in such places a long vowel would be used. But in Telugu this never is allowed.

On Dialects.

Just as happens in English and French, certain forms of expression and of spelling are in common use; others are found only in poems. Most words belong to the common stock; and those peculiar to the higher and lower dialect are altogether but few in number. Such occur even in the verb; thus "shalt not, wilt not," would be the poetical form; "shall not, will not," is the common form, and shan't, won't is the colloquial. Native grammarians condemn and neglect the colloquial forms, which they consider vulgar; though it is easy to prove their occurrence, (as in English) even in the writings of the best authors.

We are aware how totally the rules for Elision used in French, differ from those of Latin: and the difference between Sanscrit and Telugu in this respect is yet wider. What is right in one language is, sometimes, wrong in the other.

The rules for elision, permutation and softening initials are required in poetry; but not in the common Telugu we talk or write: and these poetical refinements are not admissible in books written to teach either a language or a creed. Our native teachers would willingly reject common Telugu altogether, and teach us the poetical dialect alone: which they themselves however cannot use in daily talking and writing.

In ordinary sentences, as గ్రంథము ఉన్నది *grandhamu unnadi* 'there is a book' వానికి ఇస్తిని *vaniki istini* 'to him I gave it' ఛందము అనగా యేమి *chhandamu anagā yēmi* 'what is Prosody ?' they would direct us to spell these words thus; గ్రంథమున్నది *grandham'unnadi,* వానికిస్తిని *vānik'istini,* ఛందంబనఁగనేమి *chhand-amb'anangan ēmi.* This mode of spelling would be correct in poetry; but in common life no one uses it; and if we wish to be intelligible, we must use the common dialect. The two dialects differ almost as much as ancient and modern Greek; and were a resident in Athens, to attempt to transact business in ancient Greek (using likewise poetical elision!) he would not be easily understood: nor will the Telugus understand us unless we speak and write as they do.

These remarks are made in consequence of the publication, by natives at Madras, of some small works on Grammar and on religion, which by using poetical rules are rendered hard to understand.

Writers regarding China have noticed that a similar pedantry prevails there; grammarians considering the language of common life wholly beneath their notice.

On Accent.

The accent accords with the spelling; and is easily understood. In words that consist of short syllables the accent falls on the first, thus పది *padi* 'ten' ఎనిమిది *enimidi* 'eight' పని *pani* 'work' would in English spelling be *puddy, ennimiddi, punny.*

The following instances of the accent may suffice: and to each is appended an English or Latin word of similar sound. సరి sari (Surrey) 'right' సమ sama (summa) 'even' అట ata (utter) 'they say.' మణి maṇi (money) 'a jewel.' హరి hari (hurry) 'a certain name. కళ caḷa (colour) 'a ray.' పుసి pusi (pussey) 'rheum.' చెరి cheri (cherry) 'each, apiece.' మడి madi (muddy) 'a field.' తెర tera (terror) 'a curtain.' పులి puli (pulley) 'a tiger.' శతకము satacam (shuttercome) 'a set of one hundred stanzas.'

In all these we perceive that the vowels are short in both syllables and the accent falls on the first. These words also shew that in English we express the first vowel (short a) sometimes by u and elsewhere by other vowels. But a double consonant as ల్ల or న్న or మ్మ has a different accent; as is perceived in English when the two consonants are in separate words thus; royal-lady, begin-now, unnamed, unnumbered.

When a long and short syllable come together, the accent falls on the long: thus ఈటె ītĕh 'a spear' పాము pāmu 'a snake.'

When long syllables come together the accent falls on the last. Thus కూడా kūḍā 'together.'

In reading aloud, it is the custom to open the mouth wide; and to raise the voice to a high pitch. In fact they inculcate the rules used by music masters in England.

"Those who wish to make themselves understood "by a foreigner in his own language should speak with "much noise and vociferation, opening their mouths "wide. The English ...... pursue a system diametri- "cally opposite. For example, &c." See Borrow's *Bible in Spain*, Chapter 1.

The spelling of some Sanscrit words is retained, as హరి Hari (for హరిః Harih) a name of Vishnu. కవి Kavi (for కవిః Kavih) a poet, &c., wherein the termination is but slightly altered: these are denominated తత్సమము Tatsamamu, a word more fully explained in the appendix: as well as తద్భవము Tadbhavamu or Permutations.

After making some progress in Telugu or Canarese the student should read over those chapters of Sanscrit Grammar which treat of (Sandhi, Vriddhi and Samāsa) Elision, augment, and compound words. Doubtless many read Telugu without this: but if we ever make any real progress in the language the student will require the aid of the Sanscrit Dictionary, and cannot even talk or write Telugu with any ease or precision, unless he masters the first principles of Sanscrit orthography.

Hindus and Musulmans usually mispronounce English names: and both the English and French, particularly in names of places, have equally corrupted the pronunciation of names used in India. The accent is misplaced in almost every proper name.

We call Muh'ammad, Mahomet, and Goo-da-loor, Cuddalore. We change Tee-pu టీపు into Tippoo, and Tiru-valli-keni (a suburb in Madras) into Triplicane. Cānchīpuram కాంచీపురం or కంచి is changed into Conjeveram; and Tirupati becomes Tripetty: Eranāoor ఎరనాపూరు becomes Ennore. Pudicheri becomes Pondicherry. Benglū-ru becomes Bangalore: and the name కరిమణల్ Carimanal, (a small insignificant village north of Pulicat near Madras) has been changed into Coromandel; and is applied to the entire coast. It has been furnished (by English ingenuity) with a Sanscrit root "Cholamandal or land of the Chola grain!" a name unknown to natives; who assert that the Curu race (which name some Europeans imagine to be the root of *Kuru mandalam* Coromandel) was in the north of India, not in the Peninsula.

When reading verse the Telugus like all other Hindus use a sort of vociferous chant; the Papists call it "intonation," and at the end of every stanza they are taught to drawl out the last syllable in a kind of quaver which to our ears is absurd. It is needless for us to imitate this method which a native tutor will lay aside when he finds that it does not please the English ear.

Though the learner must enunciate loudly, he need not do so after he has obtained some familiarity with the sounds.

Contractions.

The common contractions of words, (whether Sanscrit, Telugu, Hindustani or English) used in letter writing and accounts are as follows:—The Hindustani words are marked (H.)

ఆ॥	*i. e.* ఆదివారము	Sunday.
ఆ॥	ఆక్టింగు	Acting.
ఆన॥		Anno Domini.
ఉ॥	ఉత్తరము	Answer.
క॥	కసుబా (H.)	Cusbah 'a town.'
కృ॥	కృష్ణపక్షము	The dark fortnight, or wane.
ఖ॥	ఖండి *i. e.* పుట్టి	Candy or Indian ton.
గ॥	గరిశ	A Garise, or measure.
గగ॥	వరహా	A pagoda or gold coin.
గు॥	గురువారం	Thursday.
గు॥	గురించి	Respecting.
గు॥	గుమాస్తా (H.)	Gumashta, 'a writer or agent.'
గు॥	గుజారతి (H.)	In charge of.
చం॥	చందు (H.)	(Persian, *on date*) as చం॥ ౨౨ జూను on the 22d of June.
చొ॥	చొప్పున	According to, at (the rate of.)
ద్వా॥	చేత	By.
జ॥	జయవారము	Tuesday.
జ్న॥	జన or జనము (H.)	People.
డ॥	డబ్బులు	Pence.
త॥	తర్వాత	Afterwards.
తా॥	తారీఖు (H.)	Date.
తా॥	తాలూకు (H.)	Appertaining or belonging to.

తా॥	తాలూకా (H.)	A division of a district.
తా॥	క॥ తాజాకలం (H.)	Postscript.
ద॥	దస్ఖత్ (H.)	(The Persian word dastkhat) 'signature.'
ది॥	దిని	A day.
ని॥	నిమిత్తము	On account of.
నెం॥	"Number"—*i. e.*	Case, letter, field, trial, &c.
ప॥	పరగణా (H.)	Pergunnah 'a division or district.'
ప్ర॥	ప్రశ్న	Question.
ప్ర॥	ప్రథమ	First.
ప్ర॥	ప్రకారము	According to.
బ॥	బహుళ	The dark fortnight, or wane.
బా॥	బాబతు (H.)	An item, or belonging to.
బా॥ బా॥	బాకియతు బాదుండు (P.)	Be it known (to you.)
బు॥	బుధవారము	Wednesday.
మం॥	మంగళవారము	Tuesday.
మం॥ or మౌ॥	మౌజే (H.)	A village.
మా॥	మారిఫత్ (H.)	By the hand of; in charge of.
మిం॥	మింజుమలే (H.)	Out of.
మొ॥	మొకాం (H.)	A station; also, 'Dated at.'
యు॥	యుకం (H.)	An individual

యి॥ ఆ॥యిజ్జతు, ఆసారు (H.) *Izzat-i-āsar.* "Endowed with honour: Dignified." "Homage to the Tokens" See Herklots p. 236. This is a Sectarial exclamation among Musulmans of the Sheea creed. But it is used by Hindus without any idea of the meaning.

రా॥ రా॥ రా॥ Signifies రాజమాన్యరాజపూజితులైన రాజశ్రీ "His Honour" the common salutation at the beginning of a letter.

రు, రూ, రూ, రూ meaning రూపాయలు Rupees.

వ	'*Wa*' (P)	And.
వ॥	వగైరా (H.)	Etcetera.
విం॥	విన్నపములు	Letter, statements.
శ॥	శనివారము	Saturday.
శు॥	శుక్రవారము	Friday.
శే॥ or సే	శేవకుడైన	Your humble servant.
శు॥ ధ	శుద్ధము	The light fortnight.
శ్యా	శానా	Much, many.
సు॥	సదరహీ (H.)	Abovementioned.
సన్ ॥ or స్న॥	"San" (P.)	Year.
సం॥ } సం॥రం }	సంవత్సరము	A year.
సం॥రపు	సంవత్సరపు	Of a year.
సం॥రాలు is	సంవత్సరాలు	Years.
సా॥	సాకిన్ (H.)	Sākin 'Inhabitant of.'
సా॥	సాహెబు (H.)	Sāhib (a gentleman.)
సో॥	సోమవారము	Monday.
హ॥	హంగామా (H.)	Temporary.
హో॥	హొన్ను (H.)	Hunn 'a pagoda.'
+	*caret;*	denoting omission of a word.

In poetry it is customary to designate metres in the same manner. Thus క॥ సీ॥ గీ॥ ఆ॥ తే॥ ఉ॥ చ, శా॥ మ॥ denote the metres called కందము, సీసము, గీతి, ఆటవెలది, తేటగీతి, ఉత్పలమాల, చంపకమాల, శార్దూలము, మత్తేభము and వ॥ stands for వచనము *i. e.* prose; which (as in Lalla Rookh) is mingled with verse. The letter వు vu and even వ్వ will often be found written by mistake for ఉ॥ *i. e.* Utpalamala. Further details regarding metres are considered in the chapter on Prosody.

To represent Italicks in Telugu printing we can use the plan which appears in Greek books: either spacing the types, thus అ త ని కి or enclosing the word [అతనికి] in brackets.

On other Contractions used in Writing.

Where two short vowels occur in a word the second is not always written. Thus తిరిగి tirigi 'again' గనక ganaka 'therefore' తరువాత taruvāta 'afterwards' వెనక venaca 'behind' కొలిమి colimi 'a furnace' వలసిన valasina 'must, ought' అలుగు alugu 'a spear head,' &c. are pronounced as here written: though they are often written thus, తిర్గి tirgi, గన్క ganka, తర్వాత tarwāta, వెన్క venka, చోల్మి colmi, వలస్న valasna, and అల్గు algu.

In poetry such contraction is used for the sake of the metre: thus కలిగిరి may become కల్గిరి, తిరిగి may become తిర్గి, మేలుకొని mēluconi becomes మేల్కొని mēlconi, the u being dropt.

The colloquial contractions, లే for లేదు, &c. are explained in the chapter regarding those words.

The following and similar words particularly such as have three syllables and the middle syllable లు or డు or రు frequently are contracted by dropping the U of the middle syllable. Thus చిలుక chiluca becomes చిల్క chilka 'a parrot.' చాలువ cāluva becomes చాల్వ cālva 'a kennel.' This even takes place (as elsewhere stated) when two words are combined. Thus తోడు + బోతు becomes తోడ్బోతు tod-bōt, కాడు + పోతు becomes కాడ్పోతు, కోలు + పులి becomes కోల్పులి cōl-puli.

Though this does not profess to be a Sanscrit lexicon, it contains some Sanscrit words, preserved because newly explained. Thus *Putticā Vamri* and *Sithili* (పుత్తికా, వమ్రి, శిథిలి) are now proved by quotations (particularly from the Laws of Manu) to be a white ant, or termite: while all the lexicons, and commentaries (even that by Loiseleur Longchamps) on Amera have hitherto explained the words otherwise. Few Sanscrit words appear here without assuming Telugu forms: as in the English Dictionary few Latin words appear without assuming the English garb.

Note:—These remarks are reprinted with some emendations, from the Second Edition of the Telugu Grammar.

END OF REMARKS ON THE ALPHABET.

మిశ్రనిఘంటు

A DICTIONARY

OF THE

MIXED DIALECTS USED IN TELUGU:

EXPLAINING FOREIGN WORDS,

ARABIC, HINDUSTANI, &c.

THAT OCCUR IN BUSINESS, LETTERS, AND CONVERSATION.

BY CHARLES PHILIP BROWN.

అ A. Some words in this vocabulary begin with H as well as with an initial vowel.

అంకారించుట v. n. ہنکارنا *Hancarna.* To set sail. (Pritchett's Tel. version of St. Luke.) ఓడచాపలెత్తిపోవుట.

అంగరకా n. s. انگرکھا *Angarkhah.* A jacket. చొక్కాయి.

అంగియ n. s. *angiya,* A boddice that ties behind. వెనకముడివేసేరవిక.

అంగీ n. s. انگی *Angī.* A man's long jacket. నిలువుటంగి.

అంగుస్తాను n. s. انگشتان *Angushtān.* A thimble. (Tel. కుడుపు.)

అంగూరు n. s. انگور *Angūr.* A grape or grapes. ద్రాక్షపండ్లు.

అంచనా n. s. Estimate, valuation. తుకము. అంచనాదారుడు a surveyor, appraiser.

అంజాం n. s. انجام *Anjām.* End, termination, accomplishment. అంత్యము.

అంజీరు n. s. انجیر *Anjir.* A fig. సీమమేడిపండు.

అంటిసా n. s. (A bad word but much used) Connection. తగులాటము. దానికీవాడికీకొంచెము అంటిసావున్నట్టున్నది she has something to do with him.

అండబాళ్లవాడు n. s. (Nelloor) A sub-renter. See లోపాయకారి, లోపాలివాడు.

అండి Error for హండి n. s. A large pot, a kettle.

అంతరువు n. s. Interval. వ్యవధానము. అంతరువుపడ్డ annulled, suspended, intermitted.

అంతస్థ n. s. Money given secretly, a bribe. M. M. రెండోవాడికితెలియకుండాలంచముగాయిచ్చేరూకలు.

అందాజు n. s. انداز *Andāz.* Estimate, valuation. తుకము.

అందాయత్తుగావుండే, or అందాయత్తైన adj. Neat, pretty, handsome. సొంపుగావుండే. ఈబండిఅందాయత్తుగావున్నది this carriage is neat.

అందేషా n. s. اندیشه *Andesha.* Doubt, guess, conjecture. సంశయము.

అంబరసా (M.) n. s. Expressed juice of ripe Mangoes. మామిడిపండ్లరసము.

అంబారము n. s. (from انبار *Ambār.*) A heap; a heap of corn or grain upon the threshing floor. రాశి. అంబారముపోయుట to heap up grain. అంబారములుగాపడియుండుట to lie in heaps. ఉభయరాశిఅంబారము a heap of grain containing both the shares due to the Government and to the landholder.

అంబారి, or అంభారి n. s. امارى Amāri.) A howdah: the seat or throne on an elephant's back. హౌదా.

అంమ్రాయి n. s. (امراي Amrāi.) A garden or grove of mango trees. మామిడితోట, మామిడివనము.

అకస్వారీ n. s. عكسوارى Spite, malice, ill will, (కసి, అసహ్యము.)

అకారత్ adv. Akārat. Without cause. నిర్హేతుకముగా, వూరికే.

అకీకత్ for హకీకత్ n. s. حقيقت hakīkat. Account, narration, explanation, affairs, events. సంగతి.

అక్కసరి adj. عكسوارى Neighbouring, near. సమీపములోవుండే. అక్కసరివూరు A neighbouring village.

అక్కసు, or హక్కసు n. s. عكس Aks. Spite, malice. కసి, చలము.

అక్కుశాయి, అక్కుసాయి, అకాస్యాయి or అక్షాయి n. s. حق سعى Hakkussai. Commission granted to the seller of goods; or to the broker. తరుగు. See Miles's Hyder Naik, p. 143.

అఖాతివాసు n. s. (Marata, Akkha Tivasi, from అఖా whole తివాసు a carpet.) A large carpet. H. 5. 394. పెద్దరత్నకంబళి.

అగతా n. s. An advance of money. ముందరూకలు. An Udya (Ooria) word.

అగాడీ adv. اگاڑى Agārī. Before, in front, forward, further on. ముందర. n. s. The ropes with which the horse's fore feet are tied. గుర్రముపెడకుతేక ముందరికాళ్లకుకట్టేతాడు. ఆ గుర్రము అగాడీపిఛాడీలను తెంచుకొని పరుగెత్తిపోయెను The horse broke its head ropes and heel ropes, and ran away.

అగాడు n. s. Discharge, explosion. పేలుటేవడము. తుపాకినిఅగాడుచేయుట to discharge a gun. ఒకఅగాడు one volley or one shot.

అగావు n. s. اگاو Agā-ū. An advance of money. ముందరూకలు.

అచ్చారము n. s. (Tamil அச்சாரம்) Earnest money. సంచకరువు.

అచ్చిముట్టము or అచ్చుముట్టము n. s. (Tamil அச்சமட்டம்) An Acheen or Pegu poney. పైగోగుర్రము.

అజా n. s. Amount, gross product, grand total. మొత్తము.

అజాకుంచుట v. a. 'To underrate or value unfairly. To embezzle.' (Guntoor.) తకముతక్కువగాచేసిపొంగలించుట.

అజూద n. s. A certain game. ఒకఆట.

అజ్జాయించుట v. n. To doubt, hesitate. సందేహించుట.

అజ్మాయిషి n. s. آزمايش Trial, proof, examination, experience. పరిశోధన.

అట్కాయించుట v. a. from اٹکانا Atkana. To prevent, stop, hinder: check. నిలుపుట.

అట్కారి n. s. A certain caste of silk weavers. ఒకకులము.

అట్కావు اٹکاو Atkāo. n. s. Stop, prevention, hindrance. అడ్డి.

అట్టవళై n. s. (Tamil அட்டவணை) A cash-book, a ledger, an index, a register. కవిలె, లెక్కపుస్తకము.

అట్టాని for అట్టాలై n. s. A stone seat or low wall; built for carriers to place their loads on when resting: called in Tamil சுமைதாங்கி. మూటలుదించుకొనేతిన్నె.

అతావణీబంట్రోతు n. s. A revenue runner or peon. రివిన్యూబంట్రోతు.

అత్వాడ n. s. اٹھواڑا Aṭhwāṛa a week. వారము. అత్వాడలెక్క a weekly account. ఎనిమిదిదినములకు ఒకమాటు యిచ్చేలెక్క.

అడంగు n. s. Home, birth-place? ఉత్పత్తిస్థానము. అడంగువెల cost price, prime cost. పుట్టినవెల.

అడతిదారుడు n. s. (Hindi, arhatīya اڑھتیا) A broker. తరగరి.

అడదడి, or అడావడి n. s. Ravage, riot: అల్లరి, చెడబిడలు, దాడు. అడదడిచేయుట to ravage.

అడమానము n. s. (Tamil அடமானம்) A mortgage. కుదవ, తాకట్టు.

అడసట్టాలెక్క n. s. (K.) A rough estimate.

అడాయించుట v. a. To stop, sieze, arrest. నిలుపుట, పట్టుట.

అడావడి, or అడావుడి n. s. (properly) Harāharī. Confusion, uproar: routing, fright. చెడబిడలు.

అడితి n. s. Premium, commission. తరుగు.

అడితిమనిషి, or అడితిదారుడు n. s. Arhatīya (Hindi) A broker or middle-man in trade.

తరగతి. Buchanan Hamilt. Eastern India vol. 1. p. 367-380.

అడిమె n. s. (Tamil அடிமை) A slave, slavery. దాసుడు, దాస్యము.

అడియాన్ n. s. (Tamil அடியான்) A slave, a servant. దాసుడు. అడియేన్ (அடியேன்) I am (your) slave. It is a Vaishnavite word.

అడియాలము n. s. (Tamil அடையாளம்) Mark, sign, bearing. గురుతు.

అడుకు n. s. (Tamil அடுக்கு) A pile or heap. దొంతి.

అడుచుట v. a. (Tamil அடைக்கிறது) To close, to shut మూసివేయుట. అందులో నాలుగు వాకిండ్లు అడిచియున్నవి four of the gates are closed, walled up. ఆగుడ్డలనుయీపెట్టెలో అడుచు cram the clothes into the box.

అడుప్పు n. s. (Tamil அடுப்பு) A fire place, hearth. పొయ్యి.

అడ్డాకుల చెట్టు n. s. A certain tree. M. L. S. J. 1838. p. 140, 141.

అణకట్టు or అనకట్టు n. s. (Tamil அணை) A dam or embankment. అడ్డకట్ట.

అణా n. s. The sixteenth part of a Rupee. పం(డెండు పయిసాలు.

అణ్యము for అన్నము adv. (Sea term) Abaft, that is, behind. వెనక. అణ్యముఋణ్యముయెరగను I know neither good nor bad about it. Here అణ్యము is an *anuk.*

అతలసు n. s. اطلس *Aṭalas*, or *Utlus*. Satin: (formerly called in Europe "Atlas," or Damask.) వస్త్రవిశేషము. అతలసుకర్ర satin wood, or a sort of timber resembling mahogany.

అతిరసాలు n. s. A sort of sweet cakes. అరిసెలు.

అతుకుబడి n. s. Fixing, posting. Letting on a lease. అతుకుబడిచేయుట to rent out.

అతుకుబాటు n. s. Giving or letting out on rent.

అత్తరు n. s. عطر *Aṭr* 'Ottar' of roses. Perfume, essence. సుగంధతైలము, వాసనద్రవ్యము.

అత్రాపు n. s. اطراف *Aṭraf*. Quarters, country, parts. Erroneously used for surrounding, adjoining. చుట్టూ, సన్నిధి.

అదంతరము for అతంత్రము adj. Unstable, infirm, weak. అస్థిరమైన, ఐస్థైన.

అదవు or అదుపు n. s. (Tamil அதைப்பு) Swelling. వాపు.

అదబు n. s. ادب *Adab*. Respect, politeness, awe. భయము. అదబులోవుంచుట to keep in awe.

అదమాయించుట v. a. To reprimand, to admonish. గద్దించుట.

అదాచేయుట or అదాపరచుట v. a. ادا کرنا To perform, to pay, discharge. ఆచరించుట, తీర్చుట, చెల్లించుట.

అదాలతు n. s. عدالت *Adālat*. Justice, equity: (vulgarly, severe punishment, vengeance.) A court of justice. న్యాయము, న్యాయసభ.

అదావతు n. s. عداوت *Adāwat*. Enmity, hatred, spite. కార్పణ్యము, పగ.

అద్ద n. s. A stamp or seal. మట్టిముద్ర.

అద్దపుదోసిలి n. s. The fee for the looking glass. A gratuity formerly granted to barbers at harvest time. This is one of the vexatious fees now abolished by the British Government. Under the old Hindu and Musulman Governments there were numerous fees under various pretexts. ధాన్యరూపమైన పుణ్యతంత్రము.

అద్దలపాడ n. s. అనగా ఉప్పుచెయ్యడానకుఆరంభము. D.

అద్దలవాడు n. s. He who stamps or marks the salt heaps. A marker or stamper. Also a salt manufacturer. ముద్రమనిషి, ఉప్పుచేసేవాడు.

అద్దిగె n. s. Mortgage. తాకట్టు. (a Cuddapa phrase.) అద్దిగెభూమి mortgaged land.

అధర్గాము for అధర్మము adj. (Marata) Wrongful, bad, erroneous. అక్రమమైన.

అధర్గళము for అధర్మము n. s. Wrong, transgression. తప్పు, అతిక్రమము.

అధోరి n. s. ادهوری *Adhorī*. A hide, half-dressed leather. చర్మము.

అధేలి n. s. A small silver coin, a half-rupee. M. M. అర్ధరూపాయి.

అనవటిల్లుట v. n. Rice and other grain, after it is boiled and separated from the water, to *settle, dry and cool a little*, so as to be fit for eating. ఉమ్మగిల్లుట.

అనాజ్ n. s. اناج *Anāj*. Grain, corn. ధాన్యము.

అనాదీయము adj. * Immemorial, aboriginal, of unknown origin. పూర్వీకము.

అనానాసు or అనాసు n. s. The pineapple. అనాసకుండు.

అనామతు انامت *Anāmat*. A corruption from అమానతు, امانت *Amānat*. Deposit, any thing committed to the charge or care of another. సధ్యావైకరి అధీనములో వుంచి పెట్టడము. ఆ రూకలు కచ్చేరిలో అనామతుగా వుండినది the money was deposited in the office.

అనాయకము for అరాజకము n. s. Anarchy, misrule, confusion.

అనాసకుండు n. s. A pineapple: Bromelia ananas: a corruption from اناناس *Ananās*.

అనీం (from అనీ انی) n. s. The point or edge. మొన. The bows or front of a ship. వాడ ముఖముయొక్క చెంకలు.

అనుభవీకుడు n. s. He who enjoys; who is experienced. అనుభవించేవాడు, అనుభవముగలవాడు.

అనుభోగత n. s. * Enjoyment, experience. అనుభవము.

అనుభోగించుట v. a. Error for అనుభవించుట To enjoy.

అన్నవకుతి n. s. A sort of bird ?

అన్యాలు n. s. Anyāl "Cress-seed ?" (See printed Tariff.)

అకరజినుసు n. s. 'All sorts of goods ?

అకరధాన్యము or అకరాలు n. s. Miscellaneous grains. Podded grain, such as beans &c. called కాయధాన్యములు. One verse says ఉత్తరేపూర్వసస్యాని అకరసస్యాని రేవతౌ.

అకవిల్లంగము n. s. (From Tamil விவிலங்கம்) A false claim. దుర్వ్యాజ్యము.

అకసాక్షి n. s. A false witness. తప్పుసాక్షి.

అకసాక్ష్యము n. s. False evidence. తప్పుసాక్షి.

అప్పణ n. s. (K.) Permission, leave. శెలవు, ఉత్తరువు.

అప్పళము n. s. "The cut at which water is let into a field." మడవ.

అఫజూదు or అఫ్జూద్ n. s. افزود *Afzūd*. Increase, addition. adj. more, greater. అభివృద్ధి, మిక్కిలి.

అఫత n. s. for هفته *Hafta, Huftuh*. A week. వారము.

అఫరాతఫిరి n. s. for افراطتفریط Ifrāt, tafrit. Confusion, commotion. అల్లరి, కలహము.

అబ్వాబ్ n. s. See అబ్వాబు.

అబటుచేప n. s. A sort of fish, a species of Balistes. Russell, Fishes, plate 21. మత్స్యభేదము.

అబిసీ n. s. for حبشی *Habshi* An African. హబిసీవాడు, ఆఫిరికాదేశస్థుడు.

అబ్బాలాడుట v. n. To grope. దేవులాడుట.

అబ్లోసు n. s. *Ablōs*. The *wake* of a ship. వాడ పోతూవుండగా వెనకనీళ్లలో తెలిసేజాడ.

అబ్వాబు n. s. ابواب *Abwāb*. (lit; Doors, chapters.) Miscellaneous heads in Revenue accounts. "The usual heads in Revenue accounts are Māl and Abwāb. The *Māl* or *Regular* revenue is collected on land and customs, including taxes on liquor &c. The *Abwāb*, or *Miscellaneous* includes the difference of exchange (often considerable) between that of the market and the fixed rate at which the revenue of the district is paid; causal aid or support of the Government officers; fees to the shroff; and contributions to various feasts." Malcolm page 48. Vol. 2.

అఫిని n. s. from افيمي *Afīm*. Opium. నల్లమందు. But అఫినిపాలు milk opium, which is sold in leathern bags.

అమంజి or అమింజి n. s. (Tamil அமிஞ்சி) Unpaid labour, work done by people who are impressed. Drudgery. వెట్టి.

అమరకము for అమరము n. s. A feudal tenure. See the word అమరము in the T. E. D.

అమల్ or అములు n. s. عمل —— Rule, reign, sway, government. An office or post, a public charge. Execution, fulfilment, the period of one ruler's government. ఏలుబడి, దొరతనము, హయాము, నెరవేర్చడము. అతని అములులో in his reign or sway. ఆ కలక్టరువారి అములులో in that Collector's days. ఆ తీర్పు అములులోకి తేబడ్డ తరువాత after the decision was executed. వానిమీద అములుబట్టినారు they took steps against him, they accused him of embezzlement. మూడుగంటల అములు వున్నది it is about three o'clock.

అమలుదారుడు or అములుదారుడు n. s. for عملدار *Amaldār*. An officer, a native collector of revenue. A native head of Police. అధికారి.

అమాంతగాడు n. s. امانتدار An interloper. నడికొల్లగాడు.

అమాంతముగా adv. from امانت Unexpectedly, all at once. Totally, wholly. అటక్షున, యావత్తున్ను. ఆ రాళ్లను అమాంతముగా యెత్తినాడు he raised the rocks bodily.

అమాంతవర్తకము n. s. Interloping, tricks in trade. బేరములోనడమవచ్చికొట్టుకొనిపోవడము.

అమాంతవర్తకుడు n. s. An interloper in trade. నడికొల్లగాడుగా వుండేవర్తకుడు.

అమాదింసు n. s. for همجنس *Hamājins*. All goods, market wares, as grain, or vegetables. అన్నిదినుసులున్ను.

అమానత్తు or అనామత్తు n. s. امانت *Amanāt*. Deposite, charge. ఊరికె పెట్టిపెట్టబడ్డది. ఆ రూకలను అనామత్తుగా పెట్టిపెట్టినారు the money was laid without being brought into use.

అమాని n. s. امانی *Amānī*. What is in charge of a collector on the part of the Government: in opposition to that which is rented out to tenants of the soil గుత్తకివ్వకదివాణమువిచారణ కిందవుండేటిది. అమాని గ్రామములు villages which are under the immediate care of the Collector; not being rented. ఆ ముతా అమానిఅయినతర్వాత after the land was taken into the collector's own charge. ఆ శ్రోత్రియమును అమాని దాఖలుచేసుకొన్నతర్వాత after the free land was taxed. అమానిభూములు lands that like Crown Lands are in the hands of a collector on behalf of Government.

అమానిబాజీబాబు n. s. امانی بعضی باب *Amāni bāzī bāb*. Sundry farms under a collector's management. మన్నులేకుండా మేడిపాలుయిచ్చేభూమి.

అమానుదస్తు n. s. for هاوندسته Hāvandasta. A pestle and mortar for pounding betelnut. వక్కాకు కొట్టేరోలురోకలి.

అమారు, అమారుతాడు n. s. A cable. From the Portugese *amarra*. మోకు.

అమీనా n. s. امین امینا An *Ameen*. A petty revenue officer who has temporary charge of any district. A native Judge. సేధ్యాకుంపించబడ్డఅములుదారుడు, న్యాయాధిపతి.

అములు n. s. عمل *Amal*. See అమల్.

అమేష for హమేషా adv. همیشه *Hamīshā*. Always, perpetually. ఎల్లప్పుడున్ను.

అమ్రాయి n. s. See అంబ్రాయి.

అయిబు, or అయిబు n. s. عیب *Aib*. Fault, defect, blemish, disgrace, infamy. దోషము, న్యూనము, అవమానము, అపకీర్తి.

అయిందా adv. آینده Aindah. Hereafter, henceforth, next time, in future. ఇకమీదటికి. సాలాయిందా next year.

అయిను adj. عین *Ain*. Net, clear, mere, all, whole. మొత్తమైన, నికరమైన. అయినుజమ the net collected Revenue. అయినుబేరీజు grand total, the entire sum. అయినులెక్క general account. ఆ గ్రామముయొక్క అయినుబేరీజు the net produce of the Village.

అయిబు, or అయిపు n. s. See అయిబు.

అయిమా n. s. Usually యోమియా. *Ayima* Meant for یومیه Yomaya. A pension భరణము.

అయిమాయిషి, అజమాయిషి, or అజిమాయిషి n. s. ازمایش Estimate, rough calculation, or conjecture, measurement. ఒకదానుకు తుకము వేసినదిసరో కాదో అనిమరియొకడుపోయిచూడడము. అమీనా తుకము వేసినచేలను తహసీలుదారుడు అజమాయిషి చేసినాడు The Aumeen put a rate on the fields; and then the Tasceldar, estimated the same, to see whether the estimate was right or wrong.

అయివజు n. s عوض *Iwaz*. Substitute, exchange, recompence, money, property, stock, principal, capital. బదులు, చెల్లు, రూకలు, మూలధనము, బండోలము. నీకు అయివజుమనిషివచ్చేదాకా until your successor's arrival. అయివజుకు యింకావుత్తరువుకాలేదు the order for money is not yet issued. వానికేమన్నా అయివజాకరము లున్నవా has he any means of subsistence?

అయ్యాం, or హయాము n. s. ایام *Ayyām*. Days, times, period. కాలము. అతనిహయాములో in his days.

అరకట్లపుత్సవము n. s. (From Tamil அறைநிக்கட்டு) The feast of tabernacles. కిపునిగుడిలోమార్గశిర మాసములో చేసే యొకతిరునాళ్లి.

అరగడి for అరగోడ n. s. (from అర a half and గోడ a wall.) A low wall, breast high. కోట

అరగడిశింటకుందేసొరంగము the subterraneous passage under the wall of the fort.

అరగడిపతేరి n. s. The curtain wall attached to a battery. కోటబురుజులనడుమనుండే పొట్టిగోడ. See అరగడి.

అరచట్టు n. s. (Tamil அரைச்சட்டை) A jacket, a coat. అరచొక్కా.

అరజు n. s. عرض *Arz.* Price, value, estimate. ధర, విలువ. అర్జుబాజారు price current, market price. అంగటివెల.

అరణధరణశక్తిచేత adv. By every means in his power. యావత్తుప్రాణముచేతను.

అరదట్టువేయుట v. a. To imprison. ఖయిదుచేయుట, చెరలోపెట్టుట.

అరదూకు n. s. (Tamil அரைத்தூக்கு) "Half hanging:" i. e. The pillory (a Madras word.) నేరస్థులకుప్రాణముపొయ్యేంతహింసను కలగచేసేశిక్షయంత్రము.

అరదట్లుగా adv. Insufficiently. చాలీచాలనట్టుగా.

అరఫు n. s. حرف Blame, censure. నింద, అపవాదము.

అరమాయిషుఖరమాయిషు or అర్మాయిషీఖరమాయిషీ n. s. فرمائش Provision supplied gratis. దయచేసికో రిఉచితముగాయిచ్చేసామగ్రి.

అరముడి adv. "Again and again." D. మాటిమాటికి.

అరముడి, or అరమూడి n. s. (Tamil அரைமூடி) The silver or gold fig leaf worn by female infants. బిడ్డలకుకొలుకుఅడ్డముగాకట్టేబిడి.

అరాబా n. s. عرابہ *Arāba.* A wheeled carriage, a gun carriage, a cart. Bo. 1. 153. బండి, ఫిరంగిబండి.

అరితకట్లు, or పెద్దకట్లు n. s. Large dams in the saltworks. (Vizag.) పెద్దకనిమలు.

అరిమినెవాడు n. s. ارمني (Armani.) Armenian. అర్మీనియాదేశస్థుడు.

అరుపు n. s. (Tamil அறிவு) Sense. తెలివి. అరుపు తప్పిన foolish.

అర్కాటి n. s. *Arcāti.* A pilot. From the Arabic حرکت change of place.

అర్కారా n. s. ہرکارہ *Harkāra.* A messenger. దూత, తపాలవాడు.

అర్జి n. s. عرضي *Arzi.* A petition, a letter. మనవి.

అర్జిదారుడు n. s. عرضي دار *Arzīdār* for عرضي گذار Arzi guzār. Petitioner, applicant. మనవి వ్రాసుకొనేవాడు, అర్థి.

అర్జిదాస్తు n. s. عرضداشت *Arzdasht.* A written petition, address, memorial. వ్రాసుకొన్న మనవి.

అర్జు ارز *Arz.* adj. Cheap. n. s. Price, value. Breadth. The measurement, round the bottom, of the widths of a heap of grain. (See కులార్జులు.) చౌకగావుండే, ధర, వెడల్పు. అర్జు బాజారు ارزبازار *Arzi bāzār.* Price current, market price or rate. అర్జుకట్టికనుకర్చుట or అర్జుకట్టించుట To test, to thrash out one rick, as an experiment: to see whether the grain therein corresponds with the estimated quantity. అర్జుకట్టుట "to re-examine."

అర్బాబులు n. s. for ہرباب (Har, *every,* and Bab, *head.*) Various items; miscellaneous sources of revenue. ఆయాపద్దులు.

అర్రు n. s. *arru* A certain tree which is small, crooked, and bushy; called Bauhenia parviflora. Rox. 2. 323. ఒకచెట్టు.

అలంగము n. s. النگ *Alang.* A rampart. కోటగోడపైభాగము.

అలంబోతు n. s. The Ourang-outang. కోతిలో కోతి.

అలగా adj. الگ *Alag.* Separate, unconnected. ప్రత్యేకమైన. అలగాభూమి Pastures; waste lands kept for grazing.

అలగాపుల్లరి n. s. (from الگ *Alag.* separate.) Grazing tax, levied on cattle not belonging to the village. పొరుగూరిపశువులుమేసేదానికిచేరే రూకలు.

అలగాసామి n. s. الگ اسامي *Alag āsāmi.* (A *separate* man.) An inhabitant, a private individual: one not concerned. అలగాసామీలు. Loose folk, not regular cultivators.

అలబ్దు n. s. العبد *Alabd.* Signature. Countersignature. (Literally "Your obedient servant"—) or "*The Slave.*" సేవకుడు. అలబ్దురామరావు your servant Rama Rao. తమసేవకుడైనరామరావు.

అలలిసాబు, or అల్లల్ హిస్సాబు adv. علي الحساب *Alal hisāb.* According to account. లెక్క ప్రకారముగా.

అలష్ఠ error for అలసట n. s. Exhaustion, weariness, languor. పరిశ్రమ, ఆయాసము.

అలాగ్ n. s. (error for الگ Alag) Attachment, connection. సంబంధము.

అలాకు for హలాకు n. s. هلاک *Halāk.* Ruin, slaughter, death. హాని, హతము, చావు. అలాకు చేయుట to ruin, or destroy. వాండ్లు అలాకయినారు they were killed; or *half-dead.*

అలామతుకఱ్ఱ n. s. (from علامت *Alāmut*, a mark కఱ్ఱ a stick.) A buoy, for anchors. బోయాకట్టె, అనగా సముద్రములో గురుతుకై వేసి పెట్టేటిది.

అలాయిదా, or అలాహిదా adj. and adv. *alāhida* علاحده Separate, apart, distinct. వేరే, ప్రత్యేకముగా.

అలావతు n. s. Practice, custom. వాడుక, అలవాటు.

అల్కా for హల్కా adj. هلکا *Halka.* Light, mean, vile, base. తేలికైన, నీచమైన.

అల్కాబు n. s. plu. القاب *Alkāb.* The direction, superscription. A title. పయివిలాసము, కితాబులు.

అల్కాసు الکاس *Alkās.* The forecastle of a ship. ఓడముందరిభాగముయొక్క పైతట్టు.

అల్కాహా for హల్కహా n. s. (حلقه halqa) A knocker of a door, a ring, a box handle, a hasp. వలయము, పెట్టెమొదలయినవాటివలయము.

అల్గోజా, or అల్గోజా n. s. الغوزه *Alghōza* A whistle, pipe, flageolet. పిల్లంగోవి.

అల్తుంగా n. s. التمغا *Ultumgha* A diploma bearing the royal signature. రాజాయిచ్చేయోగ్యతాపత్రిక.

అల్దడి n. s. for అల్జడి (الجهاو aljhāo) *Aldaḍi.* Confusion. అల్లరి.

అల్బత్తా adv. البته Certainly, indeed. అవశ్యముగా.

అల్మాని n. s. عليماني *A'lamani* (i. e. d' *Allemagne*, German) The older kind of rupee: somewhat less in weight than the modern one. Said to have been originally coined by a native of Germany. ముసుపటిరూపాయి.

అల్మార n. s. المار *Almar.* (French *Armoire*, Spanish *armario.*) (Port *Almārio.*) An *almira.* A press, chest of drawers, book case. ఖానాలుగల పెద్దపెట్టె. అల్మారకోనేరు a well with steps down into it.

అల్లిరాగులు n. s. (*alli-ragulu.* Tel.) The fruit of the blue lotus.

అల్లీసు, or అల్లీసుకఱ్ఱ n. s. (*allis.* هليس) An oar. పడవతోసేకఱ్ఱ. అల్లీసుకఱ్ఱలుతీయుట or అల్లీసులతో నీళ్లుతీయుట to row.

అల్లెసద్దు n. s. Boundary ? limit ? land mark. సరహద్దు. See Local XVII. 200-208.

అవతప్పితము n. s. (a bad word.) A mistake, error, oversight. పొరపాటు.

అవదు This is a rude vulgar form of కాదు, "it is not so."

అవనాయము for అపన్యాయము* n. s. Injustice. అన్యాయము.

అవపథ్యము n. s. Breach of rule in eating. Error in diet. అపథ్యము.

అవాజబీ adj. (from واجبي, wajibi, justice, with the అ "privative A.") Unjust, improper. అన్యాయమైన, అయుక్తమైన. Several words thus falsely compounded, of Sanscrit and Arabic, occur in these pages.

అవాజా, or అవాదా for అవాజ్ n. s. آوازه *A'wāzā.* Voice, sound, noise, report, fame, echo, a whisper. మాట, శబ్దము, పుకారా.

అవాయిబువ్వలు n. s. Fire-arrows; sky rockets. ఆకాశబాణములు.

అవాయీ n. s. هوائي *Hawāi.* A rocket. పయికిపొయ్యేబాణపుమందు. D. ఆకాశబాణము.

అవిరేజి n. s. The English word, '*average.*' సరాసరి.

అవుటుగుండు n. s. اوت *Aut.* (Meant for) Howitzer. బాంబుసుగుండు.

అవుదు n. s. A water spout in which the stream descends: if the stream ascends, it is called పీరనుండి q. v.

అవుతుఖానా n. s. *Aut khānā.* Error for Hauzkhana, A reservoir, a cistern, pond, bath. తొట్టి, గుంట, స్నానవాటిక. Comment on Vasu. 1. 57. Satya. 2. 57.

అవుధైర్యము, or అవధైర్యము n. s. A vulgarism for అధైర్యము.

అవ్వల్ اول *aval*, adj. First. మొదటి.

అసంట for అపుంట adv. Further, or farther. అవతల.

ఆసమందము n. s. (Tamil அசமந்தம்) Carelessness. అజాగ్రత.

అసరవేసుట v. n. To delay, put off. కాలహరణముచేసుట.

అసలన్ adv. اصلا *Aslan*. (aslan An Arabic adverb.) Originally ప్రథమతః.

అసలు adj. Original, principal, excellent, real, genuine, legitimate. మొదటిదైన, ముఖ్యమైన, స్వచ్ఛమైన, నకరము కాని. అసలుదావా original complaint. అసలువాది original complainant. అసలు n. s. (plu. అసళ్లు the originals.) The principal, in contradiction to the interest. మాతృక, మూలధనమున్ను. అసళ్లు పెట్టుకొనినకళ్లు యిచ్చినాడు he retained the originals and gave the copies.

అసిమి n. s. A sack. గోనెసంచి.

అసున్నతి n. s. (from the Arabic سنت *sunnat*, circumcision; with the Sanscrit "privative A") Uncircumcision. This is the best phrase ; used in Pritchett's Telugu translation of the Gospels, printed in 1819. అసున్నతీయులు they who are not circumcised.

అస్తరు, or అస్త్రీ n. s. استر The lining (of a garment) A patch. అస్తరువేశికుట్టుట to line.

అస్తావెస్తము n. s. Foolishness, madness. చాదస్తము. అస్తావెస్తపుమనిషి a fool. చాదస్తుడు.

అస్నాదు n. s. plu. اسناد *Asnād*. (Arabic plural of Sunnad) Orders, deeds, vouchers. సన్నదులు, దస్తావేజులు.

అస్బాబు n. s. plu. اسباب *Asbāb*. Goods and chattels, furniture, tools, apparatus, baggage. Things. వస్తువులు, సామానులు, కొరముట్లు.

అహాలేకారులు n. s. plu. اهلكار *Ahlikār*. Public servants, official persons, men of business. ఉద్యోగస్థులు.

అహశాంబంట్రోతు, or అహషాంబంట్రోతు n. s. احشام *Ahshām*. A police peon. పోలీసుబంట్రోతు.

అహ్వాలు n. s. احوال *Ahwāl*. State. Particulars. స్థితి, విశేషములు.

ఆ

ఆ A ; broad.

ఆంఛ n. s. *A'nchha*. Check, coercion, restraint. Excommunication. దురాయి, వెలిప్పి.

ఆకిం n. s. حاکم *Hākim*. A ruler : governor, commander. ఏలేవాడు, నాయకుడు.

ఆఖరు, or ఆఖీరు adj. اخیرآخر *Akhir*, or *Akhīr* Last, final. కడపటి n. s. End, termination. తుద, అంత్యము. ఆఖరున adv. اخر *ākhiran*. Finally, latterly. నెలఆఖరుకు at the end of the month. ఆఖరయినది It is finished, or expended.

ఆఖీరని adv. اخرا *Akhiran*. At last. Finally. తుదను.

ఆగవేగముగా adv. *A'ga-vēgam*. With all speed. అతిత్వరగా.

ఆచూకి, or ఆజూకి n. s. *A'çuki*, *A'sooki*, (a word of uncertain origin, but in frequent use.) Trace, token, sign. జాడ, పోలిక.

ఆజీలు Error for హాజరు adj. حاضر *hazir* Ready, present. సిద్ధముగావుండే.

ఆజూబాజూ adv. آزوبازو Azūbāzū Around, about, in the vicinity. చుట్టూరున్ను, ఆప్రాంత్యములో.

ఆజ్మాయిషి, or అజమాయిషి n. s. آزمایش *A'zmāish*. Trial, proving. పరీక్ష, సరిచూడడము. ఆజ్మాయిషిచేసుట to try, test.

ఆణ, ఆణా Error for అణా (marata) n. s. The sixteenth part of a Rupee.

ఆన్యాలు n. s. *Anyāl*. "Cress-seed?" (See printed Tariff.) Perhaps meant for *Anise*.

ఆదరబాదర, or ఆదలబాదల adv. Hastily. అతిత్వరగా, అవసరముగా.

ఆదా n. s. ادا *A'dā*. Profit, gain, advantage. ఆదాయము.

ఆదాచేయుట, or ఆదాపరచుట v. a. from ادا Ada, To realize or collect the value. To pay, discharge, liquidate. రాబట్టుట, చెల్లించుట యున్ను.

ఆదాబాదా adv. آدابادا Adhā bada, Hastily, confusedly. ఆతురముగా.

ఆదాబు n. s. آداب *A'dāb*. Respects, salutation. మర్యాదలు, వందనములు. ఆదాబతస్లీమాత్వ, కూర్నిశాతి, బందగి, బజామేఆవరదు *Adābi taslimat wa cūrnishāt-i-bandagi ba-ja mē avard*,

آداب تسلیمات و کرنشات بندگی بجامی آورد a common Persian expression at the head of letters; "having duly offered his respects, salutations and prostrations, he presents his homage."

ఆదావతు for అదావతు n. s. عداوت *Adāvat.* Spite, ill will, hatred, strife. పగము, ద్వేషము, కగ.

ఆదుర్దా n. s. Alarm, trouble, distress. భయము, తొందర. ఆదుర్దాపడుట to be in trouble. తహతహపడుట.

ఆన *A'na* meant for *Anno Domini:* it answers to A. D. Thus, ఆనరాగా ౧౮౫౨ సంవత్సరము AD. 1852.

ఆనవాటుపొలము n. s. "Disputed land." కరకసాపొలము.

ఆపము n. s. (Tamil அப்பம்) *Hopper*, crumpet. అప్పము.

ఆపుచేసుట v. a. To check, stop, stay, suspend. నిలుపుదలచేసుట.

ఆఫత్తు n. s. (Arabic آفت Tamil ஆபத்து) Misfortune. ఆపద.

ఆబాదాని n. s. آبادانی *A'bādāni.* Cultivation, population. వ్యవసాయము, కాపులు.

ఆబాదు adj. آباد *A'bād.* Flourishing, thriving, well-peopled. Cultivated, inhabited. అభివృద్ధిగావుండే, బస్తీగావుండే, సాగుబడిచేయబడ్డ.

ఆబాదుచేయుట v. a. from آباد Abād. To make populous, or flourishing. బస్తీచేసుట. ఆగ్రామమునుఆబాదుచేశాను he made the village a great town.

ఆబుకారి, ఆబ్కారి, or ఆబకారి n. s. آبکاری *A'bkāri.* A tax on spirituous liquors. కల్లుసారాయీలకుతీసేపన్ను, హాసీలు.

ఆబురి and ఆబ్రూయి for ఆబ్రూ n. s. ابرو *ābrū* Honour, character, renown. బయిసి, పరువు.

ఆబ్రూ, or ఆబ్రూబు n. s. آبرو *Abru.* Honour, character. మానము, గౌరవము. ఆబ్రూబుదక్కించుకొనుట to maintain or rescue one's character.

ఆమదని, or ఆమదను, or ఆముదని n. s. آمدنی *A'madani.* Income, import, revenue. వచ్చుబడి.

ఆమదోరఫ్తు, or ఆమదురఫ్తు n. s. آمدورفت *A'mad-o-raft.* Receipt and expense. వరవుశలవు.

ఆమిషము, or హామిషము n. s. Means, property, worth, resources, gross product. అయివజు, సొత్తు, ఉత్పత్తిఅయినమొత్తము. ఆగ్రామము నకుపోయి ఆమిషముచూచుకొనివచ్చినాడు he went to the village and examined what its resources were. Pritchett's version of Acts V. 1. says తనహామిషముఅమ్మిఆవిలవలోకొంతదాచిచేసె.

ఆమీను n. s. امین *A'mīn. Aumeen.* A temporary superintendent, supervisor, surveyor. కొన్నాళ్లపనికిఉంపబడ్డఅధికారి.

ఆమిల్ n. s. عامل *Amil.* The governor of a province, a superintendent. దేశాధిపతి, అములుదారుడు.

ఆము n. s. عام People, folk. ఆమంతాచూచినారు all the people saw it.

ఆమేజాధారము n. s. (*A'mēz.* آمیز Mingled, *ādhāram* source.) Land having more than one sole resource. Such as land watered both from wells, and from a river. నదీమాతృకముగానున్నుదేవమాతృకముగానున్నుండేది.

ఆమేజు adj. and n. s. آمیز Amēz, Mixed, mixing, mixture. కలిసిన, మిశ్రితమైన, మిశ్రము.

ఆమేజుగా adv. Confusedly. మిశ్రముగా. ఆమేజుగావుండే mingled.

ఆయన్ n. s. (Tamil ஆயன்.) A shepherd (a word used in the old Telugu version of the Bible.) గొల్లవాడు.

ఆయము n. s. (Tamil ஆயம்.) Toll, tax, custom, income. ఆయము or ఆయపట్టు a vital part of the body. సుంకము, దేహములోజీవాధారమైనచోటు, వచ్చుబడి. ఆయకట్టు A yard, an enclosure. ఆయింటిఆయకట్టులోగా within the compound of the house.

ఆయా n. s. آیا *A'yah.* A waiting woman, maid, maidservant. దొరలవారియిండ్లలోవుండేదానిపేరు, పనికత్తె, దాసీది.

ఆయిందా, or అయిందా adv. آینده *A'inda*. Hereafter, henceforth. Next time, in future. ఇకమీదట.

ఆయిను జమా n. s. عین جمع *Ainjama*. The grand total. నికరం మొత్తము.

ఆరకాటి See ఆర్కాటి.

ఆరిందా n. s. آرنده *Arinda*. A porter, a carrier; one who carries the levies or taxes to the treasury. A broker; being an agent, or merchant on behalf of others. మునీబు, అడితిదారుడు, మూటవాడు, కూలివాడు, గొల్ల.

ఆరె *A'rē* The name for 'Marāta.' ఆరెవాళ్లు A certain class of farmers. ఆరెలిపి Marāta writing. ఆరెలెక్కలు accounts written in Mahratta.

ఆర్కాటి *A'rcāti*. A pilot. See అర్కాటి.

ఆలగోడు బాలగోడు గాపుండడము n. s. Roaring, yelling. పెడబొబ్బలు, మొత్తుకోళ్లు.

ఆలము n. s. عالم *A'lam*. The world; the Universe. ప్రపంచము.

ఆలుగడ్డలు n. s. plu. آلو Potatoes. ఉరలగడ్డలు.

ఆలె n. s. [Tamil ஆலை] A sugar cane press. చెరుకుగానుగ.

ఆళగాండ్లు n. s. Servants; people in an office. పాళెగాండ్ల చేతిక్రింది కొలువుడుగాండ్లు.

ఆళ్మాఘూనము n. s. (Tamil ஆள்மாகாணம்) Peons. బంట్రోతులు. తాలూకాలోవుండే పారుపత్తేదారులు తానేదారులు ఆళ్మాఘూనమువగైరా "The overseers, policemen, and subordinates." The superintendent of the district, the officers and peons.

ఆళ్లకోకి n. s. The kind of crow called stinkard.

ఆవర్జా or, (ఆవార్జా) or ఆవర్దా آوارجه n. s. A journal, a diary. దినవహి.

ఆవాయిను వాయిలు n. s. Rockets. ఆకాశబాణములు, ఆకాశచువ్వలు.

ఆషూరుఖానా, or ఆషూర్ ఖానా n. s. عاشورخانه *āshūr Khāna*. A house for the reception of the banners &c. carried during the first ten days of the Mohurram. మొహరములోజండాలు మొదలయినవిపెట్టేవాండ్లువుండేచావిడి, (పాడుకగా) పున్ర్తము, చలిమందిలి.

ఆసరా n. s. آسرا Shelter, protection, patronage, support. ఆదరువు, ఆధారము. ఈవూరికిసీళ్ల ఆసరాలేదుగనుక as this village has no resources for watering the lands. ఆసరాకళ్లులు an assurance of protection.

ఆసాను adj. (from احسان *ihsan*, kindness) Easy, convenient, commodious. సులభమైన, ఒనరైన. but this is commonly used for ఆసరా support, prop, protection. ఆవూరికిజలఆసాను లేదు that village has no resources for watering the lands.

ఆసామి n. s. آسامی *āsāmi*. A person or individual. Defendant: a contemptuous word like *fellow*; a renter, or tenant. మనిషి, పాయకారి స్త్రీ. వాడుచెడుఆసామి he is a cruel wretch.

ఆసామీవారు adj. آسامی وار *āsāmī wār*. Nominal, personal; individual. రయతువారు, యినుముబారు, నఫరుగతి. (as a settlement that is made separately with each tenant.)

ఆసు, or హంసు n. s. (At cards) the ace. కాకితాల ఆటలోవొంటిముక్కగలకాకితము.

ఆసోదా for ఆసూదా (from آسوده tranquil) n. s. *āsōda*. Rest, repose, refreshment. విశ్రాంతి, సేదదేర్చుకోవడము.

ఆస్తావేస్తముగానుండేవాడు, or అస్తావెస్తముగావుండేవాడు n. s. A fool, a simpleton. చాదస్తుడు.

ఆస్తే for ఆహిస్తా adv. آهسته *āhista*. Gently, quietly, softly. మెల్లగా, తిన్నగా.

ఆస్మానిరంగు n. s. آسمانی *āsmānī rang*. Sky blue. ఆకాశవర్ణము.

ఆస్రా n. s. See ఆసరా.

ఆహిరియుంట n. s. A pill of opium. నల్లమందు వుంట.

ఇ

ఇ The vowel I, as ఇజారా izara. ఇనాం inām For this letter the common dialect always uses యి as యిజారా yzāra, యినాం ynām.

ఇంకి n. s. "Ink." మషి, శాయి. (English ink made with galls, which fades rapidly, is always so called: to distinguish it from శిరా q. v. the common native ink made with lampblack which never fades.)

ఇంతిహాను n. s. امتحان *imtihān*. Trial, proving, examination, experiment. పరీక్ష.

ఇంసాఫు for ఇన్సాఫు n. s. انصاف *insāf.* Equity, justice: investigation. న్యాయము, న్యాయవిచారణ.

ఇక్కేరివరహా n. s. اکیری ہون The old Mysore Pagoda: coined at Ikkeri: a coin equal to nine Cantharai fanams. "It is to a gold Rupee, as 100 is to 25-884." Prinsep. ఒకనాణ్యము.

ఇఖ్తియారు n. s. اختيار *ikhtiyār.* Will, pleasure, choice, liberty. స్వతంత్రము, యథేచ్ఛ.

ఇగ్గరము n. s. Error for విగ్రహము.

ఇజరి for ఇజారి n. s. اجری *izāree.* A sort of cotton cloth. ముఖ్యముగాయిజారులుకుట్టేతెలుకగుడ్డ.

ఇజాఫా n. s. اضافه *izāfa.* Increase, supplement: complement, augmentation, surplus. వృద్ధి, అధివృద్ధి.

ఇజారా n. s. اجاره *ijāra.* A contract, a monopoly, a farm of the revenue customs &c. గుత్త.

ఇజారాదారుడు n. s. اجاره‌دار *ijāra-dār.* A contractor or farmer-general. "Tithe farmer" is the term used in Ireland. గుత్తచేసుకొన్నవాడు.

ఇజారు n. s. ازار *izār.* Breeches, drawers, trowsers. మొలనుంచి చీలమండలదాకా వేసుకొనేతిత్తి.

ఇజ్జతాసారు عزت آثار *izzat-āsār.* Marked with honour and dignity. It is a complimentary phrase used without a knowledge of the meaning.

ఇత్తరాజి n. s. اعتراضي Anger, displeasure, malice. కోపము, ఛలము.

ఇత్తిల్లా n. s. اطلاع *ittillā.* Notice, information. తెలియచేయడము.

ఇనం n. s. (Tamil இனம்) Sort, kind. రకము.

ఇనాం n. s. انعام *ināam.* A present, a gratuity to a dependant; land granted in gift, rent free for ever. బహుమానము, మాన్యము. These pensions were named, from the circumstances in which they originated: thus గ్రామమునుకట్టినయినాము land given to the founder of a village. బురుజుయినాం برج انعام to the family of the builder of برج *burj* a castle. నెత్తురుకట్టుయినాం (lit: a *blood-gift*) to such as had lost blood in battle; &c. కదీంయినాం قدیم انعام *Qadim inām* an old bequest. ఛత్రి or గొడ్డుగయినాం Gift to one who bore the umbrella. దివిటీయినాం Land given to a torch bearer. బాగ్‌మారియినాం *bāg māri inām,* a living granted to one who has killed a tiger.

ఇనాయతు n. s. عنايت *ināyat.* Bestowing, granting. ఇవ్వడము, ప్రదానము. ఇనాయతునామా عنايت نامه *ināyat nāmah.* A patent or *grace:* a warrant of donation, a respectful expression for "your letter:" your honour's letter or commands. తాకీదు. ఇనాయతుచేసుట to grant.

ఇబానామ for హిబానామా n. s. هبه نامه *Hibba nāma.* A deed of gift. దానశాసనము.

ఇమితిహాను n. s. امتحان *imtihān.* Examination, trial; proving (but not in a judicial sense.) Experiment. పరీక్ష.

ఇరాదా n. s. اراده *irāda.* Intention, design, purpose. ప్రయత్నము.

ఇరుసాలు, or ఇర్సాలు ارسال *Irsāl.* A sending, a remittance of money, sent with a guard. అంపించడము. దివాణపుసొమ్ములను అంపించడము: usually the government money sent. పంపించబడ్డదివాణపురూకలు. ఇరుసాలుచేయుట to remit gold or silver, thus ఇర్సాలునామా an invoice of the sums sent and of the coins in which the payment is made.

ఇలాకా n. s. علاقه *ilāqa.* Relation, interference. Jurisdiction, connection by business &c. (not by blood) commonly it denotes charge, possession. సంబంధము. అధికారములోచేరిన ప్రదేశము, స్వాధీనము. మాయిలాకాదారులు, మాయిలాకావాండ్లు those who belong to me, my people.

ఇలాయి n. s. *ilahi* A pole shaped like a cross, or T, bearing a light at each end of the cross bar at its head.

ఇల్ల A Canarese word for లేదు *it is not.*

ఇషారా n. s. اشاره *ishāra.* Sign, hint, suggestion. సైగ, జాడ.

ఇసుళ్లు n. s. plu. White-ants with wings. ఉసుళ్లు.

ఇస్క్రూ n. s. (E) A "screw." మర.

ఇస్తిక్బాలు n. s. إستقبال *istaqbāl.* Reception. The ceremony of meeting and receiving a visitor: a deputation sent to meet a great man. ఎదుర్కొనడము.

ఇస్తిమ్రారి adj. إستمراري *istimrāri.* Perpetual; in perpetuity, continual. ఎడతెగని, నిరంతరమైన.

ఇస్తిరి n. s. إستری *istiri.* Ironing of cloaths. బట్టలు మెరుగుగా వుండడమునకై చిన్న యినుపపెట్టెలో కట్టెనిప్పులు వేసి రాచడము.

ఇస్తిహారు n. s. إشتهار *ishtihar.* Proclamation. చాటించడము. ఇస్తిహారునామా إشتهارنامه *ishtihar nama.* A written proclamation. ప్రకటన పత్రిక.

ఇస్తీఫ n. s. إستعفا *ista-fa.* Resignation; quitting office. కొలువును విడిచిపెట్టడము, రాజీనామాయివ్వడము.

ఇస్తువ, or ఇస్తువు n. s. Property, estate. సొత్తు, ఆస్తి.

ఇస్పేటు, ఇస్పేటుకాకితాలు n. s. Playing cards.

ఈ

ఈ The vowel ī, or ee. This, in ordinary Telugu is disused: and యీ yi substituted. Accordingly in this glossary they will be found under the letter యీ *yī.*

ఈడలు n. s. plu. The sides of a pit in salt works.

ఈన For the Sanscrit హీనమైన.

ఈరట్టు n. s. (Tamil ஈரொட்டு) Uncertainty. సందేహము, సందిగ్ధము.

ఈసు, or ఈసుకర్ర n. s. The wooden cross beam of an anchor. లంగరుమొదటికి అడ్డముగా కట్టే కొయ్య.

ఈసవి n. s. عيسوي *Isavi. Eeswee.* The Christian Æra or *Anno Domini*: from عيسى *Isā,* Jesus. క్రీస్తువారి శకము. Thus ఫసలి ౧౨౩౮ ముతాబకు ౧౮౨౮ ఈసవి In the Fusly year 1238 answering to AD 1828.

ఉ

ఉ U, or OO. This initial is written వు vu, and in this glossary are placed under వు VU. The letter ఉ|| or వు|| u is used as a contraction for ఉత్తరువు answer.

ఉండది (for ఉన్నది present tense of ఉండుట) She or it is.

ఉండాడు for ఉన్నాడు He is.

ఉచ్చావచ్చముగా adv. In all sorts of ways. ఉచ్చావచ్చములాడుట v. a. To abuse in all sorts of ways. హెచ్చుతగ్గులుగా ఆడుట.

ఉచ్చి n. s. (Tamil உச்சி) The crown or top of the head. మాడు. దానికి ఉచ్చి తాకినది she is suffering from the evil imagined to be caused by letting the nipple touch the top of her child's head.

ఉజాడైన adj. أجاڑ *Ujār.* Depopulated, waste, deserted. బేచిరాకుగా వుండే, వయిరాను, పాడుగా వుండే. ఆ గ్రామము వుజాడైనది the village was depopulated.

ఉజియబాడ n. s. Starboard; (a sea phrase) కుడి పక్క.

ఉతావలి for హుతాహులి n. s. Hastiness. అతిత్వర. ఉతావలిపైనము a forced march. ఉతావలిగా వచ్చి చేరిరి they arrived with speed.

ఉడప n. s. A fish. చేప.

ఉడాను for ఉడాన n. s. اڑان *urān* Flight, rapid pace. ఎగరడము, పరుగాపోవడము.

ఉడాయించుట v. a. اڑانا *urāna* To cause to fly, to spend extravagantly. ఎగరవేయుట, దుర్వ్యయము చేసుట; but usually To make away with, usurp. హరించుట, సొత్తులో వేసుకొనుట.

ఉతాళించుట, or ఉత్తాళపడుట v. n. To be hasty or rash. ఎగిరిపడుట. Satyabhama 21. 40.

ఉదాసించుట v. a. To abuse. దూషించుట.

ఉదాసీ n. s. اداسی *udāsī,* A friar of a particular order of Gosawees. గోసాయీలలో ఒక తెగలో చేరినవాడు.

ఉదాసీనపుమాటలు n. s. plu. Abusive language. దుర్భాషలు.

ఉదాసీనుడు n. s. He who is indifferent or unconcerned. నిశ్చింతభావముగలవాడు, వాడుఅం

ఉలాకలియకవుదాసీనుడుగావుండెను he was an unconcerned spectator. A philosopher or cynic.

ఉద్దారి n. s. A superintendant (Viz.) విచారణకర్త.

ఉపరిరయ్యతు n. s. اپری رعیت *upari-rayat*. A tenant at will (Elph. p. XIV.) పాయకారి.

ఉమేజు for ఉమేదు n. s. امید *ummaid*. Hope. ఆశ, కోరిక. ఉమేజుచేసుట To live in hope, to be a hanger on, as an expectant.

ఉమేజువారి for ఉమ్మేద్వారి n. s. امیدواری *Ummaid wari*. Expectancy, waiting for an appointment. ఆశించుకొనియుండడము, ఉద్యోగమునకైకనిపెట్టుకొనియుండడము.

ఉమ్మేదువారు n. s. امیدوار *Ummaid war*. A candidate for employment: an apprentice, an expectant. ఉద్యోగమునకైకాచుకొనియుండేవాడు, ఆశించుకొనియుండేవాడు.

ఉరఫు for ఉర్ఫు n. s. عرف *urf, ooroof*, (Applied as an adverb.) Alias, otherwise called. లేక, అనే. గంగయఉరఫుచిన్నరాజు Gungaya alias Chinna Rāju.

ఉరల n. s. (Tamil உருளை) A roller.

ఉలుఫా, or ఉల్ఫా n. s. علوفه *ulfa*. Presents: supplies furnished to travellers. Batta, undressed rice, pulse &c. given to bramins or others బియ్యముమానము, బత్తెము, స్వయంపాకము.

ఉల్టా adj. الٹا *ulṭa* Reverse, the wrongside, opposite, contrary, turned back. లోతట్టు, అడుగుతట్టు. ఆశాలువను ఉల్టాగాకప్పుకొన్నాడు he wore the shawl the wrong side up.

ఉల్లంగి, or ఉల్లింకాయ n. s. The bird called a lapwing. ఒకపక్షిపేరు.

ఊ

ఊ U′ or *ōō* This initial is always written వూ. under which letter such words will be found.

ఊడాడుట v. n. (Tamil உடாடுகிறது) To be in familiar friendship with one. కూడామాడా వుండుట.

ఊదా, or వూదా n. s. اودا Brown, purple, lilac, dark flesh colour.

ఊదు n. s. (—) عود *ūd*. Frankincense, benzoin. సాంబ్రాణి. ఊదుబత్తి, or ఊదువత్తి a pastile. సాంబ్రాణివత్తి.

ఊళిగము n. s. (Tamil ஊழியம்) Service, function. కొలువు.

ఎ

ఎ E, *short*. This is commonly written యె *ye* or య *ya* when initial. Words beginning with ఎ will be found under యె. It is wrongly substituted for *a* after the letters ch, j, sh. Thus the Sanscrit words చమత్కారము, చంద్రుడు, శరీరము are written చెమత్కారము, చెంద్రుడు, శెరీరము. The Hindustani words చలావణి, జవాబు, ఝుండ become చెలావణి, జెవాబు, ఝెండ. Likewise the Telugu కత్తి, కడియ become కెత్తి, కెడియ.

ఎకరారు for ఇకరారు n. s. اقرار Admission, acknowledgement, confession. ఒప్పుకొనడము. యొకరారుకడుట to confess.

ఎకరే, or ఎక్రా n. s. The English word *acre*. నాలుగువేలమొనమన్నూటచదరగజములనేల.

ఎకాయకీ, or ఎకాయెకిగా adv. یکایکی *Yakāyaki*. Suddenly, unawares, unexpectedly, speedily. ఆకస్మాత్, వున్నట్టుండి, అతిత్వరగా.

ఎగాదిగా adv. Violently.

ఎడగరి n. s. The cold weather crop of paddy. (Raj.) చలికాలములో పండే ఫుకవరిపయిరు.

ఎతిరాజి See ఇత్తరాజి.

ఎదిరి n. s. (Tamil எதிரி) A foe, defendant. శత్రువు, ప్రతివాది.

ఎళవు n. s. (Tamil இழவு) Mourning for the dead. Damage, injury, loss. దుఃఖము, చేటు.

ఎల్లాఒితనము n. s. Cunning, guile, roguery, swindling. దొంగతనము, కేళ్ళమారితనము.

ఏ

ఏ E *long*, is vulgarly changed into yā. Thus తేప *tēpa* and కేక *kēka* become త్యాప *t-yāpa* and క్యాక *k-yāka*. The change however is not systematic, as లేరు and తేపు &c. are never so altered.

ఏకచ్చాయ n. s. A bond signed by several persons. [Ganj.] In Telugu ఉమ్మడిపత్రము.

ఏకరంగి n. s. ایکرنگی *ēkrangi*. Velvet which is of "one colour" contrasted with *dorangi*: shot silk or damask. T. 4. 202. ముఖమలు.

ఏకరి n. s. *Ekari*, A tribe similar to the ఎఱుకు వాండ్లు q. v. ఒకకులముపేరు.

ఏకాదా [Mahratta] adj. One, some one, any one ఒక, ఏదొక.

ఏకూన్ n. s. *ekōn* [Mahratta] Total, (generally) the sum total. మొత్తము, వెరశి.

ఏకోనాదారులు n. s. Fellow holders, joint partners. కలిసిపాలివాండ్లు. ఏకోను, ఏకేంద్రా total, general: the sum total. వెరశి, మొత్తము.

ఏరి-పాలి-జర-కప్పి n. s. A three sheaved pulley. మూడుచక్రములుగలకప్పి.

ఏరువ n. s. A ship's keel. వాడవెన్నుకలక.

ఏలము n. s. Auction. ఏలమువేసుట to sell by auction (see యేలాము.)

ఏల్చా n. s. ایلچہ *elcha*. The snipe, generally called however by the English name; corrupted into యిస్నాఫు *isnauf*.

ఏవరేజి n. s. Corrupted from the English word '*Average*.' సరాసరి.

ఐ

ఐ AI. For this letter the form అయి AYI is generally substituted: and the words are in this vocabulary classed accordingly.

ఒ

ఒ As an initial, O is commonly written వొ wo, or యొ yo. The vowel *A* is often pronounced *O*, as in ఒప్పగించుట for అప్పగించుట, తొల్వ for తల్వ and రొండు becomes రెండు.

ఒంట్లు n. s. A small kettle used instead of a బాన or still.

ఒగరతుమూట n. s. A certain fee, or allowance in grain, granted to reapers &c. See విల్లరుసు.

ఒప్పనము (Tamil ஒப்பனை) adv. As, like. వలె. ఆయనకుబిడ్డవొప్పనముగానున్నది she is to him as a daughter.

ఒప్పారి n. s. (Tamil ஒப்பாரி) Nominal connection: as that of two men who call each other brother.

ఒలాందావాండ్లు n. s. plu. (*les Hollandois.*) The Dutch. ఒలాందామల్లె the Dutch tuberose. ఒలాందాకములము a diamond cut in the Dutch fashion.

ఒలారదము n. s. (Tamil உலாத்துதல்) అనగా తిరుగులాడుట. To walk slowly. షికారుచేయడము.

ఒళుంగు n. s. (Tamil ஒழுங்கு) Order, a disposition of things in their proper order. Survey-measurement of land.

ఓ

ఓ The vowel O' when initial is generally written వో that is; *wo*, or *vo*.

ఓకు n. s. A telescope. దుర్భిను.

ఓళిగ for హోళి n. s. (K.) A sort of cakes. తెలుగులో పొబ్బట్లు అని అంటారు.

ఓల్ఖానా n. s. اولخانہ *olkhana*. The Prisoner's ward. Watch house. ఒకవిధమైనచెరశాల.

ఓవరి n. s. *ovari*. (Error for آبرو *ābrū* ?) Politeness. అణుకువ.

ఔ

ఔ All words beginning with AU will be found under అవు AWU.

క K, ఖ Kh, గ G. ఘ Gh.

The words beginning with these four consonants are classed together; numerous words being written with any one of the four, indifferently, as an initial. The Arabic *Kaf* and *Qaf* in Telugu become క; and *Gaf* and *Ghain* are expressed by గ G and ఘ Gh.

క|| A contraction for కస్బా قصبہ *Kasbah*, *Cusba* A town.

ఖ|| A contraction for ఖండి a Candy, or పుట్టి putti.

గ|| In accounts stands for గండు, a cant or disused name for a pagoda, q. v. గగ౨ signifies 2 pagodas and a half.

కం, or కమ్మి adj. کمی *Kami*. Less. కంకిస్ జమి౯ను کم قسم زمین *Kam Kism zamin*, Land of an inferior sort. అనగా కనిష్ఠపుతరంపొలము.

కంకర n. s. کنکر *Kamkar*. Gravel, broken bricks. జల్లి.

కంగరు n. s. کنگرہ *Kangara*. A scaling ladder. నూలునిచ్చెన.

కంగాణము n. s. (Tamil கங்காணம்) Watch, guard.

కంగాళీ for కంగాల్ adj. کنگال *Kangāl*. A miserable wretch, wretched. దిక్కుమాలిన. కంగాళీమంచము a flock bed, a wretched bed. కంగాళీబత్తెము paltry batta, a wretched pittance.

గంగుడుచెట్టు n. s. A tree called Cæsaria Tomentosa. Rox 2. 421.

కంగోరి n. s. کنگورہ *Kangora*. An arch or dome. The moulding in brick-work.

కంచాయిలు n. s. A "consignment" of goods.

కంచినీ n. s. کنچنی *Kanchini*. A dancing girl, an opera dancer, actress, courtezan. భోగముది.

గంజాయి n. s. گانجا *gānjā*. The hemp plant (cannabis sativa) The fructification when nearly ripe is bruised and smoked to produce intoxication. గంజికా, జ్ఞానపత్రము.

కంజాయింపు, or కజ్జాయింపు n. s. قضیہ *qazyah*, Quarrel, wrangling, regarding distribution of water from a stream. నీళ్లజగడము.

గంజిఫాలు n. s. گنجیفہ *ganjīfalu*. A pack of cards, a game at cards. ఒకజత ఆడేకాకితాలు, ఒకవిధమైన కాకితాల ఆట.

కంటి, or కణతిచేప n. s. A sort of fish. ఒకవిధమైనచేప. Russell plate 104 where బల్లిదుకంత is rendered A species of *sparus*: with a prickly head and large eyes.

కంఠీరాయవరహా, కంఠేరాయవరాహము n. s. کنٹھی رائی ہون A cantaroy (Kantherai) pagoda; equal to Rs. 2. 14. 8 being equal to ten cantaroy fanams: another rate gives Rs. 2. 13. 0. ఒకనాణ్యము.

ఖండిక, or ఖండ్రిక n. s. A small hamlet. చిన్నపల్లె.

ఖండికుత్త n. s. "A fixed rent." *Ganj.* శాశ్వతపేరిజు.

ఖండీ n. s. کھنڈی *Khandi*. A certain measure of grain. పుట్టి.

కండిగచేప n. s. "*Kundinga*." A sort of fish. Russell No. 203. "A species of Clupea."

కండుబాయిచేప n. s. The sepia or cuttle fish, which produces the కండుబాయిపుయిక the bone from which pounce is made.

కండ్రావి n. s. (Tamil கண்ணறாவி) A disgusting sight, a horrible spectacle. చూడఘోరముగా వుండేటిది.

ఖండ్రిక n. s. A small hamlet. చిన్నపల్లె.

ఖండ్వా n. s. *Khandwa*. A sort of cotton upper cloth, a kind of fringed cloth. దుప్పటా.

కంతరీన్ adj. کمترین *Kamtarin* Least, most humble, humblest, meanest.

కందాచార adj. کنداچار *Candāchār*, (K.) Military. దండుసంబంధమైన. కందాచారము n. s. The native militia కట్టుబడివాండ్లు.

ఖండోటి n. s. *Khandoti* (M) A bag of money. రూకలసంచి. (Bellary.)

కంబరుతాడు, or కంబారుకట్టె n. s. Coir rope; a mat made of coir. ఒకవిధమైనమోకు.

కంబళేటు n. s. From "Camlet." ఒకదినుసునాణ్యమైనకంబళి.

కంబాయి n. s. *Cambay*. A sort of cotton cloth called *charcona*. వస్త్రవిశేషము.

కంబారులు n. s. Servants, labourers. పనివాండ్లు.

కంబితీసుట v. n. (A phrase at Madras,) To run away. ఉరుకుట.

కంభర్తియినాము n. s. کم بہرتی انعام *Kam bharti inam*. A supplementary or additional grant of inam land. యింకాపుయిగాయిచ్చినమాన్యసేల.

కక్కిశచెట్టు n. s. "*Nella kakisha*." Rox. 1. 712. A tree called Posoqueria uliginosa. ఒకచెట్టు.

కచావస్ n. s. *Cachāvars*. Trickery, league, combination. మోసము.

కచేరి, or కచ్చేరి n. s. کچہری *Kach-heri*. An office, or place for publick business. A publick court. A nautch; the ceremony of dancing at a wedding &c. కొలువుకూటము, అధికారిది

చారణజరిగించేయిల్లు, పెండ్లిమొదలయినవాటిలో బహుమందికూడి బోగమువాండ్లను ఆడించబడము.

కచ్చా adj. کچا *Kach cha.* Unripe, raw, unsettled or rough, not fair, mean, low, base. కుందని, కుదరని, నీచమైన, అల్పమైన. కచ్చాసేరు the lesser seer, as defined under శేరు. కచ్చామనిషి a mean fellow. కచ్చామాట nonsense, a foolish expression. కచ్చావసూలు trial for extortion: making him account for his collections.

కచ్చుగడా, or కచ్చుకడా n. s. کچکڑہ *Kach Karah.* Tortoise shell. తాబేలుపెంకు, దీన్ని ఖడ్గమనిన్ని అంటారు.

గజము n. s. گز *gaz.* A yard. Trick. నేలకొలిచే మూడడుగులకోల, మోసమున్ను. నూరుగజాలు hundred yards.

గజరా n. s. گجرا *gajra.* Bracelets made of flowers, which at marriages are given to the guests. చేతికివేసుకొనే పూలకంకణము.

ఖజాంచి, or ఖజాంజీ n. s. خزانچی *Khazanchi,* (also wrongly spelt ఖజాంజీ) A Treasurer. దివాణపురూకల కొట్టుమీదవుండేవాడు.

ఖజానా n. s. خزانہ *Khazana.* A treasury. దివాణపురూకలకొట్టు.

కసాయి for ఖసాయి, or ఖసాయివాడు n. s. قصائی *Kassai.* A butcher. కటికవాడు.

కజ్జా for ఖజియా n. s. قضیہ *Kazya.* A quarrel, dispute, altercation. జగడము. ఖజ్జామాడుట to quarrel.

ఖజ్యా, or ఖజ్య n. s. for قضیہ *Qazya.* A quarrel. జగడము.

కటాకటి for ఖటాఖటి n. s. for کھٹپٹ or کھٹکھٹ *Khatkhat.* Wrangling. జగడము, పోరు.

ఘటాటోపు n. s. گھٹاٹوپ *Ghatātop.* Covering of a pālkī or carriage. Thick clouds. పల్లకీ లేక బండిమొక్క ఖురళా. మబ్బుఘటాటోపు చేసుకొనివచ్చినది it is overcast.

కటాయి, or కటావు n. s. کٹائی کٹاو *Katai. Katā-oo.* Cutting. కోయడము. సజురుకటాయి the money paid for leave to reap a crop. కోతకు సెలవుతీసుకోవడమునకు గానుయిచ్చేరూకలు.

కటాయించుట, or కతాయించుట v. a. from کتانا *Katana.* To enter in an account. To post in an account (Mahratta.) దాఖలుచేసుకొనుట.

కటావణి, ఖతావణి, కతావణి n. s. کتاونی A ledger, an entry, a statement.

కట్టియగాండ్లు n. s. plu. (Tamil கட்டியக்காரர்) Heralds, panegyrists. భట్టువాండ్లు.

కట్టుతూములు n. s. Allowances or remissions made in Guntoor to those who (కట్టినారు) have repaired the tanks under which they cultivate.

కట్టెము for కట్యము n. s. Proclamation, a declaration to give notice, ప్రకటనచేయడమునకై అరిచిచెప్పడము.

ఖట్లా n. s. کھٹلا *Khatla.* A bad debt (Bel.) బచ్చు బాకి.

కడంబె n. s. (Tamil கடம்பை) The Elk. కణితిమృగము.

కడపు n. s. (Tamil கடப்பு) An inferior sort of grain called సవాబింజ, వడ్లలోభేదము.

గడబడ for గడిబిడి n. s. گربڑی *garbari.* Rumour: hubbub. దడబిడలు.

గడమంచె, గడవంచి or కడవంచి n. s. گھڑونچی *gharonchi.* A frame with legs to put the things on. మూటలకుకిందవేసేపీట.

ఖడాయించుట v. a. کھڑاکرنا *Khara karna.* To erect, set up, establish, found, to pitch a tent. నిలుపుట, నిలువబెట్టుట.

ఘడి n. s. گھڑی *ghari.* An hour of twenty-four minutes. గడియ.

గడిబిడి n. s. گڑبڑ *garbar.* Confusion, puzzle. దడబిడలు. గడిబిడిమనిషి a violent man, an outrageous person. దడబిడలుచేసేవాడు.

గడిస్థలము n. s. from گڑھی *ghari.* A fortress, a hill fort. కోట, దుర్గము.

గడికారి n. s. A mason. కాసెవాడు, కొల్లపువాడు. The attendant who carries the spear before an elephant. ఏనుగ ఈటెవాడు.

గడ్డ n. s. A water course (Ganj.)

గడ్డపీలిక n. s. Tow, caulking stuff. జనుముదువ్వగావచ్చేపనికిమాలినపీచు.

కట్టాయము (Tamil கட்டாயம்) or ఖట్టాయము n. s. Violence, force, compulsion. బలవంతము. Distraint, as by government. దివాణమువారు చేసేజోరావరి. వర్తకట్టాయముపోయిననేఆజ్ఞ a government order to merchants to receive grain at a certain price which they were compelled to pay. This was a Musulman custom abolished by the English: it is similar to billeting soldiers. కట్టాయముచేసుట to constrain, to force.

ఖడ్డీ for కడ్డి n. s. A stick. పుడక.

గడ్డం i. e. గడ్డాయము n. s. Compulsion, force. బలాత్కారము.

కణజ n. s. An embankment, anikut, or dam.

కణిశము n. s. (Tamil கணிசம்) Proper weight or value. Usually. adv. about, nearly. సుమారు.

కణిశించుట v. a. (Tamil கணிசிக்கிறது) To judge of the proper weight or value. ఉజ్జాయించుట.

కతల్ చేయుట v. a. from قتل کرنا *Qatl karna.* To slay or kill. చంపుట.

కతాయించుట v. a. See కటాయించుట.

కతావణి See కటావణి.

ఖతేల్ n. s. Khatel (M.) A packet or bundle of papers.

కత్తిరించుట, or కత్రించుట v. a. from کترنا *Katarna.* To cut *cloth with scissors* or *shears.* To snuff (a candle.) To clip, to crop, to poll the head. కత్తెరతో తుండించుట, నరుకుట.

ఖత్తు n. s. خط *Khat.* A letter. జాబు. A style or school of music, రీతి, తరహా, as కర్ణాటక ఖత్తు and దేశీయఖత్తు.

కత్తువ n. s. A dam, mole or bank. ఆనకట్ట.

ఖత్ల n. s. کھتلا *Khatla.* A bad debt. చచ్చుబాకి.

కదపా n. s. An agreement, a written bond. ఒడంబడిక, పత్రము.

కదము for ఖదము n. s. قدم *Qadam.* A footstep. Twelve inches. అడుగు, పంన్రెండు అంగుళములు.

కదిర n. s. *Kadira?* ("*Kuddera*" Russell No. 175-176-277-178) A slender pipe-shaped fish. మత్స్యవిశేషము.

కదీం n. s. قدیم *Kadim.* An old servant, an old inhabitant. కదీములు the old and hereditary cultivators of a village. మిరాశికాపులు.

కదుపా n. s. See కదపా.

గర్మాయించుట v. a. گرمانا *Garmana?* To browbeat. గద్దించుట.

గద్యాణ n. s. (K.) *Gadya-anna.* A weight used in weighing silver. (Reeve) ఒకనాణ్యము, ఒక తూకకట్టు.

కనకపిళ్లె n. s. (Tamil கணக்கப்பிள்ளை) A clerk. కరణమువాడు.

కనగర్త n. s. A species of fish: a species of scomber. Russell plate 136. మత్స్యవిశేషము.

కనము, or కనముచెట్టు n. s. A tree, called Saccharum exaltatum. Rox. 1. 245.

కనముచేప n. s. *Canamu.* A fish: a species of Cyprinus. మత్స్యవిశేషము. Russell, plate 204.

కనసచేప n. s. *Canasa.* A fish: a species of Sparus. మత్స్యవిశేషము. Russell plate 109.

కనాలి n. s. *Canāli.* (French.) A canal. కాలువ.

కనిసిచేప n. s. *Canisi.* A sort of mullet. Russell plate 181. మత్స్యవిశేషము.

గనిం n. s. غنیم *Ghanim.* An enemy, an invader. శత్రువు, దాడిచేసేవాడు. T. 2. 173.

గనీబు adj. (Perhaps an error for غني Ghani) Opulent, rich. ఆ కాపులు నిండా గనీబులు they are opulent, or substantial men.

కనుకూలి n. s. *Canu-culi.* Fees taken for viewing and sorting coins.

కనుజు n. s. *Canuzu.* See కణజ.

గప్చిప్ adj. and n. s. غپ چپ *Ghapchup.* Silent. "Silence !" చిటుకుపోటుకు.

కపాతు, or కబాతు n. s. *Cabāt.* A capon. విత్తులు తీసినకోడి.

కపాయి for కబా n. s. قبا *Qabā.* A gown reaching to the ancles. తురకలుతొడిగేనిలువుచొక్కా.

కప్పరఫోలు n. s. کپڑپهول *Kaparphūl.* Gauze. గాజుగుడ్డ.

గప్పాలు n. s. plu. گپ *Gap.* Bragging, boasting. జంభాలు. గప్పాలుపడాయించుట گپ مارنا to brag, boast.

కబరు n. s. قبر *Qabar.* A tomb. గోరి.

కబురు, or ఖబురు n. s. خبر *Khabr.* News, report, a message or notice. సమాచారము. నిజకబరు certain intelligence. ఖబరుకాకితము a newspaper.

ఖబరుదారి n. s. خبرداری *Khabardārī.* Care, tending, attention. జాగ్రత.

కబరుస్తాను n. s. قبرستان *Kabristān,* A burial-ground. పాతేచోటు.

ఖబర్దారు interj. خبردار *Khabardār.* Beware! take care. Avaunt! keep off! stand off. ఖబ్రదము, జాగ్రత. ఖబర్దారుచేయుట to take care.

కబాటు, or కబ్బాటుబెంను n. s. گبات *Gabbāt.* (also called కబాడుసరుకు, కిరాణం, or ఖిరాడా.)

. Huckstery; a phrase for treacle. జీలకర, కొబ్బెర, గ్రంధ్యములు, మిరపకాయలు, మసాలా, వక్కాకు these constitute a minor source of revenue.

కబాడము n. s. A bullock load (of grass, fire-wood &c.) కబాడియెద్దులు bullocks carrying firewood or forage.

కబాతుకోడి n. s. کپات *Kabāt.* A capon. విత్తులు తీసినకోడి.

కబాబు کباب *Kabāb.* A ragout. A made dish of roast meat. వేల్చినమాంసము.

కబాయి, or కపాయి n. s. قبا *Kabā.* A shirt, an ornamental garment. శృంగారార్థముగా అన్నిటికి పైనవేసుకొనే చిన్నచొక్కా. KP. 5. 232. నవపుష్పవనము నానామణులు గ్రుచ్చిన పచ్చపట్టుకబాయి బాగునెరఫ.

కబుజ n. s. قبضه *Kabza.* Hilt, haft, పిడి. కబుజబావి a small well.

కబుజు n. s. قبض *Kabz.* A receipt for pay. రసీదు.

కబురు n. s. (for ఖబరు خبر *Khabr.*) News, tidings. వర్తమానము, సమాచారము.

కబూలు n. s. قبول *Kabūl.* An agreement. సమ్మతి. కబూలుఅయినాడు he agreed.

కబేలా n. s. for కబాలా قبالہ *Kabālā.* A document, title deeds. దస్తావేజు, యింటికిక్రమము.

కమరకాయ for కమరక్ n. s. قمرق Name of a fruit. (Carambola.) తమరతకాయ, కర్మరంగము అనేకాయ.

కమరసాల for కంయిరసాల n. s. کم ارسال The sum short in the remittance. ఇరసాల్‌కమ్మి.

ఖమాతు for గొమత్తు n. s. A leak in a ship. ఓడు. ఖమాతుపడ్డది there is a leak.

కమాను n. s. کمان *Kaman.* Meant for the French "command," a march or military journey. ఒకతుక్డీగా సిపాయీలుపోవడము.

కమాను n. s. کمان A bow, an arch. విల్లు, విల్లువంటికట్టడము. కమానుకఱ్ఱ the bow of a drill. కమానుబద్ద the spring of a watch. తీరుకమాను تیرکمان *Tīr-kamān.* A bow and arrows. కమానుదస్తా, or మాందేకులకమానుదస్తా A large bow for cleaning cotton.

కమాయషుదారుడు for కమావీసుదారుడు n. s. کمایش دار *Camayish-dar.* The officer appointed to collect the revenues of a district. తాలూకా అములుదారుడు.

కమాయిషి, or కమామీను for కమావీసు n. s. کمایش The business of collecting revenues. Period of Government: time of management. Affairs, business, details. The whole: the entire. This phrase is known to be wrong; it was introduced by the late Nabob of Masulipatam in corresponding with Asaf Jah the Vizier. దివానాపురాకలనుతందేకుని. Usually the management of affairs. నిర్వాహకము, వ్యవహారదకుత. అతని కమామీనులో in his time మాకమామీనుచూచేవాడు our agent.

గమారువాడు for గవారువాడు n. s. (گنوار *Ganwar.*) A villager. నాటుపురపువాడు.

కమిచీ n. s. کمچی *Kamchi.* A whip. కొరడా, చబుకు.

కమితరీన్ کمترین *Kamtarīn.* adj. Least, most humble. దీన.

కమితి, కంతి n. s. کمتي *Kamtī.* Less, deficiency. తక్కువ, లోటుము.

కమిలి n. s. کمل *Kammal.* A blanket. కంబళి.

కముపేషి for కంబెాబేష్ adj. کم وبیش *Kamobesh.* More or less. సుమారు.

గమేళా n. s. *Camēlā* (Portugueze, *Camera?*) The tops of masts (in which the men stand.) వాడస్తంభములో మనిషినిలిచేటట్టుగాకట్టియుండే అంతస్తు.

గమ్మత్తు n s. گمت *Gammat.* Diversion, amusement. వేడుక, తమాషా.

కమ్మర్‌పట్టి n. s. کمرپٹا *Kamr-patta.* A waist belt. నడికట్టు.

కమ్మరు n. s. کمر *Kamr.* The waist. నడుము. కమ్మ రొబందు, నడికట్టు a belt.

కమ్మలి n. s. (From کمل *Kammal.*) A blanket. కంబళి.

కమ్మి n. s. کمي *Kamī.* Deficiency. లోపము, త క్కువ.

గమ్మత్తు n. s. گمت *Gammat.* See గమ్మత్తు.

గయాళిపడ్డ adj. قيل *Gayāl.* Deserted, abandoned. పాడువేయబడ్డ, విడువబడ్డ.

గయాళుభూమి n. s. Waste, uncultivated land. పాడువేయబడ్డనేల.

గయావాళి n. s. A bramin subsisting upon the offerings made by pilgrims at Gaya. Usually, a term of reproach for a Bramin. అతి దరిద్రుడుగావుండే బ్రాహ్మణుడు, ఆఘూర్యగాడు గావుండేవాడు.

కయిసారు n. s. *Caisar.* Scissors. కత్తిరి.

కయిదు n. s. قيد *Kaid.* Restraint, prison. చెర, ని ర్బంధము, కావలి. ఆ లెక్కలుకయిదుచేసినపిమ్మట after the accounts were closed.

కయిపు n. s. کيف *Kaif.* Intoxication. మత్తు, మ యికము.

గయిరువిలియా adj. (Marata) *Ghair vilya.* Not in the class, not in order. అక్రమమైన.

కయ్యరముత్యము n. s. An inferior sort of pearl. ఒకమట్టజాతిముత్యము.

గరండీలు n. s. *Garandīl.* Grenadier. ఎత్తుగావుం డేసిపాయి. గరండీలకుంపిని a company of grenadiers. పొడుగాటిసిపాయీలదళము.

కరకసా, ఖరఖసా for కర్కసా n. s. خرخشه *Karkasha.* Tumult, riot. వ్యాజ్యము, జగడము. కరకసాభూమి Land that is debateable, as lying on two boundaries.

గరజు n. s. غرض *Gharz.* Need, want, occasion. అక్కర, అగత్యము.

ఖరడాకాకితము n. s. *Kharla, Rough,* coarse paper. ముతకకాకితము.

కరపాణి n. s. (Tamil கரப்பான்.) Scurf, eruptions on children. Ainsl. 2. 530.

కరవచేప, or కారవచేప n. s. *Carva, carava.* fish, being a species of Sparus. Russell, plates 89-125-139. కరితె Russell No. 106. A fish: a species of Sparus.

కరవాడు for కరువాడు n. s. (Tamil கருவாடு.) Dried salt fish. ఉప్పుచేప.

ఖరా adj. کهرا *Kharā.* Pure, prime, best sort, genuine, honest, candid, sincere. నిశ్చయమైన, యథార్థమైన. వాడుఖరామనిషికాడు he is not an honest man. ఖరాగా adv. Positively, assuredly, *regularly,* without error, without fail. నిజముగా, గట్టిగా, స్థిరముగా.

ఖరాజు n. s. خراج The government revenue. దివానుపువచ్చుబడి.

కరాణాజినుసు, ఖరాణాజినుసు n. s. Medical drugs. మందుదినుసు. See కబాటు.

కరాణి n. s. A scribe, a writer. లేఖరి.

ఘరానా n. s. گهرانا Family, household. ఘరానామనిషి a respectable man.

ఖరానా n. s. probably an error for کهڑاوان A wooden shoe with an iron ring worn to keep the shoes from the dirt or mud. అడుగునయినను ఉంగరముచేసినఒకవిధమైనకొప్పుకట్టె.

కరామత్ n. s. کرامت A miracle. మహిమ.

ఖరాయితులు n. s. plu. A whipper, a flogger. జేరుబంధుతోకొట్టేవాడు.

కరారు n. s. قرار Agreement, engagement. నిష్కర్ష, నిర్ణయము. కరారునామా قرارنامه a deed of agreement. ఒడంబడిక.

కరారువాక్కుగా adv. Perhaps an error for واقعی, Honestly, exactly. ఖండితముగా, సరిగ్గా.

కరాళితేజి n. s. A furious horse. దుష్టగుర్రము.

కరిడి n. s. (Tamil கரடி.) A bear. ఎలుగ్గొడ్డు.

కరితె n. s. A sort of fish: the perch with a bifid fin. Pristipoma Carissa. Cuvier. 5. 261. 331. A species of Sparus: or, Sclopsides.

గరిడి for గడీ n. s. گروي Invasion, incursion. Tour, round, rule, government. దాడు, త్రిపాటి, ప్రభుత్వము.

కరిముక్కు n. s. A fish, a fresh water fish. ఒకచేప. See in Buchanan's Mysore 3. 344.

ఖరీదు n. s. خريدي Price, value. వెల. ఖరీదుచేయుట to buy.

ఖరీదుబంది n. s. خريدبندي Settlement of price. వెలయొక్కతీర్పాటు.

గరీబు adj. and n. s. غريب Poor, mild, humble. A stranger. బీదవాడైన, తిన్ననివాడు, పరాయివాడు.

గరీబుపర్వరుసలామతు غریب‌پرورسلامت Salutation to thee, oh cherisher of the poor! (a perpetual phrase in letters, like "your obedient humble servant.") దీనరక్షకుడానికిదండము.

కరుకులు, కరుకువరహాలు n. s. plu. A pagoda worth four rupees. నాలుగురూపాయీలవరహా.

గరజు for గరజ్ n. s. غرض Want, occasion, necessity. నిమిత్తము, అక్కర, ఆగత్యము.

కరుదులెక్క n. s. Daily account, a running account. దినవహీ. లెక్కలుకరుదుచేసుట to balance or settle.

కరుబూజా n. s. خربزه A musk melon. కరుబూజాపండు.

కరుబూజాదోసకాయ n. s. A musk melon.

కరోడా n. s. An overseer, an inspector. A Collector. అధికారి.

కరోలి n. s. قرول A large matchlock. పెద్దకర్నా టకుపాకి.

ఖర్చు for ఖర్చ్ n. s. خرچ Expenditure, expense, subsistence. శెలవు, వ్రయము. ఖర్చుకులేదు I have no money. ఖర్చుకుచాలదు the money is not sufficient. ఖర్చుకుకావలసినది I want money. గ్రామఖర్చు, బాజాఖర్చు village fees. A cess levied on the villagers by the accountant and head farmer on various pretences. The money so collected forms a parish fund: which is laid out in bribes to superior servants, in feasting travellers, in feeding passing troops of dancers, or jugglers, and so forth: but the greater portion is appropriated to the private use of the village authorities. These are similar to the *Poors Rates*: both in severity of exaction and wantonness of expenditure. This wretched system is now in some degree abolished, being forbidden by Government.

ఖర్చుచేయుట, or పెట్టుట v. a. خرچ کرنا To expend or lay out, discharge, pay away. వ్రయముచేసుట.

ఖజ్జకాయలు n. s. plu. A kind of small tart. పక్వాన్నవిశేషము.

కర్నా n. s. قرنا A trumpet. పూదువాద్యవిశేషము.

కర్మాయి n. s. an error for قرمز *Krmiz.* The colour used in painting. కప్పుకర్మాయివన్నె "Lake" red. Crimson.

కలం n. s. قلم A pen (of reed) A paragraph. లేఖిని, ప్రకరణమున్ను.

కలంకారి n. s. قلمکاری A kind of chintz. (Lit: pencil work, being painted with pencils or painting brushes.) కలంకారిగుడ్డ chintz. ఒకతరహారాతవన్నెగుడ్డ.

గలంగచెట్టు, or గులుంగ n. s. A tree called Limonia Pentaphylla. Rox. 2. 381.

కళింగము, or అప్పనపొలము n. s. Land that pays no tax unless cultivated. పయిరుచేస్తేపన్నుయిచ్చేభూమి.

కలంజివిత్తులు n. s. خولنجان (Also spelt Kalōnji.) A plant, Galega maxima. Ainslie 2. 157. the Tamil word is காயவேளை or கொள்ளுக் காய்வேளை. Telugu వెంపలి.

కలందాను n. s. قلمدان A pen case; a standish; an inkstand. కలాలపెట్టె.

కలపతి n. s. Caulking. లప్పము.

కలబు for కలబ్ adj. قلب Base, adulterated. చెల్లని, తప్పు. కలబురూపాయి a false rupee. (coin) See కళవి.

కలబెట్టుట v. a. To stir, agitate. కలుపుట.

గలభ, or గలాభా n. s. غلبه Uproar, confusion, disorder, disturbance. G. 7. 30. and 7. 63. అల్లరి, తారుమారు, కలత.

గలభరించిన adj. Troubled, disordered, confused. తారుమారుచేయబడ్డ, గందరగోళముచేయబడ్డ.

కలమరచేప n. s. A fish, a species of Sparus. Russell No. 92.

కలముగాడి n. s. A great gourd or melon.

కళరుభూమి n. s. Alkaline earth. చవుటనేల.

ఖలలు n. s. خلل Ruin, mischief, harm; commonly in Telugu, disorder, confusion. చెరుపు, హాని, కలత.

కళవాసము n. s. (Tamil களவாசம்) Some grain left on the thrashing floor for the labourers in part payment for their labour. సేద్యగాండ్లకుకళ్లములోవిడిపించేధాన్యము.

కళవి for కల్బి adj. قالب Rejected, base, adulterated, bad (as coin) చెల్లని, తప్పు. See కలబు.

ఖలసా for ఖాలిసా adj. خالصه Retained under Government, not rented or alienated. దివాణమువారుస్వంతముగాపెట్టుకొన్న. Fiscal.

కలాబత్తు n. s. کلابتون *Kalabutūn*. Gold or silver thread : and it is sometimes used for *gulāb*. కులాబు. (Shak. 1286 and 2023) Handle, staple, hinge, link, hook, clasp.

కలాయి, or కళాయి n. s. قلعی The silvering at the back of a mirror. Tinning of copper pots. అద్దమునకు రసము వేయడము, సీసమువూయడము.

కలాలి, or కలాళి adj. کلالی Of or belonging to arrack. సారాయిసంబంధమైన. కలాలిపని the spirit trade. కలాలుఖానా an arrack shop, a gin shop, an arrack manufactory.

కలావరు, or క్లావర్ n. s. کلاور Clubs (at cards.) ఆటకాకితములలో సుకపాలి.

గలాసు, or గ్లాసు n. s. The "*glacis*" of a fort. Also a wine *glass*. కోటగోడతోచేరినట్టుగా యేటవాలుగావుండే ప్రదేశము, గాజుగిన్నె.

కళాసువాడు n. s. خلاصي A *Khalassy*. i. e. a sailor, a lascar, a tent-man, a gunner. తామూచికవాడు.

కలింగలు n. s. (Tamil கலிங்கல்) The sluice. అలుగు.

గలిబిలి (an error for گڑبڑی) A squabble, uproar, confusion. గందరగోళము. గలిబిల్లాడుట to squabble. గలిబిలిచేసుట to confuse.

గలీఫా, గలేబా, గలేబి for غلاف గలాఫ్ n. s. A cover, a case. ఒర.

కల్తా n. s. Suspicion, mistrust. మనోమాలిన్యము.

కల్తి n. s. Mixture, medley, confusion.

కల్దారు n. s. کلدار Granulated, crystallized, milled (as a rupee) on the edges. అంచులలోగీతలుగీతలుగావుండేరూపాయి.

గల్బతు n. s. Confusion, turmoil. అల్లరి. (Gruff goods: gruff crops as turmeric, onions. &c.) (Nelloor ?)

గల్భాయించుట v. a. غلبلکن To throw into confusion. గందరగోళముచేసుట, తారుమారుచేసుట.

కల్లా n. s. A curl. ముంగురులు? Lavanya. 3. మగువనీసొగసుకల్లాతళుక్కనినంత.

కల్మీసర్మాన్ n. s. The driver or spanker boom. A shoulder-of-mutton main-sail in a lugger. ఒకవిధమైనవాడచాప.

గల్మచ్ఛ, or గల్మీచా n. s. گلمچھا Mustachios. మీసలు.

గల్ల n. s. گلا The neck. గొంతు. గల్లుబడాయించుట to hang.

కల్లంతిరువ n. s. A fee of about twenty seers at each threshing floor, i. e. a harvest fee granted by the owner to several persons, or granted by the owner to ploughmen. కల్లమువెట్టులో వారివారికియిచ్చేరుసుము.

కల్లచేప and పరికల్లచేప n. s. A species of perch with an oblong tail. Russell on Fishes No. 123.

గల్లా n. s. غله Grain, particularly before thrashing. Also, a shopkeeper's *till*. నూర్పనిధాన్యము, అంగడిపానిపెట్టె.

గల్లి n. s. گلی A lane. సందు.

కవలచేప n. s. (Query, "*Kowal*") or కొహవ్వల్లి? Russell, No. 186. a fish: a species of Clupea.

కవాడము n. s. (Tamil கவாடம்.) A bullock load of grass or fuel &c.

కవాడు n. s. A relay or relief, as of bearers. అంచె.

కవాయితు, or కవాతు n. s. قواعد Rules; Manœuvring, evolutions. Drill, parade. సిపాయీలుకసరతుచేయడము.

గవారు adj. گنوار Gross, rude, inelegant, vulgar, dirty, coarse, foul. మడ్డి, మోటు.

కవులు n. s. an error for قول An agreement. Stipulation. ఒడంబడిక. కవులుకమ్మ, or కవులుదమ్మ An agreement, with its counterpart. Articles and stipulations exchanged.

కశము, or కశేము n. s. چشمه A fountain. బుగ్గ.

కషాల్ for కసాలా adj. کساله Bitter, salt (water) చేదైన, ఉప్పని.

కసదు n. s. قصد Pursuit, the business in which they are engaged. పూనుకొన్నపని.

కసబు n. s. کسب Trade, profession. వృత్తి, వ్యాపారము. కసబుకురానితాళ్లు palmira trees which are not fit for drawing toddy (lit: their occupation.)

కసరతు n. s. کثرت Practice, exercise. అభ్యాసము.

కసరు n. s. کثرت Excess. హెచ్చు. కసరాదాయము Surplus.

కసాయి, or కసాయీవాడు n. s. قصائی A butcher. కటికవాడు.

కసాలా n. s. Difficulty, trouble, distress, tormenting. తొందర, యిబ్బంది. వాడికియింట్లో అన్నానికికసాలాగావున్నది he is in difficulty for daily food.

ఖసిచేయుట v. a. خصی کرنا To geld, castrate. విత్తులుకొట్టుట, కచ్చికొట్టుట.

ఖసీ Apparently meant for కృషి. n. s. Cultivation, manuring. వ్యవసాయము.

కసీదు n. s. کشیدہ A kind of needle work. Flowered patterns "drawn" on silk, &c. బట్టలమీదపూలుకుట్టాలువేయడము.

కసుబా n. s. قصبہ The market town or head station. పెద్దవూరు, కడిస్థలము.

కసూరి n. s. قصور Fault, defect, failure. నేరము.

కస్తి n. s. an error for سختي Dunning, pressing often for payment. తరుపు. రూకలకునిండా కస్తిచేస్తున్నాడు he duns very much for the money.

గస్తు, or గస్తి n. s. گشت A patrol. రోందు, నగరిశోధన. గస్తుతిరుగుట to go the rounds, to patrol.

కస్థు n. s. for قصد *Qasd.* Art, trade. పని, వృత్తి.

కస్బా n. s. See కసుబా.

కస్బీ, or కసిబి n. s. کسب A trade. వృత్తి, వ్యాపారము.

కహరు n. s. قہر Order, rule, dominion, control, power. అధికారము, స్వాధీనము.

కా ఖా గా ఘా

Ka, Khā, Ga, Gha.

గా A vulgar vocative form for గాడా thus రామిగా, నర్సిగా.

ఖాం adj. خام Gross, crude, raw, unsettled, unripe, rough. కచ్చా, పచ్చి, వట్టి. (account.) ఖాంవారిజిల్లా miscellaneous or petty items.

ఖాంఖా, or కాంఖాగా adv. خواہمخواہ Positively. అగత్యముగా.

గాంగాసా (used as an adj.) Village by village. గ్రామవారి.

కాంగు n. s. Coarse cloth, dyed blue. నీలిగుడ్డ కాం?

కాంసామా for ఖానసామా n. s. خانساماں A butler or head servant. ఉగ్రాణి, కారువారి.

ఖాందాను n. s. خاندان Family, lineage, household. సంసారము.

కాంలాపండు for కమలాపండు n. s. کنولا The small orange. ఒకకిత్తిలిపండు.

కాంలెక్క n. s. (خام raw) A rough account, or memorandum. చిత్తులెక్క, దినవహి.

కాకితము n. s. کاغذ *Kaghiz.* Paper.

కాగడ for కాగ్డా n. s. A torch. దీవిటి.

గాగరా n. s. گھاگرا A petticoat (Bengali.) పావడ.

కాజి n. s. قاضی *Kazi.* A Mahometan judge. The *Cazy.* మతన్యాయాధిపతి.

గాజుగుడ్డ n. s. "Gauze." సన్నగానాణ్యముగా వుండేవొకతరహానారగుడ్డ.

కాజుదారు, or కాసుదారివాడు n. s. *Kāzdār.* قازدار A groom. (Turkish.) గుర్రపువాడు.

గాజురగడ్డ n. s. گاجر A carrot. కందపుశేషము, వొకగడ్డపేరు.

కాటకాయితనము, or కాటకతనము n. s. (K) Plundering, pillage, fowling. కిరాతకతనము, దాడు, దోపిడి. Local. ix. 304. line 16. See Reeve 415 under the word కాటక.

ఖాటా for కాటా n. s. کانٹا Large scales. ముక్కోణముచేసితూచే పెద్దత్రాసు.

కాటావారుడు, కాటాగరు n. s. A scale-man, a weigher. పెద్దత్రాసుతూచేమనిషి.

ఘాటి, ఘాటు for ఘాట్ n. s. گھاٹ or گھاٹي A hill-pass. కనమ.

గాడ adj. گاڑھ Coarse, thick (cloth) ముతకైన.

కాడ vulgar for కడ adv. At, near. దగ్గర.

కాడారంబము n. s. Dry cultivation. మెట్టసాగుబడి.

కాడి n. s. کانجی Vinegar. సిర్కా.

గాడివరహా n. s. A sort of gold pagoda worth four rupees. It is now disused. కరుకువరహా.

గాడీ n. s. گاڑی A cart, chariot, carriage. బండి.

కాణాచి n. s. Hereditary right: hereditary office or employ. The same as మిరాసి.

కాణి n. s. کانی A measure of land; 57, 600 feet square. ఇరువైగుంటలనేల.

కాతరసు, or **కాతరుసు కాకితము** n. s. 'Cartridge' paper. ముతకకాకితము.

కాతా, or **ఖాతా** n. s. Coir: cocoanut-husk fibres. కొంకాయపీచు.

కాతా for **ఖాతా** n. s. کهاتا Account, ledger. లెక్క. ఖాతా లెక్క a running account, an account current. ఖాతా Traffick, dealing. అతనితో ఖాతాకట్టాను I had dealings with him as a merchant. మాఖాతాదారులు people with whom we trade or deal.

గాతు n. s. A ship's hawser. అమారుతాడు, మోకు.

గాదక్కప్పి n. s. A two sheaved pulley. రెట్టకప్పి, రెండుచక్రములుగలకప్పి.

ఖాదా, or **ఖాదీ** n. s. کهادی An uncut piece of coarse cotton cloth. ముతకరేకు.

ఖానిగి adj. خانگی Private, domestic, household. స్వంతయింటిసంబంధమైన. ఖానిగిలెక్క a private account, not a public document. ఇంటికిందవ్రాసినదైనది. మీఖానిగికితెండి keep what follows for your private perusal.

కానుగోయి n. s. قانونگری A remembrancer or overseer. An officer of a large district acquainted with its customs and with the nature of its landed tenures. లెక్కతాలూకారివాజుమొదిగిభూములవివరలెక్కపెట్టుకొని యుండేవుద్యోగస్థుడు.

ఖానుసుమారు, or **ఖానేసుమారులెక్క** n. s. خانشماری A census or account of population.

కానూను n. s. قانون A canon, rule, ordinance. సూత్రము. కానూనుగోయి (vulgarly కానుగోయి) the remembrancer; or overseer in a village. (See Despandia Elph. page 27.)

గాభరా, **గాబరా**, **ఘాబర**, **ఘాబ్రా** n. s. گهبرا Fright, terror, uproar, confusion. భయము, కలవరము. ఘాబరాపడుట to be in a fright.

ఖావందు, or **ఖావందు** n. s. خاوند Lord, master, owner. నాయకుడు, యజమానుడు, స్వంతగాడు.

కామకా for **ఖామఖా** adv. خواهمخواه Positively, without fail. Whether or no. అవశ్యముగా, కట్టిగా.

కామరా, **కామ్రా** or **కామెరా** n. s. کمره A chamber, room; cabin or hold in a ship. గది, అర.

కామిరి Perhaps for కామరా n. s. کمره A ship's hold, a room, a chamber. అర, గది.

ఖాము adj. خام Raw, unsettled. తీరతీరని.

గాముగానా adj. See గాంగానా.

కాముగారి, or **కాంకారి** n. s. کامگاری Operations, repairs of tanks, &c. పని, మరమ్మతు.

కాయము adj. قایم Firm, fixed, established, confirmed, constituted, permanent. రూఢియైన, నిశ్చితమైన, శాశ్వతమైన, నిలకడైన. కాయపరుచుట to establish, to admit as true, or confirm. కాయపడ్డ confirmed.

కాయిదా n. s. قاعده Custom, rule, ordinance. విధి, నిర్ణయము.

కాయిలా adj. کاهلا Sick, ill. ఒళ్లుకుదురులేని.

కారంజా, or **కారంజీ** n. s. کارنجا An artificial fountain or jet d' eau. బుగ్గ.

గారతు n. s. غارت Destruction, ravage, plunder. హతము, దోపిడి.

గారతుచేసుట v. a. غارتکرنا To destroy, plunder. పాడుచేసుట, కొల్లబెట్టుట.

కారవా for కహార్వా n. s. کهاروا A dance by women dressed as boys. ఆడవాండ్లుమొగవేషము వేసుకొని ఆడే ఆట. See కార్వా.

కారవిచేప n. s. A species of perch. (Russell No. 125.)

కారికము n. s. Unbleached cloth. చలవచేయని బట్ట.

ఖారిస్తాను n. s. Enmity, bitterness. కసి, ద్వేషము.

ఖారీజులు n. s. (خارج *Kharij*) Harvest fees; being dues formerly deducted from the gross crop. ఇరుగోరులపొత్తునయిచ్చేరుసుములు.

కారు n. s. کار *Kar*. Work, employment, business, affair, labour. పని, వృత్తి.

కారుఖానా for కార్ఖానా n. s. کارخانه *Kārkhāna* Workshop, repository. Establishment, office, manufactory. దొడ్డి, పనిచేసేచోటు.

కారుబారు n. s. کاروبار *Kār-o-bār*. Business. వ్యవహారము. Plague, fuss. తొందర, యిబ్బంది. నామీదకారుబారుచేస్తాడు he plagues me much.

కారువా n. s. کهاروا *Khārwa*. A sort of red cotton cloth, used as covers for carriages, &c. ఒకతరహాముతకయెఱ్ఱరెట్టు. A dance. ఆట. See కారవా.

కారువాచేవ n. s. See కరవ.

కారువాయి n. s. کارروائی Carrying on a business, temporary arrangement. వ్యవహారమునుజరుపడము, తత్కాలమునకుబందోబస్తుచేయడము. Also (the same as కారు) a plough share. కారువాయిదోలు a demand or cess levied on estimate (Vizag. ?)

కారోబారి, usually కారుబారి n. s. کارباری An agent, a man of business. కార్యకర్త, వ్యవహారికుడు.

కార్కూను n. s. کارکن *Karcoon*. A land bailiff, an overseer, a manager. "The lowest agent or factor in managing ryots. Lit. a man of business." Malc. 1. 68. పారుపత్తి, జిల్లేదారుడు, తరుఫుదారుడు.

కార్జి for కారింజా n. s. کارنجا A fountain or *jet d' eau*. బుగ్గ. In the north (Ooria) part of Ganjam, it is a corruption for *Kazi* a judge, and is used for a munsif.

కార్జెం n. s. (perhaps meant for కలీజా.) کلیجه The liver: (jecur) గుండెకాయ.

ఖార్తిసాను n. s. (خارستان *Kharistan*, A thorny place.) Enmity, bitterness, ill will. ద్వేషము, కసి.

కార్బారు n. s. کاربار Business, affairs. వ్యవహారము. కార్బారి an agent. నామీదనిందాకార్బారుచేస్తాడు he harasses me.

కార్వా n. s. کهاروا Ooarse red cotton cloth. ఎఱ్ఱముతకరెట్టు.

కార్వా ఆట n. s. کهاور *Khārwā*. An indecent dance, so named from the town of *Carwar* in the Soonda country. ఒకవిధమైననర్తనము. (Pinkerton's Voyages, 4to vol. 8. 362.) Hamilton's East Indies 1723. chapter xxii.

గాలముచేయుట v. a. گل دینا *Gal-dēna*. To hang "on the *gallows*." తూకువేసుట.

కాలింగలు for కలింగలు n. s. (Tamil கலிங்கல்) A sluice. అలుగు, కలుజు.

ఖాలీ adj. خالي *Khālī*. Empty, vacant, unoccupied. ఉత్తదిగావుండే, పూరకవుండే.

కాలీజు n. s. A "College." పాఠశాల.

కాళి n. s. Mouldering, Mildew. పయిరు మొదలయినవాటికికుక్కేకాటుక. ఆపయిరుకుకాళికట్టినది the grain is mildewed.

కాలేయము n. s. The liver, or jecur ?

ఖాల్సా n. s. خالصه *Khālsa*. A commonwealth. The government of the Sikhs was formerly divided among a number of petty independant chieftains under the Khalsa or commonwealth fixed by Guru Govind.

ఖావందు n. s. خاوند *Khāvand*. Lord, master. ఎజమానుడు.

కావా n. s. کاوا *Cāvā*. The manege, lunging. గుఱ్ఱపుత్రిప్పట.

కావాబల్ల, n. s. *Cāvā*. A sort of planks, (mentioned in the Tariff.) ఒకతరహాపలకలు.

గావాయి n. s. *Cāvāi*. A ship's topmast. వాడకొనస్తంభము.

కావేశి, or కావేషి n. s. Spite, malice, ill will. ద్వేషము, కార్పణ్యము.

కావ్వును A vulgarism for కావచ్చును "*It may be perhaps.*"

ఖాస్దార్, or ఖాస్దారివాడు n. s. قازدار *Kāz-dār*. A groom, or horsekeeper. గుఱ్ఱపువాడు.

ఖాసా adj. خاصه *Khāsa*. Own, personal. స్వంత. ఖాసాగా personally, he himself. ఖాసా

వారి coming in person; (the phrase used for the circuits made by any ruler: as a commanding officer, a collector, or a judge.

ఖాసా n. s. خاصه *Khasa.* A slave or hereditary bondsman; such as are found among native gentlemen in the north, but they are never sold.

ఖాసు for ఖాసా adj. خاص *Khas.* Own, private, personal. స్వంత.

గాసు n. s. A sheave of a pulley. కప్పిచక్రము.

ఖాహిలా n. s. ಖಹಿಲ See ఖాయిలా.

కి Ki, కీ Kī, ఖి Khi, ఖీ Khī, గి Gi, గీ Gī, ఘి Ghi, ఘీ Ghī.

కించాటు for కించ n. s. Sorrow. వ్యాకులము. మహాకించాటుగాయున్నది I am very sorry for it.

కించాయిలు n. s. The English word 'Consignment.' అప్పగింత.

కిచాట for కీచట n. s. Quarrel, dispute. వాగ్వాదము.

ఖిచిడీ n. s. کھچڑی *Khichṛī:* (vulg. kitchery.) The dish called పులగము or boiled rice mixed with split pulse.

ఖిటికి, or ఖిడికి n. s. کھڑکی *Khirki.* A window: a little door: a ship's gangway. గవాక్షి, దిడ్డివాకిలి.

కిట్టికోల n. s. (Tamil கிட்டிக்கோல்) Thumb-screws. వేళ్లకుకుండమీదపెట్టితొత్తేదిటికోలలు.

గిడ్డంగి n. s. *Giddingi.* A *godown:* (from the Malay *gandong*) an outhouse, office, store-room, or prison. కొట్టు, గది.

కితానారగుడ్డ n. s. Canvas. కిత్తాను.

కితాని for కిత్తాను n. s. کتان *Kitān.* Canvas. కితానారగుడ్డ.

కితాబు n. s. کتاب *Kitāb.* A book. But more commonly a corruption of خطاب ఖితాబు *khitāb*, any honorary title.

కినారా n. s. کنارہ *Kinara.* Edge, border, bank. కట్ట, తీరము.

గిన్నెకాసు n. s. *Ginneh-cāsu.* (Tamil, கின்னிக்காசு) "Cup-coin." A gold coin formerly in use worth (Rs. 17-8.0) five pagodas. See వర్తమానతరంగిణి newspaper of 4th January 1849 in a list of coins.

కిఫాయతు n. s. کفایت *Kifayat.* Benefit, advantage, profits. లాభము, ఆదాయము.

కిమ్మత్తు n. s. قیمت *Kīmat.* Price. ధర, వెల.

కిమ్మత్తురవానా n. s. قیمت رونا A pass certifying the value of the goods. ఆయాసరకులవెలనుగురించినరహదారి.

గిరదా adj. گرد *Girda.* A round or circle. గుండ్రని.

గిరదాయించుట v. a. To surround, to gird in. చుట్టుకొనుట.

గిరవు, or గిరువు n. s. گرو *Girō.* Pawn, pledge, security. కుదవ, తాకట్టు.

గిరాని n. s. گران *Girān.* Dear in price. ఖరం, అధికవెల.

ఖిరానా for కిరానా n. s. کرانا *Kirāna.* Grocery. చిల్లరసామాను, పుష్పమిరపకాయమొదలగుండుకొదలయినవుసాలాలు.

కిరాయ, or కిరాయి کرایہ *Kirāya.* Rent, hire, fare. బాడుగ, కూలి, సత్తము.

గిరువు, గిరో, or గిరో n. s. گرو *Girō.* Mortgage, pawning. కుదువ, తాకట్టు.

గిర్దావరి n. s. گرداوری *Girdawari.* A circular (order) ఒట్టుహుకుము.

ఖిర్దు n. s. خرد *Khird.* Cultivation. కృషి, వ్యవసాయము. ఖిర్దు ఆబాదుచేసుకొని having cultivated fully.

గిలాబ n. s. گلابہ *Gilāba.* Plastering, applying, laying on: *paying* after caulking. గచ్చుపూయడము, వాడవులకలసందుకులప్పుమువేసినదానిమీదకీలుబొందలయినవాటనిదరమడము.

గిలాబతి See కలాబత్తు.

గిలాబతుంగ? "Gelleba tunga." Rox. 1. 199. Cyperus tenuiflorus.

గిలాబు See గిలాబ.

గిలాసు, or గ్లాసు n. s. A wine "glass." గాజుగిన్నె.

కిలింటు, or కిలేంటు n. s. A port clearance bill, taken to prove that a ship has paid all port dues. వాడతర్లిపోవడమునకైయిచ్చేశలవుచీటి.

గిల్ల, or గిల్లామాటలు n. s. Slander, scandal, tale-bearing. చాడి, అంగుడుదుడిపిమాటలు.

కిల్లటుల adv. (a bad phrase not to be used) Early, betimes. పెందలకడ. ప్రొద్దుగల్లటులతింటా ము we shall dine betimes.

కిసము n. s. قسم *Kism.* Kind, sort. విధము, తరహా.

కిస్తి n. s. قسط *Kist.* An instalment towards payment. వాయిదా.

కిస్తిబందు n. s. قسطبندي *Kist bandi.* Settlement of payment by instalments. వాయిదాలయే ర్పాటు. See జమాబందు. కిస్తిబందిప్రకారముగా in instalments.

కిస్తు n. s. See కిస్తి.

కిస్మిసు n. s. کشمش *Kishmish.* A raisin. ద్రా క్షపండు.

కిస్మిసుపండుగ n. s. "Christmas :" which natives imagine to be connected with the preceding word! కిరస్తుపండుగ.

కింకాబు, or కిన్ఖాబు n. s. کم خواب *Kam khwab.* 'Kincob,' cloth of gold : brocade, silk worked with gold or silver flowers. బుట్టాలువేసిన పట్టు.

కిలి n. s. *Kilī.* A key. తాళంచెవి.

కిలిపిట్ట n. s. *Kilī pitta* : a fish : a species of perch. ఒకచేప. Russell No. 126, 195.

కివాడ n. s. "A tract of land in which garden produce is generally cultivated, and which was formerly a part of the village." ఊరిచు ట్టూవుండేపాటిపొలము. D.

కీసా n. s. کیسه *Kisā.* A pocket in a jacket. చొక్కాలోనిసంచి, జేబు.

కు కూ ఖు ఖూ గు గూ ఘు ఘూ

కుంచ, or కుంచీ n. s. *Kuncha.* A sort of cap, with a flap behind. బిడ్డలకువేసేశిరస్త్రాణము.

కుంజరి for కుంజడా n. s. *Kunjari.* A huckster, a fruiterer. చిల్లర అంగడివాడు, పసారీదుకాణ పువాడు, పండ్లమ్మేవాడు.

గుంజాటన, or గుంజూటన n. s. Grief, regret. వ్యసనము.

గుంజాయిషి n. s. گنجایش *Gunjāish.* Capacity: profit : the usual meaning is, defect, incompleteness, imperfection. లోటు. ఆలెక్కలో గుంజాయిషీయేమిన్నిలేదు there is no defect in this account.

గుంటమాన్యము n. s. A petty manyam. (Viz.) ఒక చిన్నమాన్యము.

గుండీ n. s. گندی *Gundi.* A button : a kind of flower. బొత్తాను, ఒకపుష్పమున్ను.

గుండుసాల n. s. The circle around Madras : the jurisdiction of Madras, under the Supreme Court's authority.

కుండ్రాయిపొట్టు n. s. *Kundrai pottu.* Small dried fish. ఎండ్రొయ్యచేపలు.

కుండ, or కుండా n. s. کنده *Kunda.* The butt of a gun. తుపాకిమడమ.

కుంఫిణి, or కుంఫిణీ n. s. 'A company' of sepoys : or the East India Company. సిపాయీల దళము, ఇండ్యదేశమునుయేలుచుండేకంపెనీవారు.

గుంబజ్ n. s. گنبذ *Gumbaz.* A dome. గుమ్మటము. కలశము.

గుంజీ n. s. Bleaching (cloth) చలవచేయడము.

కుచ్చి, or కొచ్చి n. s. Cochin, a town in Malabar. ఒకపట్టణము. కొచ్చికుక్క a spaniel. కుచ్చిగుర్ర ము a horse brought from *Kutch.*

గుజరాతీ adj. Appertaining to Guzerat, made at "Guzerat." గుజరాతీవాడు an inhabitant of Guzerat.

గుజరాను n. s. گذران *Guzran.* Life, employment, livelihood, daily bread, subsistence. వృత్తి, జీవనము.

గుజరాయించుట v. a. گذرانا *Guzaranna.* To present, offer. ఇచ్చుట.

గుజరి, గుజిరి or గుజిలి n. s. A market place, thieving bazar (a Madras word.) గుజిరివేళ shopping time : about sunset.

గుజస్తా adj. گذشته *Guzashta.* Passed, elapsed, సాలుగుజస్తా last year.

గుజారతు n. s. (Error for *Guzārish.*) Possession, holding (in charge ;) వశము. Intervention. అతనిగుజారతిని by, or through him as an agent. మంగలిగుజారతినిపంపించినరూపా యీలు the rupees sent by the barber.

గుజారి n. s. An opulent man. ధనవంతుడు D.

గుజురాను n. s. گذران *Guzran.* Passing, livelihood. జరగడము, జీవనము. అక్కడగుజురానుచే యరు చాలరు they cannot prosper well there : they do not get on well.

గుజ్జెరికుక్క for గుజ్జికుక్క n. s. A shock spaniel. జుబ్బుకుక్క.

గుడిగీ n. s. گرگی *Gurgī.* Trowsers, pantaloons. (more particularly breeches.) మోకాలిదాకా వుండేచల్లడము.

గుడిగుడి, or గుడుగుడు n. s. A small hookah. చిన్న హుక్కా.

గుడిదీ n. s. A peg; a small bit of wood?

కుడివారము n. s. (Tamil குடிவாரம்) The ryot's share of the crop. See మేలువారము.

గుడ్డె n. s. (Odhra language?) A rising spot of ground.

కుతిగూర్చుట v. a. Error for కృతిగూర్చుట, అనగా పొసగించుట.

ఖుతినీ n. s. ختنی *Khtni.* Satin; so called as being brought from Khoten. It is made of silk and cotton. కుత్నిపట్టు.

ఖుద్, or ఖుద్దున adv. خود *Khud.* Self, personally, without intervention. ఖుద్రాజీ of his own accord, voluntarily. ఆయన ఖుద్దున వెళ్లినాడు he himself went.

గుదస్తె See గుమస్తా.

కుదిర్తి for కుద్రత్ n. s. Power, ability, authority. అధికారము.

కుదీలు n. s. A cant word used at cards. ప్రతిజ్ఞ, అనగా కాకితముల ఆటలో అయిదుపట్లుపట్టుతానని చేసేప్రతిజ్ఞ.

గునహ n. s. گناه *Gunah.* A sin, crime, fault. పాపము, నేరము.

గునాగారి, or గునేగారి n. s. گناهگاری *Gunahgari.* A fine, mulct. అపరాధము.

గున్నాపట్టు n. s. Gold paper or silver paper. వెండిబంగారు వర్ణము మెరిసేకాకితము.

కున్నారము n. s. Glassware? A. DK. బంగాలులు.

గుప్తి, గుంపిత n. s. A dagger.

గుబారు n. s. Rumour. పుకారా, అవాజా. వారు అక్కడికివచ్చి చేరినారు అనేదిగాయిక్కడగుబారుగా వున్నది it is reported here that they have gone there.

కుమండాన్ n. s. (A French word,) "Le Commandant." మొనగాడు.

గుమస్తా n. s. گماشته *Gumāshta.* (vulg. Gomasta) An assistant, a clerk, factor, or agent. బడులుమనిషి.

గుమానీ adj. گمانی *Gumānī.* Suspicious, suspected. సందేహించబడ్డ.

గుమాను n. s. گمان *Gumān.* Suspicion, doubt, uncertainty. సందేహము.

గుమాయించుట, or ఘుమాయించుట v. n. To spread as scent. వ్యాపించుట. ఆఅత్తరుయిల్లంతా ఘుమాయిస్తున్నది the scent of the attar is spread throughout the room.

గుమారు n. s. *Gumār.* A ship's gang-way?

గుమాస్త n. s. See గుమస్తా.

గుమిటి n. s. A sentry box. పారావాడునిలిచేగూడు.

కుముండాన్ n. s. (French word) "Le Commandant." A leader or captain. మొనగాడు.

కుమ్మకు n. s. کمک *Kummak.* Aid, help, reinforcement, assistance. సహాయము.

గుమ్మటము n. s. گنبذ (*Gunbaz.*) A dome; a balloon: a fire-balloon.

గురకాయించుట, or గురుకాయించుట v. a. To turn upon one as a hog does when struck: గ్రుడ్డుగ్రుడ్లుచుట, గుర్రుమనుట.

ఖురదా for ఖురదా n. s. خوردہ *Khurda.* Batta, subsistence: copper coin. బత్తెము, దుడ్లు, పైసాలు.

ఖురాకు n. s. خوراک *Khurāk.* Food, batta, subsistence, money. కూడు, బత్తెము, బత్తెపుకాసులు.

కురాళము, or ఖురాళము n. s. An awning. మేలుకట్టు.

కురాసానివామము n. s. خراسانی اجوان *Khurasāni ajwāyan.* Black henbane. దీప్యము, ఓమము.

కురింజి, or కురువిందము n. s. Corundum-stone. కురువిందపురాయి.

కురిచి n. s. کرسی *Kurs.* A chair: a wooden seat.

కురుజీ for కురుసీ n. s. A seat. Or, for خوگیر *Khōgir*, a pack saddle. ఆసనము, గంత.

కురట n. s. *Kurata.* A sort of fish? Russell, plate 101. "Cooroota" calls it Sparus Spinifer. మత్స్యవిశేషము.

గురదా n. s. A kind of sword. ఖడ్గవిశేషము. T. 1. 9.

కుర్తా for కుడ్తా n. s. کرتا *Kurta.* A coat; a jacket. చొక్కాయి.

ఖుర్దా n. s. خوردہ *Khurda.* Half pence, copper, small change. చిల్లర. పైసాలు.

ఖుర్దుబుర్దు n. s. (خورد و برد *Khurda wa burda.* Eaten and stolen.) Embezzlement. అపహారించబడినది.

ఘుర్ర n. s. غرہ *Ghurra.* The first day of a month. ఒకటోతారీఖు. ఘుర్రా సెప్టెంబరు on the first of September.

గుర్రపుచర్నకు (for గుర్రపుచబుకు properly చాబుకు) n. s. A horsewhip. కొరడా. A long slender fish. Russell, No. 30. Syngnathus Typhlus *Linn.*

కుల్వార్ n. s. کلوار *Kulwār.* A settlement made with the Ryots individually. రయ్యతువారి, ఆసామివారి. కుల్వారికట్టు individual settlement.

గులాపు, or గులాము for గులాం n. s. غلام *Ghulām.* A slave, "your humble servant." దాసుడు.

గులాబు, or గులాబిపువ్వు n. s. گلاب *Gulāb.* A rose. గులాబిరంగు pink, rose-colour.

కుళాయి, or కుల్లాయి for కులా n. s. کلاہ *Kulāh.* A little cap. టోపి.

ఖులాయించుట v. n. To look handsome. అందముగా అగుపడుట. ఆరంగుఖులాయిస్తున్నది the colour looks handsome.

గులాలుపొడి n. s. گلال *Gulāl.* The red powder flung about in the *Hoeli or* festival to Cupid. ఎర్రపొడి.

ఖులాసా n. s. خلاصہ *Khulasah.* Abstract, abridgement: essence, intrinsic subject. సంగ్రహము, నిగ్గు, సారాంశము. ఖులాసాగాఉండే free, open, disengaged, at ease. నిశ్చింతగాఉండే.

గులిమెంది n. s. گل مہندی *Guli mehndī.* The balsam-flower. (Impatiens balsamina. Rox. 1. 651.) A sort of fish, a species of *Sparus*: or mullet. Russell (Nos. 107. 157. 158.) mentions the లామగులిమింద, రాతిగులిమింద red mullet, and బండిగులిమింద the surmullet.

కుల్కర్ని n. s. *Kul-carni.* The village clerk: the register of a village. కర్ణము. దేశకుల్కర్ని accountant of a district, the hereditary village accountant.

గుల్లదము n. s. *Gulladām.* Pink colour. వర్ణవిశేషము. తెల్లగుల్లదము carnation, flesh-colour.

ఖుల్లసు n. s. خلص *Khulas.* Particulars, substance or essence. వివరము, నిగ్గు, సారాంశము. ఖుల్లసుగా thoroughly, essentially.

కుల్లు for కుల్ adj. کل *Kul.* All, whole. యావత్తు.

ఖుశామది, or ఖుషామత్తు n. s. خوشامدی *Khushāmadi.* "You are welcome." i. e. Flattery, a flatterer. స్తోత్రము, పొగడేవాడున్ను.

కుశిని n. s. (The french word cuisine.) A kitchen. వంటయిల్లు. కుశినివాడు a cook. వంటవాడు.

ఖుషాలు n. s. Gladness, joy. సంతోషము.

ఖుషికి, or ఖుషీగి n. s. خشکی *Khushki.* Untilled land. దున్నని నేల, బీడు. ఖుషిగిజిరాయితి cultivating untilled land. ఖుష్కీబాగాయతి dry land cultivated as garden land. తోటలువేయబడ్డ మెట్టపొలము.

ఖుషీ n. s. خوشی *Khushī.* Pleasure, delight, mirth, joy. సంతోషము.

ఖుష్కిపైకితరి n. s. (تري) *Khushki-paikī-tarī.* Wet cultivation, carried on in lands which were hitherto classed as "dry." (Bellary.) పుంజెతరం అంటె, మెట్టలోజేయబడ్డమాగాణి.

ఖుష్ఖరీదు n. s. خوشخرید *Khush kharīd* (Price, value. Reeve.) Paying in ready money (Richn. 638.) Private sale; not auction. చెయిచెలకు అమ్మడము.

ఖుష్బాషు n. s. خوشباش *Khushbhash.* He who is free. ఖులాసాగావుండేవాడు.

ఖుసూరి n. s. قصوري *Kusūrī.* Fault, defect. లోకువ.

కూంట్రాయిపొట్టు n. s. Powdered salt-fish used as a condiment. మసాలాగావేసేఉప్పుచేపపొడి.

ఖూంవారి for కౌంవారి n. s. قوموارى *Kaum vāri.* The tax levied upon different castes. అ-

యాకులాలవారిమీదతీసేసున్ను. వలకట్లఖూంవారి the fees paid for the right of fishing.

కూచిమతము n. s. Name of a sect among the Satanies. సాతానులలోనొకమతము.

కూచీచేసుట v. n. کوچ *Kūch.* To march. దండు మొదలయినవిప్రయాణమవుట.

కూజా, or ఖూజా n. s. کوزه *Kūzā.* A goglet or gugglet: a carboy.

గూడాలు n. s. (See గోడాలు and మసానీలు) The rattlins of a ship's masts.

కూడికెవాండ్లు n. s. Partners in merchandize or trade. (Vizag.) పాలికాపులు.

కూనలమ్మచీర n. s. A kind of petticoat named after a certain village rural goddess.

ఖూని n. s. خونی *Khūnī.* Manslaughter, murder. హత్య. ఖూనీఖోరు a murderer. ఖూనిరయ్యతు any delinquent.

ఖూబి خوبی *Khūbī.* Good: benefit: the real fact. ఫలము

ఖూబు interj. خوب *Khūb.* Well done! hurrah! శహబాస్.

ఖూబు adj. Good, excellent. శ్రేష్ఠమైన, బాగైన.

కూమవారి n. s. قوم *Kaum.* A tax levied as mohturfa, on a caste. ఆయాకులస్థులమీదతీసేసున్ను.

ఖూము n. s. قوم *Quam.* Tribe, sect, caste. కులము.

కూర్నిశాత్ n. s. کورنشات *Kūrnishāt,* Prostrations; homage. దండము, వందనము. This phrase is used at the beginning of letters.

కూర్మయివాండ్లు n. s. A kind of mendicants. ఒకతరహాబిచ్చగాండ్లు.

కూర్వ n. s. The ribs of a ship, or the bends. Also in carpentry, a bent piece of wood. వాడకూర్పుకువేసేవంకరకొయ్య.

కూళము n. s. (Tamil கூளம்) Chaff of straw, hem. &c కొంటు.

కె కే ఖె ఖే గె గే ఘె ఘే

ఘెండా for గైండా n. s. A rhinoceros. ఖడ్గమృగము, దీనిముక్కుమీదఒకకొమ్ముంటున్నది.

కెచ్చెళితనము n. s. "Rioting" (P† in Rom. xiii. 13.) అల్లరి, దొమ్మి.

గెడువు n. s. (A vulgar spelling for గడువు) A term, a fixed time for payment, an instalment. వాయిదా.

గెలీపు for గెలాఫ n. s. A cover. ఉ.ర. గెలీపుకత్తులు swords with covers. గెలీపుతుపాకులు muskets with covers.

ఖేటా adj. Separate. వేరే.

ఖేటాగా adv. Separately, apart. వేరేగా.

ఖేటాయించుట v. n. To separate, share out, divide. వేరుపరచుట.

కేటికప్పి n. s. A block: (a kind of pully.) ఒకవిధమైనకప్పి.

ఖేడిగావుండే adj. Adulterated, not pure, debased. మిశ్రితముగావుండే, వర్లుమొదలయినవాటిని గురించినమాట.

ఖేతు for ఖేత్ n. s. کهیت *Kheth.* A cornfield. వరిపొలము.

కేదారసింగి The D gives this as the meaning of బోదారసింగి.

కేపుమారి n. s. (Tamil) A rogue, swindler. కత్తెరదొంగ.

కేఫీవాడు n. s. A chandler, a messenger. వార్తావహుడు.

ఖేరీజు for ఖారీజు adj. خارج *Kharij.* Extra, additional, distinct. పై, జాస్తి, వేరే.

కేపు n. s. کهیپ *Khep.* Freight. వాడకూలి, వాడమీదయెక్కించేసరుకుకుకూలి.

కై ఖై గై ఘై

గైతలు n. s. A class of mountaineers in the Rajamahendry District.

కైది, or ఖైది n. s. قیدی *Quidi.* A prisoner. నేరస్థుడు.

కైదు n. s. قید *Quied.* Prison, imprisonment. కావలి. కైదుచేయుట to imprison: to close an account.

కైపు n. s. کیف *Kief.* Intoxication. మైకము.

కైఫియ్యతు n. s. کیفیت *Kifiyat.* Circumstances, particulars. సంగతి.

గైబత్తు n. s. غیبت *Ghibat.* An out-station. హుజూరులో కాకబయిట.

గైబు adj. for غایب *Ghaib.* Missing, mislaid, lost. కానకపోయిన.

ఖైరాతి adj. خیراتی *Khīrati.* Charitable, given as alms. తిరిపెముగాయిచ్చిన.

గైరాదా adj. غیرادا *Gairada.* Unoccupied, waste: due, owed. ఖాలిగావుండే, బాకీగావుండే.

కైరి for ఖైరా n. s. کهیرا *Khiera.* A grey-eyed horse: a wall-eyed horse. పిల్లికండ్లగుర్రము.

ఖైరీజులు. See ఖరీజు.

గైరు adj. غیر *Ghier.* Other, besides. excepting. ఇతరమైన. గైరువిలియాకత్తు mislaid, missing: what *is not* found. గైరు ఆదా extra collections. గైరువాజిబి unreasonable, false. గైరుమహసూలుచెట్లు trees not liable to tax. గైరుహాజరు missing, absent, not present. గైరుజవాబుజాబులు letters that require "no answer."

కైలి n. s. Of capacity: prefixed to words expressing measure.

కైలు n. s. کیل *Kiel.* Measurement of grain after thrashing and before sharing it. కైలుకాలము harvest time. కైలుదారుడు a superintendent of measurement.

కైల్లు, or కైలు n. s. Frames like the letter A used in a pent roof. పెంకుటింటికివేసేటివి.

కొ కో ఖొ ఖో గొ గో ఘొ ఘో

కొ॥, or కో॥ A contraction for కోర్జ n. s. A pack of twenty pieces of cloth.

గొంది n. s. (K.) A field. పొలము. గొందిగాడు the proprietor or renter of a field.

కొండపో for కొంచపో Take away.

కొండి n. s. A staple, or strong hook. కొక్కి.

కొచ్చె adj. (Tamil கோணல்) Wry, wrong: mispronounced. యాస.

కొట్టము n. s. A cow-house. పసులదొడ్డి.

కొట్టాయి n. s. A large shed or pent roof. కొట్టాయిఉత్సవము the feast of tabernacles celebrated in Vishnu temples.

కోటా n. s. A bale or parcel of cowries (usually 12,000) brought from the Maldives.

కొటారు n. s. A magazine or store. ఉప్పుకొటారు a salt depot.

కోఠి n. s. کوٹهی *Kothi.* A storehouse: a bank: A mercantile firm. కోఠివేయుట to set up or open a bank.

కోఠిరి n. s. کوٹهری *Kōthri.* A closet, a strong room. గది.

కొత్తవాలు, or కోత్వాలు n. s. کوتوال *Kōtwāl.* The chief officer of the police (of a city or town.) కొత్తవాలుచావడి the kotwal's hall or court.

ఖొదావందు n. s. خداوند *Khudawand.* Lord, master. స్వామి. ఖొదావందుగరీబుపర్వరసలాముత్ خداوندغریبپروسلامت

గొయ్యాకుండు n. s. The guava fruit. This is a Spanish word (guyaba) of Mexican origin. See Lockharts Bernard Diaz. Chap. 162. జాంకుండు.

గొరక and మూతిగొరక n. s. A certain fish: a species of perch. Russell, plate 132. మత్స్యవిశేషము.

కొరడా n. s. for کوڑا *Kōrā.* A whip or knot. కొంకి, జాటి.

గొరసు n. s. A shoal of fish. మత్స్యవిశేషము.

ఖొరాకి n. s. خوراکی *Khoraki.* Batta, subsistence. బత్తెము. See ఖురాకు.

కొరిచెవాడు, or కొరిచెవాడు n. s. A savage, a mountaineer.

కొర్కు n. s. The hyæna, a creature that eats horses and asses. తరసుకము, గొరవంకు, గుర్రాలనుగాడిదెలనుతినేటిది.

కొలారుబండ్లు n. s. plu. A sort of cart. ఒకతరహబండి. S. 1. 215.

గొల్ల n. s. A gôla peon; who guards or convoys money. రూకలకొట్లలోవుండే కొలువుడుగాడు.

గొల్లగారము n. s. Tax taken from the shepherds. గొల్లవాండ్లవద్దతీసేటిపన్ను.

కొల్లాయి, or కొల్లాయిగుడ్డ n. s. A kind of cloth. మడికట్టుకొనేటుండుగుడ్డ.

కొల్లత్తువాడు n. s. A mason or bricklayer. (Madras) బేల్దారివాడు, తాపీవాడు.

కొవ్వాడ్లు n. s. A sort of fish. Russell, No. 186.

ఖోగిరి, or ఖోగీరు n. s. خوگير *Khogir*. A cushion or pad used as a saddle. జీను.

కోజు, ఖోజు or ఖోదు n. s. Trace; secret; inmost meaning. మర్మము, గుట్టు, జాడ.

గోజుబాను n. s. Ox-tongue, a certain drug, being a leaf. దర్వికము, యెద్దునాలికె.

కోజా, or ఖోజా n. s. A corge or 20 pieces of cloth. This word is used among merchants. ఇరువైవస్త్రములు.

ఖోటా, or ఖోటు adj. کهوٹا *Khota*. False, not true, not real. కల్లైన, అబద్ధమైన.

కోటు n. s. A love game at cards: also "Court." a half jacket వస్త్రవిశేషము, అరచొక్కాయి, న్యాయసభయున్ను.

గోడాలు n. s. The rattlins of a ship's shrouds. నూలునిచ్చెన మెట్లు.

కోడిఋంజి n. s. A fish called gasterosteus Pterois volitans. Cuvier. Russell on Fishes No. 133.

కోతకటాయి n. s. Fees formerly paid for leave to reap a crop. కోతకలవుకైయిచ్చేరూకలు.

కోతల్ n. s. کوتل *Kotal*. A led horse: some thing which is more than absolutely necessary. మిగతగావుండేటిది.

గోదు, or గోందు n. s. گوند *Gōnd*. Gum, with which letters are secured instead of wafers. జాబులకు అంటించేబంక. గోదుచేయుట thus to close a letter. బేగోదుగావుండే unsealed, open.

ఖోదు n. s. See కోజు.

కోనముచేప n. s. The mango fish or Tupsee Muchchhee. Russell No. 185. మత్స్యవిశేషము.

కోపా n. s. A "cup" denoting a certain measure; a *cup-ful*. గిన్నె.

కోఠి n. s. A firm or mercantile house. కోఠివాడు a sorter of cloths, a ware-house man.

కోము n. s. for قوم *Qaum*. Caste, tribe. కులము.

గోరి n. s. for گور *Gōr*. A tomb; a grave. పీనుగనుపాతిపెయినకట్టినది.

కోర్వపొగాకు n. s. A superior kind of tobacco. శ్రేష్ఠమైనపొగాకు.

గోలాం, or గోలాము n. s. غلام *Gholam*. A slave. దాసుడు.

గోలి, or గోలిగుండు n. s. گولي *Gōlī*. A marble or small ball. పిల్లకాండ్లు ఆడుకొనేబచ్చెనబరిమిసవుంట.

గోరిదిబ్బ n. s. A churchyard or burying ground. పాతేచోటు

కోలుకాడు n. s. (K.) The assistant of a custom house officer.

కోల్గాడు n. s. An exciseman. See కోలుకాడు.

గోవాపండు n. s. Guava fruit. గొయ్యాకపండు.

కోవిల n. s. A pagoda or temple. గుడి.

కోవిలాళ్వారు n. s. The box in which the Vaishnavites keep their images. మందసోగము.

గోశబుర్దు n. s. Nautical phrase for coming to. వాడగోశబుర్దు అయ్యెను the ship came to.

గోషాగావుండేస్త్రీ, or ఘోషామనిషి n. s. A woman living in privacy, cloistered; as an inmate of a seraglio. రాణివాసముగావుండే ఆడుది.

ఘోషామనిషి n. s. from گوشه *Gōshā*. A woman living in privacy, cloistered as an inmate of a seraglio. రాణివాసముగావుండేటిది.

గోషుపేచు, గోష్పేచు n. s. گوش پيچ *Gōsh pēch*. A piece of cloth or shawl tied over the turban. పాగామీదనొసగనుగాకట్టుకోబడ్డవస్త్రము. H. 4. 107.

గోష్టుగుత్త n. s. The joint renting of a village by all its ryots (Ganj.)

గోష్వార, or గోష్వార n. s. گوشواره *Gōshwāra*. An abstract; an index; a tabular statement, wherein each article in a general account is reduced to it's proper head.

కోస్తా n. s. Territory: a sea "coast." (See Madras Reg. 1. of 1817.) కోస్తావర్తకము the coasting trade.

గారిశాయి n. s. A certain coin. ౧౫ అణరంజీలకు మారేనాణము.

కౌలు n. s. قول *Quoul*. A writing of assurance, agreement or engagement as granted by Government to the cultivator of the soil; safe guard or warrant to pass (as granted to an enemy.)

గ్యస్తి for గస్తి n. s. Recollection. జ్ఞాపకము.

ఖ్యాలి, ఖ్యాలు n. s. خيال *Khiyal*. Imagination; delusion: a kind of song. ఎంచడము, భ్రమ, పాట.

గ్రాది n. s. (Bengali word) A bannister, balustrade, railing or *chevaux-de-frise*. కటకటాలు.

గ్రామగ్రామసీగావుండే adj. Included in a village. ఒకవూరిలోచేరివుండే. ఆవురములోశిగ్రామగ్రామసీగావున్నపల్లె a hamlet included in the village.

క్రీస్తునుడు n. s. A "Christian." కిరస్తువాడు.

చ ఛ జ ఝ

See note on క, ఖ K Kh. The letters చ and చె generally take each other's places, as చతుర్థి, చంద్రుడు which are wrongly written చెతుర్థి, చెంద్రుడు and చాం takes the form of చేం as చాంతాడు for చేంతాడు.

జంకాయించుట v. a. To make a horse dance. గుర్రాన్ని ఆడించుట.

జంఖానా, or జంబుఖానా n. s. جامخانه *J-amkhānā*. A carpet.

జంగాల్కుచ్చు n. s. زنگار *Zangar*. The sub-acetate of lead: verditer, a greenish blue dye: semi-vitrified oxide of lead.

జంగికట్టుబడి n. s. Troops raised for war and then allowed land for subsistence.

జంజీరు n. s. زنجیر *Zangīr*. A chain. గొలుసు. జంజీరుజామీను mutual or "concatenatory" security, in which each man becomes security for the rest. (Bel.)

చండివాళము n. s. (K.) What is given to ratify a bargain, earnest money, a handsell. బయాను, సంచకరువు.

చండివాళము n. s. (Tamil சண்டிவாளம்) Loss in redeeming any article.

జంధా, జెండా or జండ n. s. جهندا *Jhandā*. A flag staff. ధ్వజస్తంభము. ధర్మజండను త్రిప్పినాడు he has established justice on its true basis.

జంత, or జంతె n. s. A machine for weeding a field. కలుపుపొయ్యేటట్టుదున్నేసాధనము.

జంత్రి n. s. جنتری *Jantrī*. An almanac. పంచాంగము.

చందా n. s. چندا *Chandā*. A *Quota* or portion of a sum due: a subscription. చందాకాకితము subscription paper. వూరిమీదచందావేసుకొనుట to raise a subscription.

జంబాడు, or జముదాడు n. s. A dagger బాకు.

జంబాళము n. s. A dagger. కటారి.

చందుకా for చందూక్ n. s. صندوق *Sandokh*. A box or trunk. పెట్టె.

చందువా n. s. چندوا *Chandwa*. The cloth of a ceiling: the top of a bed, the tester tilt of a cot. T. 3. 133.

చండోలిపిట్ట n. s. A sort of lark.

జంబుఖానా for جامخانه *Jam khana*. n. s. A carpet. కిందవేసుకొనేటిది.

చకడాలు, or చకడాబండ్లు n. s. Common carts. సామాన్యమైనబండ్లు. Bob. 1. 153.

జకాతి, or జకాయతీ n. s. زکات *Zakāt*. Custom-house duty. సుంకము. జకాయతీకుత్త a contract for custom-house duties.

చకునామా for చెక్నామా n. s. چکنامه *Chaknamā*. A map, or plan of lands. భూములుమొదలయినవాటిపటము.

జకీరా n. s. ذخیره *Zakeerah*. A store or hoard. చేర్చిపెట్టినది.

జక్కించుట v. n. Perhaps from جهکمارنا *Jhakmarna*. To be in error or fault. అపరాధియౌట. నాలుగురూకలువానిముఖముమీదపారవేస్తేజక్కించినట్టుచేస్తాడు if you pay him something he will do it submissively.

చక్రములు, or చక్రరూకలు n. s. Some small gold coin.

జగాబాకు n. s. A sort of dagger. ఒకవిధమైనబాకు. H. 5. 18. కంఠమునచేతిజగాబాకనక.

జజాయి, or జజాలి n. s. جزایل *Jazāil*. A wall-piece fired from a swivel or long swivel-musquet. ఒకవిధమైనతుపాకి.

చటాకు n. s. چهٹاک *Chhatak*. The sixteenth part of a seer. శేరులోపదహారోభాగము.

ఛట్కాయించుట v. a. perhaps from چٹکانا *Chatkana*. To whip hard. కొరడాతోబాగాకొట్టుట.

ఛట్టారి, or ఛట్టారివాడు n. s. A half caste or country-born person. Or చట్టకార but the origin of the name is doubtful.

ఛడాఛడి adv. چهڑاچهڑی *Chharā chhari*. Instantly, immediately, quickly. తటుకున, శీఘ్రముగా.

ఛడి n. s. چهڑی *Chhari*. A switch, a cane, ratan. చువ్వ, బెత్తము.

ఝర్తిచిఠ్ఠా n. s. جهرتي چٹا *Jharti chittā*. Waste book. Memorandum of daily payments. ఒకరోజువారీ లెక్క పుస్తకము.

ఝర్తిచూచుట v. a. To overhaul, review, examine. తిరిగిచూచుట, ఉండచూచుట.

ఝర్తిజాబితా n. s. An account particular; an inventory.

చఢాయించుట v. n. To raise (the price) ఎక్కుట.

చఢావణి, or చఢావు n. s. چڑاؤني *Charāoni*. An increase in price, rise: raising rent. పొడిగించబడము.

జతనము n. s. for جتن *Jatan*. Care, attention. జాగ్రత.

జత్తిగ n. s. A sowing machine. A drill plough. జడ్డిగము, అనగా విడతకుసూడుగొట్టములు అమర్చికట్టినది.

జదీదు adj. جديد *Jadīd*. New, modern. క్రొత్త. జదీదుయినాం land recently bestowed.

జనలు n. s. perhaps from جلمل *Jilmil*. i. e. *Jilmil* Shutters, venetians, any window. కిటికెలు.

జనపోసిలు n. s. The toll collection levied as a poll tax per head. మనిషికింతఅనితీసేవన్ను. (Guntoor.)

జనాబ్ n. s. جناب *Janāb*. Majesty, highness, excellency. మహాత్వము, ఘనత. Presence, as of a ruler. సముఖము. నేనువారియనజనాబులోహాజరుండగా while I was in his presence: waiting upon him.

జనాభా n. s. Population, people. జనులు. జనాభాలెక్క A census. కానేసుమారులెక్క. జనాభాపట్టి poll tax, taxes collected per head.

జనూలరు n. s. Servants of the Nizam. నిజాము వారిబంట్లు?

జన్నలు for జనలు n. s. A window. కిటికీ.

ఛపావనీ, or ఛపావణి n. s. چهپاؤني *Chhapāoni*. (Mahratta) Concealment, embezzlement. దాచడము, దివాణపుసొమ్ముతినివేయడము.

జప్తి, for జబ్తి n. s. ضبطي *Zabti*. Sequestration, attachment, seizure of goods.

చప్పా, for చాపా n. s. چهاپا *Chhapa*. A stamp, seal or impression. ముద్ర.

చబ్బూకు, for చబుకు n. s. چابک *Chābuk*. A whip. కొరడా.

చబ్బుకుచెట్టు for చౌకుచెట్టు n. s. The Cypress tree. ఒకసీమచెట్టు.

జబరు n. s. Force, violence. బలాత్కారము.

జబరుగా adv. Pompously. జంభముగా.

జబరుజంగుపిరంగి n. s. ظفرجنگ *Zafar Jang*. "The ruler of the battle"—a title bestowed on a certain cannon. Krishna Raya Vija. IV. 56. (A great gun named Zubber Jung is mentioned as being in Ghuznee.)

జబర్దస్తి n. s. زبردستي *Zabardasti*. Oppression, force, violence. బలాత్కారము.

జబాబు, for జవాబు n. s. جواب *Jawab*. An answer. ఉత్తరము.

జబితి, for జబతి n. s. See జప్తి.

చబుకు n. s. for چابک *Chābuk*. A whip. కొరడా.

జమకట్టుట v. a. To sum up, strike a total. వెరసివేసుట. ఈరుసుమునుసర్కారువారుజమకట్టుకొన్నారు this fee was sequestrated by Government.

జమఖానా جمخانه *Jamkhāna*. A carpet. జమకాళము.

జమా n. s. جمع *Jamā*. Collection, sum-total, amount. వచ్చుబడి, మొత్తము. జమచేసుట to collect. జమాఖర్చు جمع خرچ *Jamā Kharch*, the receipts and disbursements. వచ్చుబడిశెలవు. జమావసూలుబాకీ demand or assessment, collection and balance.

జమాదారు, జమాదారుడు or జమేదారుడు n. s. جمعدار *Jamadar*. A commander of a body of troops. A sergeant, the head of peons. హవాలుదారుకికిమయిదర్జాగలవాడు, బంట్రోతులపెద్దయున్ను.

జమాబంది n. s. جمعبندي *Jamabandi, Jammabundi*. Settlement of the assessments. శిస్తుయేర్పరచడము.

జమాయించుట, or జమాయించివుండుట v. n. To be in pomp. జంభముగావుండుట.

జమీందారి n. s. زمينداري *Zamīndārī*. The country or Jurisdiction of a Zemindar. ఒకజమీందారుడికిందవుండేదేశము.

జమీందారు, or జమీందారుడు n. s. زميندار *Zamīndār*. A landholder or a zemindar. A petty baron. ముతాదారుడు.

జమీను n. s. زمين *Zamīn*. Land. భూమి. జమీనుదారుడు A zemindar.

జముదాళి n. s. an error for جمدهر *Jumdhar.* A dagger. కటారి. Satyabha. 3. 53.

జరతా, జరతారు, జలతారు, or జర్తారు n. s. Gold lace. బంగారుజరిగ. H. 1. 79. జరతారుబట్టంచు చాల్చించు మేల్మిన్నా కన్నులుకప్పటంబు.

జరీ n. s. زر *Zar.* Gold or silver lace. జరిగ. జరీ ఖండువ a laced cloth. జరీబుటావలువ an embroidered cloth, tissue.

జరీబు n. s. جريب *Jarīb.* The mensuration of land, a survey-measurement. In all the northern districts this signifies garden stuff; and garden land irrigated by wells. మఘాణు, ఆనగాకోలపడము, బాగాయతి, ఆనగాతోటలుదొడ్లు.

జరు n. s. زر *Zar.* Cash, gold. రూకలు, బంగారు.

చరుచు n. s. A slap, a clap. దెబ్బ.

జరుజామీన్ n. s. زرضامن *Zarzāmin.* Money security. నగదుజామీను.

చరుకము n. s. A large metal pot. పెద్దతపేలా.

జరూరియాత్ n. s. ضروريات *Zarūriyāt.* Necessity. అగత్యము. జరూరియాత్ మరమ్మతు the necessary repairs.

జరూరు, or జరూరి adj. ضرور *Zarur.* Necessary. అగత్యమైన.

జడ్జి n. s. (E) 'Judge.' న్యాయాధిపతి.

జర్బాబు, for జర్బాఫ్తు n. s. زربفت *Zarbaft.* Gold cloth. సాదరా.

చర్హాయించుట v. a. چڑهاو *Charhāna,* To raise. చర్హావు or చఢావు چڑهاو *Charhāo,* aggravating, a higher bid.

చల్బచల్ adv. چل بچل *Chal bachal.* Gradually. క్రమముగా.

జలతారు, for జరతారు n. s. زرتار *Zartār.* Gold or silver lace, or thread. జరీ.

జలమోరి n. s. Some kind of artillery. ఒకవిధమైనఫిరంగి.

చలానా n. s. A printed list of letters paid or not paid. అచ్చువేసినజాబులజాబితా.

చలామణి, or చలావణి adj. چلاونی *Chalāoni.* Current. చెల్లే. చలామణిరూపాయి a current rupee.

జలాయి, for జులాయి n. s. جلائی *Julāi.* A weaver. నేసేవాడు.

చలాయించుట v. n. To decamp, run away. ఉరుకుట, పారిపోవుట.

జలాలి, for జలాలీ n. s. جلالي *Jalālī.* A sort of masquers at the Mohurum. మొహరంఫకీరులు.

జల్తారు, for జర్తారు n. s. زرتار *Zartār.* Gold lace or thread. జరిగ.

జల్ది, or జలిది adj. جلدي *Jaldī.* Quick. త్వరమైన. జల్దుగా Quickly. త్వరగా.

జల్లేరి, for జల్దారి n. s. A drain.

జల్ధారు, for జలదారి n. s. A drain.

ఝల్లి, జల్లీలు n. s. A sack, a bag of grain. గోతములు.

చవత n. s. An open litter or dooly?

జవాను n. s. جوان *Jawān.* A peon, a police or revenue officer. బంట్రోతు.

జవాబు n. s. for جواب *Jawāb.* An answer. ఉత్తరము.

జవాబుదారి n. s. جوابداري *Jawābdārī.* Responsibility, liability. ఉత్తరవాదము.

జవాబునివీసు n. s. جواب‌نویس *Jawāb nawīs.* A scribe, clerk or secretary. వ్రాయసగాడు.

జవాబుసవాలు n. s. جواب سوال *Jawāb sawāl.* (lit: answer and question.) Talk, discourse. సంభాషణ. అతనికిన్నినాకున్ను నిండాజవాబుసవాలుజరిగినది I had a long talk with him.

జవాహీరు n. s. جواہر *Jawāhīr.* Precious stones, jewels. రత్నములు.

చవుకము, for చౌకము n. s. Quatre or four, at games: a cloth, towel. నాలుగు, తడువము.

జహాగీరు, or జాగీరు n. s. جاگیر *Jagīr.* A grant of land revenue payable to government. Land or country bestowed as a free gift. స్వల్పపన్నుమొకరరుచేసుకొని విడిచినసీమ, ఇనాముగావిడిచినభూమి.

జహాజురవానా n. s. جهازروانه *Jahāz Rawāna.* Exportation by sea. సముద్రముమీదపంపించడము.

చా ఛా
జా ఝా

చాందిని n. s. چاندني *Chandnī.* The awning. మేలుకట్టు.

చాందినీవెండి, or చాందీవెండి n. s. from چاندي

Chāndi. Dead silver; not brightly polished. మెరుగులేనిది.

జాంపండు, or జాముపండు n. s. from جام *Jām.* The guava fruit. గొయ్యాపండు.

చాకరు n. s. چاکر *Chakār.* A menial servant. పనివాడు.

చాకరి n. s. چاکري *Chākarī.* Menial service. కొలువు. చాకరిపనిచేసే బ్రాహ్మణుడు a bramin in his private employ, a menial. చాకరీమాన్యము land given in fee for the performance of the meanest duties in a village, as the watchman, sweeper, washerman &c.

జాకీ n. s. "Jacques," "jacky" the knave at cards.

చాకు n. s. چاکو *Chākoo.* A penknife. పేనాకత్తి.

చాగలి n. s. A village officer under a potail or culcarni?

జాగా n. s. جاگه *Jāgah.* Place, land, home, dwelling. స్థలము.

జాగీరు n. s. جاگیر *Jāgīr.* A country or land given by government as a reward for services, or as a fee; a pension (in land:) a fief. The district around Madras was granted to Col. Clive by the Nizam, and hence is often called the (Jaghire) or Estate. Mill's Brit. Ind. anno. 1767 chap. 7. He retired from the service and went (ā ses terres) to his "jageer" that is to his country seat.)

జాజికాయకొయ్య, or చెక్క n. s. Deal wood. తేలికగావుండేవొకసీమకొయ్య. జాజికాయకొయ్యపెట్టె a deal case.

చాటక n. s. (K.) Witchcraft, for the purpose of ruining a foe. శత్రువును నాశనము చేయడము నుగురించినమంత్రు.

ఝూడా అయినది from جهارا *Jhāra.* It is expended, done, finished, used up, consumed. అయిపోయినది.

ఝూడాగా adv. Utterly, fully, completely, finally, conclusively, in full. పొత్తిగా.

చాడీ n. s. چاري *Chārī.* Slander, backbiting. కొండెము.

జాడీ, or ఝూడీ n. s. A large bottle or "jar."

చాడీఖోరు n. s. چاري خور *Chārī khōr.* A slanderer, a talebearer. కొండెగాడు. చాడీకత్తె a busy body; a girl that tells tales.

చాతాని plu. చాతానివాండ్లు as, (from Tamil சாத்தாதவன்.) A Sarternee, or more correctly çātānī. A caste of *Sudras,* who worship Vishnu exclusively: and whose profession is to sell flowers. They wear a female petticoat, without the కచ్చ tuck between the legs behind, which bramins use. They wear no thread on the shoulder, nor any జుట్టు top knot.

జాతాబాకీ n. s. Balance, remainder, after deductions. నిలవబాకీ.

చాతుట v. a. (from Tamil சாத்துகிறது.) To put on, dress, put vestments or garlands about an idol. సమర్పించుట. BD. 4. 37.

చాదస్తపు adj. Silly, foolish, idiotic. వెర్రి.

చాదస్తము n. s. Simplicity, foolishness. వెర్రితనము.

చాదస్తుడు n. s. A simpleton. వెర్రివాడు.

ఛాపు, for చాంపు n. s. چانپ *Chāmp.* The cock of a gun. తుపాకియొక్క గుర్రము.

ఛాపా n. s. چهاپا *Chhāpā.* A seal, print or stamp. ముద్ర, అచ్చు. ఛాపావేయుట to seal or print. ఛాపాకాకితము stamp-paper, stamps.

జాప్యము n. s. Delay, loitering. జాగు. adj. Slow, loitering. జాప్యగాడు n. s. A sloth, sluggard. జాగుచేసేవాడు.

జాఫరా n. s. for زعفران *Zāfarān.* Saffron: a light red tint. కుంకుమపువ్వు.

జాబితా n. s. ضابطه *Zābitah,* A list, inventory, paper of names. పట్టీ.

జామారు, or సాదాజామావారు n. s. perhaps from جامےوار *Jāmewār.* A long cloth without any coloured border. It is worn chiefly by widows, never by married women. తెల్లకోక.

జామీను n. s. ضامن *Zāmin.* Bail, surety, security. పూట. జామీనుదారుడు a surety, a bondsman. రొక్కజామీనుదారుడు money-security. నఫరుజామీనుదారుడు personal security.

జాయా n. s. ضايع *Zāyah.* Loss, injury, damage. నష్టము, చెరుపు. ఆచెరువుజాయాఅయిపోయినది the tank is injured. గాలిజాయాతప్పినది the wind is shifted.

జాయా adj. ضایع *Zāyah*. Dilapidated, damaged, spoilt, lost. చెడిపోయిన.

జాయాచేసుట v. a. To dilapidate, waste. పాడు చేసుట.

చారము (for چهارم *Chahārum*.) adj. Fourth (class or sort of land.) నాలుగో.

జారి adj. جاری *Jārī*. Current, proceeding, in force, continued, granted (the reverse of రద్దు *radd* annulled.) నడిచే, చెల్లే, జరిగే.

జారి n. s. جاري *Jārī*. Relieving from a state of sequestration, as land. జప్తివిడుదల. ఆభూమి నాకు జారిచేసినాడు he granted me the land. జారిచేయుట to issue, as a warrant; enact, pass a law.

చారుజామా for చార్ జామా n. s. چارجامه *Chār-jāmah*. A saddle cloth. జీనుపోసు, జీనిమీదవేసేగుడ్డ.

జాలరు n. s. جهالر *Jhālar*. Cymbals, a tambourine; fringe, net-work. పెదల్పుగానున్నగాలుం డేచెయితాళము, కుచ్చుకట్టకుందిటి అంచు మొదల యినవాటికి కట్టేటిది.

చాలాక్ adj. چالاک *Chālak*. Smart, dexterous, clever. చురుకైన.

చాలాన n. s. (Bengali) An invoice or chellaun. ఇనాన్వయిను.

చాలితి adj. (Mahr.) Incidental, occasional. n. s. A thing, item, article. ఆకస్మికమైన, వద్దు.

జాలు, or జేలు adv. زیل *Zēl*. Under. ఈజేలున hereinafter. This seems to be currupted from the Persian *dar-īn-zīr*.

జాలె n. s. Darning. రఫ్వు. జాలెతీయుట to darn. రఫ్వుచేసుట.

జాస్తి n. s. and adj. Extra, additional, increase. పై, అధికమైన. జాస్తిచేసుట to increase. జాస్తి గామాట్లాడక do not talk too freely. దౌలుజాస్తి too high an estimate. శిస్తుజాస్తి.

జాహీరు adj. ظاهر *Zāhir*. Apparent, evident, known, manifest. స్పష్టమైన. జాహీరుచేయుట to explain or represent.

జాహిలీతనము n. s. from جاهل *Jāhil*. Folly, silliness. పిచ్చి.

చి చీ ఛి ఛీ జి జీ ఝి ఝీ

జింకు A kind of inferior coin: a bad pagoda. (Bel.)

జింజీరు, for జంజీర్ زنجير *Zanjīr*. A chain. గొలుసు.

చింది plu. చిందీలు n. s. چندي *Chindī*. A shred or strip, a rag. చింపి, చింపిగుడ్డ.

జిందిగాని, or జిందిగి n. s. زندگاني *Zindagānī*. Living, bread, subsistence, property. జీవనము, సొత్తు.

చిందీలు n. s. plu. The bends of a ship: fragments. వాడకూర్పుకువేసేవంకరదూలాలు, చింపులు.

చిందువ n. s. Logwood imported from Pegu, used in dying.

చిందేలుపాము n. s. A sort of eel.

జిమ్మా n. s. ذمه *Zimmā*. Possession, charge. వశము, స్వాధీనము.

జింసి for جنس *Jins*. See the next word జింసు.

జింసు, for జిన్స్ n. s. جنس *Jins*. Article, thing, lot, property: drug, ingredients. వస్తువు, సరుకు.

జింసువారిలెక్క n. s. A catalogue, descriptive list. సరుకులవారిలెక్క.

చికినిపోకలు, for సికినిపోకలు n. s. plu. The name of the best sort of areca.

చికిలి adj. perhaps meant for صیقل *Sīqal*, Keen, sharpened, bright. పదునుపెట్టబడ్డ, మెరుగుపెట్టబడ్డ.

చికిలి n. s. perhaps meant for صیقل *Sīqal*. Furbishing, polishing. మెరుగుపెట్టడము.

చిక్కట్టు adj. Difficult, muddy. ఇక్కట్టయిన.

జిగ్ని n. s. جگني *Jigni*. A broach, worn by women at their throats. కంఠాభరణవిశేషము.

జిగ్ని, or జిగినిపీనుగ n. s. A stingy fellow. లోభి.

చిగురు and బొమ్మచిగురు n. s. A small pulley. చిన్నకప్పి?

చటాకు for ఛటాకు n. s. چھٹانک *Chhatāk.* A liquid measure $\frac{1}{16}$ of a seer. శేరులోపదునారో పాలు.

చిట్టా n. s. چٹّا *Chittā.* A rough day book; or an account taken on slips of paper before written fair. దినవహి.

చిత్తమాసము n. s. The "season" of importation by sea into the N. E. ports: it extends from August to September. ఆషాఢము, అనగా ఆడిమాసము.

చిత్తు n. s. A rough copy.

జిద్దాజిద్ది n. s. A great dispute. మహా వైషమ్యజగడము, హోటాహోటము.

చిడ్డీలు for సిడీలు n. s. plu. from سڑھی *Sirhi.* Steps, stairs. మెట్లు.

జిద్దు n. s. ضد *Zid.* Enmity, contrariety. ద్వేషము, తగ.

చిప్పె adj. Of the tailor caste. చిప్పెవాడు a tailor. కుట్రపువాడు, గోనెగొంతులుమొదలయినవికుట్టేవాడు.

జిమ్మా n. s. ذمه *Zimmā.* Charge, trust, possession, commission. వశము, స్వాధీనము.

జియాపత్తు n. s. ضیافت *Ziyāfat.* A gift to a superior in money; hospitality: invitation. నజరు, సన్మానము.

జియ్యరు n. s. A Vaishnava Sanyasee or sage. వైష్ణవసన్యాసి.

చిరా n. s. A dagger. కటారి. Naguij. 2. 209. చిగురాకుజిరాదార.

చిరాకు n. s. چراغ *Charāgh.* A lamp: anger, sudden passion. దీపము, కోపము.

జిరాతు, or జిరాయతి n. s. زراعت *Zirāat.* (written *zeroyet* and *jerrait,* and *zerahet*) Cultivation. సాగుబడి.

చిరిశీచుక్కాని n. s. The steering wheel of a rudder.

చిరునామా, చిర్నామా for శిర్నామా n. s. The direction or superscription of a letter. పైవిలాసము.

చిరునామాదారుడు n. s. The person to whom a letter is addressed. పైవిలాసమువాడు, అనగా యెవనిపేరిట పైవిలాసము వేయబడియున్నదో ఆడు నిపి.

చిలుకు, or శిలుకు n. s. వసూలుఅయినదాంట్లోయి రసాలు అయినదిపోగా మిగతరూకలు.

చిలువానము n. s. (Tamil சில்வானம்) Odd: or more than a round number specified, indefinitely exceeding it; but it commonly means money saved by a kinsman entrusted with the household affairs. S. 3. 317. చిల్లర, యింటిఖర్చుకనియిచ్చినదాంట్లోకూడబెట్టినది.

జిలేబీలు n. s. from جلیبی *Jilēbī.* A kind of sweetmeat. ఒకతరహామిఠాయి.

జిల్దు n. s. جلد *Jild.* A volume. ఒకపుస్తకము. జిల్దుకట్టుట to bind a book.

చిల్లర adj. چلرہ *Chilrā.* Sundry, various, miscellaneous. చిల్లరవాండ్లు by-standers, indifferent persons, low folk, people of no weight.

చిల్లర n. s. چلرہ *Chilrā.* Odd. చుంగుడి. నాలుగురూపాయీలుచిల్లర four rupees and odd.

జిల్లా n. s. ضلع *Zilā.* A province, district or country. A musulman author describing England says "London is in the zillah of Middlesex."

జిల్లేదారు, or జిల్లేదారుడు n. s. ضلعدار *Zilādār.* A subordinate revenue officer. తరుపుదారుడు.

జిల్లేబు for జిలేబి n. s. جلیبی *Jilēbī.* A sweetmeat like barley sugar. ఒకతరహామిఠాయి.

చిపుక n. s. A coin of the value of a quarter of a rupee. పావులా. D.

చిపుకు n. s. The rod of a ship's pump; a piston.

జీ جی *jee,* or వాలా والا *Wala.* Affixes like *man, bearer, fellow,* in the words boat-*man,* standard-*bearer,* school-*fellow.* Thus from Sett, a merchant, Set-jee, "Mr. Trader," or Sir-merchant. *Nao-wala* or *nao-jee,* a boatman, the captain of a vessel. *Garee-wala,* a carriage-man, i. e. a coachman: or, one who owns a carriage. Ghorawala, one who *has* a horse, a horseman. *Bucha-wala* one who has a child: or an animal with a young one. *Hukka-jee,* a pipe-bearer. *Sherbet-wala* or sherbet-jee, a seller of sugar-water. *Manzil,* a stage or post: *manzil-jee* the post-master.

Paisa, money : *paisa-wala* a monied man. In the feminine, wālī ; thus, *paisawalī*, a woman who is rich, &c.

చీజుబస్తు n. s. چیز بست *Chīz bast.* Furniture and baggage. మూటముల్లెలు, సామాను.

చిటి n. s. for چٹھی *Chitṭhi.* A letter or note. A bill. ఇంటిచిటి a bill of sale. లాటరిచిటి a lottery ticket. చిటివేయుట to buy a ticket.

చిడి for సిడి n. s. سڑھي *Sirhi.* Steps. మెట్లు.

జీనిగరివాడు n. s. from زین گر *Zīngar.* An artizan ; a worker in leather ; an upholsterer : they are makers of playing cards and palankeens. బట్టినబొమ్మలుమొదలైనవాటిని చేసేవాడు.

జీను for జీని for زین *Zīn.* A saddle. పల్లము. H. 1. 79.

చీపు n. s. (Tamil சீப்பு) A bunch of plantains. గెలలోనొకభాగము.

జీబి, జీబు n. s. جیبهی *Jībhi.* The area between the outer and inner walls, or gates. కోటయొక్కయాగోడకు ఆగోడకులేకగవినిమండరిగడకు కువెనకగడకుకునడిమిప్రదేశము.

జీరంగిరెక్కలు n. s. from زرنگي *Zirangi.* Beetlewings of a bright emerald hue : used in ornamenting dresses, as spangles. తళతళమనే పురుగురెక్కలు.

జీరగుండు n. s. A globe of glass filled with quicksilver in order to decorate a pandal. పందిటికి కట్టెరగుండని ప్రకరణవశమువల్లతోచినది? G. 2. 5. మెలిముత్తియంబులతోరణంబులునుకలవడంబులును మేలుకట్లునుజీరగుండ్లును.

జీరా n. s. زیرہ *Zīrā.* A flaw in a gem or coin. Armour, mail. రత్నాదులయందలిచీరిక, కవచము.

జీలాపెట్టె n. s. A leather bucket for baling a boat. ఓడవనీళ్లనుముంచిపోసేతోలుపెట్టె.

చీళితబెట్టుట v. a. To get rid of. పోగొట్టుట. T. 2. 128. జీర్ణదళసంఘముచీళితబెట్టి.

జీలు for జైల్ n. s. for ذیل *Zail.* A supplement. ఉత్తరభాగము. ఈజీలునవ్రాయబడ్డ hereinafter written.

చు ఛు జు ఝు చూ ఛూ జూ ఝూ

చుకాయించుట v. a. from چکانا *Chukana.* To complete, settle, adjust, fix the price of. తీర్చుట.

చుక్కాని, or సుక్కాని n. s. for سکان *Sukkan.* A rudder.

చుక్కి n. s. A telescope, spying glass. ఓకు,దుర్బిను.

జుజివి adj. جزوي *Juzwi.* Trivial, common, petty. అల్పమైన.

చునాయించుట v. a. from چنا *Chunna.* To plait or fold any part of a dress. పింజకట్టుట.

జుబ్బాలు n. s. from جهبه *Jhubba.* A kind of long vest resembling a shirt. ఒకతరహాచొక్కాయి.

జుమలా, జుములా or జుమ్లా n. s. جمله *Jumlā.* Total. మొత్తము.

జుమాలుపేరు n. s. A kind of necklace. ఒకవిధమైనకంఠభూషణము.

జుమికి n. s. for جهمکی *Jhumki.* A sort of pendant earring. జుమికిపువ్వు A passion flower, perhaps called Jhumka.

జుమజుములు n. s. زمزم *Zimma zimma.* A cant expression for fondness, kindness. విశ్వాసము.

జుర్మాన, or జుల్మాన n. s. جرمانه *Jurmānā.* A fine, a penalty levied. అపరాధము.

జులాయించుట v. n. جهلانا To reel about, swing about, stagger. మయికముచేతమునులుట.

జులుము n. s. for ظلم *Zulm.* Force, violence, tyranny, oppression. బలాత్కారము, దౌర్జన్యము.

జుల్ఫాలు, or జుల్ఫా n. s. for زلف *Zulf.* Locks of hair left at the time of tonsure, just above and before the ear. కాకపక్షము.

జుల్మానా n. s. for جرمانه *Jurmānā.* A fine. అపరాధము.

చుల్లా n. s. چله *Chullā.* A fire place. పొయ్యి. చుల్లావరి a hearth tax : a tax levied on forges and furnaces.

ఝూటా n. s. جهوٹا *Jhūtā.* False. అబద్ధము.

జూటు, or ఝూటు n. s. جھوٹھ *Jhuṭh*. False: falsehood. అబద్ధము.

జూతొట్టి n. s. (Tamil சூத்தாட்டி) A shambler, one who waddles along. బరువుకనిచేసేవానివలె తిరిగేవ్యర్థుడు.

జూరకత్తి, or జూరి n. s. A knife. చాకు.

జూలు, or ఝూలు n. s. جھول A painted or variegated cloth or blanket serving as an elephant's howsings. కుథము, ఏనుగమీదిబట్ట.

చె చే ఛె ఛే జె జే ఝె ఝే

చెంగలికోష్టము for చెంగల్వకోష్టము n. s. A certain drug. Costus Arabicus. Ainslie. 2. 165.

చెంగోలు n. s. (Tamil செங்கோல்) Shengol. "A royal staff: a sceptre: just government. Rottler p. 356. vol. 1. part 2. చెంగోలము.

జెండ, or జెండా n. s. جھنڈا *Jhandā*. A flag, standard, banner, colours. ధ్వజపటము.

చెండూలుపిట్ట for చరండూలు n. s. چرندل *Charandul*. The crested lark: a sort of sparrow with crimson beak and red feathers at the vent. Jerdon's Catal. No. 186.

ఛెకడా, or ఛెకడాబండి n. s. for چھکرا *Chhakrā* A cart. శకటము.

చెకముకరాయి for చెకిముకిరాయి n. s. from چقماق *Chaqmāq*. A flint.

చెక్ర, or చక్ర n. s. چکرا *Chakrā*. A small gold coin used South of Madras. చక్రరూక.

చెకలాతి, సకలాతి for సకలాతు n. s. A kind of woollen stuff. 'Chekelaton' (Chaucer in Bailey) Brocade.

చెకుతర for చకోతరా n. s. چکوترہ *Chakōtarā*. A shaddock. పంపరమూసుకాయ.

చెకునామ for చెకనామా n. s. چکنامہ *Chaknama*. A map; boundary lines in a plan, a rent roll, and descriptive list of lands: a ground plot. నేలమొదలయినవాటిపటము.

చెకుముకిరాయి n. s. from چقماق *Chaqmaq*. A flint.

చెక్కు n. s. (From the English word check) Surplus; that results from comparing different measurements of grain (Ganjam.)

చెక్కు n. s. (E) Chastisement. A draft for money on a banker. చీవాట్లు, హుండి.

చెటాయించుట v. a. To reject, refuse, disapprove. తిరస్కరించుట. వాండ్లమీదవొకఅర్జీ చెటాయించినాడు he gave a petition against them.

చెట్టాంపిళ్ల n. s. (Tamil சட்டாம்பிள்ளை) A monitor in a school. బడిపెద్ద.

చెట్వాడి for చట్టారి n. s. An "Indo Briton," vide orders of Government dated 1828.

చెడావు n. s. چڑھاو *Charāo*. Augmentation, raising the rent. పొడిగించబడము.

చెలుకు, or చెళుకు n. s. An abridgement, an abstract. టూకీ.

చెమ్మయికిస్తి n. s. The dues or instalment (Kisti) levied every (chhē mahi) six months.

జెరీబు, or జరీబు n. s. A measuring, a survey measurement, the mensuration of land. నేలకొలవడము.

చెలావణి adj. for چلاونی *Chalāoni*. Current (as applied to coin.) చెల్లే.

చెలామణి n. s. for چلاونی *Chalāonī*. Currency. చెల్లడము.

జెల్ది adv. جلدی *Jaldī*. Quickly, soon త్వరగా.

చెవి n. s. A key: (from the Portugueze *chave*: Haughton's Beng. Dict. page 1075.)

చేంది n. s. Toddy. కల్లు.

చేకు, or చాకు, or చ్యాకు n. s. for چاکو *Chākū*. A penknife. పేనాకత్తి.

చేడ n. s. (for Tamil சேடை) The wet land cultivation. మాగాణి. చేడచేయుట to make the wet land cultivation.

చేబదులు n. s. A simple loan; debt without bond or account. చేతి అప్పు.

జేబు n. s. جیب *Jeb*. A pocket. చొక్కాసంచి.

చేరా n. s. for چہرہ *Chehrā*. Features, the written description of a thief's features. పోలిక.

చేరు n. s. Spawn or roe in fishes. చేపగుడ్లు.

ఝేరుగండి n. s. An embrasure to shoot from. తుపాకిపెట్టికాల్చడమునకైకోటగోడనవుండేతూటు.

జేరుతలావు n. s. for زیر تالاب *Zērī tālāb*. Land lying "under a tank." చెరువుకిందిభూమి.

జేరుదస్తు adj. زيردست *Zerdast*. Weak, powerless, abject. దుర్బలమైన.

జేరుబందు n. s. زيربند *Zerband*. A martingal, a saddle girth, a whip. కళ్లెమునకు గుర్రముముఖమునకు కట్టు కున్న టంగువారుకున్న కట్టేవారు, టంగువారు, రఘాటి.

చేర్లాబడ్డ adj. Leaning, sloping. గోడచేర్లాబడ్డది the wall has sunk.

జేలి for ذيل *Zel*. A supplement (See జీలు) ఈజేలిన hereinafter, as follows. ఈజేలినవివరిం చినప్రకారము as follows.

చైవ్రాలు for చేవ్రాలు n. s. Signature.

చొక్కబాన n. s. The bonfire. కామన్ననాడుకాల్చే కుప్ప.

చోంగ n. s. from چنگاني *Chungānī*. A tobacco pipe.

జోఖ్యము n. s. جوکهم *Jokham*. Loss, risk, danger, hazard: goods, merchandise. నష్టము, అపాయము, సరుకు. వాదజోఖ్యము peril of the sea: risk of shipwreck.

జోడి n. s. A favourable quit rent. సుళువుగా యేర్పరచబడ్డకప్పు.

జోడు n. s. for جوڑي *Jōrī*. or جوڑا *Jōrā*. A pair or couple: shoes. జత, పాపోసు.

జోనంగి, or జోనంగివాడు n. s. One of the lowest tribe among the Mahometans. A sort of Musulman merchant on the Malayalam coast, who are also called Cholias or Lubbees. A corruption of the Tamil சோனகர் *Shonahar*. లబ్బెవాడు.

చోబుదారు, or చోబుదారుడు n. s. چوبدار *Chōbdār*. A macebearer. వెండిబెత్తమువాడు.

జోరావరి n. s. زورآوري *Zōrāwarī*. Violence, outrage. బలాత్కారంది.

చోరీ n. s. چوري *Chorī*. Theft, robbery, stealth, smuggling. దొంగరికము. A revoke at cards. చోరీపట్టీ a list of stolen goods.

జోరు n. s. زور *Zōr*. Force, violence. బలాత్కారము.

చోళా for చోలా n. s. چولا *Chōlā*. The upper part of a man's jacket (the body of a gown or ungaraka.) చొక్కాయిపయిభాగము.

చోళి n. s. چولي *Chōlī*. A woman's jacket or bodice. రవిక.

జోళ్లు n. s. (plural of జోడు a pair) Shoes. చేతి జోళ్లు gloves.

చౌక n. s. چوک *Chouk*. Bazar. అంగడివీధి, కు జరి.

చౌక n. s. A square, court, or area. A quarter of a rupee. చవుకా, పావులుండేజనము, చోటు న్న.

చౌకండి for చౌఖండి n. s. A closet built alone, like a sentry box. వేరేగాకట్టినచిన్నగది.

చౌకట్టు n. s. چوکهٹ *Choukhat*. A window frame: any square frame. చట్టము.

చౌకి n. s. چوکهي *Choukhi*. A watch or guard. A party of persons &c. stationed. The station or post. See Balarama IV. 257.

చౌఖండి adj. Square, quadrangular. చౌకమైన, న ల్చదరమైన.

చౌథాయి n. s. چوتهائي *Chouthāī*. A quarter, one-fourth. పాతిక, పాతికపాలు.

జౌదరి, చౌదరి, or చౌదరి n. s. چودري *Choudri*. The head man of a trade, the head merchant who manages a town market. అంగళ్లకంతాపె ద్దగావుండేవాడు.

చౌని n. s. چهاؤني *Chhāonī*. A cantonment or lodging for troops. దండువుండేచోటు.

జ్ఞప్తి n. s. (a vulgar word) *jnapti*. Remembrance. జ్ఞాపకము.

జ్మా n. s. (contracted for జమ) The receipts.

ట ఠ డ ఢ

డ|| A contraction for a Dubboo. Twenty cash.

ఢంకా n. s. ڏنکا *Danka*. A pair of kettle drums carried on a horse. గుర్రముమీదవేసికొట్టేచర్మ వాద్యము. వాడుఢంకాకొట్టినాడు he died.

టంగుమైదాను for తంగుమైదాను n. s. تنگ ميدان *Tang miedān*. A narrow or small plain, a valley. ఇరుకుగావుండేతావు.

టంగువారు n. s. from تنگ *Tang*. A horse's girth. జీల్లముసుబిగించేపట్టు.

ఢక్కణము for ఢక్కను n. s. دکهن *Dhakkan.* The Deccan (a word of unknown origin.) It is also the name of a village where Hyder lived in his youth.

ఢక్కాముక్కీ, or ఢక్కాముక్కి n. s. ڈهکامکهی *Dhakkā mukkhi.* Difficulty, time of trouble. ఇరుకు, సంకటము.

టక్కుబాజీతనము n. s. from ٹهگبازی *Thagbāzī.* Trickery. మోసము. (From this word *Takku*, is derived the word Thug, one who deludes and strangles.)

డజన్ adj. Dozen. పండ్రెండు. (English "A dozen") This is often used for an indefinite number of stripes: a flogging.

టపాయికు for తుపాంగు n. s. A musket, a fowling piece. తుపాకి.

టపాలు, or టప్పాలు n. s. (plural టప్పాలులు) ٹپال *Tappāl.* The post or mail (అంచె.) టప్పాలు పెట్టుకొనిపోయి travelling post.

టపాసు n. s. A cracker in fireworks.

దబాయించుట for దబాయించుట v. a. from دبانا *Dubānā.* To press, oppress, crush. అణుచుట, అదుముట.

డబ్బి n. s. ڈبی *Dubbi.* A little box, as a snuff-box. భరణి.

డమాను n. s. (perhaps meant for బాద్బాను بادبان *Bādbān.*) A sail; *bara damanu* the main-sail. డమానుమాసము (i. e. mausim) Sailing season: the months of February and March, when the northern ports are open.

టముకు for తముకు n. s. from تمکی *Tamki.* A small drum. తుడుము.

ఢమ్మనుట v. n. To die suddenly. గచ్చకొట్టుట, వాడుఢమ్మన్నాడు he died suddenly.

డయలి, or డయరి n. s. (E) A "*Diary.*" దినచర్య.

టరాయించుట for తరాయించుట v. a. To settle, adjust or fix. నిర్ణయించుట.

తరావుబేరీజు n. s. Assessment fixed by the estimation of the produce of a village.

టరిణి or టరణి n. s. (E.) The word "Attorney," wherein the initial is mistaken for the article A. లాయరు.

టరీఫు n. s. تعریفه A *tariff* or table of quotations of prices or duties. వెలచిట్టీ.

డలాయతు or ఢలాయతు n. s. ڈهليت *Dhalait.* A dalait or armed attendant: a body guardsman. వెంటివిళ్లబంట్రోతు.

టలాయించుట for తలాయించుట v. n. ٹلنا *Talana.* To walk about. ఇటుఅటుతిరుగుట.

డల్లి n. s. ڈلی *Dallī.* A lump (of sugar, force-meat, &c.) ముద్ద.

టబాయి for తబాహీ n. s. تباهي *Tabāhī.* A foul wind: an unfavourable breeze. చెడుగాలి.

డవాలి n. s. دوالی *Dawalī.* A peon's belt on which a badge is worn. బంట్రోతువిళ్లనుతగిలించేపట్టి.

ఠస్సా n. s. ٹهسا *Thassa.* A stamp or chop or print. అచ్చు. ఠస్సాచేయుట to stamp, to print. దాన్నినీవుయిస్తేనేగానికదలననిఅక్కడఠస్సావేసుకొనికూర్చున్నాడు he insists upon your paying it, and is rivetted to the spot.

టాకనా, or టాకణా n. s. ٹاکن *Tākan.* A pony. అశ్వమట్టము.

టాకనాగుర్రము for టాకణా n. s. ٹاکن *Takan.* A Pegu pony. అశ్వమట్టము.

ఠాకాడొంగ n. s. A gang robber. దీవిటిదొంగ.

టాకేటాకు adv. for ٹاکے ٹاک *Takē tak.* Speedily, without delay. అతిత్వరగా.

టాచిమెంటు n. s. An "attachment" or seizure of goods. జప్తిచేసుట.

ఠాణా n. s. ٹهانا *Thana.* A watch house; a police station; garrison in a fort. పోలీసుబంట్రోతులుఉండేచోటు, కోటలోకావలియుండేరాణువ.

ఠాణాదారుడు n. s. ٹهانادار *Thanadār.* A head police officer. విళ్లబంట్రోతు, పోలీసుబంట్రోతు.

టాపు n. s. An island. The *top* or hood of a gig, cot &c. దీవి, బండిపయికప్పు.

డాబు n. s. A list or catalogue. A physician's recipe; a female's zone. చిట్టీ. డాబామొలతాడు a broad belt.

డామా n. s. A false charge, a groundless claim. Meant for దావా *dāwā.*

ఢామ్మనుట, or ఢమ్మనుట v. n. To expire, to die suddenly. అటక్కునచచ్చుట. ఢమ్మకొట్టిచచ్చె, వాడుఢమ్మనెను he died suddenly.

ఠారు, or ఠారుమునడము n. s. تهار *Thār*. Sudden death. చావడము. పదిమందికి ఠారున్ను యిరువైమందికి గాయాలున్ను అయినది ten died and twenty were wounded.

ఠారుఠారవుట v. n. To be afraid, or alarmed. నిండా దిగులుపడుట. నాకు ఠారుఠారు అయినది I was very uneasy. ఠారుమనిచినిగినది it tore with a loud crash.

డాలరు n. s. A "dollar." In the Mysore List is ఢాలరివరహా.

టాలాటోలితనము, or ఠాలాఠోలితనము n. s. Knavery, trickery, ill behaviour. టక్కు, పితలాటకము. ఠాలాఠోలిమనిషి a rogue, a vagabond.

డాలి n. s. ڈالی *Dālī*. A pottle or small fruit basket. బుట్టిక.

ఢాలు n. s. ڈهال *Dhāl*. A shield. కేడెము.

ఢావుబోడు n. s. Larboard. ఎడమఅట్టు, ఎడమపక్క.

డింకమల్లి n. s. A sort of jessamine.

ఠికానా, or ఠికాణా n. s. ٹهکانا *Thikānā*. Place of residence; resort, abode, station: "his where about." Prospect, chance, likelihood; means, resources, funds. తిండిచోటు, గతి. కూటికి ఠికాణా లేదు there is no means of getting food. వానికియివ్వడమునకు నాకుయేమిన్ని ఠికాణా లేదు I am not able to give him any thing.

డిల్లి n. s. دهلى *Dehli* or دلى *Dilli*. The city called Delhi.

డివిజను n. s. The English word Division: this is used for a small or subordinate district; and also for a police station or guard house. భాగము, తుక్కుడి.

ఠీకు adj. ٹهیک *Thik*. Proper, just, fit, exact, complete, true, precise. సరియైన.

టీపు n. s. ٹیپ *Tīp*. A banker's bill, which is transferrable by endorsement. A grant or assignment of revenue given to a creditor. Money deposited as security for good conduct. హుండి, తనఖా, జామీనుగాపెట్టినరూకలు.

డుబాయించుట v. a. ڈبانا *Dubānā* To ruin. ముంచుట, అనగాచెరుపుట.

డుమారము for దుమారము n. s. Dust. దుమ్ము, ధూళి.

టూకరించుట for టూకీకరించుట v. a. To abridge, or abstract. సంగ్రహముచేసుట.

టూకి adj. Compendious, short, brief, contracted. సంగ్రహమైన. టూకిచేసుట to abridge.

టూకిగా adv. Briefly, in brief. టూకిగావ్రాసుట to abridge.

డెంకణ n. s. The flag-staff on the bastion of a fort. కొడికంబము.

టేకు, or టేకుచేప n. s. A skate or ray fish. One species is called అంబటిటేకు.

టేకుమాదిరి n. s. Teak timber. టేకుచెక్కదూలము.

డేక్చా for డేక్చా n. s. دیگچه *Dekchah*. A boiler or great brazier, or large kettle. అండా.

ఠేటు, or థేటు adj. The best, pure. శ్రేష్ఠమైన, మొదటితరమైన.

టేపు n. s. The English word tape. నాడా.

డేరా, or ఢేరా n. s. ڈیرا *Dērā*. A tent. పటకుటము.

ఠేవణి, or ఠేవణాతి n. s. ٹهیونی *Thevanī*. Monied security, advance, deposit, putting money into a bank. రొక్కరూకలనుజామీనుగాపెట్టడము.

డైమను n. s. "Diamonds" at cards. ఆటేకాకితములలోశకటాలి.

టైము n. s. The English word Time. కాలము.

తైలి for థైలి تهیلی *Thailī*. n. s. A small bag; particularly of paper. సంచి.

టాక్కుజీగాడు n. s. The bird called coppersmith. It's note is like the sound of a small hammer striking a rock. Jerdon. No. 216. ఒకపక్షి.

డొల్ల, or డొల్ల n. s. A great basket placed on a cart. The cheek. A lie. డొల్లలు withes, straw ropes that gird in a stack of grain. వెంటిని డొల్లకిటిగాచుట్టిచేశిరి they made a basket of twisted straw.

డోకడా, or డోక్రా, or ఢోకడాలు n. s. A cent, or hundredth part of any coin. డోకడాలప్రకారముగా Per cent. పదకొండుడోకడాలు is $\frac{11}{100}$.

ఢోకా n. s. Perhaps an error for ڈهکا *Dhaka*. Injury, defect, impediment. Fear. చెరుపు, ఖరాబు. మీకుయేమిన్ని ఢోకాలేదు you have nothing to fear.

టోకుకట్టుగాకొనుట v. a. To purchase by whole sale. జట్టుగాకొనుట.

టోపి n. s. توپی *Tōpi.* A hat, a cap. జాతివాండ్లు తలకువేసుకొనేటిది, కుళ్లాయి.

డోరియాచీర n. s. from ڈوریا *Dōryā.* A double or single striped cloth. ఒకవిధమైనచీర.

టోలా n. s. ٹولا *Tōlā.* A family; a crowd; a band. గుంపు. యేకటోలాఅయి in a mob.

టోలా n. s. تولا *Tola.* The weight of one rupee. రూపాయియెత్తు.

టోలి, or తోలి n. s. تولی *Tolī.* The eighth of a pice పైసాలోయెనిమిదోభాగము.

డోలి n. s. ڈولی *Dōli.* A dooly or litter.

ఢోలు n. s. ڈھول *Dhōl.* A great drum. ఒకచర్మవాయిద్యము.

డౌలు n. s. ڈول *Doul.* Manner, form, appearance. Estimated revenue: probable produce. The amount of the Government demand. Fixed rate of assessment. డౌలువసూలుబాకి demand, collection, and balance.

త థ ద ధ

ద|| Stands for దస్తఖత్తు Signature.

తంఖా for తన్ఖా n. s. تنخواه *Tankhāh.* An assignment on the revenue. An assignment or billet on lands: an order on the treasury for the payment of a stipend. తనఖాపత్రము a bond transferred by endorsement. తనఖాకాకితము the order for an assignment on the revenue.

తంఖాజాస్తి or తనఖాజాస్తి n. s. Excess (in a crop) proved after the amount has been re-examined. Detection of underrating.

దంగిడి n. s. A coarse cloth; dowlas, so named from a village near Bombay.

తంట, తంటా for టంటా n. s. ٹنٹا *Tanta.* Difficulty, puzzle. Dispute, squabble. Debt. తొందర, సంకటము, అప్పు. తంటాలుపెట్టుట to torment or plague. తంటాకోరుతనము Quarrelsomeness. తంటాకోరు a makebate: a quarrelsome wretch. తంటాలేని undisputed, indisputable.

తండ n. s. The bottom of a ship.

తండ for తాండా n. s. A mass, heap, or multitude. గుంపు.

తండలు n. s. (Tamil தண்டல்) Collection, the money collection.

తండా, or లంబాడితండా n. s. A troop of Brinjaries or Lumbadies.

దండాలుతీయుట v. n. To perform exercises, or feats of strength. కాళ్లుచేతులునేలమోపిముందుకువెనకకుపూగుట.

దండుగయినాం n. s. ڈنڈگاانعام *Dandgā Inam.* Land formerly granted as compensation for extortions.

తండుట v. a. (From Tamil தண்டுதல்) To collect (the money due on bills.) వసూలుచేసుట.

తండుపాళము n. s. Cast iron. పోతయినుము.

తండేలు n. s. A tindal or boatswain. పడవవాండ్ల పెద్ద.

దండోరావేయడము, or తండోరావేయడము n. s. (from ڈھنڈورا *Dhandōra.*) Proclamation by beat of drum.

దండ్యా, or దండియా n. s. ڈنڈیا *Dandyā.* A particular petty officer of the bazar. A bailiff, or constable. బంట్రోతు.

తంబాకు n. s. A metal, pinchbeck. సొగసా.

తంబి n. s. تنبیه *Tambīh.* Punishment. శిక్ష.

తంబు n. s. تنبو *Tambū.* A small tent. చిన్నడేరా.

తంబుర, or తంబురా n. s. تنبور *Tambūr.* A drum. A sort of guitar or lute. చర్మవాద్యవిశేషము. తంత్రీయుక్తవాద్యము.

తంబూలిదుకాను n. s. A huckster's stall. పసారిదుకాణము.

తకద్దమా n. s. Adjustment. (Vizag.)

తకరారు n. s. تکرار *Takrār.* Dispute, altercation, quarrel. వివాదము. తకరారుచేయుట to specify: to resist.

తకావి n. s. تقاوی *Taqāvī.* Money advanced to a cultivator for the purchase of seed &c. సాగుబడిచేయడమునకై కాపులకు సహాయముగా యిచ్చేరూకలు.

తగాజా n. s. تقاضا *Taqāza,* usually తగాదా Dunning. రూకలుచెల్లించుమనికక్షసింపడము.

తక్కాలిపండు, or తక్కాళిపండు n. s. The Brazil gooseberry. బుడ్డమునిసిరిపండు.

తక్సీంం for తక్సీం تقسیم *Taqsīm.* Sharing out. Dividing, apportionment. పంచడము. తక్సీంచు చేయుట to allot.

తక్యా for తక్కియా n. s. تکیہ *Takyā.* A pillow. A mosque. తలగడ, మసీదు.

తక్తా n. s. تختہ *Takhta* A plank, a table; a sheet of accounts. పలక, బల్ల, ఒక తావులెక్క కాకితము.

తఖ్తు n. s. تخت *Takht.* Throne, a royal seat. సింహాసనము.

తక్రారు n. s. تکرار *Takrār.* Dispute, altercation, puzzle, objection. వివాదము.

దఖలు n. s. دخل *Dakhl.* Insertion; entering; taking possession of. దాఖలుచేసుకోవడము, స్వాధీనముచేసుకోవడము, ప్రవేశించడము.

దఖినీ n. s. دکھنی *Dakhnī.* The southern dialect: i. e. the Hindustani spoken in the Peninsula. తురకభాష.

తఖీదు for తఖీకు adj. Correct, true. నిజమైన. తఖీకువర్తమానము a true report.

తఖీయ్యతు for తఖీయ్యదు n. s. تقید *Taqiyad.* Injunction.

తగద్దమా for ముకద్దమా n. s. مقدمہ *Muqadama.* Matter, affair. వ్యవహారము.

దగల్‌బాజి, or దగల్‌బాజీ n. s. دغلباز *Daglbaz.* A rogue, a cheat. మోసగాడు.

దగలా or దగళా n. s. دگلہ *Daglā.* A coat of mail.

తగల్లూబీ n. s. تغلبی *Tagallubi.* Irregularity. అక్రమము.

దగా n. s. دغا *Daga.* Fraud, cheating, trick, deceit, chicanery, imposture. మోసము.

తగాదా n. s. تقاضا *Taqāzā.* Claim, suit or dispute. Dunning: the same as Dhurna. వ్యాజ్యము. See notes at the end of Sir W. Jones's paper (As. Res. iv. 364) "On some customs of the Hindus." See Malcolm's Memoir 1. 559 and Elph. 93.

దగాబాజి n. s. دغابازی *Dagabāzi.* Fraud, craft, knavery. మోసము, వంచన.

తగాయత్తు usually తాగాయత్ adv. for تغایت *Tagkayat.* Until, up to, since ఆతగాయత్తు ever since.

ధగిడీ n. s. for دھگڑ *Dhagar*, or *dhagra*, A jade, slut, wretch. ధగిడీకొడుకు a villain.

తగిడీ n. s. Cloth of gold. బంగారువస్త్రము.

తగులూఫు for తగాఫలూ n. s. تغافل *Taghaful.* Neglect, carelessness. అశ్రద్ధ.

తగ్యైరు or తగ్యైరు n. s. for تغیر *Tagheer.* Dismissal, turning out. బరతరఫు. జాగీరుతగ్యైరుచేశిరి they sequestrated the land.

తజావజా adv. Upside down, in confusion, in dismay. కలవరకంతుగా, తారుమారుగా. MM. 442.

తజువీజు n. s. تجویز *Tajwiz.* Considering, contriving, planning. ఆలోచన, యుక్తి.

దటాయించుటfrom دٹانا *Datāna.* v. a. To chide, snub, rebuff. అదమాయించుట. Sh. 843.

తట్టు n. s. ٹٹو *Tattoo.* A pony. తట్టువాజిగుర్రము.

తట్టుబడుట v. n. To incur debt or expense (Ganj.)

తట్టువాడు n. s. (Tamil) A goldsmith. కంసాల వాడు.

తడమాడుట v. n. for تارمار *Tārmār.* To stagger, waver in speech, perplex. తడబడుట.

దడారము n. s. (Tamil) Courage. ధైర్యము.

దడాయిసు v. a. (K.) To sound (a drum) దణదణమనివాయించుట.

ధణీ n. s. دھنی *Dhani.* Master, owner, lord. యజమానుడు.

తతిమ్మా adv. تتمہ *Tatimma.* The remainder, the rest. తతిమ్మారూపాయలు the balance. తతిమ్మావాండ్లు the rest of the people.

తత్తరము adj. (Tamil தத்தளம்) Shattered, ruinous, leaky. శిథిలమైన.

తత్తరించుట v. n. To vacillate or to be agitated, to be in trouble. సంకటపడుట.

తద్బీరు n. s. تدبیر *Tadbīr.* Opinion, advice, counsel. అభిప్రాయము, ఆలోచన.

తనఖ్ఖీ, or తనకీ n. s. تنقیح *Tanqih.* Ascertaining, examination. విమర్శ. తనఖ్ఖీచేయుట to compare, check, or audit accounts. తనఖ్ఖీమశాతు *tanqīh mashāt.* The proof measurement or trial measurement.

తనఖా n. s. تنخواہ *Tankhah.* Assignment of the revenue. See తంఖా.

తనాబి or తనాబితుండు n. s. A block of wood. సదరముగాపుండేమొద్దు.

తనిఖి, or తనఖా n. s. تنقیح *Tanqih.* Examination, ascertaining. విమర్శ, విచారణ.

తఫసీలు n. s. تفصیل *Tafsīl.* A detailed account or statement. వివరము.

తప్తి n. s. An earthen seal on a stack to prevent theft. మంటిముద్ర.

తప్పెట్టు adj. Lonely, out of the way. ఎడారిగా వుండే. తప్పెట్టుతాలు a lonely distant spot.

తఫసీలు n. s. تفصیل *Tafsīl.* Detail, particulars, analysis. వివరము.

దఫా n. s. دفعہ *Dafā.* Time, occasion, turn : a company of armed peons. తడవ, బంట్రోతులయొ మూహము.

తఫాత్ for దఫాత్ n. s. for دفعات(*dafaāt* plural of dafa) Items.; a head containing various details : extra or sundry collections. దఫాత్ ఖర్చు *dafaat kharch,* various expenditures. Miscellaneous sums paid.

దఫాదారు, దఫేదారుడు, or దబేదారుడు n. s. دفعدار *Dafādār.* The serjeant or head of a company of policemen.

తఫావత్తు n. s. تفاوت *Tafawāt.* Difference, disparity. Fault, defect. భేదము, లోపము. తఫావత్తులేదు there is nothing the matter : there is nothing wrong : no matter ; never mind !

తఫిసీలు or తఫసీలు n. s. تفصیل *Tafsīl.* Detail, particulars. వివరము.

దఫ్తరు, or దస్త్రము n. s. دفتر *Daftar.* A bundle or packet of papers. A register or record : the budget or seals of a ministry.

తఫ్రకా, or తఫరకా n. s. تفرقہ *tafraqa* A time. తడవ, తేప. See తబరకా.

తఫ్రీకు n. s. تفریق *Tafriq.* Allotment, division into shares ; the allotment of the shares forming a total sum contributed. It is generally applied to extra collections thus shared.

దబకతనము n. s. Backbiting, trickery. అంగుడు దుడిపితనము.

దబకాయించుట v. a. from دبکانا *Dabkānā.* To press down, to snub, chide, frighten, reprove. అదుముట, గదమాయించుట.

తబకు, or తబుకు n. s. طبق *Tabq.* A tray or large salver for cups &c. తట్ట.

తబరకా for తఫరకా n. s. تفرقہ *Tafraqā.* A time. తవడ, తేప. ఒకతబరకా once.

దబరా n. s. A ship's capstan ? a basin.

తబలకు n. s. Packthread to tie up bundles of papers : a packet so tied. కాకితములకట్టకట్టే దారము.

దబశీరు n. s. See తవషీరి.

దబాయించుట v. a. from دبانا *Dabana.* To press down, to snub, chide, frighten, reprove. To bully, brow-beat, beat down. అదమాయించుట.

తబీయ్యతు n. s. طبیعت *tabiyat* Nature, genius, disposition, constitution ; obedience. Generally used for health. But *tabiyat* تبیعت Following, dependance.

తబుకు n. s. طبق *Tabq.* A salver or tray for paun &c. it is also spelt దబ్బుకు, తట్ట.

దబేనా, or దఫీనా n. s. دفینہ *Dafīnā.* Hoard, buried treasure. Property. నిక్షేపము, ధనము. నీఅబ్బదబేనానావద్దలేదు I don't owe you a farthing. This perhaps is a false pronunciation for దమ్మిడి even a farthing.

తబేలా n. s. for طویلہ *Tawaila.* A stable. అశ్వశాల, గుర్రపుశాలయము.

తబ్దీలు n. s. تبدیل *Tabdīl.* Exchange ; transposition ; transfer. మార్పడము.

తబ్లక్కు n. s. See తబలకు.

దమదమా n. s. دمدمہ *Damdama.* A battery. బురుజు. M. M. Local. xix 74

తమాను n. s. تمان *Tamān.* Trowsers, long drawers, ఇజారు.

తమాము adj. تمام *Tamam.* The whole. తమాముగా adv. Wholly, utterly.

తమాయించుట v. a. from تھمانا *Thamana.* To check, to stop. To sustain ; to save himself from falling. శమించుట. తమాయింపు checking, stopping.

తమాశా, or తమాషా n. s. تماشا *Tamashā.* Shew, spectacle, exhibition, sport, fun. వేడుక. తమాశా.

గా వ్రాయుట to write neatly, finely, prettily. మంచితమాషా a fine scene, a pretty sight.

తమ్మడు, తమ్మయ్య n. s. (K.) A simpleton or dummy. వెర్రిముఖము. HN. 4. 110. అనగాఅయ్య.

దమ్మష్, దమాస్, or దమాసు n. s. دمش *Damash* Damask. దమాసు.

దమ్మిడి n. s. دمری *Damrī.* A pice, a farthing. five cash. అరదుడ్డు.

తయారు n. s. تیار *Tayār.* Readiness, ready. సిద్ధము, సిద్ధమైన. తయారచుట to make ready.

తయినాతి n. s. تعیناتی *Tayināti.* Attendance, service, waiting.

దర్ در *Dar.* In. దర్బందగిహజరత్తు dar bandagi hazrat. (Let this letter appear) *in* the presence (lit: service) of his honour &c. This is the usual superscription of letters.

తరఃదారి adj. for తరహాదారి Classed in kinds, diverse. తరహారి

తరక్కీ n. s. ترقي *Taraqqi.* Advancement in office. ఉద్యోగములోఅభివృద్ధి.

తరగతి n. s. Sort, kind. Classification, arrangement. స్థాను.

తరజాస్తి adj. درزیادتي *Dar Ziyadati.* "In addition", as an extra tax. Over and above.

తరదూదు, or తరద్దుదు or తర్ద్దూదు n. s. تردد *Taraddud.* Effort, labour, struggle, striving, exertion, application, toil, fag, pains-taking; cultivation of land. కృషి, ప్రయత్నము. తరద్దుదుఖత్తు a memorandum specifying the crop intended to be raised in a field.

తరఫయిను n. s. طرفین *Tarfain.* Both sides. ఉభయవాదులు.

తరఫు n. s. طرف *Tarf.* Side, quarter, district. పక్క, దేశము.

తరఫుదారి طرفداري *Tarfdāri.* Partiality. See తరఫయిను.

తరఫుదారుడు n. s. طرفدار *Tarfdār.* Ruler of a district. One who has the superintendence of a small district. జిల్లేదారుడు, పారుపత్తి

దరబారు n. s. دربار *Darbar.* A court, cutchery or hall of audience. కచ్చేరి. దరబారుఖర్చు a kind of extra tax levied by the head farmer &c.

తరబియ్యతు n. s. تربیت *Tarbiyat.* Education, training. తనుకరచడము.

తరలచేప n. s. A fish. మత్స్యవిశేషము. Russell, plates 80. 81.

తరహా n. s. طرح *Tarah.* Sort, kind. విధము. పెద్దమనిషితరహాగా like a gentleman.

ధరా n. s. Price, rate, value.

తరాజు, or తరాసు n. s. ترازو *Tarazu.* A pair of scales. తక్కెడ.

ధరావత్తు n. s. for دهروت *Dharōt.* (Mahr.) Deposit. Money given in pledge, or security. డిపాజిట్టు.

తరాసు n. s. ترازو *Tarazu.* A pair of scales. త్రాసు.

తరి n. s. تری *Tarī.* Wet cultivation (మాగాణి) irrigated land producing rice.

దరిజీ n. s درزی *Darzī.* A tailor. కుట్టువాడు.

తరిబియ్యతు n. s. تربیت *Tarbiyat.* Education, training. తనుకరచడము, అలవరచడము.

దరివేసి, దరవేసి or దర్వేసి n. s. درویش *Darwaish.* A beggar; poor.

దరిమిల, దరివిల్ల adv. درینولا *Darinwila.* Subsequently; hereinafter. దానికిదరిమిల since that date. దరివిలవడ్డి Interest that subsequently accumulated. దరివిల్లవడ్డితో with the subsequent interest. This word like "*To Wit*" is used at the commencement of a letter or order.

తరీకు n. s. طریق *Tarīq.* Manner, way, custom, fashion: a rule, a canon. రీతి, వాడుక, నిబంధన.

దరు n. s. درو *Daroo.* A large well. దొరువు.

దరుజామీన్ for زرضامن *Zarzamin.* Money-security. రొక్కజామీను.

దరుజు, or దురుజు n. s. A cornice, a frieze, a joining, a seam, in carpentry or masonry. గోడకానగాని స్తంభముమొక్క కొననగాని చేసియుండేచిత్రము. దురుజునున్నము Plaister made of lime.

తరువాయ, or తరువాయి n. s. Seasonable time, opportunity. తరుణము.

దరోగ for దరోగ్ دروغ *Darogh*. Fraud, a lie. మోసము.

దరోబస్తు adv. and adj. دروبست Wholly, completely, entirely, all. యావత్తు.

దర్ఖాస్తు n. s. درخواست *Darkhast*. Proposals, application, offer. అడగడము, చెప్పుకోవడము.

దర్గావజా n. s. درگاه *Dargah waza*. Allowances for ceremonies at a (dargah) Musulman tomb.

దర్జ n. s. درجه *Darja*. Rank, grade. మెట్టు. దర్జావారి classification.

తర్జుమా, or తర్జమా n. s. ترجمه *Tārjuma*. A translation. భాషాంతరము.

దర్బారు n. s. دربار *Darbar*. A hall of audience; a court, a public office. కచ్చేరి. దర్బారుఖర్చు "Court charges" A fee or sum exacted on various pretexts; formerly demanded to pay for the petty charges of an office.

తర్బియ్యతు n. s. تربيت *Tarbiyat*. Education, training. చెనుకరచడము, అలవరచడము.

దర్మహా, or దర్మా n. s. درماهه *Darmāha*. Monthly wages, salary. జీతము.

దర్మ్యాన, or దమ్యాన, దరిమేన n. s. درميانه *Darmiyana*. Meddling. జోలి. వానిదరిమేనాపో బోకు do not meddle in his concerns, or do not meddle with him.

దర్యాఫ్తి, or దర్యాప్తు n. s. دريافت *Daryaft*. Enquiry, trial. విచారణ.

తర్వాడి, or తర్వాణి n. s. Vinegar?

తర్వాయి n. s. A lesson in the Vedas. The rest, the continuation. తర్వాయినెంబరు the next or preceding case.

తర్వారి, or తరవారి n. s. A settled measurement of fields or villages. తరపడి. తరవారిగ్రామము లు the villages which have got the ryotwar system.

తర్వారు, or తలవారు n. s. تلوار *Talwar*. A sword. కత్తి.

తలపరిగినాలా n. s. A water course from a spring. కశంకాలవ.

తలబుదీవానిగ్రామములు n. s. طلب‌ديوانی Villages granted on quit rent for service.

తలమరలుగా (Tamil) adv. From generation to generation. వంశపరంపరగా. అనేకతలమరలు గా from generation to generation.

తలాబు n. s. تالاب *Talab*. A tank. చెరువు.

దలాయతు, or ధలాయతు n. s. ڈهلايت *Dhalayat*. An armed personal servant. A peon. వెంటివి ళ్లబంట్రోతు.

దలాలి n. s. دلال *Dallal*. A broker, a salesman. తరగరి.

తలావు n. s. تلاو *Talao*. A tank. చెరువు.

తలాషు n. s. تلاش *Talash*. Search, enquiry. విచా రణ.

తళిగ, తళియ or తళిహ n. s. A brass dish, full of rice, used in a Vaishnava temple. నివేదనము నకైకళ్లములోవుంచినఅన్నము.

దలీలు n. s. دليل *Dalīl*. Argument, proof, demonstration. న్యాయము, రుజువు.

తల్లాశి for తలాషు n. s. تلاش *Talash*. Inquiry. విమర్శ. తలాషుచేసుట to make inquiry into, to look after.

దళ్వాయి, or దళవాయి n. s. Dalwai: also written Delavoy. Dulwoy. A general: a minister or regent. (Wilks.) The general of an army: the manager of a state. సేనాధిపతి, కార్యకర్త.

దవతి, or దవితి n. s. دوات *Dawat*. An ink-stand. సిరాబుడ్డి.

దవర, for దబర n. s. ڈبره *Dabra*. A basin. బోగిణె.

తవషీరి, or తవషీర n. s. طباشير *Tabāshir*. Manna of bamboos. వెదురుప్పు.

తవాయి for تباهي *Tubahi*. An incursion of plunders, war, battle, contest. A cross wind, a foul breeze. Misfortune, hazard, peril. వాడత వాయిపట్టినది the ship missed stays, or fell out of it's course. క్రమూడము, ఉపద్రవము.

తవుకూఫు n. s. توقف *Tawaqquf*. Delay. ఆలస్య ము.

దవుడు n. s. دور *Daur*. Running, galloping: an inroad, incursion, or invasion. సవారి, తవా యి, తల్లి, అవాంతరము.

దవె n. s. A title like Esquire, used by Guzaratees, as, Cheyanalu Dhaveh.

దశరామశరగా adv. Without observing the stops

and meaning. తారుమారుగా. వాడు దాన్ని తరారా మురారాగా చదివినాడు he read it confusedly.

తశరీమంచె n. s. A sort of silk cloth. ఒకతరహాపట్టుబట్ట.

తశ్రీఫుఫర్మాయించుట v. n. تشريف فرمانا *Tashrif-farmana* To condescend (to come or go.) దయచేసిరావడము, లేకదయచేసిపోవడము.

తష్ఖీషి n. s. تشخيص *Tashkhis.* Valuation, estimation, reckoning. మదింపుచేయడము.

తసదీక, తస్దీకు for తసద్దుకు n. s. تصدق *Tasadduq.* ("Receiving contributions for pious uses" *Richn.*) "A fixed sum paid by Government to a pagoda, a mosque, or the officers in an establishment, as consolidated allowance in lieu of assumed lands" &c. It is also erroneously used for మొయిన్యాను. దేవాలయములు మొదలయినవాటికి దివాణమువారు నిష్కర్షగా యిచ్చేరూకలు.

దసరా, or దస్రామండగ n. s. The Dasara or నవరాత్రి *Navarātri* feast in honor of the goddesses Durgi, Laxmi, and Saraswati: it is also called విజయదశమి. It falls on the tenth day of the light fortnight in Aswija. Throughout India it is celebrated with great pomp, and all weapons, implements and books are consecrated. The name is also spelt దశహరా, but that seems erroneous. It lasts ten days, beginning on the last new moon of the rainy season: varying from the end of September to the beginning of November. See Moor's Pantheon, page 156-350.

దసరి, దుసరి or దశిరీమంచె n. s. A sort of silk cloth. ఒకవిధమైనపట్టుమంచె.

తశరీఫు, or తశరీఫు n. s. تشريف *Tashrīf.* A present. బహుమానము.

తసర్రపు, for తసర్రుఫ్ n. s. تصرف *Tasarrūf* Embezzlement, use, usufruct. Enjoyment. అపహరించడము, హరించడము, అనుభవించడము. నా చేనుఫలంబిరుతసర్రఫు చేసినారు they have seized on my crops.

దసిరిపట్టుమంచె n. s. A sort of silk cloth. ఒకతరహాపట్టుమంచె.

తసుకు n. s. Trick, wile, deceitful promises. టక్కు. తసుకుచేసిపోవుట to slip out of the hand.

తష్ఖీసు, తష్కీసు for తష్ఖీస్ n. s. تشخيص *Tashkīs.* Ascertainment, valuation. Appropriation. నిశ్చయించడము, మదింపుచేయడము.

దస్ఖతు n. s دستخط *Dastkhat.* Signature. చేవ్రాలు.

దస్తు, అంబులదస్తు n. s. دستہ *Dasta.* A quiver. అమ్ములపొది.

దస్తక్ n. s. دستک *Dastak.* A pass or order: a summons. ఆజ్ఞ, సమ్మను, పిలుచుకొని రమ్మనే ఆజ్ఞ.

దస్తగిరి n. s. دستگيري *Dastagiri.* Patronage. సంరక్షణ. దస్తగిరిచేయుట to patronize.

దస్తవజు, దస్తావేజు for దస్తావీజ్ n. s. دستاويز *Dastawīz.* Voucher, document, a paper. సాధకము.

దస్తా n. s. دستہ *Dastā.* A quire of paper. ఇరువదినాలుగుకాకితములకట్ట.

దస్తావజు, or దస్తావేజు for దస్తావిజ్ n. s. دستاويز *Dastawīz.* Voucher, document, written instrument. సాధకము.

దస్తు n. s. دست *Dast,* Gross collections: money realized. దస్తుచేయుట to collect. చోరీదస్తు embezzled rents, money collected but not brought into the public accounts. A hand at cards. దస్తుబాకీ the balance of collections.

దస్తుగరదా To make up a deficiency. (Ganj.)

దస్తుగిరిచేయుట v. a. from دستگيري *Dastgiri.* To patronize, or take by the hand. సంరక్షించుట, ఆదరాచేయుట.

దస్తుబదస్తు adv. and n. s. دست بدست *Dast badast.* From hand to hand. ఈచేతిలోనుండి ఆచేతికినగదుగాచెల్లించడము.

దస్తుబాజు n. s. دستباز *Dastbāz.* Collection of revenue?

దస్తూరి n. s. دستوري *Dastoorī.* Customary fees. A person's usual hand writing; autograph, signature. వాడుకగాయిచ్చేటిది, చేవ్రాలు, దస్ఖత్తు. దస్తూరిదారుడు he in whose hand-writing the paper was.

దస్తూరు, or దస్తూరి n. s. دستور *Dastoor.* Custom, manner. (In sailor's language) Studding sails.

దస్త్రము (for దఫ్తరు دفتر *Daftar.*) n. s. A budget: a portfolio; being a handkerchief or cloth full of papers, and tied up as a bundle. ముద్రద్దీలకాకితాలకట్ట.

తస్రీఫు n. s. See తశ్రీఫు.

తస్లీం n. s. تسليم *Taslīm.* An assignment or draft for money. "Balance remaining in the hands of Tahsildars." (Ganjam.)

తస్లీము n. s. Reward, present. బహుమానము.

దస్వందము n. s. See దశబంధము.

దస్వారా adv. (K.) دسوارہ *Daswārā.* Once in ten days. పదిదినములకు ఒకమాటు.

దస్వారాపోర్టు n. s. from دسوارہ *Daswārā.* A ten-days Report. పదిదినములకు ఒకమాటు వ్రాసే సమాచారము.

దస్సాల adj. دس سالہ *Das sāla.* Decennial: lasting ten years. పదియేండ్లు.

తహా, or తహ n. s. Consent, agreement. సమ్మతి. తహాపడుట v. n. To be proved: to be settled. వీండ్లు చెప్పినదివానికి తహాపడలేదు they did not believe what he said.

తహతహ n. s. Grief, vexation, weariness. వ్యాకులము, వేసట.

తహతహపడుట v. n. To be vexed, be grieved. వేసటపడుట, వ్యాకులపడుట.

తహద్ది, తజద్ది for తఅద్ది n. s. تعدي *Taaddī.* Trouble, disturbance; affair; extortion, wrong, violence. (Shak.) తొందర, వ్యవహారము, దండగతీయడమున్ను.

తహద్దు for తఅద్ది n. s. See తహద్ది.

తహబంది n. s. تهبندي *Tahbandi.* An agreement. ఒడంబడిక. (Reeve.)

తహబందిచేయుట v. a. To subdue. జయించుట.

తహమ్ముల్ n. s. تامل *Ta ammul.* Delay, waiting. సావకాశము, కాచుకొనియుండడము.

తహరీరు n. s. تحرير *Tahrīr.* Percentage or allowance made to superintendents of public works.

తహవారి n. s. تواري *Tahwari.* Specification, classing, arrangement. తరహావారి, ఏర్పాటు.

తహవీలు n. s. تحويل *Tahwīl.* Comparison. సరిచూడడము.

తహసీలు n. s. تحصيل *Tahsīl.* Collection, exaction of money, restraint.

తహసీలుదారుడు n. s. تحصيلدار *Tahsīldār.* A collector of revenue. A native revenue officer. అములుదారుడు.

తా థా దా ధా

తా|| A contraction for (H.) తాగాయతు since, and also for (H.) తాలూకా a district. Also in letters signifies తాజాకలం *tāzā Kalam* Postscript, or literally, A fresh paragraph.

తాండా, or తండా n. s. تانڈا *Tānḍā.* A troop or camp of Lambadies or gypsies. లంబాడీలగుంపు.

ధాక్, or ధాక n. s. for دهاک *Dhāk.* Awe, dread. భయము.

తాకత్తు n. s. طاقت *Taqat.* Ability, power, strength. శక్తి, బలము.

తాకీదు n. s. تاکيد *Takīd.* A written order by authority: a precept. ఆజ్ఞాపత్రిక.

తాక్లు n. s. (Tamil தாக்கு) A place. చోటు. తాక్లువారుగా ఉండే లెక్క an account of the different divisions of the field.

దాఖల, or దాఖలా n. s. داخله *Dakhila.* Insertion, entry in an account, verification. Ground, basis, authority, proof. Instance, example, precedent, comparison. A schedule. దాఖలచేయుట to file, or enter. వ్యాజ్యముదాఖలఅయినది a suit was filed. దాఖలపడినది it proved true, it was verified. దాఖలచూచుట to compare. దాఖల్ ఇచ్చుట to answer, or tally.

తాగాయత్తు prep. تاغايت *Tā Ghāyat.* Since, until, up to. వరకు.

తాజం for తాజీం n. s. تعظيم *Tazīm.* Reception of a guest. Treating with ceremony and respect. సన్మానము. తాజంఇచ్చుట to receive or welcome a guest.

తాజా adj. تازہ *Tāzā.* Fresh, new: pleased, cheerful; not sickly. కొత్త, నవీనమైన. తాజాకలం Fresh paragraph; postscript. తాజాచేసుట to make [illegible]at or pleasing.

థాడ or థాడా n. s. A swarm, a group, a mob. గుంపు.

దాడవ n. s. A run of good luck, a flush at cards. జాకీదాడవ a flush of three from the knave. (దాడవస్తోకు whist?)

దాడి n. s. داڑھی *Darhi*. A beard. గడ్డము.

దాణా n. s. دانا *Dānā*. Horse-gram. ఉలవలు, సెనగలు.

తాపటమేకు n. s. A two pointed spike nail joining two boards edge to edge. See నెమ్ములు.

తాపి n. s. Ballast in a boat. వాడఅడుగున బరువుకై వేసేటిది.

తాపిదారుడు n. s. A spy. వేగుచూచేవాడు.

తాపిత, or తాఫితా n. s. تافتا *Tāftā*. A sort of stuff: taffety. పట్టువస్త్రము.

తాఫా n. s. طایفه *Tāifā*. A set or company, as of dancers. భోగంమేళము.

తాఫ్తా n. s. "Taffety:" also *Tartan*. పట్టువస్త్రము.

తాబందు for تہبند *Tahband*. A sort of petticoat. పావడ. తాబందుబల్ల a shelf or ledge.

తాబాజారి n. s. Tax paid by venders in bazars. అమ్మేవాండ్లుయిచ్చేపన్ను.

దాబు for దాబ n. s. داب *Dāb*. Subjection, control, keeping under. దాబులోవుంచుట to keep under control.

తాబే n. s. تابع *Tabe*. Dependance. ఆయనతాబేను under his orders. (A wrong phrase. Shak. 479.) తాబేదారునవుకరు A menial or private servant. A dependant or follower.

తామాను n. s. See తమాను.

దామాషాయి, or దామాషా n. s. for داماساهی *Damasahi*. Appointment, equitable allotment, dividends. The proper name of a merchant, who died insolvent and his effects were divided. (Shak.)

దాయతి, తాయిత్తు n. s. An amulet. రక్ష.

దాయి n. s. داعی *Dāī*. Plaintiff. ఫిరియాది.

తార n. s. The long straight trumpet used at funerals. చావుకువూదేటిది.

ధారణ n. s. (Mahr) Price, valuation. ధర.

తారము n. s. The "Tare" or difference allowed for the weight of package. కట్టలుతూచడములో గోనెదారముమొదలయినవాటికిగానుతోసియిచ్చేటిది.

తారీఖు n. s. تاریخ *Tārīkh*. Date of the month, day of the *English* month. తేది.

తారీఫు n. s. تعریف *Tārīf*. Praise, commendation. పొగడడము, బుజ్జగింపు.

దారు adj. دار *Dār*. Substantial, having money or funds పుంజిగావుండే. నాదారు having no money or funds. దారునాదారు the rich and poor.

దారు or దారుడు دار *Dār*. As an affix; keeper, overseer, or holder. దఫేదారు دفعدار *Dafēdār*. A head man of peons, a serjeant. తండాదారుడు A Lambadi chief: the head man of a gypsey camp.

దారు n. s. دارو *Dārū*. Spirituous or vinous liquor. Gun powder. సారాయి, తుపాకిమందున్ను.

దారోగా n. s. داروغه *Dārōghā*. An agent or superintendent. పెద్దగావుండేవాడు.

తార్వారి for తరవారి n. s. A settled dimension of fields or villages. పైమాయిషి, మసాహతు. తరవారిలెక్క The "*survey*" accounts. (Bel.)

తార్వాళము for తాళ్వారము n. s. (Tamil தாழ்வாரம்) A balcony. వసారా, మంచపాళి.

తాళా n. s. (Mahr.) Similarity, match. దాఖలా. ఈలెక్కలుతాళాపడ్డవి these two reckonings correspond.

తాళాబందు for తహాబందు (Usually తాహాబందు) n. s. An account epitomised from the ఖాతావణి A complete abstract of the actual receipt and expenditure of the revenues for the past year. From it is formed the *āzmāish* or estimate for the next or current year.

తాళీశపత్రి most commonly తాళిశపత్రి for తాళీశపత్రము * n. s. A plant (Flacourtia cataphhracta); the leaf of this plant is used in medicine.

దాళువా n. s. "The black crop." A technical phrase in Ganjam, Vizag. and Rajamundry.

తాలూక్ or తాలూకా n. s. تعلقه *Taalluqa*. A dependancy: a district, a sub-division. పరగణా.

తాలూకా adj. تعلق *Taalluqa.* Belonging to, pertaining to. నాతాలూకా పెంకుటియిల్లు a house of mine. ఆతాలూకా regarding that, under it, appertaining thereto. ఆతలకాయతాలూకాపుర్రెయిదేను This is the scull of that sheep's head.

తాళబందు n. s. See తాళాబందు.

దాల్చిని or దాల్చిన్ని n. s. دارچینی *Darchīnī.* Cinnamon. ఒకమందుదినుసు.

తాళ్వారము (for Tamil தாழ்வாரம்) n. s. Veranda, a balcony, an open portico. వసారా.

తావత్తు n. s. Solvency, capability. శక్తి. తమరియొక్క తావత్తునుగురించి regarding the means you possessed to pay the debt.

దావత్తు for దవాత్ n. s. دوات *Dawāt.* An inkstand, a standish. సిరాబుడ్డి.

ధావళి n. s. Serge, a kind of woollen. కంబళి.

దావా n. s. دعوی *Dāwā.* A claim, a lawsuit, a complaint. వ్యాజ్యము. దావాదారుడు a prosecutor, a complainant.

తావీజు n. s. تعويذ *Tawīz.* A magic knot. An amulet or charm against sorcery. తాయెత్తు.

తావు n. s. تاو *Taū.* A single sheet of paper. ఒకబందుకాకితము.

దావుని n. s. داونی *Daūnī.* The slip worn over a gown. పైట.

తావేలు for تحویل *Tahwīl* తహవేలు n. s. Trust, entrusting. తహవేలువేయించుట To give in trust: usually, to collate or compare. సంప్రతించుట.

ధావత్తు n. s. for دهشت *Dahshat.* Fear, terror, dread. భయము.

దాసనపొడి (most commonly దాసుపొడి) n. s. Black powder applied to blacken the teeth. పండ్లపొడి.

తాసికమాసికలు for తాచికమాచికలు n. s. Cheating, defrauding. పిత్తలాటకము, మోసము.

తాసు n. s. طاس *Tas.* An hour of 20 minutes. గడియ. (Cuddapa.) సగంతాసు half an hour.

తాహతు or తాహత్తు n. s. Dignity, rank, respectability. పరువు, గౌరవము.

దింగడి adj. Wretched, lean, thin. బక్కచిక్కిన.

దింసు or దినుసు for జినస్ n. s. جنس *Jins.* A thing; article; goods, wares, different species. వస్తువులు. రెండుప్రతులలొకటేదినుసు There is the same reading in both manuscripts. దినుసువారి sundry, divers. H. 2. 216. వియ్యంపుగరితలుదినుసులుగలకోకారు.

తిక్కడి n. s. A word used (in the Belari Christian Tract XII. p. 9.) for the cross (కొఱ్ఱు.) తిక్కడిపెట్టుట To kill or strangle. To embarrass.

తిగ n. s. (in chess) Three, trois. మూడు. తిగపంటు or తీపంటు trois ace, a part of a game at dice.

దిగరు adj. دگر *Digar.* Another. ఇతర, మరొయి.

తిజాయి adj. and n. s. تیجا *Tijā.* A third part, a third. మూడోభాగము, మూడోవంతు.

దినుసు n. s. for جنس *Jins.* Thing, article, goods. వస్తువు.

దిప్ప n. s. The wad of a gun. బిళ్ల, అనగా మందుగుండువేసినతరువాత గట్టించడమునకైవేసేకాకితము.

దిమాకు n. s. for دماغ *Dimāgh.* Pride, hauteur, arrogance. గర్వము, హామిక్.

దిమిచె for దిమ్మిసు n. s. A pavior's beetle. గట్టనపలక.

దిమిటి n. s. A heap, a pile? కుప్ప, రాశి.

ధిమ్మతు n. s. Charge, trust, custody: control, or authority over things, business or persons. దిమ్మతునన్నదు A written authority or warrant for collecting revenue.

తిరగటివాడ n. s. A brig, a two masted vessel. ఒకతరహావాడ.

తిరస్తు n. s. An alienated village. (Vizag.) Perhaps from *tah* inferior (left) and *rast*, gone, passed.

తిరిగొండ n. s. The town of Mangalagiri. మంగళగిరి.

తిరు adj. *Tiru* (Tamil திரு) is equivalent with శ్రీ. Blessed and is used in numerous phrases in the Vaishnavait dialect: as తిరుమాళిగ which means a house. See several of the following words.

తిరుకొళము n. s. (Tamil திருக்குளம்) A tank with flights of stone steps. మెట్లుకట్టియుండేకోనేరు.

తిరుగుళి n. s. A turn screw. ఇస్క్రూలాగులుతిప్పేఆయుధము.

తిరుచూర్ణము n. s. (Tamil for திருச்சூர்ணம்) Powder of different colours made into paste used to mark the forehead by votaries of Vishnu. శ్రీచూర్ణము. తిరుచూర్ణపరిపాలనము a ceremony among Vaishnavas, on removing a dead body from the house.

తిరుచూర్ణములు n. s. (Tamil திருச்சின்னம்) plu. A kind of trumpets usually blown in pairs before a guru in the temple or in other places. ఒకవూదువాద్యము.

తిరుతోళ్లు n. s. Cant for *ganja* or *bang*. గంజాయాకు.

తిరునామము n. s. (Tamil திருநாமம்.) The Vaishnava mark on the forehead. A sacred song. వైష్ణవబొట్టు, వైష్ణవులుదేవునిమీదచెప్పేపాటలు.

తిరునామచెట్టు n. s. A plant. Artemisia vulgaris. ఒకచెట్టు.

తిరునామకత్తి n. s. A plant. ఒకచెట్టు.

తిరునామపాలచెట్టు n. s. A plant. Periploca tunicata.

తిరునాళ n. s. A festival. ఉత్సవము.

తిరుపుగూడు n. s. (Tamil திருப்பக்கூடை) The basket in which the followers of Vishnu keep their clothes, rosary, sectarian seal, box, salagram, &c., వైష్ణవులుదేవంకరుకగిలించుకొనేబుట్ట.

తిరుపతి n. s. (Tamil திருப்பதி.) A Vishnu fane. The town of Tripity. విష్ణుస్థలము, తిరుపతిఅనేవూరున్ను. నూటయెనిమిదితిరుపతులు The hundred and eight Vishnu fanes in the peninsula.

తిరుపళి n. s. (Tamil திருப்பள்ளி) Lit: A place of repose. A Vaishnava cant for a tomb.

తిరుమంగలియము n. s. (Tamil திருமங்கலியம்) A kind of neck ornament tied on the bride by the bridegroom. అరవవాండ్లుకట్టేతాళిబొట్టు.

తిరుమంజనము n. s. (Tamil திருமஞ்சனம்) The bathing of a Vishnu image &c. The water itself. అభిషేకము, అభిషేకోదకమున్ను.

తిరుమణి n. s. (Tamil திருமணி) A kind of white clay used in making the sectarian mark, or the mark itself. నామము.

తిరువిళక్కు n. s. (Tamil திருவிளக்கு) Vaishnava cant for a lamp. దీపము.

తిరోకుకర్ర n. s. A block (a sort of pulley: sea term.) ఒకతరహాకర్ర.

తిర్నీరు n. s. (Tamil திருநீறு) Holy water. The holy ashes of burnt cow-dung worn on the forehead by Saivas. తీర్థము, విభూతియున్ను.

తిర్యాకు n. s. A drug called Theriacum. ఒకమందుదినుసు.

తిర్యాపాలు n. s. A certain foreign drug. ఒకమందుదినుసు.

తిర్యాదరము n. s. (Tamil திரியாவரம்) Deceit, fraud, trick. మోసము.

తిల్లిక for తిరువిళక్కు n. s. (Tamil திருவிளக்கு) A Vaishnava cant for a lamp. దీపము.

తిర్వళిక్కులు n. s. (Tamil திருவிளக்குகள்) plu. (A Vaishnava cant) Lamps. దీపములు. H. 3. 31.

దిలాసా n. s. دلاسا *Dilasa*. Encouragement, assurance. Comfort, confidence, reliance, hope, trust. దిలాసాచెప్పుట to encourage or cheer.

దిల్బరి n. s. دلبری *Dilbarī*. Encouragement? (Ganjam.)

ఢిల్లి for ఢిల్లి n. s. دهلي *Dehli*. The city of Delhi.

దివానము n. s. A court, a hall of audience: tribunal. Usually, Government. న్యాయసభ, సర్కారు. దివానపువారు persons belonging to Government. దివానాజ్ఞ a public or Government order.

దివాలా n. s. دوالا *Diwala*. Bankruptcy. దివాలాతీయుట (or యెత్తుట) To become bankrupt: or to declare himself bankrupt. దివాలాతీసినవాడు A bankrupt. Corrupted from the Bengali దెవులియ dēo-līya.

తివాసి n. s. A sort of carpet. రత్నకంబళి.

తిస్సాల adv. Triennial: once in three years. మూడుసంవత్సరములకు ఒకమాటు.

తింతేరగా for తీతేరాగా adv. تینتیرا *Tintēra*. In confusion. తారుమారుగా.

దీగరు adj. دیگر *Dīgar*. Another. ఇతరమైన, వేరే.

దీటు n. s. Rate. దీటువారితక్తా Classification of lands according to value.

తీతారవుట v. n. To be dispersed, spoiled, frustrated. తారుమారవుట.

తీతారుగావుండే adj. Dispersed, spoiled, frustrated. తారుమారుగావుండే.

దీనారు from దీనారము * n. s. دینار *Dinar*. A gold coin. ఒకనాణ్యము.

టిఫిని n. s. (Tamil டிபன்) Dinner, tiffin. భోజనము.

దీపాకంటు n. s. "Half produce" (Ganjam ?)

ధీమత్తు n. s. See దిమ్మతు.

తీరుకమానులు n. s. تیرکمان *Tīr Kaman.* Arrows and bows. విల్లంబులు.

తీరువజాస్తి n. s. An additional or supplementary assessment. నిర్ణయించబడ్డతన్నకంటె పైగావుంచేరూకలు.

దీవాను for దివాన్ n. s. دیوان *Dīwan.* A minister. మంత్రి.

దుంపరాష్టకము n. s. A medical root. ఒకమందుదినుసు.

దుంబాలా n. s. دنباله *Dūmbala.* A permit or written permission: sanction: warrant: a deed or grant. దుంబాలాయినాం the same as జోడియినాం. In the Royal As. Soc. Transac. No. 4, p. 219, a wrong etymon *dō-māl* is given and the word is stated to mean Alienated.—In the "Madras Journal" No. 22, p. 177, it is spelt *Doomaleh,* and explained "two properties" the chief part of the revenue being alienated, but the government having a quit rent; the same as జోడియినాం Tennant (Vol. XI. p. 393. says "An order to the farmer to reap the corp is called *Dumbala deron* which means taking or seizing by the tail." In Molesworth's Mahratta Dictionary, p. 513, it is spelt దుమాలా *dumālā* and is stated to be the Persian word Dunbaleh *a tail* (Shak. p. 1997, says this means) Pursuit: and it is interpreted Reversionary, granted for life. The Canarese Dictionary p. 799, says దుంబాల means Trouble, sorrow, vexation.

తుకము or తుఖము n. s. (Tamil தொகை.) A total, an estimate. అందాజు, అంచనా. తుకముచూచేవాడు one who estimates. తుకముచూచుట to value or estimate a field.

దుకాణము n. s. دکان *Dūkan.* A shop. అంగడి.

తుకిడి or తుక్కుడి n. s. ٹکڑی *Tukrī.* A district, a division; a province, or country. తాలూకా.

తుఖమి or తుఖము n. s. Money advanced for seed corn to a cultivator. See తకావి.

దుగారుబగారు n. s. Prodigality, wasteful folly. దూబరదిండితనము.

దుజిది for دزدی *Duzdi* దుజ్ది n. s. Robbery, plunder.

తుజుకు n. s. Probably an error for (*tuzk* Retinue, regulation: this is a Turkish word: Shak.) Haste, hurry ?

తుటాయించుట v. a. To violate, transgress, disregard, contemn. తప్పుట, మీరుట, తిరస్కరించుట.

తుట్రా, తుట్రగా or తుట్రమర adv. Utterly. బొత్తుగా.

తుడుపు n. s. (Tamil துடுப்பு) An oar, a paddle. A wooden flat spoon like a raquet, to stir a boiling liquid. (A spatula. Rottler) అర్ధకర్ర, కడవతోసేకొయ్య, కెలికేటిదిన్ని.

తుతార n. s. A kind of trumpet. ఒకవూదువాద్యము.

తుత్తినాగము n. s. Tutenague, pewter. లోహవిశేషము.

తుని n. s. A bed in a salt pan. (Vizag.) కళ్లి, మళ్లి.

తుపాకి n. s. for تفنگ *Tufang.* A musket, or matchlock. తుపాకిగట్టించుట to load a gun. తుపాకికాల్చుట to fire a gun.

తుపాసి n. s. Lord, master. దొర. OG.

దుప్పటి n. s. (for دوپٹہ *Dupatta.*) A garment (properly one with a seam down the middle.) పైబట్ట, చలికికప్పుకొనేదిన్ని.

తుప్పలి n. s. Thorns ? brambles ? (See Gordon on Luke. VIII. 7)

దుఫసలి adj. دوفصلی *Do fasli.* Yielding two crops in the year. ఇరుగారులుకుండే.

తుఫాను n. s. طوفان *Tūfān.* A storm, a tempest. గాలివాన. adj. Vexatious, idle, groundless, litigious, light as air ?

దుబారా adv. دوبارہ *Dobāra.* Twice, two times. రెండుమాట్లు.

దుబాసి n. s. A Dubash:—a title given to a "man of business;" a manager, agent, head clerk, an interpreter. Various etymons of this word have been given: some say it is *dobahsi* (Persian and Arabic) a man of "two modes of speech." (Tyriosque *bilingues,* Æneid. 1. 661. who spoke two tongues.) More probably *do bhashi*, one who speaks two languages.

దుబాసీతనం n. s. The office of interpreter : agency.

దుముకి or దుమికి n. s. A cotton press?

దుముదారు دمدار n. s. *Dumdar*. The rear of an army. T. 4. 64. ఏదిక్కు జూచినయెలదేటిదుముదారు.

దుయ్యం adj. (دويم *Duyum.*) Secondary, subordinate. రెండో. దుయ్యంశిరస్తేదారుడు the second Seristadar.

దురంగి adj. دورنگي *Do Rangi.* Double coloured as some cloths. రెండువన్నెలుగల. T. 4. 202. పేల్దురంగిచందువలు.

తురంజి n. s. ترنج *Turanj.* A citron. మాదీఫలపుకాయ.

తురక adj. (from ترک *Turk.*) Of or belonging to Musulmen. తురష్కులసంబంధమైన.

తురక n. s. ترک *Turk.* A musulman. తురష్కుడు.

తురకరాయి n. s. The stone called laterite. జొంతరాయి.

తురకాణ్యము n. s. The Musulman rule. తురకప్రభుత్వము.

తురకుట v. a. To caulk. ఓడకులల్పుము వేసుట.

దురస్తు or దురుస్తు adj. درست *Durust.* Right, in good order, well in health. దురుస్తుచేయుట to repair.

తురా, తురాయి n. s. طره *Turrah.* A feather, a crest, a nosegay. Gun metal made of copper &c.

దురాయి n. s. for دوهائي *Dohai.* A protest or adverse declaration. A caveat or veto : arrest of proceedings : used thus యీపనినీవుచేస్తేనీకు రాజుమీదదురాయిఉన్నది I adjure you to desist *on your allegiance.* నీకురాజరుదురాయి "if thou do this, thou art not Cæsar's friend." It was an *adjuration* or warning, like the Norman *Haro.* This warning was given by any one, even a private individual unknown to the king.

తురికి n. s. ترکي *Turki.* A turkish horse. ఒకదేశపుగుర్రము.

తురుపు n. s. "Trumps" at cards. A "troop" of cavalry. ఆటఆడేకాకితములలోనొకటి, గుర్రపుదండు.

దుర్గాపు n. s. Persons who watch at the salt pans? (Vizag.)

దుర్బీని or దుర్బీను n. s. دوربين *dūr-bīn.* A telescope. దూదు.

తుల n. s. طول *Tūl.* Length. తులార్జులు طول ارض the length and width. The measurement of a heap of grain with a cord, both *tula*, over the top and ارض *arz* round the bottom.

దులాబు n. s. دولابه *dulāva.* A recess in the wall with shelves and shutters, a cupboard. అరమాలు, అలమారు.

దులాబి n. s. A spend-thrift, a prodigal. దూబరదిండి. వాడుయిప్పుడునిండాదులాబిగావున్నాడు he is now become poor.

దులాబితనము n. s. Prodigality, profligacy, wild waste.

తులులు n. s. A sort of herrings called sardinias. మత్స్యవిశేషము.

తువాలా or తువాలాగుడ్డ n. s. (French touaille) A towel. తడువము.

దుశాలు or దుశ్శాలువలు n. s. دوشاله *Do shālah.* A double shawl, or pair of shawls. జోడుశాలువలు.

దుసిరి or దుసరా adj. (دوسرا *Dūsra*) Another. ఇతరమైన, మరియొక.

దుస్తు n. s. A suit of clothes. ఒకజతబట్టలు.

దుస్సలహా n. s. (From the Sanscrit *Dus* and the Arabic صلاح *Salāh.*) Evil counsel, bad advice. దురాలోచన.

తూకు n. s. (Tamil தூக்கு) Hanging. తూకుమాను the gallows. అరతూకు the pillory.

తూము రాతి, తూము రాతి n. s. A drain, a water-course. నీళ్లుపారేతూము. OG.

తూమారు n. s. (طومار *Tumār.*) A certificate of conduct. యోగ్యతాపత్రిక.

ధూము n. s. (دهوم *Dhum*) Disturbance, fray. Plague, pestilence. తొందర, సంకటము. హయిదరుధూము the inroad of Hyder. అమ్మవారిధూము Cholera Morbus. వాడునామీదనిండాధూము చేస్తున్నాడు he is hard upon me.

దూర్బీను n. s. دوربين *Durbīn.* A telescope. దూదు.

ధూళికుత్త n. s. Rent paid for a field yet unsown? From ధూళి dust?

తూలు adj. طول *Tul.* Prolix, long, lengthy, verbose, protracted, voluminous, tedious. పెంచి వ్రాసిన, పెంచిచెప్పిన.

థూళ్లతాళ్లు n. s. plu. The hauling ropes of a mast.

దూసరా usually దుసరా adj. (دوسرا *Dusra*) Another. ఇతరమైన.

తెంకాశి n. s. (Tamil தென்காசி.) Also called తెంకోడు The name Southern Benares; a Hindu shrine a few miles north east of Kottalum on the river Sittaru north west of Tinnevelly. In the map it is spelt Thencaussee. Sir Thomas Munro in a letter dated 5th September, 1826, says, Here is an ancient pagoda and choultry, with figures, of which the sculpture is far superior to any thing at Madura.

తెండా n. s. (Ganj.) A picota, a pump or swape. ఏతాము.

తెలవలేదు A vulgarism for తెలియలేదు it is not known or understood. See తెలియుట.

తెలింగ n. s. تلنگ *Telinga.* This is a *foreign* name: the Telugus are called Telingas by the Musulmans and by the Malays. తెనుగువారు, ఆంధ్రులు.

తెల్లాకులవాడు n. s. One who sells a kind of betel leaves. తెల్లతమలపాకులుఅమ్మేవాడు.

దేకచా or దేక్చా n. s. (دیگچه *Dēkcha.*) A brazier, a kettle. అండా.

దేఖిల్ or దేఖీలు (Marata language.) Of or belonging to, together with. కూడా, సహ.

తేకడ adj. (Tamil தேய்கடை) Wearing away. అరిగిన. తేకడరూక a worn fanam.

తేగా n. s. (تیغه *Tēghā*) A broad sword, a scymitar. పట్టాకత్తి.

తేగుభోగము a vulgar phrase for త్యాగభోగము n. s. (Lit: generosity and enjoyment) తేగభోగములకుగాను for the support of a temple.

తేజి n. s. (تیزی *Tēzi*) An Arab horse. గుర్రము.

తేడ n. s. Profits, surplus, balance. మిగులు.

తేదారు (Perhaps an error for تعداد *Tēdād.*) Quantity, sum. మొత్తము.

తేయాకు n. s. (French word Th'e) Tea: tea-leaves. జాతివాండ్లువేన్నీళ్లలోవేసితీసుకొనేఆకు.

తేరీజు n.s. (بیریج *Tērij.* an error for تیریج *Bērij*) An account specifying the particulars and afterwards the amount.

తేరుమహాల్ or తేరుమూలు n. s. (تیرمحل *Ter mahal.*) Name of an old prison at Chingulput.

తేరె n. s. (Tamil தேரை.) A flying frog. ఊరుకప్ప.

తేలి n. s. (تیلی *Telī.*) An oilman. గాండ్లవాడు, నూనెలమ్మేవాడు.

దేవడీ, దేవిడీ n. s. (دیوڑهی *Dēorī.*) A fort-gate, the gate of the palace. కోటవాకిలి, నగరువాకిలి. usually the palace of the Nabab.

దేవరాయము n. s. Error. దేవాదాయము.

దేవాలి n. s. (دیوالیا *dēwāliya.*) A bankrupt.

దేవుడీ, or దేవిడీ n. s. (دیوڑی *Dēorī.*) A gate way, the gate of the palace. కోటవాకిలి, నగరు వాకిలి. See దేవడి.

దేశకులకర్ణి n. s. (*Dēsh-kul-Karni.*) A public accountant or clerk. కర్ణము.

దేశపాండ్య, దేశముఖి n. s. (K.) *Desapandya, Desamukhi.* A clerk, a record keeper, a register: also called *Potail,* or *Carnam.* In some places, it is the same as a zemindar, or small baron. Under the Mahomedan government this office was hereditary: the head revenue-officer of a district. These words are written *Despondeah* and *Deshmook* by Colonel Munro.

దేశాయి n. s. (*Desai.* Marata) A chief man among Lingavant merchants; the head man among people of the right hand caste. కుడిచేతిబాణమునకుపెద్దగాఉండేవాడు.

దేహాయ n. s. (*deh,* a village) Land revenue. (Vizag.)

తైలంగ or తైలింగ n. s. (تلنگ *Talanga, Tylung.*) Tailanga, the name given by the Musulmans to the Telugu people.

తోండు n. s. (Tamil தொண்டு) A quantity of straw to be sold.

తోంబ n. s. A mob, a tumultuous rout, a rabble. తుక్కుమూక, దొమ్మి.

దొంబ్లాసు or దొంబ్లాసుగావుండే adj. Hulking, overfed, loutish. అట్టాపొట్టగావుండే.

తోషము, తోకము n. s. Estimation. ఉజ్జాయింపు.

తోగ n. s. (Tamil தொகை.) The total. మొత్తము.

తోగడా or తౌగడా n. s. Exchange. తౌగడాపొలము one field exchanged for another?

తోడపము n. s. (Tamil துடைப்பம்.) A besom, a broom. చీపురు.

తోన్ని n. s. An albino, or person of a fair complexion: such persons among the Telugus are quite as fair as Europeans. తెల్లపాటి?

తోరపగము n. s. (Tamil துரப்பணம்) A gimlet. బరమా.

తౌకరా n. s. (توكرا Tokra.) A large basket. A basket-work *ferry boat.* గంప, పుట్టియున్ను.

తౌగడా n. s. See తోగడా.

తోటా n. s. توٹا *Tota.* A cracker, squib, cartridge. తుపాకిమందుపొట్లము.

దోదమ్మి n. s. (دودمي Do Dummī) Two edged (a sword.) This is sometimes wrongly interpreted as being *two blades* in one haft. రెండంచులకత్తి.

తోబరా n. s. (توبرا Tōbrā.) A horse's nose bag for gram. ఉలవలసంచి.

తౌపా or తోఫా n. s. (تحفه Tohfa.) Tribute. షేష్కిస్తి, కప్పము.

తోపి for టోపి (توپي Tōpī) A hat, a cap. కుల్లాయి.

తౌపు n. s. *Towf.* A red or brown colour, bistre. తౌపుచీర a red petticoat. అంచులేనిముష్ఠచీర.

తౌఫా n. s. (تحفه Tohfa.) Boon, present. బహుమానము.

తౌమత్తు for తోహమత్ n. s. (تهمت Tohmat.) Aspersion, imputation. దూషణ.

దోరస్తు n. s. دورست *Do rast;* Gross produce. ఇరుగోరులు. (Ganj.)

తోలుఫారా n. s. A kind of fish. మత్స్యవిశేషము.

తౌషాఖానా or తోశేఖానా n. s. توشخانه *Tosha. Khana.* A treasury, a place where clothes and furniture are kept. రూకలకొట్టు, వస్త్రాభరణములుఉంచేకొట్టు.

తోస్తానం for తోజ్దాన్ توزدان *Tōzdan.* A cartridge box, pouch. కృష్ణాజినపుసంచి. OG.

దోహాదము n. s. (*do-adha.* دوادها) The dividing into two halves.

తౌజీ (توجه *tawajjuh.* or తౌజీయత్) n. s. Pension, allowance. A kind of allowance to landholders. భరణము, వర్షాశనము.

దౌడు n. s. (دور *daur,*) or దవుడు, Inroad, invasion. దళ్లి.

దౌతి n. s. (for دوات *Dawāt.*) An inkstand. మసిబుడ్ర. H. 1. 158.

దౌరు or దవురు n. s. (دور *daur.*) The flaps or skirts of a coat. చొక్కాయిక్రిందుట్టువేలాడేగుడ్డ.

దౌలత్ ఖానా دولت‌خانه (lit: The Abode of fortune) a respectful phrase for (your, his, their) House, Mansion.

దౌలత్తు n. s. (دولت *Daulat.*) Fortune, wealth. Power, authority. భాగ్యము, అధికారము. ఆరుదుఆర్కాటిదౌలత్తుచేసేటప్పటికి during his reign: while he ruled Arcot. In his days.

తౌలు n. s. (*taul.* طول) A kind of drum. డక్కవాద్యవిశేషము.

త్యాహీంతిగా adv. (*Mahr.*) Voluntarily, at one's will, as one pleases. యథేచ్ఛగా, మనసువచ్చినట్టు.

త్రష్టి n. s. (K.) Loss, defect, damage. నష్టము, లోటు.

త్రష్టించుట v. a. To grieve, torment, reprimand?

త్రావి n. s. (ترائی *Tarāi.*) A rafter, a small beam. మిద్దెయింటికివేసేసన్నదూలము.

ధ్రూపైరు (for ధ్రువపైరు) n. s. Permanent crops; groves of trees &c.

న

నంజ n. s. (Tamil நஞ்சை.) Land artificially watered. Irrigated fields. Land in which wet crops are raised. A field adapted for the growth of rice corn. మాగాణి.

నంబరు n. s. (E) (Usually spelt నెంబరు and written నెం॥) A "Number." This word is used for "Article:" sometimes for a law case, elsewhere for a field. Numberdars or Lumberdars, "are proprietors of land." Buchanan's Eastern India 2. 430.

నకరాయి n. s. (perhaps meant for ناقرار *na Kirār*) A forfeit or penalty levied on a dishonored hill. మూడుసికిగ్రమగ్రమిరాంచిల్లించనదర్కె పెట్టు కొనేదంటుగ.

నకలు n. s. (نقل *naqal.*) A copy or transcript. నకలుచేయుట to copy. వాణ్ని ఆపిల్లకాయలునక లుబట్టిస్తున్నారు they tormented or teased him.

నకశా or నకాశా for నక్షా n. s. (نقشه *naqsha.*) A drawing, a map, a plan. పటము.

నకార adj. (ناکار *Nākār.*) Useless. Vile, contemptible. తుచ్ఛమైన.

నకాసి adj. نقاشی *Naqāshī*. Ornamental, variegated, as sculpture. Satyabha. 3. 49. 4. 8.

నకిశి for నక్షి n. s. Figured work in enamel, painting, embossed gold or embroidery.

నక్కుటంటుగ n. s. A superstitious rite performed for luck when the salt pans are prepared. పా మురులుచేసేశుకటంటుగ.

నక్కీలు n. s. (from (نکهی *Nak Khī.*) Gold or silver lace for trimmings. Brocade. జరిగ.

నఖుకొంఖూల adv. (Marata.) Every where, up and down, in every corner. అంతట.

నఖురి or నగరి n. s. A palace or mansion. Pal. 257.

నగదాగాజులు n. s. plu. Bracelets of lac and gold leaf. లక్కతోకలుంగారుతో చేసేగాజులు.

నగదియాతు n. s. نقدیات *Naqdiyāt*. Coin, money, cash. రొక్కము.

నగదిలెక్క n. s. (*naqdi hisāb*) Money accounts, cash accounts. రొక్కలెక్క.

నగదు n. s. نقد *Naqad.* Cash, money in coin. రొక్కము.

నగారా n. s. (نقاره *Naqāra.*) A large kettle drum. చర్మవాద్యవిశేషము, పెద్దఢంకా. D.

నచ్చికొట్ట n. s. (from the Tamil word நச்சுக்கொட்டை) The drug called (కాకమారి) Cocculus Indicus. ఒకవిషవిత్తు.

నజరాన or నజరాణి n. s. (نذرانه *Nazrānā.*) A forced tax levied on all the people under the title of free presents: as Charles I. used to do in England; an unjust fine. దండగ.

నజరు n. s. (نذر *Nazr.*) A present offered in homage. (In old days in England this was called a fee.) It originally meant *sight*: hence. నజరుగల Shapely, handsome, sightly.

నట్టుకొనుట v. n. (Tamil நட்டுக்கொள்ளுதல்) To be checked, come to a stand. మూడునెల లు అక్కడనట్టుకొన్నాడు he tarried there for three months.

నట్వాలు n. s. An ambling pace. గుర్రపునడక. D.

నడమాడుట v. n. (Tamil நடமாடுதல்) To take moderate exercise, to move about after sickness.

నతరాలు n. s. (نترالو *Natrālu.*) The sweet potato (Convolvulus batatas.) చిలగడదుంప.

నత్తము n. s. (Tamil நத்தம்) A village, a town. ఊరు.

నత్తు n. s. (H.) (نت *Nat.*) A nose-jewel. ముక్కుపోగు.

నదరు n. s. Vulgar for నజరు.

నదారదు v. a. (ندارد *Nadarad. he hath not*) A blank, "none" ఉత్త.

నన్న adj. (for ننها *Nhannā*) Short? అనగాకురచ. OG.

నఫరు n. s. (نفر *Nafar.*) Person, individual. ఆసామి. నఫరుగరి (adj.) Individual. (Settlement &c.) నఫరుజామీను personal bail. నఫరుగరిలెక్క Each customer's account at a shop. H. 4. 43. నఫరుగరిగా Individually.

నఫా or నఫా n. s. (نفع *Nafā.*) Profit, gain, advantage. లాభము.

నబీ n. s. (نبی *Nabī.*) The prophet: an epithet of Mahomed. మహమ్మదు

నఫిరి n. s. A sort of trumpet. ఒకవూదువాద్యము.

నమూదు or నమోదు adj. (نمود *Namud.*) Shewn, mentioned, specified, exhibited, particularized, headed. అగుపరచబడ్డ, చెప్పబడ్డ, వివరించబడ్డ. నమూదుచేయుట to shew, to bring to notice. వానిమాటనమూదుచేయలేదు they took no notice of his statement.

నమూనా n. s. (نمونه *Namuna.*) A specimen, sample. A form, pattern, or model. A skeleton account. మాదిరి.

నమ్మకస్థుడు n. s. He who is faithful. నమ్మదగ్గవాడు.

నమ్మకు n. s. نمک *Namak*. Salt. ఉప్పు. so called in official papers.

నల n. s. (نلی *Nalli.*) The barrel of a fusil. తుపాకిగొట్టము.

నల్లకూను n. s. ("Black wood") called *Rose-wood* in the Tariff. ఒకకొయ్య, దారువిశేషము.

నవటాకు or నవటాకు n. s. (Bengali) One-eighth of a seer.

నవసిర n. s. نوسر (*Nao sir.* "New head") A fresh commencement. Afresh, anew. ప్రథమారంభము, కొత్తది. "*Nao sir talāo* cowl" A grant of land to a person who has built a new tank or well.

నవాడ n. s. See నివాడా.

నవారు n. s. نوار *Nawār.* Strong broad tape. కట్టెమంచానికిఅల్లేది.

నవాసాగరము, నవాసారము n. s. *Nousāgar* for نوشادر *Noushadar.*) Sal-ammoniac.

నవితి n. s. A measure of twelve seers. (Ganjam?)

నవీసింద, నవీసు n. s. (نویسنده *Nawīsindah*) "The writer." This word is generally added to the name of the clerk who wrote a paper. See జవాబునవీసు.

నవుకరి n. s. نوکری *Noukri.* Service. కొలువు.

నవుకరు n. s. نوکر *Noukar.* A servant. కొలువుడుగాడు.

నసీహతు or నసీయతు n. s. نصیحت *Nasīhat.* Punishment. శిక్ష.

నాంకారు n. s. نانکار *nan-cār.* Subsistence: land granted as a pension.

నాంచారు n. s. (From Tamil நாச்சியார்.) A lady, a goddess. నాచ్చారు.

నాకారు adj. ناکاره *Nākārā.* Useless, unprofitable. పనికిమాలిన.

నాకాల్, నాకాలి n. s. (For Tamil நாற்காலி.) A chair, a stool. నాలుగుకాళ్లపీట.

నాఖిర్దు for నాకర్దా adj. (ناکرده *Nakardāh.*) Unploughed, waste, fallow. బీడుగావుండే.

నాగ n. s. ناغه *Nāghā.* None, naught, nothing: a cypher or blank: omission in an account. Discount. నాస్తి. నాగాలేకుండా without intermission, without fail.

నాగుబారిదేశము n. s. The "Nicobar" Islands.

నాజూకు adj. (نازک *Nazuk.*) Delicate, fine; nice, easily hurt or offended: touchy, crusty, fretful, peevish. సున్నితమైన, నాజూకైన.

నాటు n. s. A blemish or defect in coin?

నాటుపుఱము n. s. (Tamil நாட்டுப்புறம்) Up-country. The inland country, but the Telugus call it *outlands* బైటిసీమ.

నాడా n. s. (ناړه *Nārā*). Ribbon, tape, string. నేసినపట్టె.

నాణాతోటా n. s. Rejection, rejected coin?

నాదారు adj. (نادار *Nā dār,*) Indigent, bankrupt, destitute. లేమిడిగల.

నాదావాసన్నదు n. s. (for لادعوی سند *La dawa sanad.*) An acquittance or receipt in full. ఫారిఖత్తు.

నానబొర n. s. A breast of mutton? See బోర.

నాపసా n. s. A "knapsack." సిపాయీలవీపుమూట.

నాపు, or నాము n. s. One skimming or "crop" of salt: one "*measuring.*"

నాబూతు for నాబూద్ adj. نابود *Nabud.* Devastated, annihilated. పాడైన, నాశనమైన. నాబూతైన or నాబూదుఅయిన Pauperized, ruined, beggared.

నాముకా, నాముకాకు or నాముకా adv. By name, specifically, nominally. పేరుకు.

నామర్దు adj. (نامرد *Nā Mard.* Impotent, effeminate, a coward. పుంస్త్వములేని, పిరికైన.

నామా n. s. (نامه *Namah.*) A deed: letters patent. Hence కరారునామా قرارنامه *Karār namah.* An agreement. రాజీనామా قرارنامه *rāzī namah.* A deed of an amicable settlement. వకాలత్తునామా وکالت‌نامه *Wakālāt namah.* A deed of attorney: a written power.

నామిరూపాయి n. s. (نامی روپیا *Nami Rupayah.* A kind of rupee, not now in use, which was somewhat triangular. In Mahratta *nāmī* is noble, superior.

నాముషి, నామోషీ or నామూషీ n. s. (for ناموس *Namus.*) Disgrace, shame. అవమానము.

నాయంకరము n. s. Mastery ? power ? sway ? యాజమాన్యము ?

నాయకవాడి n. s. The militia. కట్టుబడివాండ్లు.

నారసీదు adj. (نارسید *na rasīd*) "Not expended." A head in accounts regarding money not laid out on the work originally intended. కలుపుకానిది, ఖర్చుకానిది.

నారింజా n.s. (نارنج *Naranj.*) An orange. కిచ్చిలి పండు.

నాలము n. s. (for نعل *Nāl.*) A horse shoe. లాడము.

నాలా n. s. نالا *Nālā.* A rivulet or water channel. కాలువ.

నాలాయకు adj. (نالايق *Nalayaq.* Unfit, improper. తగని.

నాలింషు or నాలీసు n. s. (نالش *Nalish*) Reproach, blame, a complaint. నింద, నేరము, ఫిరియాదు.

నాలికి, నాలకి or నాల్కి n. s. (نالكي *Nalkī.*) A state palankeen. The bottom is eight sided and has eight legs: there is over it a canopy like a parasol: it is borne on the shoulders by means of crossed sticks placed before and behind.

నాపు or నాము n. s. (for ماپ *Māp*) Measurement (of salt) కొలత.

నాసు or నాస్ n. s. (ناس *Nas.*) Snuff. పొగాకు పొడుము.

నాస్తా n. s. (ناشتا *Nashta.*) Breakfast: luncheon: refreshment. చద్ది, ఫలహారము.

నాహక్కు for నాహక or నాహక్ adv. (ناحق *Nahaq*) Wrongfully, unjustly. అన్యాయముగా.

ని

ని॥ A contraction for నిమిత్తము.

నింకళ, నీముకళా adj. (from نیم کلا *nīm cālā.*) Unfinished, incomplete. తీరని. ఆపుస్తకముయింకా నిముకళాగావున్నది the book is unfinished.

నిందాయము adj. Free of freight (Masulipatam.) కేవులేని.

నిక్కచ్చి n. s. Force, violence. నిర్బంధము.

నిగరిబాను for నిగాబాను n. s. نگهبان *Nigahbān.*) An overseer; the head or manager. సంరక్షణకర్త.

నిగా, or నిఘా n. s. (نگاه *Nigāh.*) View, superintendence, control, care. దృష్టి, విచారణ. నిగాచేయుట v. a. To bully or browbeat. బెదిరించుట.

నిగాబాను n. s. (نگهبان *Nigahban.* An overseer, the head or manager. విచారణకర్త, సంరక్షణకర్త.

నిగారించుట v. n. (نگره *nigrah, aversion.*) To be angry. ముఖముగాండ్రించుకొనుట ?

నిఘాలుపెట్టుట v. a. See నిగాచేయుట.

నిషాన్కొయ్య for నిశానుకొయ్య n. s. (نشان *Nishān.*) A flag staff. ఝుండాకొయ్య.

నిజాను, నిశాను for నిషాను A flag or standard. ఝుండా.

నిజాయత్తుగా adv. Rightfully? న్యాయముగా ?

నిట్రుచేయుట v. a. (Tamil) To get by heart. హృద్గతముచేసుట.

నిభాయించుట v. a. (نباهنا *nibāhna.*) To suffer, endure, bear, tolerate. తాళుట, ఓడుట.

నిభావు n. s. (نبهاو *Nibhao.*) Enduring, success, happy progress, and end. నిర్వాహకము.

నిమకళ adj. (نیم کلا *Nim Kālā.*) Unfinished, still in progress, half done, unconcluded, on hand, unsettled, not closed, running on, as an account. కొరతగావుండే, తీరకుండావుండే.

నిముబడి or నిమేబడి adj. Half and half. సగములో సగము ?

నిమాజు for నమాజ్ n. s. نماز *Namāz.* Worship, divine service. పూజ.

నిమూన for నమూనా n. s. نمونه *Namūna.* A pattern, a model. మాదిరి.

నిమిండగాడు n. s. (Tamil திமந்தக்காரன்) A servant at a pagoda. A servile person employed as a porter in carrying an image.

నిమినిమాలుగా or నిమానిమాలుగా adv. About enough; more or less than enough. చాలీచాలక.

నిముకాయించుట v. n. To be obstinate: refuse to listen ?

నిముచెకత్తి, నిమ్చాకత్తి n. s. (نیمچه *Nīmcha.*) A dagger. కటారి.

నిమే n. s. (نیم *Nīm.*) Half. సగము.

నిరఖు n. s. (نرخ Nirkh.) Market-rate (as fixed by the Police) price current. అంకవెల.

నిరఖుగా adv. Definitely, positively: as a result.

నిరఖునామా n. s. (نرخنامه Nirakh-nāma.) A tariff or rate of prices. పోలీసువారునిర్ణయించిన అంకవెలలపట్టీ.

నిరుకు n. s. Certainty. నిర్ణయము. Thus, జీతము నిరుకులేదు there are no settled wages.

నిరూపము n. s. (Marata) Command, warrant. A letter. ఆజ్ఞ, ఉత్తరువు, ఉత్తరము.

నిర్హేతుకైన for నిర్హేతుకమైన adj. Causeless. Vulgarly this is used for "poor."

నిలితము n. s. Postponement. నిలుపుదల. మూడుదినాలనిలితముమీదయిస్తున్నాను I will give you in three days.

నివాడా n. s. (Marata) Decision, settlement, decree, award. Bargain. తీర్పు. See ఏర్పాటు. Elph. Appx.

నివీసు n. s. (نويس Nawīs.) A writer as; జవాబునివీసు he who writes down an answer. వ్రాసేవాడు.

నిశాను n. s. (نشان Nishān.) Flag, banner, mark, sign, signature. ఝండా, గురుతు, చేవ్రాలు.

నిశానుదారు n. s. (نشاندار Nishāndār.) Any one of the regular village authorities. (Literally, one of the signers.) కవ్వల్యగ్రామాధికారి.

నిషా n. s. نشه Nasha. Intoxication. మత్తు, మైకము.

నిసింద for నివిసిందా n. s. نويسنده Nawisindah. A clerk or writer. వ్రాయసగాడు. నిసిందవ్రాత an odd scrawl.

నిసాబు for నిసాబు n. s. (نصاب Nisab.) Stated estimate or valuation. మదింపు. so as నిసాబుజాబితా is a rate of values.

నిస్ఫ adj. (نصف Nisf.) Half, as నిస్ఫర్యాయతి. In Guntoor this is ignorantly used for a middle number, a proportional or average. Thus నిసాబుజాబితాలు the average lists. అనగానిరాకరిజాబితాలు.

నిహేంగులు for నిర్హేతుకులు n. s. The poor. బీదవాండ్లు.

నీచి from నీచము * adj. (نيچے Nīchē) Mean, low, degraded.

నీమా n. s. نيمه Nīmā. A sort of jacket. ఒకతరహాచొక్కా.

నీము adj. نيم Nīm. Half. సగము.

నీముకళ, నీముకళా or నిమ్కళా adj. نيم كار Unfinished, incomplete. కొరవ.

నీముచా or నిమ్చా نيمچه Nīmchā. A dagger. కటారి.

నీరారంబము n. s. (Tamil.) Wet cultivation. నీళ్లుపారింపుండేవరి.

నీరావరి adj. Well watered; having good wells?

నీల్గరు n. s. (نيلگر Nīlgar.) An indigo dyer. నీలిచాయఅద్దేవాడు.

నీల్పాని n. s. An emerald worn on the top of the ear?

నీళ్లుముట్టు n. s. An allowance of grain granted in harvest to various persons. (Masul.)

నెం|| Meaning నెంబరు i. e. the English word "Number:" which is used to denote a field; a lawsuit; a person; a letter. In Bengal Lumbardars are holders of fields. See Act I. of 1842.

నెట్రుచేయుట v. a. (Tamil) To get by heart. వల్లించుట.

నెరిప్పు or నెరుప్పు n. s. (Tamil நெருப்பு) Fire. నిప్పు.

నేజా or నేరిజము n. s. (نيزه Nēzah.) A spear. ఈటె.

నేఫ n. s. (نيفه Nēfā.) A gusset or gore put in to lengthen, widen, or strengthen a dress.

నేమకము Error for నియమింపడము n. s. Fixing, appointing. ఏర్పరచడము.

నేమించుట Error for నియమించుట v. a. To appoint, fix. ఏర్పరచుట.

నేరంపూటము n. s. Ballast. వాడలోఅడుగుబరువువైవేసేటిది.

నేరుజా or నేజాఁ n. s. (نيزه Nēzah.) A spear. ఈటె.

నేవళీగ (for నైవేద్యము *) n. s. An offering or oblation to the deity.

నైజా Error for నేజా n. s. نيزه Nēzah. A spear.

నొస్ట (Vulgar for నొసట abl. of నొసలు) On the forehead. లలాటమునందు.

నౌకర్లు, పల్లినౌకర్లు n. s. (نوکر naucar, a servant.) The name assumed by intruding beggars who, while using civil language, take free quarters in a man's house. They are civilly treated. మేళతాళములుబిరుదులువేసుకొని ఇంటిముందుగావచ్చిజోరావరిచేసేబిచ్చగాండ్లు.

నోక్ర్రు n. s. Mountebanks. కనుకట్టువిద్యలుచేసేవాండ్లు, వీండ్లుబహుజంభముగా మేళతాళములతో వూరూరబిచ్చమెత్తుకొంటారు.

నోటగాడు n. s. (Tamil நோட்டக்காரன்) An examiner of coin, a shroff. సరాఫు. D.

నోటము n. s. (Tamil நோட்டம்) Examination of coin by looking on it. నాణెముమంచిదో చెడుదోచూడడము.

నౌకరి n. s. (نوکری *Naukrī.*) Service. చాకిరి, కొలువు.

నౌకరు n. s. (نوکر *Naukar.*) A servant. సేవకుడు.

నౌబత్తు or **నౌబతు** n. s. (نوبت *Naubat.*) A large kind of kettle drum. చర్మవాద్యవిశేషము. Bobbili. 2. 213.

న్యాదర్లు for **నాదారులు** (نادار *Nādār.*) n. s. The poor. బీదవాండ్లు.

ప P, ఫ Ph, బ B, భ Bh.

ప and ఫ. Some words beginning with these letters are sometimes spelt with బ and భ and are placed accordingly.

బంకడీ n. s. A stall, bench, or form?

పంకా, పంఖా n. s. (پنکها *Pankha.*) A fan. విసురుకర్ర. Lavania 49.

బంటు n. s. A guard at the gate. తలవాకిటిపహరా.

బంకోలు n. s. 'Bencoolen.' ఇదిఒకదీవిపేరు. బంకోలుదొంగ A 'gallows rogue.'

బంగళ or **బంగాళా** for **బంగ్లా** n. s. (بنگلہ *Bangla.*) A bungalo or small house standing alone: a summer house. విలాసార్థముగాకట్టిన వొంటియిల్లు.

బంగాళదేశము or **బంగాళాదేశము** n. s. Bengal.

బంగి n. s. (بانگی *Bāngī.*) The bangy post, or mail. *Bhangi*, An eater of *bangue*. బంగితపాలు, బంగిముచ్చున్ను.

బంగి n. s. (بنگ *Bang or* بهنگ *Bhang.*) The bang or ganjah plant, a species of hemp. Cannabis Sativa. గంజాయి. బంగిమాజూము bang made into cakes. బంగిముచ్చు an eater of bangue.

బంగిటివాడు n. s. A villain, rascal?

బంగీను n. s. A "banyan" or flannel shirt. ఒకచొక్కా.

పంగు n. s. (Tamil பங்கு) *Pung*, or *Bang* (thus written in the Travancore list) Part, portion, division, sub-division. భాగము.

పంచకేలిజరుకు n. s. The aggregate of articles. కొన్నిబిల్లరదినుసులు.

పంచరంగి or **పంజరంగి** n. s. (پنچرنگی *Panchrangī.*) A variegated silk of five colours. అయిదువన్నెలపట్టుచీర.

పంచవాద n. s. A cess levied from the inhabitants?

పంచాణంవాండ్లు n. s. plu. Artificers. కరణుల, కంసల, వడ్ల, కంచర, కాసెకునివాండ్లు.

పంచాయతి n. s. پنچایت *Panchayat.* Arbitrement, a court of five persons; chosen as umpires to decide between two parties. అయిదుగురుగాయేర్పడ్డతగవరులసభ.

పంచోత్ర or **పంచోత్తరా** n. s. (پچهتره *Pachhatra*) Interest at the rate of five per cent per mensem. A tax or duty of five per cent. Also, "The head sayer station."

బంజరు for **బంజర్** n. s. (بنجر *Banjar*) Waste land. బీడునేల. అనాదిబంజరు land which is immemorially waste.

పంజాయి n. s. (پنجه *Panjah.*) A sort of torch. ఒకతరహాదీవిటి. H. 3. 31. జగతిజ్యోతులుకాగడాలు, బలుపంజాయీలులో బత్తులు.

బంజారి n. s. (بنجاره *Banjārah.*) The name of a tribe of gypsies who trade in grain; usually called Brinjarries or Lumbadees. లంబాడివాండ్లు

పంజెరూకలు n. s. అనగానామూలరూపాయీలు?

పంటిగచెట్టు n. s. A tree called Briedelia Montana. Rox. 3. 735.

పండ, పండా or **పండావాడు** n. s. The officiating priest in the temple of an idol at (Juggernaut) Jagannath. A head man in particular castes in Bengal. జగన్నాథములోపూజచేసేవాడు.

బండవలము, బండాలము, or **బండోలము** n. s. (K.) Stock, capital, funds, means, treasure. Capacity, dependance, basis, ground. ముల్లె, సొత్తు.

బందారము n. s. An assembly of caste people held to try cases. కలతలుతీర్చుటకునకైకూడిన బంధుజనము.

పందర మోడీవరహా for పంద్రా మోడీవరహా n. s. A sort of gold pagoda formerly in use : valued at "15 quarters." i. e. Rs. 3-12-0. ఒకనాణెము.

పందరవాడు or పంద్రావాడు n. s. A hucksterer or seller of herbs. So పంద్రాపొలం garden land.

పంటసేవ n. s. A festival celebrated in honor of Venca-teswara-swami. ఉత్సవవిశేషము.

బందాఖోరు n. s. A slave, one bound to the service of another, dependant drudge, slut. దాసుడు, బద్ధుడుగావుండేవాడు.

బందారుచెట్టు n. s. A tree called Cinchona Excelsa. Rox. 1. 529. S. 2. 369.

బందిముద్దత్ n. s. The number of days named in a bill of exchange. హుండీమీదవ్రాసేవాయిదా.

బందిషుచేసుకొనుట v. a. To have one on his side. కట్టుకొనుట, తనపక్షముగావుండేటట్టుచేసుకొనుట.

బందీఖానా for బందెఖానా n. s. (بندیخانه Bandī Khānā.) A prison. చెరశాల.

బందీవాను n. s. (بندیوان bandīwān.) A prisoner, captive. ఖయిదీ.

బందు n. s. (بند Band.) A tie, band, bank, hinge, hoop, clasp, clamp, fastening, a half sheet of paper. బందుచేయుట to close an account. బందుఅయినహిసాబు A closed account,

బందుకు or బందూకు n. s. بندوق Bandoq. A musquet. తుపాకి.

బందుగులు n. s. plu. Vulgar for బంధువులు.

బందువాడు (for బందూకువాడు) n. s. A musqueteer. తుపాకివాడు.

బందేశరానా n. s. An account of fines and forfeitures ?

బందోబస్తు n. s. (بندوبست Bandobast.) Arrangement, settlement, management, regulation, order, security. భద్రము, జాగ్రత, పరిష్కారము.

పంద్రా See పందరా.

పంపరపనసపండు or పంపరమాసపండు n. s. The fruit called pomelnos, or shaddock. (Citrus Decumana.) It was introduced from Batavia by the Dutch.

పంపకి, పంపణి for పంపకము n. s. Sharing, distribution.

బంబాళీ or బాంబును n. s. The name given to a mortar gun, because it discharges "bombs." రోటివంటిఫిరంగి.

బక్షాయించుట v. a. from بخشانه Bakhshānā. To forgive, pardon, excuse, remit. క్షమించుట.

ఫకతు for ఫకత్ adv. (فقط faqat.) Only, merely, simply. మాత్రము.

బకాయు n. s. (بقایه baqaya. Plural of باقی bāqi.) Arrears, net balance. Outstanding balance. నిలువ.

బకాయి n. s. (بقایه Baqaya.) Arrears, outstanding balance. నిలువ.

పకాలి n. s. پکهال Pakhal. A leathern water bag carried on a bullock. Usually, a *Puckally*, or a water-drawer : or bearer of a (mussuck) skin water bag : called in Bengal a Bihishtee or beesty. From the old Canarese పఖాల *pakhale* a water-pot. తోలుసంచితోనీళ్లుతీసుకొనిపొయ్యేవాడు.

బకాలు n. s. بقال Baqāl. A chandler. నానావస్తువులుఅమ్మేవాడు.

ఫకీరు usually పక్కీరు n. s. فقیر Fakir. faqīr. A *fakir* ; poor ; a beesty, dervise, or religious mendicant.

బకీరు, బఖీరు for బఖీలు n. s. بخیل Bakhil. A miser. లోభి.

బకేడా for బఖేడా n. s. Contention, disputing, quarrelling. Applied to any business or occurrence considered as troublesome or vexatious. రచ్చ, పీకులాట.

పక్కా adj. (پکا Packā) Ripe, ready : downright, prepared, fair, revised. పక్వమైన, సిద్ధమైన, పచ్చి. పక్కాచిట్టా a ready draft or prepared statement. పక్కాదొంగ a hardened rogue.

బక్కాల్ n. s. (بقال Baquāl.) A chandler. నానావస్తువులుఅమ్మేవాడు.

భక్తి n. s. Manner, way, fashion. విధము, రీతి.

పక్కెచేప n. s. A sort of sprat.

బక్రా n. s. (بکرا *Bakra.*) A he goat. మేకపో తు.

బఖేరా n. s. (بکھیرا *Bakhērā.*) Contention, quarrelling, disturbance; breach of the peace. పోకులాట, రచ్చ, తొందర. adj. Contentious, quarrelsome, troublesome. పోకులాటైన, రచ్చైన, తొందరైన.

ఫకత్తు adv. (فقط *faqat.*) Only, merely, simply. మాత్రము, ఊరక.

బగరు for బగర adj. (for بغیر *Baghair.*) Without, devoid of. లేని. బగరుపేసుబడి not liable to pay the tax on trades. బగరుశర్తు without reference, unconditionally, devoid of any agreement.

బగలు n. s. (بغل *Baghl.*) The armpit. చంక. బగలుమే *baghal-mēn* under his arm. Mrityunjaya. 1. 97.

భగాయించుట v. n. (from بھگانا *Bhagānā.*) To put to flight. ఉరుకుట.

పగోడా n. s. (پگورا *Pagōra.*) A kind of sweet meat. మిఠాయివిశేషము.

బుక్కండి n. s. A red powder which the Hindus throw over each other during the Hoeli feast. గంధపొడివసంతమల్లుకొనేయుద్రవపొడి.

పగ్రీసు adj. The same as *lakheraj.* (Malcolm.)

బచాయించుట v. a. (from بچانا *Bachānā.*) To preserve, save or rescue. రక్షించుట, కాపాడుట.

పచారి, పచారువాడు for పసారి for پنساری *Pansarī*) n. s. A vender, a druggist. మందుదినుసులుఅమ్మేవాడు.

పచారు n. s. An airing. పచారుపోవుట to take an airing. పచారుచేయుట to walk up and down.

బచావు n. s. (بچاو *Bachāo*) Protection, preservation, security. సంరక్షణ.

బచ్చాలు for బచ్చాల్ n. s. (for بدچال *Badchāl.*) Bad behaviour: ill conduct. దుర్మార్గము, దుర్నడత.

బచ్చెగానిపంచె or బచ్చెకానా n. s. A small cloth woven for 'bache' children. (Guntoor.) పిల్లలకుకట్టేచిన్నపంచ.

బజాంత్రి or భజంత్రి (بجنتری *Bajantri.* Music. A musician. మేళము, మేళగాడు.

ఫజలుజ్యాస్తి n. s. (فصل زیاستي *fasl zyāsti.*) The second or extra crop; generally taxed only half as high as the regular crop is rated.

బజా adj. بجا *Bajā.* In its proper place; fitting, proper. యుక్తమైన, తగిన.

బజారు n. s. (بازار *Bāzār.*) A market. అంగడివీధి.

పజీతి, ఫజీతి usually బజీతు n. s. (فضیحت *Fazihat.*) Disgrace, ignominy: annoyance, harrassment. A. 5. 52. అవమానము, అల్లాటము.

బజీతుచేసుట v. a. (from بجد *Bajid.*) To urge or press importunately. నిర్బంధముచేసుట. Usually, to annoy, harass. సంకటపెట్టుట.

బజ్జి n. s. A mess of vegetables. అనుపానవిశేషము.

బజ్జింసు for బజ్జిన్సు adj. (for بجنس *ba-jins.*) Ipso facto: with the article. దినుసువారి. Sort by sort, kind by kind.

పటం n. s. A ship's chains: the "bottom."

పటక or పట్కా n. s. (پٹکا *Patka.*) A belt or sash: One width of cloth. నడికట్టు.

పటాకి or పటాసు n. s. (for پھٹاکھا *Phatākha.*) A squib or cracker. టపాసు.

పటాణి n. s. A 'pathan' horse. దేశవిశేషపుగుర్రము.

బటానీలు or పటాణీలు n. s. Peas: (pisum sativum.) ధాన్యవిశేషము.

బటాయి n. s. (H. بٹائی *Batāī.*) Dividing: i. e. yielding one half the crop to the landlord (from بانٹنا bānttna.) పంపకము.

పటాలం n. s. (English) A 'battalion,' సిపాయీలదళము.

పటాయించేయుట v. a. To make him run. ఉరికేటట్టుచేసుట.

బటాసాలు n. s. (for بتاشہ *batāsha.*) A sort of cakes. సింధుఫేనమనేభక్ష్యములు. D.

ఫటాసు n. s. (for پھٹاکھا *phatakha.*) A cracker టపాసు.

పటికము n. s. A basin. తమ్మపటికము a spitting pot.

పటేల n. s. A potail or head man of a village. A Mahratta title for the head man of the village. The managing proprietor. రెడ్డి. గ్రామముఖ్యజమాని.

పట్టా n. s. (for پٹا *Patta*.) Information, traces. A lease roll: a "pottah" a grant. జాడలు, దివాణమువారుయిచ్చేపట్టాచీటి.

పట్టాదారుడు n. s. An informer. A lease holder, a farmer who holds a "pottah." జాడలుచెప్పేవాడు, దివాణములోపట్టాతీసియుండేవాడు.

పట్టామణియగాడు n. s. A village authority whose business is to collect the revenue. దివాణరూకలువసూలుచేసేగ్రామాధికారి.

పట్టీ n. s. پٹی *Pattī*. A list. జాబితా.

బట్టీ n. s. for بھٹی *Bhatti*. A still for drawing spirits. సారాయికాచేబాన.

పట్రవాండ్లు n. s. A certain tribe who live in the forests. ఒకవిధమైనఅడవిమనుష్యులు.

భటవృత్తి adj. See భట్టవృత్తి.

బటువార n. s. بٹوارہ *Batwārah*. Allotment, distribution. Partitioning. Disbursement. పంపకము. (Butwarra. Act. XX. of 1836.)

బట్వాడి n. s. (Canarese) The village clerks: called Curnum or Shanbogu?

బట్వాసంచి n. s. بٹوہ *Batwāh*. A wallet made of striped ticken. పట్టువసము, జోల్నా.

పడచా for పార్చా n. s. پارچہ *Parcha*. An extract, a summary: order, decision. నకలు, సంగ్రహము, తీర్పు.

పడవాజి for పర్వాజ్ n. s. پرواز *Parwāz*. Flight, being carried away, or blown away. ఊరకడము, కొట్టుకపోవడము.

బడవ or బడవా n. s. بھڑوا *Bharwa*. A pimp; a base scoundrel. ముండలనుతార్చేవాడు, లుచ్చా.

బడానాగరుతకావి n. s. بڑاناگرتقاوی *Barā Nagar taqawī*. Sums granted to those who use the "great plough" in bringing fresh land into cultivation. పెద్దనాగలికట్టియున్నదమునకైదివాణమువారుముందుయిచ్చివెనకతీసుకొనేరూకలు.

బడాయి n. s. بڑائی *Barāī*. Boasting, egotism, bragging. జంభాలు.

బడాయి n. s. بڑھئی *Barhai*. A carpenter. వడ్లవాడు.

బడాయించుట v. a from بڑھانا *Barhānā*. To advance or put forward, to promote. ముందుకుతెచ్చుట, అభివృద్ధిచేసుట.

బడాయిఖోరు n. s. بڑائی خور *Barāi Khōr*. A boaster, a braggart. జంభాలఖోరు.

పడావు n. s. پڑاو *Parāo*. Falling into the hands of an enemy. Defeat. శత్రువులచేతిలోబడడము. పడావుఅయినవాండ్లు those who have fallen into the hands of the enemy. పడావుచిక్కినారు they were taken prisoners. (Reeve.)

పడితరము n. s. Order, general rule: daily allowance at a pagoda. Annual grant or income: stipend. దేవళములోనానాటికిశలవయ్యేదిట్టము, ఏటావచ్చేఅయివజు.

పడియా n. s. Fallow or waste land. బీటిపొలము. వృద్ధపడియా Land immemorially waste. అనాదిబంజరు.

బడుగులు n. s. *Badagas*. The name of a tribe in the Nilgheri hills: whom the English call Burghers. Correctly Vadagar.

పడుమాడు n. s. Stock on hand?

పడువరి n. s. Sprouts from grain unintentionally dropt. చిందినగింజలుమొలిచినఅయినపైరు.

బడేకము n. s. Brag, boast. బడాయి.

బణజిగ or బణిజిగ n. s. (K.) The name of a certain tribe of Sudras. See. లంబాడి.

బణిజారి n. s. بنجارہ *Banjāra*. A Brinjari. See లంబాడి.

పతంగ n. s. پتنگ *Patang*. Red wood or yellow wood used in dying? చేవమాను.

బతారీఖు adj. بتاریخ *ba tārīkh*. Dated: on the date. తేదిగల.

పతేకారి n. s. Weavers of silk and tape. Throwsters.

పత్తడము or పత్తళము n. s. The collar round a bullock's neck under the yoke. జోటా?

పత్తా n. s. پتا *Patta*. Signs, traces. ఆచూకు, జాడ. పత్తాదారు a spy, or an informer.

బత్తాయి n. s. from 'Batavia.' ఒకదేశము: also written బతావి whence బత్తాయినారంజిపండ్లు

a kind of orange. బత్తాయినిమ్మపండ్లు The fruit called pomelnoses.

బత్తీ for బట్టి n. s. A still. సారాయికాచేకుండ.

పత్తు n. s. (Tamil பத்து.) Land or place. నేల. మెరకవారపత్తు dry land the produce of which is shared. మెరకతీరువపత్తు dry land settled on a money rent.

భత్తేరి for బత్తేరిn. s.(بتیری Batērī. Une batterie.) A battery of guns. ఫిరంగులుపెట్టికాల్చడమునకుయుత్తుగావేసినదిబ్బ.

భత్యం or బత్తెము n. s. from بھتا bhatta. Batta, daily food, sustenance.

పత్రబంది for పత్తర్ బంది adj. (پتھربندي pathri bandi.) Built of stone. రాతికట్టుడు.

బత్రి n. s. See భత్తేరి.

ఫత్వా n. s. فتوی fatwā. Legal decision according to Mahomedan law, sentence. తీర్పు.

బదనామి n. s. (بدنامي bad-nāmī.) Bad name, disgrace, infamy. Also wrongly used for responsibility. అవమానము, అపదూరు, జవాబుదారి.

బదరకా n s. بدرقہ Badarqa. A convoy or guard on the road. That which accompanies. దారితోడు. బదరకాలెక్క the account (or invoice) accompanying goods.

బదర్విసి n. s. Auditing or retrenchment of charges?

పదలము n. s. A weight of 20 dubs. ఇరువైడబ్బులయెత్తు, అరవీశఅంటారు.

బదలాయించుట v. a. (from بدلانا badlāna.) To change, exchange, substitute. మార్చుట.

బదలు or బదులు n. s. بدل badl. A dedt: what is given on pledge. Exchange, return: retaliation, other. అప్పు, మారు, ప్రతి. చెయిబదులు a debt of hand, a simple debt, without account or bond.

బదస్తూరు adv. (بدستور ba-dastūr.) According to custom. మామూలుప్రకారముగా.

బదిలి or బద్లీ n. s. He who is in charge of. బదులుగానుండేవాడు. రంగయ్యకుబదిలీగానున్నాడు he acts for రంగయ్య.

బదులు adj. In answer to, in place of, in lieu of. ప్రతి. బదులుజాబు an answer to a letter. బదులుమాట a word in reply.

బదులుగా adv. In lieu of, in stead of. బదులుపలుకుట to reply.

పదూర n. s. A female's under garment, like a petticoat. గాగర. D. అనగాపావడ.

పదూలు n. s. The cock of a gun?

బద్నామి n. s. (بدنامي Badnāmī.) Ignominy, disgrace, infamy. In Telugu, Odium: responsibility. అవమానము, జవాబుదారి, ఉత్తరవాదము.

బద్మామిలా n. s. بدمعاملہ bad-muāmila. Bad management, mismanagement, unfair dealing, misconduct. దుర్మార్గము, నిర్న్యాయించచేతకామి.

బద్లామి n. s. See బద్నామి.

బద్లాయించుట v. a. from بدلانا Badlana. To exchange, change, substitute. మార్చుట.

పనతాడు n. s. A leather rope. తోలుమోకు.

బనసు n. s. Brown colour. ఊదారంగు?

పనసమాను n. s. (lit: a beam of jack wood) The outrigger of a boat. పడవపొర్లకుండాపక్కనకట్టేమాను.

బనాతు n. s. بانات Bānat. Broad cloth, woollen. సకలాతు.

బనామె بنام Bāname (See Benami and Banami in my Zillah Dictionary) "To the name of: To so and so." బనామెతహసీలుదారు A letter to the Taseeldar.

బనాయించుట v. a. and v. n. from بنانا Banāna. To fabricate, make up, feign, put out (coin,) trump up. (Also) To obey, mind. To suit: agree. కల్పించుట, సరిపడుట. వానికీనాకుబనాయించలేదు he and I did not agree.

బనాయింపు n. s. from بنانا Banāna. Fiction, fabrication. కల్పన.

బనారసు n. s. بنارس Banaras. Benares. కాశీ.

బనావని n. s. بناوني Banawanī A fabrication, a made up story. కల్పించడము, కట్టివిడువడము, కట్టుకథ.

పనిబాబులు n. s. Error for పనిపాటులు jobs.

పన్న n. s. A frame used in weaving.

బన్నసు or బన్నసు n. s. A deep purple, or shade of black. ఊదావర్ణము.

పన్నా n. s. The frame on which paper is made. కాకితాలుచేసేచట్టము. పెద్దపన్నాకాకితాలు paper of a large size.

ఫన్నాలు n. s. Widths or strips of cloth cut out, as for a jacket. గుడ్డతునక. నిలువుఫన్నాలుగా చేయుట to cut a cloth lengthwise, not across.

ఫపయ or **ఫప్పాయపండు** n. s. The Popya fruit. The "Carica Papeya" or Pappaw fruit (as called in America. Rox. 3. 825.)

ఫప్పిళము, ఫప్పిళిచీర n. s. (Engl.) 'Poplin' cloth. ఎరుపు తెలుపు పట్లుపట్లుగా వుండేచీర.

బబ్లాసు for దొంబ్లాసు n. s. A simpleton, a fat fool.

ఫబ్లీకు adj. (Engl.) Public. దివాణపు, బాహిరంగమైన, అందరికి సామాన్యమైన.

బమవుజీబు for బమోజీబు adv. بموجب *Bamojib.* According to; in obedience to. చొప్పున.

ఫముచాయించుట for (پونچانا *pōnchānā*) పొహంచాయించుట v. a. To deliver, give. చేర్పించుట.

బమై prep. بمعه *Bamae.* With, together with. కూడా.

బయవర్దు or **బయావర్దు** for బయాంవారి n. s. بیانوار *Bayanwar.* Details, particulars. వివరము.

బయాజు n. s. بیاض *Bayā* Disbursements not yet charged in the ledger. ఖర్చుఅయియుండగా వహీలో దాఖలు కానికద్దులు.

బయానా n. s. (بیعانه *be-ana.*) Earnest money, handsel, an advance of money. సంచకరువు.

బయాను n. s. بیان *Bayān.* Details, particulars. వివరము.

ఫయాల్ or **ఫయాలు** n. s. A "piali" that is a dais, or *bulk:* a small terrace; a raised floor before a door. తిన్నె.

బయావరి for బయాంవారి adj. بیانواری *Bayanwari.* Detailed, with particulars, distinctly. వివరమైన.

ఫరంగి n. s. فرنگی *Farangi.* plu. ఫరంగులు or ఫరంగీలు Europeans. జాతివాండ్లు.

ఫరంగిచెక్క n. s. The drug called China Root (Smilax China; Ainslie. 1. 70.) ఒకమందుదినుసు.

ఫరంగిపేట n. s. The name of Porto Novo. ఫరంగిపేటవరహా a certain gold coin.

ఫరంగిమనిషి or **ఫరంగివాడు** n. s. A half caste. చట్టారివాడు.

ఫరంజ or **ఫరంజా** n. s. A scaffold. సారవ (Tamil சாரம்.)

భరంతు n. s. (for بهرت *Bharat.*) The flooring of a room. భరంతుదిబ్బ an earthen floor?

బరంది n. s. A veranda?

బరకతు or **బరఖత్తు** n. s. برکت *Barakat.* Prosperity, thriving, keeping in good condition. (శ్రేయస్సు).

ఫరకళ్లాపి n. s. Seals or marks (of clay) set on heaps of grain to prevent theft. అంబారములమీదవేసేగురుతు.

ఫరకాయి n. s. پرکهائی *Parkhai.* Examination, trial. ఫరఖావణి.

ఫరకాలా or **ఫరకాలాగుడ్డ** n. s. Long cloth, a cotton cloth fine in texture. అరిటిమోవివంటిగుడ్డ.

ఫరకావణి n. s. From پرکهنا *Parakhna.* Shroffing, examining money. రూకలనాణ్యముచూచుట.

బరక్సు for బర్అక్సు n. s. برعکس *Baraks.* Contrariety, variance. విరుద్ధము.

ఫరఖాయి, ఫరఖావణి n. s. From پرکهنا *Parakhna.* Proving coin, shroffing or trying money by sight. రూకలు నాణ్యముచూడడము.

ఫరగణా n. s. پرگنه *Pargana.* A sub-division of a district. తాలూకా. A pergunna.

భరణము n. s. A load or measure of twenty తూములు.

బరతరఫు n. s. (برطرف *Bartarf.*) Discharge, dismissal. తోసివేయడము, తగరైరు.

బరతరఫుచేయుట v. a. To discharge or dismiss. తోసివేయుట, తగరైరుచేసుట.

బరదస్తు n. s. برداشت *Bardasht.* Embezzlement. కచ్చావసూలు, సిద్దాయముచేయడము. బుచ్చనమీదబరదస్తుతీసేనిమిత్తము to enquire into the charge of embezzlement against Buchanna.

ఫరదా n. s. پرده *Pardah.* A curtain, blind, screen. తెర.

ఫరదాబాతు n. s. Wild duck. ఒకవిధమైనబాతు.

ఫరదారు n. s. Trotting?

ఫరనిషా n. s. Consignment, assignment. సాటించడము.

భరనె, భరణి n. s. A casket, a small box for jewels &c. డబ్బి.

పరభారి, పరభార్లా n. s. Assignment. Reference for payment. తనఖా.

పరభారిగా adv. Indirectly. పరస్పరముగా.

బరమా n. s. برما *Barma.* A drill turned by a bow. తొరకణము, or తొరపడము.

పరమాను n. s. A ship's yard?

పరమాయషు n. s. See పర్మాయిషి.

పరమిచెట్టు n. s. Name of a tree. Rox. 1. 614. The spelling is doubtful.

బరమొక్కి n. s. برمکی *Barmakhi.* A perfume, resembling *frankincense.* ఒకపరిమళద్రవ్యము.

పరవ n. s. for پرہ *Parra.* A line of soldiers or by-standers. Dress, garb, habit of a sect. పర వకట్టుట to arrange troops in a line. పరవఆట a line of hunters round a wood.

భరవసి for భరోసా n. s. بھروسا *Bharosa.* Confidence, trust, belief, pledge. నమ్మకము, తాకట్టు.

పరవానా n. s. پروانا *Parwānā.* Mandate, precept, written permission, warrant. రాజాజ్ఞ, రాజశాసనము.

పరష n. s. People assembled at a festival in the temple. తిరునాళ్లకువచ్చేజనము.

పరషు for ఫరష్ n. s. فرش *Farsh.* A carpet. రత్నకంబళి.

పరసు n. s. Means, way, mode, opportunity.

బరాతము n. s. برات *Barat.* A peremptory demand or dunning for payment, an assignment or written order. తరుపు, తనఖాచీటి.

పరాపు n. s. A charge of cavalry?

బరాబరి adj. برابری *Barabari.* Right, just, proper. సరియైన. n. s. Good order, arrangement. క్రమము. బరాబరిచేసుట to make equal. Bmj. 2. 119. HN. 4. 13. HK. 5. 111.

బరాబరిగా adv. In a straight line. Pal. 218.

ఫరామోషి n. s. فراموشی *Furamoshi.* Forgetfulness, oversight. మరిచిపోవడము, పొరపాటు.

పరాయి adj. پرایا *Parāyā.* Strange, foreign, other. ఇతర, అన్య. పరాయిదేశస్థుడు a foreigner.

పరాయిది n. s A strange woman. అన్యురాలు.

ఫరారి, ఫరారియైన adj. فراری *Farārī.* Fled; run away, absconded. పారిపోయిన. ఫౌతి ఫరారి فوتي وفراري dead or fled: killed or missing చచ్చినలేకపారిపోయిన.

పరావణిబంగారు for పదహారువన్నెబంగారు n. s. Fine gold. అపరంజి.

బరావతు for బరావర్దు n. s. براورد *Barāwurd.* Calculation, estimation. మదింపు, ఉజ్జాయింపు.

పరాసుడు n. s. From فرانسیس *Farānsīs.* A Frenchman. ఫ్రాంసువాడు, ఫ్రెంచివాడు.

పరాష్కం, పర్యాచకం n. s. An error for పరిహాసము ridicule. ఎకసెక్కము.

బరిచి n. s. برچی *Barchī.* A spear. ఈటె.

పరిచ్ఛితము adv. (a wrong word) Utterly, at all, absolutely. ఎంతమాత్రమున్ను, శుద్ధముగా.

పరిధవణ or పరిద్ధవణ n. s. Ostentation, display. జంభము. ఛత్రచామరములుమొదలైనసమస్తపరిద్ధవణతోకూడా with all the ostentatious display of umbrella, chowries &c.

పరిబార్లా for పరభాలాణ n. s. A reference or assignment for payment.

పరియంతరము adv. Error for పర్యంతము.

పరివట్టము n. s. (Tamil பரிவட்டம்) A cloth or head band used on various ceremonial occasions. వస్త్రము, కొన్నిసేవకాలములయందుతల కుకట్టేగుడ్డ.

బరుజు n. s. A small iron bar like a knitting needle, with each end formed into two points: used by carpenters.

భరుజు n. s. The haft of a dagger, the hilt or handle. పిడి.

భరువసి, భరవసి or భరోసా n. s. بھروسا *Bharōsa.* Confidence, reliance, trust, dependance. Encouragement. భరోసాచేయుట to encourage.

భరోసా n. s. بھروسا *Bharōsā.* Trust, confidence, belief, dependance. నమ్మకము.

భరోసాచేయుట v. a. To confide in, to believe. నమ్ముట.

పర్ఖావణి, పరఖావణి n. s. from پرکھنا *Parakhna.* Shroffing. i. e. trying or proving the goodness of coin. నాణ్యముచూడడము.

బర్ఖాస్తు n. s. برخواست *Barkhāst.* Rising or breaking up; as a court. (Repeated inquiry, minute investigation. Reeve) కలియశకము, పరి తవిమర్శ.

బర్ఖాస్తుచేయించుట or బరఖాస్తుచేయుట v. a. To raise or remove (a guard.) To withdraw a warrant.

పర్గణా, పరగణా n. s. پرگنہ *Parganā.* A division of a district or Zillah. తాలూకా.

పర్చా n. s. پرچھا *Parchhā.* A decision, a settlement. పరిష్కారము.

బర్జా or బజా adv. (برجا *Barjā* on the spot.) In its proper place. తమరుచెప్పేమాటబజాగానున్నది you are right.

భర్జించుట v. a. To strike, to beat. కొట్టుట, వాయించుట. Codandrama. 10. విలుదాల్పనినుము గోలలుబట్టగానేలకంజెసిరవము భర్జించనేల.

బర్తరిఫ్, బర్తరుఫు for భర్తరుఫు n. s. برطرفی *Bartarfī.* Discharge, dismissal from employ. కొలువులోనుంచి తోసివేయడము. బర్తరఫుచేయబడ్డ dismissed. బరతరఫుచేయుట to dismiss or turn out.

భర్తి n. s. بھرتی *Bharti.* Fulness, completion, filling up. సంపూర్తి. భర్తిచేసుట to make up a deficiency, to fill up gaps in a manuscript.

ఫర్ద n. s. فرد *Fard.* A long slip of writing; a roll, catalogue, list, inventory &c. A sheet, or quarter sheet of paper. ఫర్దినివీసు *fard nivis* فردنویس ("writer of the scroll") A secretary: this is corrupted into "Furnavees" the Mahratta minister of finance. Malcolm, Memoir vol. 1. p. 351.

బర్దస్తు See బరదస్తు.

పర్దా n. s. پردہ *Parda.* A screen or blind. తెర.

భర్మదు n. s. بھرمد *Bhar Mad.* The mark *madd* (a black line drawn across the page,) was used to mark the commencement of a paragraph in a Persian statement: and the *Bhar-madd* or line drawn quite across the page denoted a new chapter. Hence it formerly denoted a fresh head: chapter in accounts.

బర్మా n. s. برما *Barma.* A kind of auger or gimlet worked with a string. తొరపడము.

ఫర్మానా n. s. فرمان *Farmān.* A warrant: letters patent. A royal mandate: a command. శాసనము.

ఫర్మానుబర్దారు adj. فرمانبردار *Farmānbardār.* Obedient, obsequious. విధేయుడైన.

ఫర్మాయించుట v. a. From فرمانا *Farmāna.* To direct, order, appoint. To speak. Lit: to command. ఆజ్ఞాపించుట. Colloquially applied as an auxiliary; thus ములాయిజా ఫర్మాయించుట To please to attend, to lend an ear.

ఫర్మాయిషి n. s. فرمایش *Farmaish.* Order, commission. A levied contribution: an order to make up an article. ఆజ్ఞ, వసూలుచేయబడ్డధం దారూకలు, ఇదిఅట్లాచేయమనేఉత్తరువు.

పర్వా or ఫర్వా n. s. پروا *Parwā.* Regard, respect, care for. లక్ష్యము. పర్వాచేసుట to esteem, regard, care for. బేఫర్వా disregard, contempt. ఫర్వాలేదు (From پروا *Parwā.*) Never mind. No matter. చింతలేదు.

ఫర్వానా n. s. پروانہ *Parwānā.* A warrant, letters patent. A royal mandate: a command. శాసనము, రాజాజ్ఞ.

ఫల్ n. s. پھل *Phal.* Fruit. పండు.

ఫలం n. s. فلم *Falam.* A fanam. రూక. See on కంతేరాయరూక.

పలంగపోష్ for పలంగుపోశ n. s. پلنگ‌پوش *Palangpōsh.* A counterpane or coverlet. పరుపుమీదిదుప్పటి. H. 5. 97.

ఫలంపాటు n. s. Profit, advantage. లాభము.

పలక n. s. The plank on which toddy-drawers sit when perched on the cocoanut or palm tree.

పలకట్టడ or పలకట్రె adj. (Tamil பலபட்டறை) Promiscuous, mixed. చిల్లర. పలకట్రెజనము rabble.

పలవరకాయ n. s. پلورپھل *palvar phal.* The name of a fruit: described in Kasi Yatra (date 7th September 1830.) పలవరఆకులు the leaves, used for manure.

ఫలప్రాయి n. s. Produce, crop, fruits. ఫలసాయము, ఫలము.

పలసరుకు n. s. "Gruff goods" (Reg. I. of 1816.) Spiceries, pepper, tamarinds &c. ఉప్పు మిరపకాయచింతపండుమొదలయినవి.

ఫలసాయము n. s. Produce, crop, fruits. ఫలము.

బలా n. s. بلا *Balā.* Evil: misfortune. చెరుపు, చేటు. బలాదూరు. بلادور *bala dur!* away with the pest ! A sacrifice (because used to avert evil :) the same as దిగదుడుపు. సిలుసా మీదబలాదూరుఅయిపున్నాలు i. e. 'the grapes are sour.'

ఫలాన, ఫలాని adj. فلانا *falna.* Such a one, such and such. ఒకానొక, అట్టి. ఫలానివాడు such a man. ఫలానిపని such a work. ఫలానికార్యము such and such an affair. This Arabic word "fulano" "such an one" has even become Spanish. See Mem : of Suchet 1. 301.

పలాములుచేసుట v. a. To ravage or spoil. దోచి డిచేసుట. దేశమంతాపలాములుచేసిరి they plundered the country.

పలాస్తరు or పలా స్తిరి n. s. (the English word) A 'plaister' for a wound. గుడ్డకుదరిమిచ్చుంటికి వేసేటిది. పొక్కుపలా స్తిరి a blister.

బలిచేటు n. s. A fee in grain from the threshing floor : claimed by వెట్టివాండ్లు.

ఫలీతా n. s. پلیتا *Palita.* A volley, a number of darts, balls or words sent together. ఒకదెబ్బ.

బలూతి n. s. (for బలావతి.) A trade. కులకాయిక ము. బారాబులావతీలు, అనగావడ్ల, కమల, మొదలయినపండ్రెండుకుల కాయకములు.

బలోద్బంది or బలోబందీ n. s. (Marata) Force, violence, compulsion. బలవంతము, నిర్బంధము.

బల్కాయించుట v. n. From بلکنا *Balkana.* To take hold : to acquire strength. బలిష్ఠమగుట.

బల్ద n. s. بلده *Baldah.* The City ; The "*Capital.*" i. e. Hyderabad. ప్రధానసగరము.

బల్లము, బల్లెము n. s. بلم *Ballam.* A dart, a hog spear. ఈటె.

పల్లా n. s. پلا *Palla.* The measure of 120 pucka seers, or ten mercals. పందుము, పదితూములు.

భల్లారె for భళారే بهلارے *Bhalāre.* Well done ! Ila. 2. 168.

పల్లికూటము n. s. (Tamil பள்ளிக்கூடம்) A school. బడి.

పల్లెవాండ్లు n. s. A certain tribe of Hindus. ఒక కులస్థులు.

భవంతుబుట్టారుమాలు n. s. A square handkerchief with a pattern in each corner. నలుమొనలాబు ట్టాలువేసినపెకిలరుమాలు.

భవనాసి n. s. A poor's box, an alms dish. అక్ష యపాత్ర.

ఫవుతి adj. فوتی *Fauti.* Dead, deceased. చచ్చిన. See పరారి.

బస n. s. Home, abode, lodging. జాగ. బసచేసుట to lodge. నాబసవాండ్లు my family ; those under my roof.

పసందు n. s. پسند *Pasand.* Comeliness : an ornament or decoration. సొంపు, సొగసు. పసం దవుట to become handsome. పసందుచేసుట to make handsome, pretty, well or nice. ఆయన దీన్నిపసందుచేసినారు he likes this.

పసందు adj. پسند *Pasand.* Comely, handsome, well, pleasing, nice. సొగసు.

పసందుగా adv. Agreeably, trimly, nicely, fashionably. సొంపుగా, సొగసుగా.

బసమా n. s. بسمه *Basma.* (Arabic) Staining, colouring or gilding the breasts or legs so as to seem covered with tight silk. పురస్త్రీలు కాళ్లమీదవ్రాయించుకొనేరంగు.

ఫసలు, ఫసలీ for ఫసల్ n. s. فصل *Fasl.* Literally a crop or harvest. Hence a season : one year. Land producing one crop *per annum* was called *ek fusli* and that which yearly bore two, was *do fasli.* The فصلی *fasli* (or *fusly*) year furnishes the official date : the revenue year : which begins on the fourteenth of July : being the beginning of the Tamil month *A'di,* or Karkatacam. But it is not divided either into quarters or months.

ఫసలుకమ్మీ n. s. فصل کمی *Fasl Kammi.* A deduction on account of a deficiency in the crops.

ఫసలుజాస్తి n. s. فصل زاید *Fasl Zayad.* The second or extra crop raised in the year from the same land. The revenue demand upon it is proportionately less : usually one half less.

బసాయించు n. s. (بچانا *bachāna.*) "An advance of money" (Ganjam.)

పసారం n. s. (for *pansar* پنسار) The trade of a పసారి *pasari* (pansāri) druggist (correctly pansārī.) పసారదుకాను *pansari dukan* a dispensary or doctor's shop. The name is also applied to the trade of a corn chandler, or grocer.

బసి n. s. A mess, dinner, common dish ?

ఫస్కి n. s. (پھسکی phaski.) A fee paid by a shopkeeper in a fair or market.

బసుమాబుతేదారు adj. بسمہ بوتیدار Basma Butedar. Flowered, embroidered. బుట్టాలు వేసిన.

బస్తన్ n. s. بستن Bastan. Reduction: conversion or exchange in arithmetic?

బస్తా n. s. بستہ Basta. A bale of goods. సగ, కట్ట, మూట.

పస్తాయించుట v. n. From پچتانا Pachtana. To regret, sorrow. పశ్చాత్తాపపడుట.

బస్తి n. s. بستي Basti. A town. పట్టణము. బస్తిగావుండే populous. పట్టణస్థలముగావుండే.

బస్మా n. s. بسمہ Basma. Painting (the skin: so that it looks as if covered with silk.) కురక స్త్రీలు కాళ్లకు బట్టుబట్టతొడిగినట్టుగా వేసేరంగు.

బహాత్తరి n. s. A set of (Bahattar) "Seventy-two." ద్విసప్తతివర్గము, అనగా పురోజతగావుండే డెబ్బదిరెండు. కీరబహాత్తరి The name of a set of stories like the Cent nouvelles. The tales of the Parrot.

పాదుషా for పాద్షా n. s. پادشاہ Padshah. A king. రాజు.

బహాలు for బహాలు n. s. بحال bahl whence బహాలి بحالي bahlī Enlistment. Appointment, restoration to office. మళ్లీకలవు, మళ్లీజారిచేయడము. బహాలుభర్తరఫులు entertaining and dismissing.

బహాదరవాంతరము n. s. Hyder's Invasion: which happened in the year శార్వరి or AD. 1780. This is often alluded to as an æra.

బహాదరిహొను n. s. بہادری ہون Bahaduri hun. A four rupees pagoda. కరుకువరహా. బహాదరీపూలు Gold pagodas strung in a necklace.

బహాదరు n. s. بہادر Bahadar, Behader. "The Most Noble." "His Lordship." "This is a Tartar word, meaning Noble, Brave: but it now accompanies every military title." Batouru Yang (Behauder Jung) was the name of a certain victorious general. See Hue's Travels in Tartary, chap: XI. A title equivalent with Count. కుంపిణీబహాదరు the Hon'ble Company. బహాదరువారు "His Lordship." This is a usual phrase for Hyder Naik, father of Tippu Sultan.

బహానా or బహానా n. s. بہانہ Bahānah. Pretence, pretext, excuse. సాకు.

బహుషా for బహుశః adv. Of course. Usually: probably.

బహోరా n. s. Table of receipts and demands. See తాళాబంది?

పా ఫా
బా భా

బా|| i. e. బాబత్తు بابت babat. Or, for బాగాయతి بغايت baghayat.

బాం n. s. بام Bām. Three cubits and a half. (Harris.) ఏడుజేనలు.

బాంకా n. s. بانکہ Bankah. A long trumpet. (Campbell.) ఒకపూరువాద్యము.

బాంకు or బాంక్ n. s. بانک Bank. A dagger. కటారి.

పాంజేబి or పాజంజేలు for పాజేబ్. n. s. پازیب Pāzēb. A silver anclet. గజ్జెగొలుసు.

బాందీ n. s. باندی Bandi. A female slave. పనికత్తె, ఆడబాపు.

బాంల్లి n. s. Error for బాణలి n. s. A frying pan.

బాకా n. s. See బాంకా.

బాకి n. s. باقي Baqi. Debt, a remainder. అప్పు. నాకు బాకీవున్నాడు he owes me money. నూరురూపాయలు తనకుబాకీచేసుకొన్నాడు (or) బాకీయేర్పరచుకొన్నాడు he struck a balance of 100 Rupees in his favour.

పాకీరేజంతువులు for ప్రాకేజంతువులు n. s. plu. Reptiles.

బాకు n. s. بانک Bank. A dagger.

పాగ n. s. A stable. లాయము. Among Mahrata horse signifies a troop.

పాగా n. s. پاگا Paga. A turban. తలకుచుట్టుకొనే బట్ట.

బాగాతు or బాగాయత్తు n. s. باغات Baghat. Groves, gardens, plantations. Garden land on which herbs alone are raised; not corn or grain. తోటపొలాలు.

భాగినగరము *Bhāgi-nagar.* The ancient name of Hyderabad near Golconda. ఒకపట్టణము.

బాఘు or భాగ్ n. s. A tiger. పులి. బాఘుమాన్యము land granted to a man for killing tigers. (Bellary phrase.)

బాజరా n. s. باجرا *Bajra.* (Holcus spicatus) A sort of grain; the same as సజ్జలు.

ఫాజిల్ n. s. فاضل *Fazil.* Surplus. Whatever is realized over and above the estimated produce.

బాజా n. s. باجا *Baja.* Music. బాజాబజంత్రీలు drums and trumpets: a musical band. బాజాఖర్చు sundry expences (error for Bazee.) See బాజి.

బాజారు n. s. بازار *Bazār.* A market. అంగడివీధి. బాజారుఖబరు rumour, talk, news.

పాజీ adj. پاجی *Pajī.* Vile, worthless, despicable, base, contemptible, rascally. తుచ్ఛమైన, క్షుద్ర.

బాజీ adj. بعضے *Bazē.* Miscellaneous, trifling. చిల్లర, స్వల్ప.

బాజుబందు for బాజూబందు n. s. بازوبند *Bazuband.* An armlet. భుజములకుకట్టుకొనేసొమ్ము.

ఫాజిల్ n. s. فاضل *Fazil.* Excess, surplus. అధికము. ఫాజిల్ వసూల్ Extra collections.

బాజీబాబు for బాజేబాబు n. s. بعضےباب *Baze bab.* A miscellaneous head in account. చిల్లరబాబతు.

బాజూ n. s. بازو *Bazu.* Side, quarter, part. Verge, margin. పక్క.

బాజుగస్తు adj. بازگشت *Bazgasht.* Refunded. Diverted from its original purpose (surplus.) మళ్లీయిచ్చివేయబడ్డ, మరొకపనిలో వినియోగము చేయబడ్డ.

బాజుతీరుధాన్యము n. s. Sweepings of grain.

భాజే adj. بعضے *Baze.* Miscellaneous. చిల్లర.

బాజేఆఫ్తు n. s. بازیافت *Bazyaft.* Money refunded as being more than the right collections. మళ్లీయిచ్చివేయబడ్డజాస్తివసూలురూకలు.

బాజేఖర్చు n. s. بعضےخرچ *Baze kharch.* Extra expences, expences for sundries not included in the regular account or estimate. పైశలవులు.

బాజేదఫ్తరు n. s. بعضےدفتر *Baze daftar.* Waste book: miscellaneous record. చిల్లరపద్దులువ్రాసేలెక్క పుస్తకము.

బాజేబాబు n. s. بعضےباب *Baze bab.* A miscellaneous head in accounts. చిల్లరబాబతు.

బాజేయాఫ్తు بازیافت *Bazyaft.* See బాజేఆఫ్తు.

ఫాట for ఫాంటా n. s. پهانٹا *Phanta.* The cancelling mark or dash, the check in the accounts, shaped equivalent with ✓. Erasure. కొట్టివేయబడ్డదనిగుర్తు. పాటకొట్టుట to blot out.

ఘాట n. s. for باٹ *Bat* A road. పథము. ఘాటవాండ్లు female swindlers and murderers, called Thugs.

పాటకాలు n. s. Rent of Moturfa.

పాటదా n. s. (Mahratta) A kind of జీరా or సం తేరము.

ఘాటదారు n. s. Spokesman, representative. అనగామాటరి,మాటకారి, కలమండికిబదులుగామాట్లాడేవాడు. See Maratta Dictionary, page 771. బాట.

బాటలువన్నె or బాటిలువన్నె n. s. The colour called "bottle" green.

ఘాటసారి or ఘాటస్వారు n. s. A passenger or traveller. దోవనడిచేవాడు.

బాటి n. s. (Bengali) A brick-kiln: a still. ఇటికరాళ్లఆవము, సారాయికాచేబట్టి.

బాడాసుపు n. s. A broad-axe: from which English word, this seems to be a corruption. గండ్రగొడ్డలి.

బాడు n. s. بهاڑ *Bhār.* Money paid to a whore; a harlot's portion or hire. ముండకుయిచ్చినరూకలు. బాడుకాసులంజ a hedge whore.

బాడు n. s Drudgery. బాడుగాపు a drudge. బాడుకాసు pittance: hard earned wages.

బాడుఖోరు n. s. بهاڑخور *Bhār Khōr.* A pimp. బడవా.

బాడుగోలు n. s. A pimp. బడవా.

బాణము n. s. (Sepoy's phrase) A worm-pricker: a bullet-screw.

బాణా, బాణాకఱ్ఱ or బాణాకట్టె n. s. A foil used in fencing, an iron mounted mace, a cudgel. దుడ్డుకఱ్ఱ. బాణాకత్తి a two handed sword.

పాణారంవక్కలు for పానారంవక్కలు n. s. Betel nuts of a certain superior quality. శ్రేష్ఠమైన ఒకజాతివక్కలు.

పాణి, రంగుపాణిచీర n. s. A woman's cloth, the colour of which will last long.

పాజీదారుడు n. s. (Bengali.) A bailiff: a police runner.

పాతాఖాని or బాతాఖాని మనుష్యుడు n. s. باتان خاني *Batan Khāni* n. s. A loquacious man. వదురుబోతు, వాగేవాడు.

పాతి n. s. A garden-bed. A salt-bed. పాదు.

బాతినీ adj. باطني *Bātinī.* Secret, underhand: A spy. మర్మమైన, వేగువాడు. బాతినీనిమిత్తము పంపిరి they sent him to find out the plot.

బాతిల్ or బాతుల్ adj. باطل *Bātil.* Vain, fruitless. నిష్ఫలమైన.

బాతు n. s. بات *Bat.* A duck: (borrowed from the Portugueze word bato?) ఒకజలపక్షి.

బాతులాడుట v. n. (At games) To lose?

పాత్రసామాను n. s. (Telugu) Plate, hardware, gold plate, silver plate: gold silver and brass ware. Coppers and brasses.

పాత్రాంగము n. s. The minister, the manager. దివానుగిరిచేసే పెద్దమనిషి.

బాదంకాయ or బాదాం n. s. بادام *badam.* An almond.

బాదజుసలాం adv. بعدازسلام *badaz Salum.* After compliments. దండములు పెట్టి.

బాదాం n. s. بادام *badam.* An almond.

బాదామిరూపం adj. بادامی *badami.* Almond shaped: oval: oblong. కోడిగుడ్డుఆకారము గావుండే.

బాదు, బాదులు n. s. (Said to be meant for the Persian باد *bad.* i. e. wind, mere emptiness, nothing. Fees in grain, paid to the village servants, before the division of the crop. ఉభయ రాశిఅంబారములోపనివాండ్లకుయిచ్చేమిరాశిలు. బాదుయినాము or బాదుమాన్యము land in free tenure, given to the washermen, barbers &c.

బాదుగా adv. (meant for بد *bad*?) Perpetually; from the beginning: beyond the memory of man.

బాదుపోయినపొలము n. s. Land not available for cultivation; as the sites of villages &c. సాగు బడికిపనికిరాకపోయేలేకయిండ్లు కొండలుఘాటలున్ను చిక్కిందపోయిననేల.

పాదుషా n. s. بادشاه *Badshah.* King, emperor. రాజు, సార్వభౌముడు.

పానవట్టము n. s. The lower or female part of a Lingam. లింగములోనికిందభాగము.

పానారము n. s. A sort of areca nuts. శ్రేష్ఠమైన వక్కలు.

బాను, బానుజీ n. s. A lady. దొరసాని. భానుజీఅ ప్పారాయనిపారు the wife of Appa Rao.

పానుబాగు n. s. پان باغ *Pan bag.* A betel garden. తమలపాకులతోట.

పానుమూడు n. s. The self planting tree. కట్టెపా కుర or ఆకుపెంలకాకు better known as the సీమజిల్లేడుచెట్టు.

పానుసోరి n. s. (Bengali) A sort of fennel (Anethum sowa Rox.) మధురిక, ఒన్నసోంపు.

బాబతువారితఫసీలు n. s. بابت واری تفصیل An account particular of different heads. ఆయా సంగతివివరము.

పాపోసులు n. s. from پاپوش *Paposh.* Slippers. ముచ్చెలు.

బాప్రె interj. n. s. باپرے *baprē Huzza!* O dear! ఆహారే.

బాఫ్తా n. s. بافته *Bafta.* A kind of silk cloth. వస్త్రవిశేషము.

బాఫీయతుబాషండు باعافیت باشند *ba afiyat, bashand.* May they be prosperous! This Persian salutation is still often used in official letters, written in Telugu, Tamil or Oanarese: the meaning of the words being unnoticed even if known.

బాబతి n. s. The shares (out of the revenue) which belong to the head officers of the state or of district &c. MM. p. 726.

బాబతు n. s. بابت *Babat.* Matter, item, affair, head in accounts. విషయము, పద్దు. దానిబాబతుగా concerning it, belonging to it. యీబాబతుకాకితము paper of this sort.

బాబమ్మ n. s. Grandmother, father's mother. నాయనమ్మ.

బాబు n. s. باب *Bab.* Head in accounts, point, matter, subject, item. బాబతు, కద్దు.

బాజెయాఫ్తు n. s. بازيافت *Bazyaft.* Classification (of lands.)

పామంచము n. s. Stone steps, a landing place. రేవు.

పామిణి n. s. Probably for پاوني *Paoni.* An advance of money.

ఫామీదా adj. فهميده *Fahmidah.* Familiar, expert. కనుకడ్డ, తెలియిరిగిన.

పాయంఘాటు n. s. پائين گهات *Pāin Ghāt.* Payenghaut. The name given to the Carnatic as being "below the (Ghats) mountain passes;" as opposed to the Carnatic Balaghat, or high lands. కనుమకిందిదేశము.

పాయకట్టు n. s. A district. కరగా. (పాయగట్టు A spot redeemed from jungle.) (Guntoor.)

పాయకారి n. s. A temporary tenant (called in France 'Metayer') who usually receives a larger share of the crop than would be granted to the permanent tenant. (Fifth Report, page 719.) సుఖవాసి.

పాయఖానా or పాయిఖానా n. s. پائخانه *Pāi Khānah.* A privy or necessary. మరుగుపెరడు.

పాయా n. s. پايه *Fāyah.* A foundation. బునాది. అస్తిభారము. పాయావేసుట to lay a foundation.

భాయి n. s. بهائی *Bhāi.* Brother. తోడబుట్టినవాడు.

ఫాయిదా n. s. فايده *Fāedah.* Profit, gain. Interest or gain on money. లాభము.

పాయిదారు adj. پايدار *Pāedār.* Fixed, stable, lasting. శాశ్వతమైన.

పాయిమాలి n. s. پايمالي *Pāimālī.* Depredations, ruin of crops by violence: particularly such as is caused by flood, or marching troops. Allowances made to farmers on plea of such depredations.

బార adj. بارہ *Bārā.* Twelve. పండ్రెండు. ABS.

భారంగి n. s. A medical root. గంటుభారంగి. Ainsl. 2. 112.

బారకాసు or బార్కసు n. s. The English word "Barracks." సిపాయీలుండేశాల. బారకాసు లంజ a common whore.

పారడిపొలము n. s. Pasture land. పసువులుమేసే పొలము.

పారకత్తి, పారుపత్యగాడు n. s. A superintendent, a manager. అమలుదారుడు.

బారబలోతి for బారాబులావతి n. s. 'The twelve (بلاهت *Bulāhat.*) callings'; that is the village servants in general. In Elph. Appx. page 10 the "*baloot* of the balooties." గ్రామపనివాండ్లు.

ఫారము n. s. Meant for the English "form" or tabular statement.

పారసి adj. پارسي *Pārsī.* Persian.

పారా n. s. پهرا *Pāhrā.* A guard, a sentry. కావలి.

బారాపాటకము, బారాబటి n. s. A coalition of Musulman or Hindu Rulers, similar to the Heptarchy. The name of the town of the Odhra princes.

పారావాడు n. s. A sentry, or watchman. కావలివాడు.

భారి adj. بهاری *Bhārī.* Weighty, respectable, opulent. Plump, stout, fine. ఘనమైన, బరువైన, గొప్ప, బలిసిన.

బారిక n. s. A village servant, a low caste peon. (Vizag.) పొలముకాచేతలారి.

పారిగోడ n. s. Error for ప్రహరీగోడ.

బారిషికట్టీ n. s. بارش *Bārish.* A 'rain table' or statement shewing the amount of rain that has fallen. వానకట్టీ, వాననుగురించినవివరము.

పారిఖత్తు or ఫారిఖత్తు n. s. فارغ خطي *Fārigh Khatti.* A deed of partition. A receipt, or acquittance, or release, a writing testifying the receipt of a debt. విభాగపత్రము, సమాప్తిగా దాలున్నతీర్చివ్రాసుకొన్నచీటి.

పారిశము Error for పార్శ్వము n. s.

బారుకాసులుతినుట v. n. To live by pimping. బడవాతనముచేసిజీవించుట?

బారుఖోరు n. s. بهارخور *Bhār Khōr.* A pimp. బడవ.

బారుగీరు n. s. بارگير *Bārgīr,* or *more properly,* بهاگير *Bahāgir.* A trooper, a horseman who does not find (produce, supply) a horse for himself. తురుపువాడు, గుఱ్ఱముగలవాడు.

పారుచా or పార్చాజినుసు n. s. پارچه Clothier's goods, drapery. జవిళి.

బారుచేయుట v. a. To load (a gun) తుపాకిలో మందుగుండు వేసికట్టించుట.

బారువాడు n. s. بارواﻻ *Bārwālā*. A soldier. సిపాయీవాడు.

బారూదు n. s. باروت *Bārut*. Gunpowder. తుపాకిమందు.

బార్కసు n. s. The English word "Barracks." సిపాయీలుండేశాల.

పార్గాచేసుట v. a. To drive out. వెళ్లగొట్టుట.

బార్కుచు or బార్కసు n. s. The English word "Barracks" సిపాయీలుండేశాల.

బార్డుము n. s. Card, pasteboard?

బార్యావాడు n. s. (An Odhra word) A menial village servant?

భాల్గా n. s. Riot, disturbance?

భాల్గాచేయించుట v. a. To clear, make smooth, make defenceless. తెరపిగానుండేటట్టుచేసుట.

బార్హా adv. for بارها *Bārhā*. Repeatedly, several times. పదేపదే, మాటిమాటికి.

పాల్కి or పాలకీ n. s. پالکی *Pālki*. A palankeen. అందోళిక.

పాలకతండ్రి n. s. A foster-father. సాకినతండ్రి.

పాలకి n. s. پالکی *Pālkī*. A palankeen. అందోళిక.

బాలణి for పాలణి n. s. A cradle. తొట్ల.

పాళయము, పాళెంపట్టు, or పాళెపట్టు n. s. The country under a petty chieftain. The suburbs of a city. పాళయగాడుయేలేదేశము. పాళెగాడు A petty chieftain.

బాలాంబియ్యము n. s. Rice imported from the port of Balong.

బాలాజి n. s. The name used among Bairāgīs (byraggees) for the god at Tirupati (Tiripetty.)

బాలాబందు or బాలబందు n. s. بالابند *Bala band*. That is, "closed above" by a transverse line: as Marata writing is. One of the Indian alphabets which differs a little from the Devanagari character.

బాలిది or బాల్ది for బాలిత n. s. بادلی *Bādlī*. (Bengali) A bucket, a tub. కొయ్యతొట్టి.

బాలీసు n. s. بالش *Bālish*. A bolster or large round pillow for the back in a throne. ఒరుగుదిండు.

పాలు for పాల్ n. s. پال *Pāl*. A small tent used by private soldiers.

పాలువాసి n. s. A bonus or extra grant. బహుమానము.

బాలే n. s. The head of a still?

బాల్డీ, బాడ్లీ for బాలిత n. s. بادلي *Bādlī*. A wooden bucket (A Bengali sea term.) కొయ్యతొట్టి.

భావంజి n. s. A certain plant: it has a bitter medicinal seed of a brown colour. Ainslie 2. 447?

పావణి n. s. See పామిణి.

పావతి for పావుతి n. s. پاوتي *Paoti*. A receipt for money. రసీదు.

బావనాలు n. s. Feats, pranks, outrages, gambols?

పావాడము n. s. A vow, promising to cut off his own tongue or any limb, if the god will grant a prayer: self mutilation. Mountebank tricks.

బావిడి n. s. باورى *Bāori*. A stone-built well. బావి.

బావిరిగడ్డము for బావురుగడ్డము n. s. A thin beard, like that of a goat. పిల్లిగడ్డము.

పావు n. s. پاو *Pao*. A quarter; a quarter of any coin; a rupee, as being one-fourth of a bahādari-pagoda: a quarter pagoda. రెండుబదవలములు.

బావు for బావే (Bengali) n. s. The helm of a rudder, a tiller of a ship or boat. చుక్కాణి.

బావుట n. s. باوتا *Bāota*. A flag. ధ్వజపటము, కొడి.

పావుదార or పావుజరు for n. s. پاوزهر *Pāozahr*. Camel's gall: a drug so called. ఒకవిషము.

పావులా n. s. پاولا *Pāolā*. A quarter rupee. పావులురూపాయి. పెద్దపావులా Half a rupee.

పాశనాలుపాయుట v. a. To level or smooth ploughed land. దున్నిననేలనుసమముచేయుట.

పాశరము or పాశురము n. s. (Tamil பாசுரம்) A hymn, a sacred chant. అరవపాట.

ఫాశిల for **ఫాసిల** n. s. فاصله *Fāsilah.* Distance. దూరము.

ఫాసికపెట్టికూర్చుకొనుట n. s. A cross legged attitude in sitting. పద్మాసనముపెట్టికూర్చుండడము.

బాసికము or **భాశ్యకాల్లు** n. s. A nuptial crown or an ornamental patch of pith or soft wood or paper made by potters, and fastened in the forehead of the bride and bridegroom at the time of marriage. బెండుతోచేసిపెండ్లిలోతలకుకట్టుకొనేటిది.

ఫాసిగర్లు n. s. Plu. from پهانسی گیره *Phansi Girā.* Thugs. తగ్గువాండ్లు, గొంతుపిసికిచంపే దొంగలు.

బాహత్తరి adj. بهتری *Bahattari.* (Bengali) Seventy two. డెబ్బదిరెండు.

పాహాడిగుత్త n. s. پهاری گتا *Pahāri guttā.* "Hill rent" paid for pasture. కొండపుల్లరి.

పాతెషా for **పాదుషా** n. s. پادشاه *Padshah.* A prince. రాజు.

పి ఫి బి భి

పింగటించుట v. n. To brag.

పింగటిమురకట్టుట v. a. To pinion. పెడరెక్కలువిరిచికట్టుట.

పింగాణి n. s. *Pingani.* Crockery. China: a China plate. Apparently derived from పింగాణి the Mahratta or Canarese word for a butterfly or moth: because common crockery is generally painted with figures of these insects.

పింగాణి n. s. A plant resembling the lotus. పింగాణికాయ its fruit is large and edible. అల్లిదాగులు.

బింగసెరా n. s. A flint. చకిముకిరాయి. బింగసెరావంటి Stubborn (a western word.)

పింగు n. s. అనగాశిక్షము which see.

పింజరి, పింజారి for **పింజార** n. s. پنجاره *Pinjāra.* A cotton cleaner: a poor miserable wretch. దూదేకులవాడు, దిక్కుమాలినకుక్క.

పింజాఖోరు or **పింజేరి** n. s. (K. H.) A scamp, rascal, blackguard. లుచ్చా.

పింజరి n. s Flounce, hangings. జాలరు.

పింజుట v. a. To card cotton with the fingers. కర్దకర్దలుగాపుండేప్రత్తినిచేతితోచిన్నముగాతీసుట.

బిందువాలు or **బిందుకలకలు** n. s. A sort of small timbers. Letters vol. 6, p. 66. చెక్కలబిందువాలు.

బికలం for **బకలం** n. s. بقلم *Baqalami.* (Literally written by the pen of.) Signature of the clerk who drafts a document. జవాబునివీసుచేవ్రాలు.

భికారి or **బికారి** adj. بهکاری *Bhikārī.* Indigent, lean, debilitated. దరిద్రుడైన, బక్కచిక్కిన.

భికారి n. s. بهکاری *Bhikārī.* A poor man. బీదవాడు.

బిక్క adj. Abject. దిక్కుమాలిన. బిక్కఫకీరితనము abject poverty.

బిక్కలం n. s. for بقلم *Ba qalami.* Signature of (the clerk who writes a document.)

బిగాడాయించుట v. n. from بگارنا *Bigārnā.* To break with, become on bad terms with. విరోధమువచ్చుట.

ఫిగులుమనిషి n. s. (From the English word A "flugel" man.) A well drilled soldier, appointed to stand in front of the line and give the time in the manual and platoon exercises. కవాతుచెప్పేసిపాయి.

బిచానా n. s. بچهانا *Bichhānā.* A bedding. పడక.

పిచ్చలబాకి for **పిచ్లాబాకి** n. s. پچهلی باقی *Pichhli bāqi.* Old balances; outstanding. Former debts. పాతఅప్పు.

పిఛ్వా adj. پچهوا *Pichhwa.* Former, of old standing.

బిఛ్వాక for **బిచ్వా** n. s. بچهوا *Bichhwa.* A dagger. ఒకతరహాకటారి.

బిజినిగొడ్డు, బిజినివాడు n. s. A miser. లోభి.

పిటార for **పిటారా** n. s. پتهاره *Pithara.* A hamper. A basket-work box, with lid and hinges. పెడరపెట్టె.

బిడలవణము or **బిడాలవణము** n. s. Black salt or Bitloben, prepared by fusing fossile salt with emblic myrobalans; the produce is muriate of Soda with small quantities of muriate of lime ulphur and oxide of iron. ఒకఉప్పు.

బిడా or పాన్ బీడా n. s. بیڑا Bira. A roll of betel. చుట్టి, తాంబూలచుట్టి.

పిరాయించుట for ఫిరాయించుట v. a. from پھرانا Phirānā. To turn round; to return.

బిరాయించుట v. a. from بھرانا Bhirānā. To fold up (a letter.) To enclose in a packet. ఒకటిగ మరొకట్లో పెట్టుట.

బిరారు n. s. برار Birār. A party or caravan of Lumbadies. A cargo of grain carried on bullocks. A herd of loaded cattle. లంబాడీదండా, లంబాడీసరుకు.

పిడిదరిపిడి or పీడీదర్ పీడి n. s. پیڑی در پیڑی Pīri darpīrī. From father to son, in succession. పుత్రపౌత్రపారంపర్యముగా.

పిడివాదము n. s. (Tamil பிடிவாதம்) Contention, obstinacy, pertinacity. మూర్ఖము.

పితలాటకము n. s. Trickery, roguery, fraud. మోసము.

ఫితూరి n. s. فتور Fitūr. Intrigue, plot, treason, conspiracy, underhand proceeding. కుట్ర, కృత్రిమము.

ఫితూరివాడు or ఫితూరిఖోరు n. s. from فتوری Fitūrī. A rebel, a traitor, a makebate, a conspirator. ద్రోహి, కలహకారుడు.

బిత్తరపోవుట v. n. To shirk or twist so as to elude darts? Perhaps bhītar jāna, to go in.

పిత్తరకాసు n. s. for پتل کاس Pittal cass. A sort of fish? మత్స్యవిశేషము.

పిత్తళి for పిత్తడి n. s. for پیتل Pital. Brass. రాగి తుత్తినాగములకలిపి చేసినలోహము.

ఫిదివి n. s. فدوی Fidwī. A servant. Your humble servant. నౌకరు, తమదాసుడు.

బిద్దెలు n. s. plu. The cross bars supporting the deck of a boat?

బిన్ adv. بن Bin. Without లేకుండా. బిన్ముసవిదా بن مسوده Bin musawadah. In original; without any rough draft.

బిన్నాణి n. s. A deceitful female. మాయలాడి.

బిన్నాహము for బిన్నహ n. s. (K) A request, a petition. విన్నపము.

బిబ్బీ for బీబి n. s. بیبی Bībī. A lady. దొరసాని.

పియ్యతోలు for పితోలు n. s. The epidermis? or outward skin? ఈచర్మముదోగితేనెత్తురురాదు.

ఫిరంగి, or ఫిరింగి n. s. فرنگی Farangi. A European. A cannon. జాతివాచక, శతఘ్ని, ఖడ్గము.

ఫిరంగి adj. فرنگی Farangi. A European. Generally used as a word of scorn, andparticularly applied to the black Portugueze. Corrupted from Franc or François.

ఫిరంగిచెక్క n. s. China root (Smilax China) a certain medicinal drug. Ainslie 1. 70.

పిరాట్టి n. s. (Tamil பிராட்டி) A lady goddess. దేవతస్త్రీ, అమ్మవారు.

బిరాకా n. s. Quarrel, spite, ill-will, disagreement?

బిరాదరి n. s. برادری Birādāri. A brotherhood: band (of peons &c.) a company.

బిరాన adj. برانه Birana. Alien, foreign. పరాయి.

పిరాయించుట v. a. from پھرانا Phirāna. To change, to turn, exchange. మార్చుట.

ఫిరాయింపు n. s. Lending money. Money returned to the payer, discount. అవసరానికియిచ్చి మళ్లీతీసుకోవడము, అప్పుయిచ్చేమొత్తములోనూ వడ్డీకియింతనిపట్టుకొనేరూకలు.

పిరం, పిరెం for ప్రియము adj. Dear in price. గిరాకి.

ఫిరింగి, పిరంగి, ఫిరంగి n. s. A cannon శతఘ్ని.

పిరింగికత్తి n. s. An European sword, i. e. a cutlass. జాతికత్తి.

పిరింగిచెక్క for ఫిరంగిచెక్క n. s. China root. Smilax China. ఒకమందుదినుసు.

బిరింజి n. s. A kind of pudding.

ఫిరిస్తు for ఫేరస్తు n. s. فهرست Fehrist A list, a catalogue.

ఫిర్కా n. s. فرقه Firqah A part, a sub division. తగిలు, ముక్కుడి.

పిర్యాది n. s. فریادی Faryadi A petitioner, or complainant, plaintiff. ఫిర్యాదుచేసుకొన్నవాడు.

ఫిర్యాదు n. s. فریاد Faryad. A petition or complaint. మొర.

బిల్కుల్ adv. بالکل bilkul. At all, in the least; also used for wholly, totally. బొత్తిగా, కుట్రమర, ఎంతమాత్రమున్ను.

బిల్ ఫైలు adv. بالفعل *Bilfĕl.* For the present. తత్కాలానికి.

ఫిల్ హాలు or పిలాలు adv. في الحال *Filhal.* At present, for the present, just now, for the mean while; in fact. ప్రస్తుతము.

పిలాస్తరు for ప్లాష్టరు n. s. (E) "Plaster." గుడ్డకుచరిమిళ్ళుంటికివేసేటిది.

ఫిలాహాలు adv. في الحال *Filhal.* At present, &c. (See ఫిల్ హాలు) ప్రస్తుతము.

బిల్మక్తా or బిల్మూక్తా n. s. A fixed annual rent. గుంపుగుత్త.

బిల్మక్తాగా or బిల్మూక్తాగా adv. بالمقطع *Bilmaqta.* Altogether, by the bulk, in general. మొత్తముగా.

పిళ్ల n. s. A termination used with some names of men; as Sri Nivasa Pilla. It is confined in general to people of the గొల్ల caste (herdsmen) or కరణములు clerks.

బిళ్లసాదము n. s. The phrase used for rice given to the menials in a pagoda. బిళ్లబిళ్లలుగాచేసి గుడిపనివాండ్లకుయిచ్చేఅన్నము.

పిల్లాంగ్రబము Error for పిల్లమురిగము n. s. A summerset or leap heels over head. వేశ్యాకన్యలు మొదలయినవారువేసేలాగులుఅనగాలఘువు.

పిళ్లారి n. s. (Tamil பிள்ளையார்) A name of the god Ganesa. వినాయకుడు. D.

పిశానా, బిసానా for బిచానా n. s. (An error for بچهنا *Bichana.*) A bedding. పడక.

పిశినారి n. s. A miser, a covetous wretch. లోభి.

పిషాణివడ్లు n. s. A fine sort of rice. సంబావడ్లు.

పిసురు n. s. A dovetail. పావురాయితోకవలెవుండే కుసి.

బిసాత్ n. s. بساط *Bisat.* Power: breadth, width. Means, capital, stock, estate (same as ఆస్తి, సొత్తు) అదియెంతబిసాత్ what great matter (or affair) is that? అదినీబిసాత్ that was your luck, or chance, or lot. నీఅధికారమేమి దానిబిసాతేమి What chance has she with you? Pretence is one thing and performance another.

బిసానా for బిచానా n. s. (An error for بچهنا *Bichhana.*) A bedding. పడక.

బిస్తి for బిహిస్తి n. s. An error for بہشتی *Bihishti.* A water man; who leads an ox that carries water in goat-skins. పఖాలి.

పింగాణి n. s. Chinaware, crockery. See పింగాణి.

పీక or పీకె n. s. The refuse or stump of a cigar. తాగిమిగిలినచుట్ట.

బీజకె n. s. (Turkish بیجک) Invoice, inventory, list. Label, ticket?

బీజబంక్ n. s. Bird-lime, made from (బీజము bij) the seed of the tamarind. A close fisted miser. జిగురు, లోభిష్ఠి.

బీజువరి n. s. Paddy seeds with germs, being ready for sowing. మొలకవడ్లు.

ఫీటా for పీత n. s. پیتا *Pita.* Tape; ribbon; (*vitta* in Latin) a fillet. నాడా.

పీడీదర్ పీడి adv. پیری در پیری *Pīrī dar pīrī.* From generation to generation. తరంతరగా.

బీబీ n. s. بی بی *Bībī.* A lady. దొరసాని.

బీభత్సు n. s. Disgust, abhorrence. అసహ్యము, చీదర. దాన్నిబీభత్సుచేసినాడు he has spoiled it. బీబత్సుగావుండే for బీభత్సుగావుండే adj. Out of repair, damaged, confused.

బీమా n. s. بهیما *Bhīma.* Insurance, money paid for insurance. ఇన్సూరాన్సు.

పీరాంజుట or బీరాంజుట v. a. (Tamil சேராம்பிறது) To collect, gather grass &c. పోగుచేసుట.

బీరువ n. s. 'A bureau,' chest of drawers. అంతస్తులంతస్తుగావుండే పెద్దపెట్టె.

పీరునుండి n. s. A waterspout at sea? మేకగము. If descending, it is called అవుకు, అవుకుఖానా.

ఫీరోజి for ఫీరోజా n. s. فیروزہ *Fēroza.* A Turquoise. ఒకరత్నము.

పీర్లు n. s. An image in the form of a hand, used by Mussulmans at the Mohorum. తురకదేవుడు. పీర్లపండుగ The Mohurrum (as being the "anniversary of the (*pīrs*) Saints") "All saint's day" which in the Madras country has degenerated into All Fool's Day: being a street masquerade annually held among the mobility: and is just as popular among Hindus as among Musulmans.

పీల, ఫీలా, పీలశిరంగు n. s. The lues venerea.

బీలు n. s. بیل A sort of spade. ఒకతరహాపార.

పీలుకాడవ for పీలుకాడ్వాఆట n. s. The flush of four cards?

బేలుదారు for బేల్దార్ n. s. بیلدار *Beldar*. A digger, a labourer, a pioneer. తవ్వేవాడు.

బుంగ n. s. بھنگا *Bhunga*. The baggage belonging to a camp. పరంజాం.

పుంజజమాన్ n. s. Dry grain land. మెట్ట. మెట్టపొలము.

పుంజె n. s. A phrase for *four* (as we call twelve a dozen) నాలుగుపుంజెడురూపాయీలు four rupees. తొమ్మిదిపుంజెరూపాయీలు 36 rupees.

పుండాఖోరు n. s. A wrangler, a quarrelsome wretch. తంటాఖోరు.

పుండాయితనముచేసుట v. n. To do mischief. కొతముచేసుట.

పుకారు n. s. پکارا *Pukārā*. Outcry, rumour, report, alarm, an uproar. రట్టు, రగ్బ.

బుకా adj. بھوکا *Bhuka*. Hungry. ఆకలిగొన్న. బుకాఫకీరితనము utter poverty.

బుక్కీస, బాక్సాస for బక్షా n. s. بقچه *Bakhsha*. A bundle, a pack of cloth. వస్త్రములమూట.

బుక్కు n. s. (English word) "*A book*:" as distinguished from కవిలె and గ్రంథము.

బుటా or బుట్టాపని n. s. بوٹا *Buta*. Flowered pattern in cloth. జరిబుటా a gold pattern. బుటేదారుబట్ట بوٹےدار *Butēdār*. Embroidery.

ఫుటాయించుట v. n. To split, separate (one cause or lawsuit into several.)

బుడేలు or బుడ్యాలు n. s. The roots of the ears. చెవులమొదళ్లు. నీ చెవులుబుడేలమట్టుకుకోసెగకోస్తాను I will cut your ears off.

బుత్ పురోషి or బూతుపురోశి n. s. A sort of tax, or cess levied for the maintenance of a pagoda. In Guntoor this signifies the same as Mohtarfa. ఇలువరుసవన్ను Fees or small penalties levied under Musulman governments, on various tradesmen to defray the expenses attendant on festivals. Supposed, but wrongly, to be meant for بت پرورش *but parvarish*, or sustenance for the idol. Also penalties levied by a guru or confessor on certain breaches of caste: such as permitting a widow to marry again. The Mohtarfa being levied on merchants alone: this is levied on all classes except merchants.

బుతాము or బొత్తాం for బొత్తాను or బొత్తాసు n. s. (French, *Un bouton*) A button. గుండి.

బునాది for బనియాద్ n. s. for بنیاد *Bunyad*. The foundation of a building. అస్తిభారము.

పునాస n. s. The first crop in the Hindu year: the dry-grain crop, or light crop: consisting of the grains called పునాసలు (that is, పునర్నవులోవిత్తినవి) viz, కొఱ్ఱలు, బొబ్బర్లు మొదలయిన ధాన్యము.

బుయ్యారం for బుయ్యార n. s. for بھنیارہ *Bhunyarah*. A dungeon. చెరశాల.

బురకలు n. s. (A low word) Empty ears of corn.

బురకా n. s. برقع *Burqah*. A covering or veil for a palankeen &c. గవిసెన.

పురజ for పుర్జా n. s. پرزه *Purzah*. Note, memorandum. లెక్కచిట్టి or daily account. రోజుపురజ A shopkeeper's day book. పురజా A small piece of paper. చీటి. (M M. p. 651.) *A wharf* at a sea custom house?

బురడా n. s. Bragging, a lie. జల్లి.

పురబ్జీ or పురబ్జీలు n. s. A kind of soldiers. ఒకతరహాదండువాండ్లు.

బురదుక్కు n. s. A kind of fish.

బురసా A certain colour or tint used in chintzes, also called చారిణి. Charu Chandrod. 588.

పురారుకులక for పూరారుకులక n. s. (H.) Clap boards used in building. సన్నకులక.

బురుజు n. s. برج *Burj*. A bastion, a tower or fortalice. పిరంగిపెట్టికాల్చేదిబ్బ, గడి, చిన్నకోట.

బురునీసు for బూర్నీసు n. s. Flannel, woollen. నిండామెత్తగావుండేదళమైనకంబళి.

బురుమ for బరమా n. s. برما *Barmā*. A carpenter's augre. తొరపుడము.

ఫురుసత్తు n. s. فرصت *Fursat*. Leisure. సావకాశము.

బురుసా n. s. (i. e. Bursa, a town in Anatolia) the name given to a sort of woollen goods: and also to the (blue or yellow) colour. బురుసారుమాలు a blue or yellow handkerchief, for which they are prized. These are also called పైఠిణి Paithinī and బురహాన్‌పురి usually బురాన్‌పురి Burhan puri.

బురుసు n. s. A brush (A jar :) a large pot. A sort of firework. తూలిక (జాడి ?) ఒకబాణవిద్య.

ఫురోక్త or ఫురోఖ్తు n. s. فروخت Furōkht. Sale, selling, vent. అమ్మకము. ఫురోఖ్తుచేయుట to dispose of, sell.

పురోణి n. s. (M) A note. చీటి.

పురావు n. s. Proof, written documents. సంద ర్భమును చూపేరుజువు, దస్తావేజు, అనిఅర్థమవుతున్నది. This word often occurs in Duhur. Local III. 84, line 13, ib. III. 94, line. 19.

బుర్నీసు for బూర్నీసు n. s. A blanket or thick felt. మెత్తగాదళముగాఉండేకంబళి.

బులాకి n. s. بلاق Bulāq. A jewel worn (chiefly by unmarried girls and courtesans) on the middle of the nose between the nostrils. నాసాభరణము. Herklots, page XXI, of Appendix. Borrowed from the name of the port of Cairo. Boulak is a suburbs of Cairo.

పులావు or పోలావు n. s. پلاو Pulāo. The dish called pillaw. ఒకతరహావంటకము.

పులిహోరn. s. (Tamil புளிசோறு) Rice dressed with acid sauce. పులుసుఅన్నము.

పుష్టి n. s. پشتي Pushtī. Support, aid, assistance. ప్రోద్బలము.

బుసక, బుసర n. s. Chaff: the dust of thrashed corn. బుసకభూమి chaffy soil. అనగారబడుదు, తువ్వనేల.

భూసాజింసుn. s. بهوساجنس Bhūsā Jins. Grain of any kind: so termed in the Bellary accounts. ధాన్యము in reality grain in husk. వడ్లు, కాయధాన్యములు.

పుసాలున adv. Suddenly. లటక్కున.

పుసేల n. s. The seventh lunar mansion. పునర్వసు is called పెద్దపుసేల, and the eighth పుష్యమి is called చిన్నపుసేల.

పుష్తబంది n. s. پشتبندي Pushta bandi. "Back fastening." Stone work executed at the back of a tank. చెరువుకట్టకు వెనకతట్టుఆధారంగాకట్టినది.

పుష్టి n. s. پشتي Pushti. Encouragement, backing. ప్రోత్సాహము, అండ, సహాయము. పుష్టిచేసుట to second, to support.

పుస్తీలు n. s. plu. Mustaches. కల్పెచ్చా.

ఫుస్లాయించుట v. a. from پهسلانا Phuslānā. To coax, wheedle, persuade. బుజ్జగించుట.

ఫుస్లాయింపు n. s. (From the same) Coaxing, persuasion. బుజ్జగింపు.

పూచి n. s. Business, affair. Penal responsibility. ఆపూచినామీదకాదు I am not responsible for it. ఆపూచికడిపించినాడు he carried on the business. పూచిచేయుట to undertake.

పూజు n. s. (Ganjam dialect ?) A yoke. See Acts, XV. 10. P†. నొగ.

పూటము n. s. Lading, burden. ఎగుమతియైనసరుకు.

బూటాలు for బుట్టాలు n. s. from بوٹا Būtā. Flowered patterns in chintz or muslin. వస్త్రముమీదవేసేపూలు.

పూటుట v. a. అనగాకుదురుబాటుచేసుట To establish ? (Ganjam.)

బూడిదెకట్నము or బూడిదెపన్ను. n. s. A tax levied in the Kannadi country, on every wedding. Elsewhere on every funeral. Local. V. 229, line 6, & 7.

పూడ్చుట or పోయివచ్చుట v. n. To go. These words are used at Madras instead of పోవుట.

బూతాదు, బూతాత్ n. s. for بيوتات Buyūtat. Household expenses: also an account of them. మనోవృత్తి, మనోవృత్తిలెక్క. బూతాత్‌నవీసు clerk of the household. One letter says మాబూతాదు(వ్యయం మొదలయినవాటికిచాలా శ్రమనుపొందుచున్నాముగనక as we suffer very much for want of subsistence.

బూతుపురోహి n. s. See బుత్‌పురోషి.

బూబందులెక్క n. s. An account (in England called a *terrier*) of boundaries of fields. గుడికట్టుభూమిడా, పొలములసరహద్దులెక్క.

బూబు or బూబుసాని n. s. بوبو Būbū. A musulmani lady. తురకాబిడ.

పూరా adj. پورا *Pūrā*. Full, complete. సంపూర్ణమైన.

బూర్నీసు n. s. A blanket, or thick woollen. దళముగా మెత్తగావుండేకంబళి.

ఫూలిహొన్ను n. s. پهولي هون *Phuli hun.* A star pagoda of the sort worth 3½ Rupees. ఫూలవరహా.

భూసాజింసు n. s. بهوسا جنس *Bhūsa Jins*. Grain in the husk. వడ్లు, కాయధాన్యములున్ను.

భృగు n. s. Traces: secret, concealed fact. ఆనవాలు, సామర్థ్యము, జాడ, రహస్యము.

బెంగిటప్పాలు for బంగిటపాలు n. s. بانگي تپال *Bāngī Tappāl.* The Bangy, or mail that conveys parcels. మూటలుపొయ్యేతపాలు.

పెండారి or పెండేరి for పిండారి n. s. پنداره *Pindarā*. (Mahr.) 'A Pindaree' or plunderer, freebooter or mosstrooper. In Mahratta పెండారి is, a gang of mounted robbers.

బెద్దకిస్తు n. s. The revenue charged on the summer crop?

భెత్రి n. s. بيتي *Betī.* Threes. A term at dice, or dominos. దచ్చి.

పెద్దాపురి n. s. A fine soft sugar mixed with lime: which is made at Peddapore. పెద్దాపురిచక్కెర.

పెద్దింటమ్మ n. s. A certain rural goddess. ఒకక్షుద్రదేవత.

పెయ్యర n. s. A certain forest shrub called Grewia Orientalis. Rox. 2. 586. అల్లిపెయ్యర a species called Grewia Didyma. ibid 2. 591.

పెరుంబడిగావుండే adj. (from Tamil பெரும்படி) Unfinished, as a painting. Sketched. చిత్తుగావుండే.

పెరుమాళ్లు n. s. A Tamil name of Vishnu.

పెరె n. s. A reservoir for water at the salt pans. నీరువుంచేమడి. (Vizag.)

బెల్లపాకుచెట్టు n. s. Said to be a name of the తుత్తిరిచెట్టు.

పెళ్లీళ్లాట n. s. Picquet at cards?

పెళ్లు n. s. (Madras phrase) A privy. A backyard. మరుగుపెరడు, పెరడున్ను.

బే adv. بے *Be.* (Pers:) Without; as అదబు *adab* manners, బేఅదబి _ *be-adbi* contempt, unmannerliness. బేరీజనుగా '*bē-reason-ga*' without reason. (Rajahmandry dialect.)

బేంబేరు n. s. Fright or alarm. దిగులు, భయము.

బేగారి n. s. بيگاری *Bēgarī.* an error for بيكار *Bēkar* without work, idle. A hackney. Stray folks impressed, without pay, to carry loads. From the Persian *bīgar*. Employing any person without remuneration. వెట్టికిపనిచేశేవాడు.

బేగి adv. بيگي *Bēgī.* Quickly, without delay. త్వరగా.

బేగిరావు n. s. A dromedary. بيگي رو From *Begi* swift and *rao* going. పెద్దలొంటిపిట, తపాలుఒంటె.

బేగోదుగా adv. بےگوند *Begond.* Unsealed. See గోదు 'without gum:' because it is the custom to secure the envelope of a letter with gum.

పేచి or పేచు n. s. (K.) Pecuniary embarrassment, trouble on account of arrears in taxes. (Reeve, page 953.) Responsibility.

బేచిరాకు adj. بيچراغ *Be charagh.* Desert, ruined, devoid of a single lighted lamp: depopulated. ఇండ్లులేనిదిగానున్నుపొరుగూరికాపులచేత సాగుబడిచేయబడేదిగానున్నవుండేటిది. బేచిరాకు గ్రామము a depopulated or deserted village.

పేచీకోరి adj. Litigious, roguish. తంటాలమారి.

బేచెడ or బేచెడావు adj. for బేచిరాకు which see.

బేజరూరు adj. بےضرور *Be zarūr.* Useless, needless, superfluous, unnecessary. ఆవశ్యకములేక, అక్కరలేని.

బేజా adj بيجا *Bējā.* Bad, wicked. Groundless, for which there is no room; inadmissible. నిరాధారమైన, కనికిమాలిన. బేజాపని injustice, wrong.

బేజారు n. s. بيزار *Bēzār.* Fatigue, weariness, annoyance. అలుపు. బేజారవుట to become fatigued. బేజారుచేసుట to weary, dun, teaze, drive a man desperate, torment or put him out of his wits.

బేజుమాలు adj. بيزمال *Bēzmāl.* Bright, polished, set, as a sword.

బేజురూరు adj. See బేజరూరు.

పేట n. s. پيته *Pēth.* "Pettah," suburbs, market. శాఖానగరము, పట్టణస్థలము, బాజారు.

భేటి n. s. بهيت *Bhēt.* Interview, visit. దర్శనము.

బేడా n. s. A break, for teaching a bullock. గాడీయెద్దులనుకట్టిమరిపేటిది.

బేడా n. s. بيرا *Bērā.* Siege, besieging. ముట్టడి. బేడావేయుట to besiege.

బేడాస్తంభము n. s. A pillar made of a sort of black marble. ఒకవిధమైననల్లరాతిస్తంభ మేమో?

బేడిగ n. s. A tax or a favourable assessment. పన్ను.

బేడీలు n. s. بيرى *Bērī.* Fetters. సంకెళ్లు.

బేడౌలు adj. بيڈول *Bē-doul.* Wretched, irregular, incorrect. Shapeless, ill-formed, clumsy; విరూపమైన, వికారమైన.

భేత్రి n. s. بيتي *Beti.* The throw of threes, which makes six on the dice or dominos. దచ్చి.

బేద for బైద్ n. s. بيد *Baed.* A plunderer. కొల్లగాడు. బేదవారులు plunderers.

బేదఖలు adj. بيدخل *Bēdakhl* Ousted or dismissed from office. తోసివేయబడ్డ.

బేదరు n. s بيدر *Bēdar* A class of savages. బోయవాండ్లు. The *Katbadi* peons are mostly of this caste.

పేదా or ప్యాదా n. s. پيادہ *Piyādah.* A peon or armed messenger. బంట్రోతు.

భేడా n. s. Money levied as a contribution from the neighbours of a bankrupt farmer, to pay the rent due? (Ganjam.)

బేదాన n. s. Meant for بہيدانہ *bihi-dāna* (Persian) Quince-seed, sold as a drug. ఒకచెట్టు, దానిమందుచన్ను.

బేదిల్ adj. بيدل *Bedil.* Disheartened. ధైర్యము తప్పిన. కాపులు బేదిల్ అయిపోయి the farmers being disheartened.

పేనా n. s. (the English word) A quill 'pen.' కలము.

బేపర్వాగా adv. بيپروا *be-parwa,* Heedlessly, carelessly. అలక్ష్యముగా.

బేపర్వాయించుట or బేపర్వాచేసుట v. a. To despise, disregard. అలక్ష్యముచేసుట.

బేపార్ n. s. Traffic, trade, commerce. వర్తకము, వ్యాపారము.

బేఫహము adj. بےفہم *Be fahm.* Careless, unmindful. జాగ్రతలేని.

బేబందుగావుండే adj. بےبند *Be band.* Disordered, confused, irregular. తారుమారుగావుండే.

బేబాకీగా adv. بےباقى *Be bāqi.* 'Without balance' as a complete payment. బేబాకీగాచెల్లించినాడు he paid it in full.

బేమంజూరు adj. بےمنظور *Be manzur.* What is not approved, discountenanced. ఒప్పుకోబడని. ఆ అర్జీ బేమంజూరుఅయినది the petition was discountenanced.

బేమరమ్మతుగావుండే adj. بےمرمت *Be marammat.* Out of repair, damaged, broken. శికస్తుగావుండే.

పేమిలిచీటి n. s. *A "family"* chit.

బేమొలాజా for బేమొలాహిజా n. s. بےملاحظہ *Be mulahazah.* Treating with sternness, or rigour, not showing favour. నిర్దాక్షిణ్యము. బేమొలాహిజాగా without favour or partiality.

పేరణికటాకణి n. s. Sowing and reaping. విత్తడము, కోయడము.

ఫేరస్తు or ఫేరిస్తు n. s. فہرست *Fehrist.* A list or catalogue. పట్టీ.

పేరాముట్టి n. s. (Tamil பேராமுட்டி) A certain plant called Hibis-cus Zeilan. ఒకమందుచెట్టు.

పేరిస్తు n. s. فہرست *Fehrist.* List, catalogue. పట్టీ, జాబితా.

బేరీజు n. s. بيرج *Berij.* An amount of assessment, the total assessment of a village or district. దివాణపుపన్ను మొత్తము. శాశ్వతబేరీజు permanent assessment.

బేరోజుగారు or బేరోజుగావుండేవాడు n.s. بےروزگار *Bē rōzgār.* He who is unemployed. నిరుద్యోగముగావుండేవాడు.

బేలాయఖు adj. بےلايق *Be layaq.* Unfit. తగని.

బేల్దారు n. s. بيلدار *Bēldār.* A pioneer, a mason. కాదూటివాడు, కొల్లత్తువాడు.

బేవారిసు adj. بےوارث *Be wāris.* Without heir or claimant. నాధుడులేని. బేవారుసుగొడ్డు a stray cattle. బేవారిసుయినాము. An 'Inaum' that has fallen in, to which no heir has appeared.

పేవిడి, పేవుడి or పేమిడి n. s. پیوڑی *Pēorī.* The colour called imperial perfect yellow, or bright *golden yellow*: distinct from Gamboge. ఒకతరహాపసుపువర్ణము.

బేశక్కు or బేషక్కు adv. بےشک *Bēshak.* Undoubtedly. నిస్సంశయముగా.

పేశానుపువడ్లు properly పిశానుపువడ్లు n. s. The name given to the rice which is reaped in February and March. Ainslie 1. 340.

బేశుమారు for బేషుమార్ adv. بےشمار *Be shumār.* Without being reckoned, vastly, abundantly, countlessly. విస్తారముగా, లెక్కలేక.

పేశ్వాజు for పేష్వాజు n. s. پیشواز *Peshwāz.* A gown. ఒకచొక్కా.

బేష్ or బేషుగాఉండే adj. بیش *Bēsh.* Best, superior. శ్రేష్ఠమైన.

బేషకు adv. بےشک *Bē shak.* Without doubt; certainly, doubtless. నిస్సంశయముగా.

బేషకుము for బేషోకం adj. بیش وکم *Besho kam.* Unrivalled. అసమానమైన.

పేషిగి n. s. پیشگی *Peshgī.* Advance of pay. ముందుగాకూలియివ్వడము.

పేష్కషి or పేష్కస్తి for పేష్కషు n. s. پیشکش *Pesh kash.* (Present, fee, donation.) Tribute paid by a zemindar &c. బహుమానము, కప్పము.

పేష్కారు n. s. پیشکار *Pēshkār.* A revenue officer, secondary to an Amildar. ఒకఅధికారి.

బేసబబు adv. بےسبب *Bē sabab.* Without reason, causelessly. నిష్కారణముగా.

బేసరి n. s. بیسر *Besar.* A jewel worn by women on one side of the nose. ముక్కుపుడక.

బేసరిదుంప n. s. A plant with a red flower: the root is eaten as a pickle.

పేసికి n. s. Pride, presumption. బడాయి ?

బేహారి or బేపారి n. s. An individual of a particular distinction among Musulmans. They are pedlers or retail sellers చిల్లరబేరగాడు.

బేహాలుగాఉండే adj. from بےاحوال *Bēahwāl.* Bankrupt, beggarly. దరిద్రముగాఉండే.

పైంటు n. s. (E) 'Appoint.' పైంటుచేసుట to appoint.

పైకారి properly పాయకారి n. s. A sub-renter or under tenant: a tenant at will. This word is opposed to కదీం; and in Cadapah it is explained పరస్థలపురైతు a man who cultivates land lying in another village.

పైకి (Mahr.) Out of, from amongst, of, from, under the head of, in, belonging to, appertaining to; the same as సంబంధము. Thus బాగాయతుపైకితరి A rice field which properly (or originally) belongs to 'garden land.' అపైకి means అందులో, అనగామించుజమలి.

పైగస్తి n. s. پیگشتی *Paigashti.* A patrole. ఆమలుకట్టడమునకైతిరిగేవాడు.

పైజారు n. s. پیزار *Paizār.* A slipper or leather sandal. జోడు.

పైజారుమట్టు n. s. The remora or sucking fish. ఒకచేప.

పైతాణి or పైఠిణి n. s. A cloth partly silk and partly cotton. పట్టుప్రత్తికలసినేతగుడ్డ. (A silk stuff striped red and yellow ?)

బైదరులు for బేడరులు n. s. from بیدر *Bēdar.* A kind of plunderers. The savages called Beders, or Veddahs.

బైదా, బైద్ n. s. بید *Baid.* Insurrection, rebellion, mutiny, tumult in a state or army. తిరుగబడడము. బైదాగుర్రము predatory horse. పిండారిగుర్రము.

పైమాయిషి n. s. پیمایش *Paimāish.* The survey-measurement of lands. నేలలుకొలవడము.

పైమాలి n. s. پایمالی *Paimālī.* Ruin, ravage. చెరుపు, చేటు.

భైరవచక్రము* n. s. 'Rioting.' C†. in Rom. XIII.

భైరవి, బైరిడేగ n. s. The peregrine falcon. జాట్టుభైరి the white crested eagle. (Jerdon) See M. Journ. X. 79. భూతభైరవి the name of a tree called Premna Serratifolia. Rox. 3. 77.

బైరాగి or వైరాగి n. s. بیراگی *Bairāgi.* A monk, a friar. విరాగముగలవాడు.

పైలాదికర్ర n. s. A see-saw ?

పైలుమాను for పైలువాను n. s. پہلوان *Pahlwān.* A boxer or wrestler. జెట్టివాడు.

పైవస్తు most commonly పైవస్తు n. s. پیوست *Paiwast.* The date of the arrival of a letter. The mark denoting "Received" సాలిపైవస్తు the year before last. (Bellary.)

ఫైసలా n. s. فیصله *Faisalah*. Settlement, decision, sentence, decree. తీర్పు, పరిష్కారము.

బొంకప్ప n. s. A certain fish, *Tetradon hispidus*: it is nearly spherical and covered with prickles.

పాంచి n. s. The cooling drink made from jaggory, lime juce and water mixed. ఒకతరహాపానకము.

బొంగ్లాంకాయ n. s. A young cocoanut. ఎళనీరుకాయ.

బొంత n. s. The mullet fish. (*Mugil cephaleius.*)

బొండిలి n. s. Name of a certain caste. ఒకజాతి.

బొకనాయిరోగము n. s. Caries caused by lues venerea. కనుబొమ్మలలో రెప్పలలో వుండే వెంట్రుకలు రాలిపొయ్యేయుండరోగము.

బొకారు n. s. بخار *Bukhār*. Steam, glowing heat: eruption on the skin ఆవిరి, ఒంటిమీదపేలినది.

బొచ్చు n. s. Doublets, at dice?

పొడబారుటorపొడగొనుట v.n (from Tamil புடை) To sink or become hollow, as a sore. పొడబారిన full of holes. గుంటలోకలవేసుట.

బొణిగె n. s. A kind of wooden bell, hung at a bullock's neck. సొడక, ఆవగాచెద్దమెడ్డ మెడలో లాడుకులాడుకు అని ఆడే ఒకతరహా గొయ్య గంట.

బొనగుబు n. s. See బొణిగె.

పొన్నారుతాళము n. s. (error for పొన్నరిదళము) Orpiment.

బొప్పరమీను n. s. A whale. ఒకమత్స్యము.

పొప్పళి for పప్పళి n. s. A plaid or chequered garment worn by women. The stuff called "poplin." A plaid of a square pattern alternately green and red. విరుతపొప్పళి. S. 1. 176. పచ్చరపొప్పళి a green and white tartan.

పొప్పాయిపండు n. s. The fruit called papaw. Rox. 3. 825. Carica papaya.

బొముక n. s. Corruption of ఎముక a bone. (Masul.)

బొమువిగురుకప్పి n. s. A block or large pulley. ఒకతరహాకప్పి?

పొరంబోకు or పొరంబోకునేల n. s. Waste land, utterly unfit for cultivation. సాగుబడికిరాని భూమి.

బొరిగము, బొరిగె n. s. A hoe used in digging up grass. (Vizag.) తొల్లిక?

పొరివట్టు, పొలివట్టు n. s. A heap of boiled rice offered to a god. తిరుప్పవళము, తిరుప్పావడ.

పొల్లాయి n. s. Certain fees paid on every thrashing floor. (Ganjam.)

పొస్తకము n. s. error for పుస్తకము a book.

బొహు adj. error for బహు Much.

భొంచావణి or పొహంచావణి پهنچاونی *Pahunchāwuni.* Insurance: on goods or on lottery tickets.

పోంచి, పోంచీలు for పొంచీలు n. s. پونچی *Paunchi.* A sort of bracelets. కరభూషణము.

భోంట్లాంకాయ n. s. A young cocoanut. A cocoanut with the husk on. ఎళనీరుకాయ, పట్టు పులువని టెంకాయ.

పోక n. s. A heap of salt. (Vizag.) Apparently an error for పోగు?

భోక్తముగా adv. Gently, delicately.

భోత్రా n. s. Respect, regard, honour. గౌరవము. భోత్రాచేసుట to respect. భోత్రాగా respectfully.

భోగబంద n. s. (from భోగబంధము) Mortgage on land; which till the debt is paid is enjoyed by the creditor (Ganjam) Usufruct. భోగ్యము.

బోగాణి or బోగిణి n. s. A sort of copper bowl. పాత్రవిశేషము.

భోగాట్ట, భోగవట్ట n. s. Enquiry. విచారించుట. ఆసంగతిబొక్కగాభోగవట్టా చేసినాను I enquired into it properly.

పోచీలు for పొంచీలు n. s. پونچی *Paunchi.* A sort of bracelets. కరభూషణము.

బోజు for బోజ్ n. s. بوجھ *Bōjh.* Weight, responsibility. బరువు, ఉత్తరవాదము.

పోటాపోటి n. s. پوٹاپوٹی *Pōtāpoti.* Rivalry, emulation, outbidding. (Bellary.) నాకంటేనా కనిపయుబడడము.

పోటు for పోట్టు n. s. A raised hearth built in a Vishnu temple. గుడిలో చాల్యాగావుండే పొయ్యులు.

పోతా for పోత n. s. (Mahr.) A book, a work, a writing &c. పుస్తకము M. M. page 663. (A leaf in an account book: a folio?)

బోద, బోదము for బోళము n. s. A sort of medicine.

బోద n. s. (in sea language) A board, i. e. side. ఉజియబోద Ujiya boda, starboard. దావుబోద *dāoo bōda* larboard.

పోదుచుట error for పోయివిడుచుట v. n. To go away. This is a Madras phrase. పోయి for పోయి (past p‖ of పోవుట) Having gone.

బోణి n. s. Hansel or the first money a seller receives in the morning. The luck-penny: a shopkeeper's first receipt in the day. అమ్మేవాడు మొట్టమొదటనేరుకు అమ్మి తీసుకొనేరూక. బోణిచేసినాడు he took hansel.

పోతి or పోతిబిళ్ల n. s. پوتي *Potī* (Mahratta) A piece of cotton steeped in red ink: which is wetted and squeezed into the inkstand. ఎర్ర యింకిదూది.

బోదారసింగి n. s. A medical drug. కేదారసింగి. D. ఒకమందుదినుసు.

పోదిన, పోదిని most commonly for پودينه *Pudīnā* పుదీనా n. s. Mint. ఒకమొక్క.

భోధాయకము n. s. Instigation, temptation. దుర్బోధన.

బోనాంపెట్టె, బోనంపెట్టె n. s. A round box or basket, covered with leather. దయినతోలుచేసినగుండుపెట్టె.

బోనుపొయ్యి n. s. A portable oven, formed by placing a deep dish as a cover on a bowl?

బోనేశ్వరాలు n. s. (a low word) A suite of rooms?

బోముబిగురుకప్పి n. s. A large block or pulley. ఒకపెద్దకప్పి.

బోయడు for బోయవాడు n. s. (from بهوئی *Bhōi.*) A savage, a man of the woods. A palankeen bearer. చెంచువాడు, బోయిన్ని.

పోర, పోరకాడు, పోరడు n. s. from پور *Pōr* (K.) A boy. Reeve page 962. పిల్లకాయ.

బోర or పోర n. s. A slip or piece of land appertaining to a field. The breast, or chest. దుండు నేల, రొమ్మున్ను.

పోరకాడి n. s. Puzzle, intricacy.

పోరడి n. s. A hedge?

పోరడు n. s. from پور *Pōr* (K.) A boy, a child. పిల్లగాడు.

పోరవ or పోరువ n. s. (from Tamil போர்வை) A cover. పైనకప్పేవస్త్రము.

బోరింపోతు n. s. A great jar: a glutton?

పోరిల్లు n. s. A gambling house? Paln. Vira. 22.

పోరుడు for పోర్ n. s. پور *Pōr* (K.) A boy. పిల్లగాడు.

పోరువ or పోర్వ n. s. (from Tamil போர்வை.) A cover. పైనకప్పేవస్త్రము.

బోర్గణము, బోర్గాణము for బొక్కణి n. s. A horse's nose bag.

బోళా adj. Unreserved, frank. కపటికాని, మనసులోదాచని. బోళామనిషి he who is not reserved.

పోలాద్ n. s. for فولاد *Fōlād.* Steel. ఉక్కుపోలాదిగంట a bell made of steel. ఉక్కుగంట. Ila. 1. 148.

పోవిడి most commonly పోవిడి n. s. (Tamil போக்கு.) Traces, signs. జాడ, ఆనవాలు.

భోషాణము n. s. A large chest. పెద్దపెట్టె.

పోస, పోచ, ప్రోచ n. s. A fibre, a bit. లేశము.

పోస్తుకాయ or పోస్తకాయ n. s. پوست *Pōst.* Capsules of the poppy used medicinally. (Madras "Tariff.") ఒకమందుదినుసు.

పౌంచాయించుట for పహుంచాయించుట v. a. from پهنچانا *Pahunchana.* To cause to arrive; to deliver.

ఫౌంజు for ఫౌజ్ n. s. فوج *Fauj.* Army, troops. దండు.

బౌగుణి, బౌగోణి or బోగిణి n. s. A sort of copper bowl. పాత్రవిశేషము.

ఫౌజు n. s. for فوج *Fauj.* Army, troops. దండు.

ఫౌజుబంది n. s. فوجبندي *Faujbandī.* Collecting or levying troops. దండుకూర్చడము.

బౌటా for బావటా n. s. باوٹا *Bāotā* A flag. ఝండా.

పౌర్ణిమి Error for పూర్ణిమ * n. s. The full moon.

ఫౌతు n. s. فوت *Faut.* Death. చావు. ఫౌతుఅయిన తర్వాత after his death. ఫౌతుఫరారి killed and missing, the dead and those who fled.

పోర్తులు a vulgar error for ప్రవర్తులు. ఎన్నిమాట్లు పోర్తులైనవి how many evacuations took place.

ప్యాకేజి n. s. The English word a "package;" మూటలుకట్టడము.

ప్యాదా n. s. for پیاده *Piyādah.* A peon or footman. బంట్రోతు.

బ్యామనుడు for బ్రాహ్మణుడు n. s. (برهمن *Birahman.*) A Bramin.

ప్రమోసము n. s. Error for మోసము which see.

బ్రమ్మత్తె Error for బ్రహ్మహత్య n. s. Bramin slaying. బ్రాహ్మణునిచంపడము.

ప్రయాయించుట n. s. A sea term for *making the shore.* వేరియప్రయాయించుట *veriya prayainçu* or వేరియచేయుట to tack about. Perhaps meant for *phirānā* to turn?

ప్రసాపడుట v. a. To eat. భోజనముచేసుట.

ప్రసాపాటు n. s. Food, eating. భోజనము.

ప్రస్తావన for ప్రస్తావము n. s. Incidental reference to a person or thing. ఒకరినిగురించిలేక ఒకటినిగురించినమాటయెత్తడము.

ప్రహరితిరుగుట v. n. To go the rounds, to patrol. గస్తువచ్చుట.

బ్రమ్మత, బ్రమ్మత్య error for బ్రహ్మహత్య n. s. Bramin slaying. బ్రాహ్మణునిచంపడము.

బ్రాంది n. s. (E) "Brandy." ఒకతరహాసారాయి.

ప్రాక్సంవత్సరము n. s. (This is an ignorant phrase in common use.) Last year. పోయినసంవత్సరము.

ప్రాథేయపడుట error for ప్రాధేయపడుట v. a To entreat. వేడుకొనుట.

బ్రాహ్మార్థం* n. s. (a vulgar phrase) Invitation to a dinner on the anniversary of a death. See నిమంత్రణము.

బ్రాహ్మణీకము* n. s. (vulgar phrase.) Braminship, the rank or state of a Bramin. బ్రాహ్మణత్వము.

ప్రోవ, పోవాలు n. s. Trick; imputation: gibing, quizzing?

మ.

మం॥ A contraction for మంజె meant for మవుజా موضع *Mauzā.* A hamlet.

మంజళ్, మంజళి, మంజెళు n. s. (Tamil. மஞ்சள்.) Turmeric: yellow as turmeric. పసుపు. మంజళ్ పట్టు yellow silk.

మంజూరు adj. منظور *Manzūr* Approved, ratified. అంగీకరించబడ్డ, రూఢిచేయబడ్డ. మంజూరుచేయుట to sanction or approve.

మంజూరు n. s. منظور *Manzūr* Approval. అంగీకారము. మంజూరుచేసుట to approve.

మంజె for మౌజా n. s. موضع *Mauzā.* A hamlet.

మండడీడు n. s. A groom? a horsekeeper. Pal. 50. గుర్రపువాడు.

మండాడుట v. a. (from Tamil மன்றாடு) To beg, to pray. బతిమాలుకొనుట. Pativr. 13.

మండి n. s. مندی *mandi.* A wholesale shop. భారీగాసరుకులుఅమ్మేచోటు.

మండిగలు n. s. A biscuit made of wheat. భక్ష్యవిశేషము.

మండువ n. s. مندوا *Mandwā* A booth. పందిలి, పాక, అనగానేంతతిరునాళ్లమొదలయ్యినవాటిలో అంగటివాండ్లువేసుకొనేటిది. H. 4. 104.

మంత్రాంగము* n. s. Agency, machination, trickery. మంత్రిత్వము, తంత్రము, కుహకము.

మందాసము or మందాసనము n. s. An ark, chest, box. Reeve page 1067.

మందుభాయి n. s. An opium eater. A phrase like "Tom pottle" or *Jack Tosspot.* నల్లమందుతినేవాడు.

మంసబ్దారు for మనసబ్దారు n. s. منصبدار *Mansubdār.* A ruler. A military officer of rank. దొర.

మకందిబ్బె or మకబిబ్బి n. s. (K.) A buffalo's horn filled with gunpowder and let off, as a firework. (Reeve 1068.) ఒకబాణవిద్య.

మకాం n. s. مقام *Muqām.* Place, lodging, station. బస, స్థలము. మకాముగానుండే situated.

మకుటము n. s. A sort of cloth, worn after purification, or worn by bramins when at meals. మడిగుడ్డ.

మకురుతనము n. s. Obstinacy, pertinacity, contumaciousness, stubbornness. మొండితనము. ఆబిడ్డనిండా మకురుతనముచేస్తున్నది the child is very stubborn.

మక్కికిమక్కి or దేశికిదేశి Rogue versus rogue; diamond cut diamond.

మక్కివన్నె n. s. Gamboge, bright yellow. హారిదళవర్ణము.

మక్తా for మక్తా Sometimes మఖ్తా مقطع *Maqtā.* Rent, tenure, farm, usually, a contract. గుత్త. మక్తాదారుడు a contractor. మక్తాసరుకులు contracted goods. Rate or standard. Rent. a fixed rate, proposal, estimate, or offer, a bid. Fixed money tax: like compounded taxes. మక్తాకాలు a special agreement given to a tenant. మక్తాపూరు a village which pays rent at a fixed rate without reference to the crop raised. మక్తాశిస్తు (in Guntoor) a particular settlement with each farmer by the Government or the Zemindar.

మక్దూరు n. s. مقدور *Maqdūr.* Power, ability, authority. అధికారము.

మఖఫి for మఖ్ఫీ مخفی *Makhfī.* Secret. రహస్యము, గుప్తము. మఖఫిగా for మఖ్ఫీగా secretly, clandestinely.

మఖము n. s. (Tamil மகமை) A donation by merchants or cultivators to a fane. A revenue granted as a privilege. రుసుము.

మఖమల్ n. s. مخمل *Makhmal.* Velvet. ఒకరకపుపట్టు.

మగరూరి for మగ్రూరు n. s. مغرور *Maghrūr.* Haughtiness, arrogance, pride. గర్వము.

మగ్గానివాడు n. s. A weaver. నేసేవాడు. మగ్గదరి for మగ్గవరి n. s. A tax on looms: (used in Masulipatam.)

మగ్దూరు for మక్దూర్ n. s. مقدور *Maqdūr.* Power, authority, ability. అధికారము, శక్తి.

మగ్మా or మకమ n. s. (Tamil) *makhamei* A donation by merchants or cultivators to a fane, a revenue by privilege. రుసుము. మగ్మాదారు he who enjoys a revenue by privilege. This word occurs in Persian documents granted by Tippoo and some other rulers.

మచిలీపన్ను, మచ్చిలీసం n. s. The tax formerly paid by fishermen, being a branch of the మోతర్ఫా *mōtarfa.* చెంబడిపన్ను.

మచిలీకూలు n. s. مچھلی *Machhli.* A fishery. (Raj. and Ganjam dialect.) చేపలవర్తకము.

మచ్చుడ n s. Love-powders, poison, drugs?

మచ్చిపింజె n. s. A dovetail, in carpentry. కుసి.

మచ్చిలీసం n. s. The tax paid by fishermen. (Vizag.) చెంబడిపన్ను.

మజకూరు for మజ్కూరు adj. مذکور *Mazkūr.* Abovesaid, aforesaid. సదరహూ. See—జా—.

మజర for మజరా n. s. for مزرع *Mazrā.* A hamlet, a cluster of huts belonging to some village, but separate from it, for the facilitation of agricultural purposes. ఒకపెద్దగ్రామములోచేరినచిన్నపల్లె.

మజిలీ n. s. منزل *Manzil.* One stage: a halt. A day's journey. మజిలీచేయుట to halt, stop for the night. ఒకదినంప్రయాణము.

మజుందారుడు for మజుముదార్ n. s. مجموعدار *Majmu dār.* A head accountant in the Talook cutcherry. తాలూకుశిరస్తేదారుడు.

మజుకూరు مذکور *Mazkūr.* 'Aforesaid' abovementioned. Vulgarly this means the said village. *Here, There.* It is even applied thus, మజుకూరికాపురస్థులు the inhabitants of this village. మాహేమజుకూరు the present month. రోజుమజుకూరు this day. మజుకూరిలో. Here in this town.

మజుకూరు or మజుకూరి n. s. (error) A village peon or bailiff?

మజుబూతు adj. مضبوط *Mazbūt.* Strong, valid. గట్టిగావుండే.

మజుమూను n. s. مضمون *Mazmūn.* Purport, contents, substance. మతలబు, సంగతి.

మజూరి n. s. for مزدوری *Mazdūrī.* Hire, the wages of a day labourer. కూలి.

మజూరు for మజ్దూర్ n. s. مزدور *Mazdūr.* A workman, a labourer. కూలివాడు.

మట్ట adj. Moderate, inferior. జబ్బైన. మట్టబియ్యము rice of a poor sort. మట్టయిల్లు a mean or small house.

మట్టపలక n. s. A flat ruler, a bricklayer's level. కొల్లత్తువాడు, అనగా తాపీపనివాడు గోడకట్టడము నకై పెట్టుకొనియుండేటిది. మూలమట్టపలక a carpenter's ruler.

మట్టము n. s. A pony. మట్టగుఱ్ఱము. జంబురుమట్టము A sort of cloth.

మట్లగడ్డ n. s. Name of a certain snake. ఒకపాము.

మఠంకూర్చుకొనుట for మఠకవేసుకొనికూర్చుండుట v. n. To squat like tailors, or as the images of Buddh are seated. పద్మాసనమువేసుకొనికూర్చుండుట.

మడయ adj. (Tamil மடைய) Dull, inelegant. మడ్డి, కొంట.

మడయుడు n. s. (from Tamil மடையன்) A stupid fellow, an idiot. మడ్డివాడు.

మడిచారు n. s. (Tamil.) అనగా వైష్ణవస్త్రీలుకట్టే కోకలో వెనకటికచ్చ.

మడియతనము or మడయతనము n. s. (Tamil மடையத்தனம்) Dullness, inelegance, rudeness. మడ్డితనము.

మడిరూపనోల్లు n. s. error for మడ్డియవుసోల్లు, or బోల్లు? See Rox. 1. 143, 244.

మడుపు adj. Appointed, select, ready. మడుపుభూమి land assigned to a man?

మణాగాపసలక or మణియాకపలక n. s. (Tamil மணியாசப்பலகை) A wooden tool for polishing a chunam wall. గోడకుగచ్చుచదరచేసేపలక.

మతిగ or మథిగ n. s. A wholesale shop. మండి.

మతలబు for మత్లబ్ n. s. مطلب *Matlab.* Purport, meaning. Topic, subject. తాత్పర్యము, సంగతి.

మతాబు or మత్తాబు for మహతాబ్ n. s. مهتاب *Mahtāb.* Blue-light in fireworks. A white flame: the kind of firework called Roman candles, which give a brilliant white flame. పగులువత్తి.

మతించుట v. a. To esteem, respect, regard. To estimate, appraise. గౌరవించుట, ఉజ్జాయించుట.

మతింపు n. s. Valuation, rating. ఉజ్జాయింపు.

మదద్గారు usually మద్దద్గారు n. s. مددگار *Madadgār* An assistant. సహాయుడు.

మదాం n. s. (The French word *Madame.*) The Queen at cards. కుయుసు.

మదారీసు, మదాలీసు n. s. probably an error for مجلس *Majlis*, or مجالس *Majālis*. A concert of music?

మదాళించుట v. n. (from Tamil மதாளித்திருக்க.) To luxuriate, grow rank as plants. To flourish, bloom. మదాళించినచెట్లు Rank weeds.

మదింపు n. s. Rate, valuation, appraising, supposal, estimate. ఉజ్జాయింపు.

మదిప్పు n. s. (Tamil மதிப்பு.) An estimate. మతింపు, ఉజ్జాయింపు.

మదుగు n. s. (Tamil மதகு.) A sluice. తూము.

మదుపువన్నె n. s. Dark emerald green. ఒకవర్ణము.

మదుము n. s. (Tamil மதகு) A sluice or flood gate. తూము.

మదుర n. s. A vulgar error for మజరా or మత్రా which see.

మద్దతు n. s. مدد *Madad.* Help, aid, assistance. సహాయము.

మద్దతుగారు or మద్దదుగారు n. s. مددگار *Madadgār.* An assistant. సహాయి.

మద్దు n. s. مد *mudd.* An item, head or column, in an account. The Persian word *Madd* denotes a horizontal line, placed at the commencement of a paragraph, and sometimes running quite across the page. ఒకతొడ్డు, ఒకకత్తెము.

మధ్యాన్నం n. s. A mistake for మధ్యాహ్నం Noon. రెండుఝాములవేళ.

మనమి n. s. vulgar for మనవి or మనివి.

మనవర్తి, మనువర్తి or మనోవర్తి n. s. Stipend, pension, allowance. యింటికొలవు.

మనసుబి for మన్సూబ్ adj. منسوب *Mansūb.* Related, belonging to. సంబంధించిన, చేరిన.

మనాయించుట v. a. (If from مانا *Mānnā.*) To mind, or obey; (and if from منع کرنا *Manā karna*) To forbid. వినుట, లక్ష్యపెట్టుట, అతిగి నడుచుకొనుట.

మనేల Most commonly మనీలా n. s. A sort of oranges; "*Manilla*" fruit. మనేలవాండ్లు Pedlars who deal in jewels and gems (because originally from *Manilla*.) మనీలపాము or మన్నిలపాము The Manilla snake, which is harmless, thick and lumpish in shape. Russell, plate. XVI.

మన్సానుబేదారు or మనస్సుబేదారుడు Perhaps an error for منصبدار *Mansabdār*. n. s. A chieftain. సరదారు, నాయకుడు, వెంకటగిరివారి హస్తియాలాగంటిసమస్తానికుడు.

మన్నా for మనా n. s. منع *Manā*. Prohibition, hindrance, prevention. అభ్యంతరము, అడ్డి.

మన్మానిగా adv. Selfwilledly, wilfully. స్వేచ్ఛగా, యథేచ్ఛగా.

మబ్బేము, మభ్యం for ముబ్హేం adj. for مبهم *Mubham*. Doubtful. సందిగ్ధమైన.

మభ్యపెట్టుట v. a. To delude, slur over. మబ్బుతాళము వేసుట, ఉపాయముగా దాటవేసుట.

మయక్కము, మయికము or మైకము n. s. Confusion or distraction of mind. Intoxication. మత్తు, భ్రమ.

మయానా n. s. میانہ *Miyānā*. The title of the old Nabobs of Kadapa.

మయూరు n. s. (French, *majeure*.) Major in the army. Ranga Rao. 1. 157. సమరోజ్జ్వలధిత శౌర్యధుర్యులగు సర్జంతుల్ మయూరుల్ కుమందములు కాకీరులు సోలుదారులు.

మయ్యం n. s. (Tamil மையம்) The middle. మధ్యము.

మర n. s. A screw. మలుచుట్టు.

మరకాల్ n. s. (Tamil மரக்கால்) A mercall: eight puddies or measures. తూము.

మరచుట్టు n. s. A turnscrew. తిరుగాణి.

మరడివ్యాధి n. s. The cholera morbus. వాంతి భ్రాంతి. (Rajamahendri.)

మరకు n. s. A quantity of land: an acre. కుచ్చెల, కత్తివతకొంతలెక్క భూమి.

మరత్తబు for మురత్తబ్ adj. مرتب *Murattab*. Closed, as a settled account. పరిష్కారమైన, తీరిన(ఇదిలెక్కనుగురించినమాట.)

మరమేకు n. s. A screw. ఇస్క్రూలాణి.

మరమ్మతు n. s. مرمت *Marammat*. Repair, mending. బాగుచేయడము.

మరవ n. s. (Tamil மரவை) A wooden bowl, a pot or cup. ముంత.

మరవలి n. s. A final entertainment given by the bride's parents to the bridegroom, after the conclusion of the whole marriage ceremonies. మనుగుడుపు.

మరహమ్మతు for మరమ్మత్ more correctly మరమ్మతు n. s. مرمت *Marammat*. Repairs. చక్కబెట్టడము.

మరహూం adj. مرحوم *Marhūm*. Deceased, late, dead, as نواب مرحوم *Nawabi marhūm* the late Nabob. చనిపోయిన.

మరాటి or మహారాటి adj. *Marātī*. i. e. Mahratta. మహారాష్ట్రసంబంధమైన.

మరాటితీగ n. s. A certain aphrodisiac drug, called Spilanthus Amella. Rox. 3. 410.

మరిడి n. s. Name of the goddess of cholera. మరిడిసంకటము cholera.

మరియాకానుఆట n. s. 'Maria's game.' Playing at cards. A word perhaps of Portugueze origin.

మరూడి n. s. مروڑی *Marōri*. (H.) A turnscrew?

మర్కారి n. s. A head boatman. పడవవాండ్ల మేస్త్రీ.

మర్ఖూము adj. مرقوم *Marqūm*. Written. వ్రాయబడ్డ.

మర్జి n. s. مرضی *Marzī*. Pleasure, determination, will. Temper, disposition. తాత్పర్యము.

మర్తబాను n. s. مرتبان *Martabān*. A black Pegu jar; so called because imported from Martaban. నల్లజాడి.

మర్తబు adj. for مرتب *Murattāb*. Closed, as a settled account, concluded, finished, settled. తీరిన, పరిష్కారమైన. మర్తబుచేయుట to close. పరిష్కారముచేసుట.

మలచటి adj. (error for మరసటి) Next. మలచటినాడు next day.

మలచము adj. Cheap, fine. నయమైన.

మలపత్ or మల్వతీ n. s. Extra assessment; an increased demand or additional exaction. (Vizag. and Bellary dialect.)

ములాము or మొలాము n. s. ملمع *Mulammā*. Plating, silvering. బంగారుమొలాము gilding.

ములి adj. Next. ములినాడు next day. తొలిధర the original price, ములిధర the second or higher price?

ముళిగ n. s. (Tamil மளிகை) A warehouse or shop of grocery, excluding cloth &c. మండి.

ముల్ఫాపుచేయుట v. a. from ملفوف کرنا *Malfūf karna*. To enclose (a letter in a cover) అందులో ముల్ఫాపుఅయినజాబులు The letters enclosed therein.

ముల్లగొల్లాటము or ముల్లగొల్లాలము n. s. Squabble, rumpus. రచ్చ, జగడము.

ముల్లగుల్లాలుపడుట or ముల్లగుల్లాలాడుట v. n. To wrangle, squabble. జగడమాడుట.

మువంజ n. s. Vulgar for మౌజ موضع *Mouzā*. A hamlet.

మువకూఫు most commonly మొకూబు. adj. for موقوف *Mouqūf*. Stopped, suspended. నిలుపుదలచేయబడ్డ.

మువాసిగిరి for మువాషీగిరి مواشی گیری *Mawāshī girī*. Rebellion, plunder of the country, outrage. మువాసిగిరీచేయడానకు అక్కడికివెళ్లి. Local. XIX. 40, line 1.

మువుంజె for మౌజే n. s. موضع *Mouzā*. A hamlet, a dependancy of a village. ఒకవూరితోచేరినచిన్నపల్లె.

మువుకూఫు usually మొకూబు n. s. موقوف *Mouqūf*. Ceasing, termination. మానుకోవడము. లడాయిమువుకూఫుచేసిరి they stopped fighting.

ముశాత్తు n. s. See ముషాత్.

ముశ్రూగుడ్డ for ముష్రూగుడ్డ n. s. مشروع *Mashrū*. Satin: literally 'Legal,' according to the Sharah or law: cloth woven of cotton mixed with silk is *Mashrush* or legal. Hence, a name of satin.

ముశ్రూత్ adj. مشروط *Mashrūt*. Conditional, exacted. ఒడంబడికెగల.

ముషరు n. s. مشروع *Mashrū*. Satin. పట్టువస్త్రము.

ముషాకత్తు for ముషాత్ n. s. for مساحت *Masāhat*. Square measurement; mensuration. కొలవడము.

ముషాఖత్తు n. s. for مشقت *Mashiqat*. Pains taking; labour, toil. వ్యవసాయాదులయందు పడేపాటు, శ్రమ. Improvement of land. The repairing of fields or water courses (Ganjam.) Manuring (Vizag.) Hire, cooly, as వడ్లముషాఖత్తు carpenter's hire.

ముషాతు for ముషాత్ n. s. for مساحت *Masāhat*. Measurement of land; the same as పైమాయిష్ (*Paimayish*.) Survey. నేలకొలవడము.

ముషాలు n. s. مشعل *Mashal*. A torch or flambeau. దివిటి.

ముషాల్చి most commonly ముసాల్జి n. s. مشعلچی *Mashalchī*. A torchbearer, a lamplighter. దివిటివాడు, దీపాలుపెట్టేవాడు.

ముసబుజమీను n. s. Mixed soil, not so productive as the black soil but superior to the common red land. Red soil: light, not solid. See ముసవ్వభూమి or దుమ్ములురేగేభూమి.

ముసలతు for ముసలహత్ n. s. مصلحت *Maslaht*. Counsel, advice. ఆలోచన, బుద్ధి.

ముసవిదా most commonly ముసోదా for مسوده *Musawadā*. A rough draft or copy. ముతలబుకు దిద్దిచిత్తుగావ్రాసినది.

ముసానీలు, ముసాని n. s. مسان *Masān*. The rattlins of a ship's shrouds. గోడాలు?

ముసాల n. s. مصالح *Masālah*. Spicery, seasoning drugs. Horse physick సంభారము, గుర్రానికిచ్చేమందున్ను.

ముసాలిజి n. s. for مشعلچی *Mashalchī*. A lamplighter. A torchbearer. దీపాలుపెట్టేవాడు, దివిటీవాడు.

ముసి n. s. Ink made with lampblack. శాయి.

ముసీదు, ముశీది for ముసీద్ n. s. An error for مسجد *Masjid*. A mosque or Musulman place of worship.

ముసుబుభూమి n. s. See ముసబుజమీను.

ముసూదా for ముసోదా n. s. for مسوده *Musawadah*. A rough draft. చిత్తుగావ్రాసినది.

ముసూరు for ముష్రూ n. s. مشروع *Mashrū*. A Satin vest పట్టువస్త్రము.

ముస్తకి n. s. مصطکی *Mastaki*. రూమిముస్తకి Gum Mastic. ఒకమందుదినుసు.

మస్తు n. s. Pride, presumption, arrogance. గర్వము. కొవ్వు. మస్తుపట్టిన headstrong, ungovernable.

మస్తు adj. Abundant, plentiful. అధికము. మస్తుగా abundantly, plentifully, profusely.

మస్విదా for మసోదా n. s. مسوده *Musawadah.* A rough draft of a letter.

మహంతు n. s. A title assumed by some teachers (gurus) or Confessors. మఠాధిపతిగావుండేబయిరాగి.

మహాజను for మహాజన్ n. s. مهاجن *Mahajan.* A Mayor or head merchant, a substantial banker. సాహుకారు.

మహజ్జరునామా or మహజరునామా n. s. for محضرنامه *Mahzar namah.* A general affidavit; a certificate signed by all present at a transaction. A general petition signed by a town. A title deed. A written award or decision.

మహాద్వారము n. s. The mouth of a river. నదీప్రవేశమహాముఖము. (A bad phrase though common.)

మహారాజులాగు adv. Of course, by all means.

మహార్నవమి n. s. error for మహానవమి which see.

మహాలు or మాలు n. s. محل *Măhal.* A district in a province, a ward in a town. A spot of land. A fund producing revenue to government. (Malcolm: Index.) మహాలుదారుడు a small laird or landlord.

మహాలారుజా for మాల్ వజా n. s. مال وجه *Mālwajah.* Goods on hand or "in view." Crop, harvest. Revenue, income, rent, estate. వాజరులోవుండేసరుకు, పంట, వచ్చుబడి.

మహసూలు n. s. محصول *Mahsūl.* Produce, crop; product of a field, grain.

మహసూలుదార్లు n. s. محصولدار *Mahsuldār.* Watchmen set over crops. కంగాణముగావుండేవాండ్లు, ఒప్పిడిచేయించేవాండ్లు.

మహాగణులు n. s. A title assumed by jangam Gurus.

మహాజరు n. s. See మహజ్జరు.

మహాదేవి n. s. (a term used in Ganjam.) Lady, baroness. దొరసానిగారు.

మహాదేవులు n. s. plu. Lords, courtiers. దొరలు.

మహానాడు n. s. (Tamil மகாநாடு) A witenagemote, or council held by headmen.

మహారాజులాగు adv. Of course, by all means.

మహారాష్ట్రము n. s. Mahratta. A name given without any proper authority to the *Marati* language.

మహారోగము or మహావ్యాధి n. s. A sort of leprosy. Buch. Ham. (E. I.) 3. 485.

మహితాబు most commonly మతాబు n. s. مهتاب *Mahtah.* A sort of firework called Roman candles. పుష్పవత్తి.

మహ్లా n. s. See మహాలు.

మా

మా॥ A contraction for మారీఫత్.

మాందాళిగాయి or మాందాళిపచ్చ n. s. A dark green emerald. పచ్చ.

మాంలతుదారు usually మాములీతుదారుడు n. s. معاملتدار *Moamalah.dār.* The Tahsildar or managing native officer of a district.

మాగడి n. s. Supineness, careless neglect, disregard of duty. అశ్రద్ధ, అజాగ్రత. మాగడికాలము a sickly season. యీవూరిలో మహామాగడిగా వున్నది this village is unhealthy.

మాగాణి n. s. Wet cultivation, i. e. rice, which cannot be cultivated without the fields being flooded. నీరారంభము. మాగాణిపొలము land artificially irrigated.

మాచికాయ n. s. Gall nut.

మాచెనపక్షి n. s. A sort of carp fish. ఒకచేప.

మాజా, మాజుఫలము for మాజూ n. s. مازو *Māzū.* Gall nut. మాచికాయ.

మాజీ adj. ماضى *Māzī.* Former, late, last, past, gone by, cancelled. మునుపటి, మునుపటి, గడిచిన, కొట్టివేయబడ్డ. మాజీచేయుట to cancel.

మాజు, మాజుం n. s. for معجوم *Mājūm* or معجون *Mājūn.* An inebriating preparation of Bhang with sugar, spices &c. formed into cakes and eaten. బంగాకుబెల్లము మొదలయినవి వేసిచేసిన ద్రవ్యము.

మాజూ n. s. See మాజుఫలం.

మాజూలు adj. معزول *Māzūl.* Dismissed, turned out. తోసివేయబడ్డ.

మాటి n. s. ماٹی *Māti, more properly* مٹی *Mitti.* Mud, clay. మట్టి which see.

మాటిపోగులు for మట్టిపోగులు n. s. plu. Refuse heaps of grain, so named because mingled with bits of earth and stone.

మారు n. s. مارو *Maru.* A pair of antelope horns joined at the roots, resembling a dagger?

మాతాది or మొహతాదు usually మహతాదు or మహతాదుబంట్రోతు n. s. مهتاوي A village bailiff or petty collecting officer.

మాతాబు n. s. for مهتاب *Mahtab.* Roman candles, blue lights, silver cloth: of which some caps are made మతాబు, జరిబట్టయున్ను.

మాతుబరు adj. معتبر *Motabār.* Trustworthy, substantial, honest, respectable. నమ్మదగిన. మాతుబరుజామీను Good security. నేను ప్రస్తుతం మాతుబరు కాకపోయినాను I am no longer in good circumstances.

మాత్బరి n. s. معتبري *Motabari.* Goodness of bail. Responsibility or *Respectability.* Good circumstances as those of a substantial farmer. నమ్మకము.

మాద n. s. A disease. ఒకరోగము.

మాదా n. s. The Portugueze word "Madre." The Roman catholic chapels are called మాదా కోవిల్, మాదాగుడి i. e. Chapel to St. Mary.

మాదిరి n. s. مادري *Madri.* A pattern, model, or example, sort, kind. The original; as opposed to a copy. A large beam of timber. మచ్చు, తరహా, చదరముగా వుండే పెద్ద శేకుమాను.

మాధవకరము, మాధోకరము, మాధుకరము or మాధవళబళ్లము n. s. Begging boiled rice; the rice so given. అన్నపుతిరిపెము, బిచ్చగాడికి వేసేఅన్నము.

మానమాత్ర n. s. Period, time, occupied by a reign. అయ్యాం, హయాం, ప్రభుత్వముచేసిన కాలము.

మాని معني *Mani.* Meaning, import. A secret. అర్థము, అభిప్రాయము.

మానేజరు n. s. (E) A "manager." నిర్వాహకుడు, వుదిమందికి పెద్దగా వుండేవాడు.

మాళు n. s. A husband?

మాఫల్ కాయ n. s. from ماپهل *Māphal.* The gall-nut used in ink and used to dye the teeth black. మాచికాయ.

మాఫిణి for మాపణి n. s. ماپني *Mapnī.* Measurement. కొలవడము.

మాఫీరవానా n. s. معافيروانا *Muāfirawana.* A certificate of tax being paid. A pass given for goods on which no duty is payable at the place from whence they came. A permit allowing goods to pass free. A certificate of payment.

మాఫు n. s. معاف *Muaf.* Pardon, excusing. మన్నింపు, క్షమింపు.

మాఫుచేయుట v. a. from معاف *Muāf.* To forgive or excuse. మన్నించుట, క్షమించుట.

మామిలియ్యతు n. s. معاملت *Muāmalāt.* Management of public business. Affairs of state. నిర్వాహకము.

మామూదుచేసుకొనుట or మామూర్ చేసుకొనుట v. a. To take possession of. స్వాధీనముచేసుకొనుట యనితోచినది.

మామూలు n. s. معمول *Māmūl.* Use, usage, custom. Fashion, mode, practice. వాడుక.

మాయామాతి n. s. మాయామాతిమనస్సుకుతెచ్చుకొనిసై కోమాటకుఅర్థముతోచలేదు.

మాయి n. s. Slate colour; whitish blue, or dark grey?

మారకమ్మ n. s. Name of a certain fury. ఒకక్షుద్రదేవత.

మారాటము n. s. (Tamil மாராட்டம்) Trickery, guile, fraud. మోసము.

మారిడి n. s. Confusion?

మారిఫత్తు n. s. معرفت *Mārifat.* Trust, charge, possession. వశము. ఒకనిమారిఫత్తులోయిచ్చుట to entrust or commit to one.

మారు for మార్ n. s. مار *Mār.* A blow. దెబ్బ. మారుమారు At him! smite him! Beat him! Ila. 3. 195.

మారేడుగడ్డ n. s. A bulbous root resembling a truffle. It has little or no appearance above the surface of the ground. బల్లిగడ్డ?

మాల్ n. s. مال *Mal*. Property, goods. సొత్తు. మాలుజామీను money security, real security; a jewel &c. put in deposit. In Revenue, Māl (i. e. stuff) includes every thing connected with land, crops, and ploughing.

మాలకు for మాలిక్ n. s. مالک *Malik*. Owner, master, proprietor. స్వంతగాడు.

మాలీయాసువరలు n. s. A certain class of savages.

మాలి n. s. مالی *Malī*. A gardener. తోటవాడు.

మాలి (error for మాటు) n. s. One time. ఒకమాలి once, one time.

మాలి n. s. مالي *Mali*. The same as ముల్కి i. e. Revenue; thus మాలిపేష్కారు the assessment accountant.

మాలిక్కు n. s. مالك *Malik*. A heir, owner, proprietor. స్వంతగాడు.

మాలిగ n. s. (Tamil மாளிகை) A house, a building. ఇల్లు. నేలమాలిగ a cellar. తిరుమాలిగ (a cant phrase, among the Vaishnavas) a house.

మాలిష్ مالش *Malish*. most commonly మాలీసు n. s. Rubbing down a horse. Thrashing or treading out of corn. గుర్రమునుతోముట, కయిలుచేయించుట. మాలీసుచేసుట to curry, dress or clean a horse.

మాలిస్తా See మాలిష్.

మాలిస్తిదారుడు n. s. Superintendent of thrashing the crop. కయిలుచేయించేఅధికారి, నూర్పించేవాడు.

మాలీస్తు for మాలీసు n. s. مالش *Malish*. Thrashing corn. నూర్పడము.

మాలు n. s. مال *Māl*. Property, goods. సొత్తు. See మాల్.

మాలు for మహాలు n. s. محل *Mahal*. A palace. A division of a district containing ten or twelve villages. నగరు, తాలూకాయున్ను. Vema. 1205, 1546, 1725.

మాలుకరణము n. s. A revenue clerk. కరణంవాడు.

మాలుగుజారి n. s. مالگذاري *Mālguzārī*. Land liable to pay rent or revenue. దివాణానకుకిస్తు చెల్లించేనేల. See Reg. 3. of 1802. Such land as is not *Lakhirāj*.

మాలుశిబ్బంది n. s. probably an error for محلسیبندی *Mahal sibandī*. The revenue establishment of peons, శివిబ్బంది్గ్రోణులు.

మాలూము adj. معلوم *Mālūm*. Known. అతనికిమాలూముచేసినతర్వాత after this was made known to him.

మాలేరు n. s. A certain tree ?

మాలోరుజా for మాల్వజా n. s. مال وجه *Mal wajah*. Property, goods. సొత్తు.

మావడమరవడ n. s. (Tamil மாவிடைமரவிடை) Beasts and trees. గొడ్లుగోడలుచెట్టుచేమలు. Rottler. IV. 51.

మావలి for మాలి n. s. A gardener.

మావు n. s. (Tamil மா) One twentieth. ఇరువైయింటిలోనొకభాగము.

మాష్టి n. s. A certain tribe of beggars among pariars. ఒకతరహామాలవిచ్చగాడు.

మాష్టీడు or ముస్తీడు n. s. A teacher ? q. v. An elephant driver. ఏనుగవాడు.

మాసం for మౌసీం n. s. موسم *Mausim*. The season. ఋతువు.

మాసం or మాసా n. s. (from Sanscrit మాషము.) A jeweller's weight of eight goonju (seeds of the Abrus precatorious) ఎనిమిదిగురిగింజలయెత్తు.

మాసురా or మాసల n. s. A specimen or muster. మాదిరి ?

మాసి for మనిషి n. s. A man: this is a boorish pronunciation like *mon* or *mun*, in Scotch.

మాసూలు for మహాసూల్ n. s. محصول *Mahsūl*. That which is collected. Income, product. Produce, crop, collections. పంట, ఫలము.

మాహా n. s. A month. నెల. మాహాహజుకూరు In the present month.

మాహావారి adj. Monthly, that happens every month. నెలనెలకువచ్చే.

మింగిమిరము, మింగిమిర్యము n. s. A certain herb (పొంగా A tree; pentaptera arjuna.) నింగిమిర్యము, క్రుకార్య. Q ?

మింజుమల adv. منجمله *Minjumla*. In part payment: *out of this sum*. అందులో. ఆమింజుమలా, అందుమింజుమలే out of that sum or number.

మిజాజు for మిజాజ్ n. s. مزاج *Mizaj*. Pride. గర్వము.

మిజాజు n. s. for مزاج *Mizaj.* Temper, humour. Health; tastiness, elegance. గుణము.

మిర్జా n. s. مرزا *Mirzā.* A title among Mahomedans. తురకలలో ఒకజాతి.

మిటికీలు n. s. Some sort of grain. ధాన్యవిశేషము.

మిటుకులాడి n. s. A pretty girl, a belle. సొగసుకత్తె.

మిట్టవరహా n. s. A pagoda, or gold coin worth four rupees. ఒకనాణెము.

మిఠాయి n. s. مٹھائی *Mithai.* Any sweetmeat. పిండివంట.

మిడిమిల్లాడుతున్నది (A phrase having the meaning) It is excessively hot.

మిడిముల్లు n. s. Spurs. గుర్రంకడుపులోపొడవడమునకైకాళ్లకుకట్టుకొనేముల్లు.

మినహా n. s. منہا *Minha.* Subtraction, deduction. తోసివేయడము, భాగారించడము.

మినహాచేసుట v. a. from منہا *Minha.* To subtract, deduct. భాగారించుట, తోసివేయుట.

మిన్నా for మిహీన్ adj. مہین *Mihīn.* Fine, delicate, or elegant. దివ్యమైన, సొగసైన.

మిరాశీ or మిరాసి n. s. میراثی *Mirasī.* میراث *Miras.* Hereditary right, hereditary property. తరంతరగావుండేబాధ్యత, తరంతరగాఅనుభవములోవుండేసొత్తు. కాపులకుకలమిరాశీ the right of the inhabitants. మిరాశీదారుడు one who possesses such a privilege.

మిలమిలలాడుట v. n. To abound, swarm, be rife. నీళ్లలోచేపలు మిలమిలలాడుతున్నవి the fishes tumble over one another. ఆకలిచేతమిలమిలలాడుతున్నారు they are exhausted with hunger.

మిళాయించుట v. a. from ملانا *Milana.* To mingle: to introduce. కలుపుట.

మిసల్ n. s. (probably meant for مثل *Misl.* Turn, time, occasion.) A visit of ceremony or friendship. దర్శనము. తాశీలుదారుడునన్నుమిసలుకుపంపినాడు the Tasildar sent me to pay the collector a visit. Post, department, station. "Seat, place, chair. The Seiks were divided into twelve *missuls* or tribes: each under its own headman. అతడుమిసల్ తాకమునుపే before he was employed (in that duty.)

మిసల్ కరణము n. s. *Misl carnam.* The curnum who is in power: his name being on the commission or List. Hence he is also called లిస్టుకరణం.

మిసలురెడ్డి n. s. The Reddi or farmer who is in the commission, or in power. దివానమునకున్నమూడుగావుండేరెడ్డి.

మిహానతు usually మెహనత్తు n. s. محنت *Mehnat.* Trouble, pains. కష్టము, ప్రయాస.

మీరజా or మీర్జా n. s. مرزا *Mirza.* A *Mīrza.* (A certain title) prince. ఒకకితాబు, యువరాజు.

మీరాసి n. s. میراثی *Mīrasī.* See మిరాశీ.

మీరుబక్షీ n. s. میربخشی *Mīrbakhshī.* A commandant of troops, a General. సేనాధిపతి.

ము

ముంగాచీర n. s. A kind of silk worn by Hindu women. ఒకరకపుపట్టుచీర.

ముంగిముశౌతనము n. s. Stubbornness, stupidity. మొసరుమూతితనము.

ముందిరివిత్తులు n. s. Cashew nuts. ముంతమామిడివిత్తులు. ముందిరిపప్పు the kernel of cashew nuts.

మున్షీ usually మునిషి n. s. منشی *Munshī.* A tutor, clerk, secretary. Reader. చదువుచెప్పేవాడు, వ్రాయసగాడున్ను. Blackstone, 3. [320] says, quoting Sir John Davis "he understood the law language in ten days almost perfectly without a *reader*."

ముకద్దం n. s. مقدم *Muqaddam.* The headman of a village same as (*qadīm*) kadeem. Presupposition, supposal. ప్రామాణికారి, అనుకోవడమున్ను. Thus ముకద్దంచేశీ Taking it for granted. On the ground that. పోయినారనిముకద్దంచేశీవ్రాశీనాను Imagining they had gone, I wrote to him.

ముకద్దమా n. s. مقدمہ *Muqaddama.* Affair, business. వ్యవహారము, పని.

ముకర్రరు usually మొకరరు adj. مقرر *Muqarrar,* Fixed, established. స్థిరపరచబడ్డ.

ముకర్రరు or మొకరరు n. s. مقرر *Muqarrar.* Determination, certainty. నిష్కర్ష. మొకర్రరుచేయుట to determine.

ముకాబిలా n. s. مقابله *Muqabala.* Confronting. Comparison of a copy with the original. సరిచూడడము, సంప్రతించడము.

ముకాసా or మొఖాసా adj. Granted. మొకాసా గ్రామము A *mocasa* village is one that is granted either free (as a reward) or on a light rent. It is a spurious phrase fabricated by the Hindu clerks, by some corruption of an Arabic word. జీవనానికియిచ్చినగ్రామము.

ముకాహిరా n. s. Guardianship. సంరక్షణ.

ముకూతకోరు (perhaps for ముక్కుపాలు) n. s. A lease granted generally by Enamdars: in which the farmer employed, has three-fourths, and the landlord one-fourth of the crop.

ముక్కిడి or ముక్కిడిపిట్ట n. s. A snipe. See ఉల్లి.

ముక్కిడిచేప n. s. A certain fish.

ముక్కుకోపము or ముక్కోపము for ముంగోపము n. s. Sudden passion. ఆలోచనలేకుండావచ్చేకోపము.

ముక్కుటము n. s. Caudle, food for infants గంజియు. లుసాంబ్రాయినసాలాకలిపిబిడ్డలకుపోసేటిది.

ముక్తసరు adj. مختصر *Mukhtasar.* Abbreviated, abridged, brief, short, succinct. సంగ్రహమైన.

ముక్తాయించుట v. n. To close, To quaver in music. సంగీతములో ముగియుట.

ముక్తాయింపు n. s. A close, conclusion, in music. ముగించడము.

ముక్తార్థము n. s. Import, summary, purport. ఫలితార్థము.

ముఖాబిలా or మొకాబిలా n. s. مقابله *Muqabalah.* Comparison, collation. సంప్రతించడము.

ముఖీం n. s. مقيم *Muqīm.* A resident. ఉండేవాడు, కాపురముండేవాడు. (A valuer of cloths. (తరగరి) an appraiser.)

ముకెల్వ n. s. A snipe?

ముఖ్తారు for ముఖ్తియారు usually ముక్త్యారు n. s. مختار *Mukhtar.* He who is free: his own master. Plenipotentiary. స్వతంత్రుడు.

ముఖ్మల్ or మొకమల్ n. s. مخمل *Mukhmal.* Velvet. మెత్తగాదళముగానుండేవొకతరహాబట్ట. H. 1. 73.

ముగర n. s. A lot of, the number of. ఆరుముగర నుఅష్టము a lot of 6 is half a dozen?

ముగల్, మొఘల్ n. s. مغل *Moghal.* A mogul or Musulman. తురకవాడు.

ముగులు n. s. The sheathing of a ship. వాడఅడుగునీళ్లలోనానిపురుగులుబట్టి చావకుండా ఉండడమునకైవేసేటిది.

ముగ్డ plu. ముగ్డలు n. s. Dumb-bells. లోడ్లు.

ముచిల్కా or ముచ్చిలికా for ముచల్గా n. s. مچلكا *Muchalga.* (Turkish) A penal bond or money security. An Indulto, (as called in Spanish) or indemnity. A bond or written agreement of any sort: an agreement of truce. ముచిల్కామీదవచ్చిచేరడము To come in *on muchilka* is, to come into camp on truce. ముచిల్కాయిచ్చిపోయినవాడు one who is out on his own recognizances.

ముచీలు or ముశీలు n. s. (Masulipatam) Leave, permission?

ముచ్చి n. s. A Moochey; a bookbinder: who makes pens. కచ్చేరిలోపుస్తకములుకట్టికలములుచెక్కియిచ్చేవాడు.

ముచ్చిలికా or ముచ్చెలికా n. s. for مچلكا *Muchalga.* A deed of settlement, a final agreement in writing. ఒకదస్తావేజు, సాధకము.

ముచ్చివాడు or ముచ్చెవాడు n. s. A painter: who makes toys and images of paper or pith.

ముజములీ adv. مجمل *Mujmal.* Briefly, in an abridged form. ముజుములిపట్టీ. Abstract, heads of accounts.

ముజుముదారుడు usually ముజాముదారుడు n. s. مجموعدار *Mujmuadar.* The head accountant in a Talook Cutcherry. తాలూకుశిరస్తేదారుడు.

ముజరదు adv. مجرد *Mujarrad.* Instantly. వెంటనే, తోడుతోనే.

ముజరా n. s. مجرا *Mujra.* Allowance, subtraction, reduction, remission. A bow or a salam. తోపుడు, తోశియిచ్చినది. ముజరాఖర్చు donations by government for religious purposes. ముజరా

చేసుట to make allowance: to make a salam. ముజరాయిచ్చుట to deduct, to subtract, to give a donation for religious purposes. నాకుముజరా రావలెను I am to be refunded, repayment is due, allowance must be made to me.

ముజాహిం adj. مزاحم *Muzahim*. Obstructing, hindering. అభ్యంతరముచేసే, అడ్డిచేసే, ఆటంకకరచే used mostly in notes and passports.

ముజిమిలిజుమా n. s. مجمل جمله *Mujmal jumla*. Grand total. వెరసి, మొత్తము.

ముజుముదారుడు n. s. مجموعه دار *Majmudār*. The head accountant in the Talook Cutcherry. తాలూకుశిరస్తేదారుడు. An auditor: a clerk who checks the accounts.

ముజుమూలుగా adv. from مجمل *Mujmal*. Completely. సంపూర్ణముగా.

ముటుమర్దాగి, ముట్మర్దాగి n. s. متمردگی *Mutmardagi*. Disobedience, stubbornness. అలక్ష్యము, తిరస్కారము.

ముటాలు n. s. plu Faggots. కట్టెలు.

ముట్టకోసుకూర n. s. Cauliflower.

ముట్టా or ముఠా n. s. مٹھا *Muttha*. A portion of a district, a subdivision. కొన్నిగ్రామములు.

ముట్టి n. s. Rogue, wretch, villain ?

ముఠా n. s. A sub-division: a party in politicks. కొన్నిగ్రామములు, జమాయిత్తు.

ముఠాఖు or ముట్టాఖు n. s. A fool; a simpleton. చేతకానివాడు.

ముడిజామ్వారు for ముడిజామూరు n. s. An entirely white cloth without any coloured border. తెల్లగుడ్డ.

ముతయ్యను, ముత్తైను adj. متعين *Mutaaiyin*. Posted, appointed, placed, entertained, fixed, deputed. నియమింపబడ్డ, పెట్టుకోబడ్డ.

ముతల్లకు, ముతలఖ్ adj. مطلق *Mutlaq*. Whole, entire. adv. Utterly, entirely. యావత్తు, బొత్తుగాఅన్ని.

ముతసద్దీ usually ముసద్దీ n. s. متصدي *Mutasaddi*. A clerk, accountant, writer or scribe. లెక్కవాడు, వ్రాసేవాడు.

ముతాబకు مطابق *Mutābaq*. Answering to, corresponding with (in dates.) సరియైన. See under యాసిది. This is the phrase used when two dates are mentioned, one English and one Indian, thus ౧౮౪౫ది సం॥ ముతాబకువిశ్వావసునామసంవత్సరములో In the year 1845 corresponding to Vishvavasu.

ముతాలికు adj. متعلق *Mutaalliq*. Appertaining to, pertaining. చేరిన.

ముదాం adj. مدام *Mudam*. Perpetual, eternal. Fixed, established. శాశ్వతమైన. ముదాంసిబ్బంది *Mudām sibbundi*. A fixed establishment. (village police men?)

ముదారుశింగు n. s. See మురుదారు.

ముద్దతు n. s. مدت *Muddat*. A period or time. ముద్దతునుంచియిట్లాగున్నది It has long been so.

ముద్దతుకౌలు n. s. مدت قول *Muddatqaul*. A conditional agreement. కరారునామా.

ముద్దతుక్రయము n. s. A foreclosed mortgage, in which the pawn after a certain time is forfeit. A conditional sale with penalty attached. అవధిక్రయము?

ముద్దతుండుగ n. s. A feast observed among salt makers, when beginning the year. ఒకపండుగ.

ముద్దాయీ n. s. مدعي *Muddai*. The defendant; the prisoner; the accused. ప్రతివాది, ఖయిది. ముద్దాయీపడుట to be liable, to be prosecuted.

ముద్ది, కరముద్ది n. s. A sort of fish. Russell plate 48. మత్స్యవిశేషము.

మునగానాంతేలానాంగా adv. In all sorts of difficulties. వానికినిమునగానాంతేలానాంగావున్నది he is in danger.

మునసబు or మునిసీపు n. s. منصف *Munsif*. A native judge. ఒకతరవరి. గ్రామమునసబు the village justice, the head farmer.

మునాది n. s. منادي *Munadī*. A proclamation. (Bellary) ప్రకటన.

మునాశబు for మునాసిబ్ adj. مناسب *Munasib*. Proper, fit, due. Suitable. తగిన.

మునిషీ n. s. منشي *Munshī* A writer, a secretary. A teacher or tutor in a language. రాయసగాడు, చదువుచెప్పేవాడు.

మునిసిఫి for మున్సిఫ్ usually మునిసీపు n. s. منصف *Munsif*. A native civil judge. మునిసీపు.

మునీం, మునీబు n. s. منيب *Munīb.* A principal or master, one who appoints a నాయబు or deputy. An agent or constituent; a mercantile correspondent, an executor. (From *Nāyib.*)

ముప్పంచీర n. s. A cotton cloth, which is white, with a red border, a cubit deep at the ends.

ముప్పావు n. s. Three quarters of a pagoda. మూడుపావులు.

ముప్పావులా n. s. Three quarters (of a rupee.)

ముప్పిరిచేప n. s. A certain fish or ముంగముప్పిరి? A species of sparus, or, Mesoprion quinquelineatus.

ముఫదరా for ముఫ్రద్ n. s. مفرد *Mufrad.* An abstract: a summary. సంగ్రహము.

ముఫస్సల్ adj. مفصل *Mufassil.* Distinct, full, ample, detailed. Clear, perspicuous, plain. స్పష్టమైన, విశదమైన, వివరమైన.

ముబలక adj. Abundant, copious, plentiful, numerous. విస్తారమైన, యథేష్టమైన.

ముబాదలా adj. مبادلا *Mubadala.* Changed, exchanged, altered. మార్చబడ్డ, బదలాయించబడ్డ.

ముబాదిల n. s. مبادلا *Mubadala.* A loan, an advance. Exchange or barter, sums lent and paid on running accounts without the use of receipts or documents on either side: being merely a temporary accommodation. ముందుగా యిచ్చినది, చెయిబదులుగా యిచ్చినది.

ముబాహము or **ముభావము** adj. مباح *Mubāhan.* Doubtful, indeterminate. Unknown. సందిగ్ధమైన. ముబాహంగా Indifferently. Briefly, in the gross, anonymously, without going into names or particulars. Cursorily, by guess.

ముబ్లక్కు usually ముబల్లగు n. s. مبلغ *Mublagh.* A mount, sum. మొత్తము.

మురబ్బీ n. s. مربي *Murabbi.* An usher, introducer, recommender. సిఫార్సు చేసేవాడు.

మురాదిజల్లి n. s. مرادجلي *Murade jalli.* A fine kind of rice. ధాన్యవిశేషము.

మురుకు n. s. (Tamil முறுக்கு) A sort of cake in coils. చక్కిలము.

మురుకుశాలి n. s. A kind of grass. Rox. 1. 228.

మురుదారు or **ముర్దారుసింగు** n. s. مردارسنگ *Murdarsing.* "Sulphate of copper" says Burnes (Bokhara. p. 207. Vol 3.) Others say, Litharge, semi-vitrified oxide of lead.

ముర్తిజానగరు n. s. مرتضى نگر *Murtuza nagar.* The Persian name of Guntoor. గుంటూరు.

ముర్దారుసింగు n. s. مردارسنگ *Murdar sing.* See మురుదారు.

ముర్ర n. s. The foot or lower corner of a sail?

ములాజిమత్ n. s. ملازمت *Mulazamat.* Paying respects to a superior. భేటి.

ములాయిజా for ములాహిజా n. s. ملاحظه *Mulahiza.* Regard, notice. Observation, consideration. దాక్షిణ్యము. బేములాహిజా *Be-mulahiza,* without partiality.

ములికినాడు or **ములికినాటిసీమ** n. s. A district lying south and east of Gandicota. ఒకదేశముపేరు.

ములుము n. s. The *grain crop* from land as distinguished from జరీబు *zarib.* The *zarib* land produces tobacco, chillies and betel, all other land is *mulumu.* The two together form *bāghāyat* or "garden cultivation."

ముల్కి adj. ملكي *Mulki.* Appertaining to revenue. రివిన్యూసంబంధమైన.

ముల్తవీ, or **ముల్తవి** n. s. ملتوي *Multawi.* Trickery, cunning.

ముల్తవీ, ముల్తవి adj. ملتوى *Multawī.* Delayed, postponed, spun out, protracted.

ముల్తవీమనిషి n. s. A rogue. పేచీకోరు.

ముల్లా n. s. ملا *Mullā.* A schoolmaster, a doctor: one who administers an oath. ఉపాధ్యాయులు, సత్యముచేయించేవాడు.

మువాను n. s. A ringleader?

మువ్వ adj. Single-masted (a doney or vessel.) మువ్వదోని a single canoe as opposed to a సంగడి or double canoe.

ముశరపు for ముషరఫ్ مشرف *Mushraf.* An account keeper. ముసద్దీ, లెక్కమనిషి.

ముశీలు n. s. Permission, warrant, license. సెలవు. కోతముశీలు leave granted for reaping.

ముష్టాకట్టుట v. a. To pinion or bind. విరిచికట్టుట.

ముస్తాజరు n. s. مستاجر *Mustāgir.* A renter; revenue-contractor or farmer-general. ఇజారా దారుడు.

ముసమ్మాతు n. s. مسمات *Musammāt.* Named, 'Dicta, nominata.' (The feminine adjective derived from Ism, name) A word equivalent to 'Mrs.' This word is only used in Bengal, as Musammāt Rami; i. e. a woman named Rami. 'Nominata Rami.' It was used in writing down Persian depositions wherein it shewed which of the Hindu names denoted females. పేరుగలది.

ముసెర n. s. A hillock. Refuse of food. ముసెరతేనె a sort of honey: but Reeve says ముసెరె Any thing boiled, or dressed ready to eat.

ముసల్మాను n. s. مسلمان *Musalmān.* A Musulman. తురకవాడు.

ముసెవ్విద usually ముసోదా n. s. مسوده *Musavvadah.* A rough draft of a letter, a memorandum చిత్తు, చిత్తుపుస్తకము.

ముసాంబ్రం usually మూసాంబ్రము n. s. مصنبر *Musambar.* Bitter aloes. ఒకమందుదినుసు.

ముసాబు n. s. (from Tamil முசாப்பு) Constant rain, drizzling. ముసురు.

ముసుకుబెండ n. s. A certain herb, the seed of which has a "musky" scent.

ముస్తకుబులు n. s. مستقبل *Mustaqbil.* Future, the future tense. (Anticipated payments or collections; a part of the revenue due, taken forcibly in anticipation of the full time. Equivalent to the forced loans exacted by the Charleses and Jameses in England.)

ముస్తరురూపాయాలు n. s. A monthly stipend?

ముస్తాజరు n. s. مستاجر *Mustajir.* A revenue contractor, or farmer-general. ఇజారాదారుడు.

ముస్తాదు adj. مستعد *Mustaid.* Prepared, ready, fit, capable, worthy, adept. సిద్ధముగా ఉండే, తయారుగా ఉండే.

ముస్తీదు, ముస్తైదు, ముస్తీబు adj. See ముస్తాదు.

ముస్తీబు n. s. Equipment, accoutrements. ఉపకరణము.

ముస్వీద or ముసెవ్విద usually ముసోదా n. s. مسوده *Musavvada.* A rough draft of a letter. చిత్తుగా వ్రాసినది.

ముహాజరునామా n. s. محضرنامه *Mahzar namah.* A general certificate signed by all present. A presentment, or declaration signed by all. An affidavit, a general petition, a declaratory deed. కదిమందిన్నిచేరి ఒక సంగతికి సాక్ష్యముగా లేక తీర్పుగా వ్రాసియిచ్చిన దస్తావేజు.

ముహాబ్బతు n. s. محبت *Mohabbat.* Friendship, love, affection. స్నేహము, విశ్వాసము.

ముహీము n. s. مهم *Mohim.* Important affair, urgent business. అగత్యమైనపని. Battle, assault. యుద్ధమున్ను.

మూజబాని n. s. منهزباني *Muh zabānī* Words of mouth. మూజబానిగా adv. By word of mouth.

మూటం n. s. (Tamil மூட்டம்) A fire covered, so as to yield much smoke, also, a bonfire. భోగి మూటము a bonfire, usually kindled the day before the Pongal festival.

మూటంవేసుట v. n. To heap fuel on a fire or bonfire.

మూడుమంచు (for Tamil மூடுபனி) A mist, a thick fog. పొగమంచు.

మూరి n. s. The sort of cloth called Salampore?

మూర్తం Error for ముహూర్తము which see.

మూష n. s. A framework of bricks over which an arch is turned?

మూసా n. s. Monsieur. This word is used in the Ranga Rao Charitra wherein Monsieur Bussy is called మూసాబూసీ Book 2. 66. ఒక ఫ్రెంచి సరదారుని పేరు.

మెత్తాది adj. A simpleton, a coward. తెన్నని వాడు, మేదకుడు.

మెరటుట v. a. (Tamil மெரட்டுகிறது) To frighten, bully. బెదిరించుట.

మెహందా n. s. A kind of sword. Swa. 4. 36. మిహికసిందికురంజు మెహందాకెలం కులాలుగుజ్జరిస్తేతకేవడంబు. టీ॥ అడ్డకత్తి. ABA. 2. 404. కట్టనునామముల్ కుక్టైమున మెహదాయనయడ్డకత్తినాన లరుచుండు.

మెహానతు n. s. محنت *Mihnat.* Labour, toil, trouble, difficulty, exertion, pains, industry. పాటు, కష్టము.

మెహమానము n. s. مهمان *Mehman.* Good will. కృప.

మెహమానుదారు n. s. مهماندار *Mehmandar.* A host or landlord. ఇంటియజమాన

మేండబనావని for మేరాడ్ బనావని n. s. The "mending" and repairing the bank of a tank. కట్టమరమ్మతుచేయించడము.

మేంథి n. s. مندی *Mundi*. A herb called Fenugreek, saintfoin. మెంతికూర, మెంతులున్ను.

మేకు n. s. میخ *Mekh*. A nail, tent-pin, peg, a hook. వసి, చిల, కూటము.

మేజవాని n. s. میزبان *Mezban*. An entertainment with an exhibition of dancing girls. చదురు. మేజబాన్ *Mezban*. the host or entertainer. చదురుచేసేవాడు.

మేజా, మేజు n. s. میز *Mez*. A table, a dinner, mess. బల్ల.

మేజువాని n. s. میزبانی *Mezbāni*. An entertainment. చదురు. మేజుబాను a host or entertainer. చదురుచేసేవాడు.

మేజోడు, మేజోళ్లు n. s. Stockings.

మేటి n. s. A Maty; or helper. A certain menial servant. It is merely the low English *mate* as cook's *mate* and the "y" in matey seems to be vulgarly added as in slavey, cookey. A menial who cleans plates, dishes, lamps and shoes.

మేతరాంగము n. s. Seniorship, the office of an alderman, headmanship. పెత్తనము ?

మేతరు n. s. مہتر *Mehtar*. A headman, an alderman. పెద్ద, పెద్దగావుండేవాడు.

మేవ n. s. Stuff, solidity. Profit, advantage, gain. సత్తు.

మేధావంతము n. s. Fineness of grain.

మేనేజరు n. s. (The English word) "Manager." నిర్వాహకుడు, పెద్దఉద్యోగస్థుడు.

మేరచేటు n. s. Certain fees granted to pariars in harvest time. మిరాశీగింజలు.

మేలువారము n. s. (Tamil மேல்வாரம்.) Government share of agricultural produce. మేలుకోరు.

మేస్తు n. s. Column, head or item in accounts (Bellary) A form in accounts. A model or pattern ?

మేస్తరి or మేస్త్రి n. s. *Maistre*. (French or Portuguese.) A head workman. పనివాండ్లపెద్ద.

మేస్తరు adj. That is, Mr.

మై prep. مع *Mai*. With. తో, కూడా.

మైకము n. s. (Tamil மயக்கம்) Confusion or distraction of mind. Intoxication. చిత్తభ్రమ, మత్తున్ను.

మైజారు n. s. مجار *Mejar*. A skirt or selvage of a woman's cloth. మైజారుచీర a woman's cloth having the మైజారు.

మైదాను or మైదానము n. s. میدان *Maidan*. Plain, meadow. బైలు.

మైనరు n. s. (E.) A '*Minor*.' అప్రాప్తవ్యవహారికుడు, వ్యవహారదశరానివాడు.

మైల adj. میلا *Mailā*. Dirty, foul, soiled. మురికియైన.

మైలారివాండ్లు n. s. A certain class of beggars ?

మైలారు n. s. Name of a certain feast among whitsters during which they abstain from work. చాకలవాండ్లపండగ.

మైలి or మైలిరూక n. s. A single silver fanam.

మొకద్దంచేయుట v. a. from مقدم *Muqaddam*. To prefer. (To assume or take for granted. ఇది మొకద్దంచేసి assuming this as a ground ?)

మొకద్దమా n. s. مقدمہ *Muqaddamā*. Matter, affair, business. వ్యవహారము.

మొకరరు adj. مقرر *Mukarrar*. Certain, fixed, appointed. రూఢియైన, నిర్ణయించబడ్డ, నియమించబడ్డ. మొకరరుచేసుట to fix, appoint.

మొకస్సరు for ముకస్సరు adv. مکسر *Mukassar*. Full, as full ten yards. పూరా.

మొకాం n. s. مقام *Maqām*. A halting place in a journey. A dwelling, residence, station. మజిలి, నివాసము, బస.

మొకాబిలా n. s. مقابلہ *Muqābalā*. Comparison, collation, setting face to face. సంప్రతించడము, ఎదురెదురుగాపెట్టడము. మొకాబిలాచేసుట to compare.

మొఖమల్ or ముఖమల్ n. s. مخمل *Makhmal*. Velvet. దళముగామెత్తగావుండేపట్టువస్త్రము. H. 1. 73.

మొఖాలిఫ్ for ముఖాలిఫ్ n. s. مخالف *Mukhālif*. An enemy, a foe, usually (meant for *mokhālif*.) Opposition, opposing ?

మొఖాసా n. s. See ముకాసా.

మొగదాలిఅమ్మ n. s. Name of the tutelar goddess of salt pans.

మొగలాయి adj. from مغل *Mughal.* Mogul, Moghlai. కర్నాటకపు.

మొట్టచేప ? or మొత్తచేప ? n. s. A fish, a species of Scomber. Rox. pl. 84. 153. 162. 171. 172.

మొదలియారు or మొదలారి n. s. A Tamil title.

మొఫర్దు for ముఫ్రద్ مفرد *Mufrad.* An abstract, a summary. సంగ్రహము.

మొబలగు for ముబలగ్ n. s. مبلغ *Mublagh.* A sum of money. రొంరరూకలు, ఒక మొత్తము.

మొబాదలా or మొబాదిలా adj. مبادلا *Mubādalā.* Borrowed, as a loan. చెయిబదులు గా తీసుకొన్న. See ముబాదలా.

మొబాదలా or ముబాదిలా n. s. مبادلا *Mubādalā.* Exchange, interchange. మార్పు.

మొబాదిలాఅయివజు for ముబాదిలాఅయివజు n. s. مبادلا *Mubadāla.* A loan. చేబదులు.

మొయీన్జాబితా n. s. معين ضابطه *Mueenzābita.* The red book, monthly abstract of salaries, fixed statement. జీతాలకట్టి.

మొయ్యాను or మోయీను n. s. معين *Mueen.* Manner, mode, way batta. రీతి, విధము, బత్తెము న్న. యా మొయ్యానుకువచ్చె matters came to such a pitch.

మొయ్యానుగా adv. from معين *Mueen.* Moderately, as much as suffices. మితముగా, మట్టుగా.

మొరబండి n. s. A timber-dray ?

మొరసవాండ్లు n. s. (Tel.) A certain caste of Sudra farmers ?

మొలాజా for ములాయిజా n s. ملاحظه *Mulāhazah.* Looking at, regard, notice. Perusal. కటాక్షము. See ములాయిజ.

మొలామకడు n s. A sort of melon.

మొలామా adj. ملمع *Mulammā.* Plated, covered with gold or silver. వెండిబంగారుపూతపోయబడ్డ.

మొలామా n. s. ملمع *Mulamma.* Gilding. Application of medicine to a wound. బంగారు వెండిపూయడము, పుంటిమీద వేసేటిదిన్ని.

మొలాయిజా or మొలాహిజా n. s. ملاحظه *Mulahazah.* Regard, notice. Partiality, favour. దాక్షిణ్యము. మొలాయిజా చేయుట To condescend.

మొస్తరు or మోస్తరు n. s. Muster (an Indian word for sort, pattern or specimen.) మాదిరి.

మొహజ్జరునామా for మహజరునామా n. s. محضرنامه *Mahzarnama.* A presentment or statement made by many persons acquainted with the facts.

మొహతరఫా or మోతర్ఫా محترفه *Mohtarifah.* A tax on houses, looms, shops, or trades. ఈన్న, పరి.

మొహంతాది or మహంతాదబంట్రోతు n. s. A village peon employed to watch crops.

మొహందా n. s. A broad sword, a hanger. కట్టాకత్తి. See ఆంధ్రశబ్దార్ణవము 2. 206. quoted in note on Jaimini 5. 124.

మొహమలు for మాక్మాల్ usually మొహమూలు n. s. for مخمل *Makhmal.* Velvet. పట్టుముగా మెత్తగా వుండే పొకపట్టు.

మొహంచంగు usually మోర్చింగు n. s. منهچنگ *Monhchang.* A kind of jew's harp.

మొహరము n. s. محرم *Moharram.* An annual Musulman festival in commemoration of the death of two heroes called Hussun and Hoosein. తురకలపండగ.

మొహరా or మోహరా n. s. مهره *Muhrah.* Any piece or man at chess, except pawns. చదరంగములో బంట్లు తప్పకదము కాయలు.

మొహరాయించుట v. a. from مهره کرنا *Mohra karnā.* To polish cloth, in mangling. ఇస్త్రీచేయుట.

మొహరి or మోహరం n. s. for مهر *Muhr.* A gold coin. వరహాబంగారునాణెము.

మొహరు n. s. مهر *Muhr.* A seal. ముద్ర.

మొహసీలు for మొహస్సల్ usually మోసూలు n. s. محصل *Muhassal.* Restraint, placed on a person to prevent his escape, or to enforce the payment of a demand. కావలి, తరుపు. వారిమీద మోసూలు పెట్టినారు they kept him in guard.

మొహిం n. s. مهم *Muhim.* See ముహిము.

మోక్షకచట్టు n. s. అనగాముద్రకారు. Q.

మోకూపు n. s. موقوف *Mauqūf.* Abolishment. తోసివేయడము, ఎత్తివేయడము. మోకూపుచేయుట to abolish.

మోచి n. s. See ముచ్చి.

మోజా n. s. موزه *Mauzā.* A boot. బూట్సు.

మోజాత్, మోజాతు, మోజుదాతు n. s. موجود *Maujud.* Stock in hand, store, provision. కట్టుబడ, ఇరువు.

మోజు n. s. Ardent desire. నిండా ఆశ. వానికి యిప్పుడు వేటమీద నిండా మోజుగా వున్నది his thoughts are now all bent on hunting.

మోజుబా n. s. perhaps an error for محاسبه *Muhasaba.* Giving up charge, yielding office to a successor. తనవుద్యోగము తనకువచ్చినవానికి ఒప్పగించడము.

మోటాటికాపులు n. s. (Tel.) A certain caste of the farmer tribe.

మోడి n. s. A name for the Marata character. In Colebr. Essays, 2. 29. he spells it మూరు Mūru.

మోడిని adv. "At the rate of" (చొప్పున) A word used in the salt permits printed at Madras, but unknown in the north.

మోడిహొన్ను n. s. مہری هون *Muhri hun.* A certain coin?

మోతదోని n. s. A canal, a channel? కాలవ.

మోతబరి usually ముతుబరి adj. معتبر *Mutabar.* Substantial, confidential, trustworthy. వీడవాడు కాని, నమ్మదగిన.

మోతరఫా n.s. محترفه *Mohtarifa.* The moturfa tax, levied on merchants and artisans. In Ganjam it is a tax on houses. It includes both that which is called వీసుబడి and బగైరవీసుబడి.

మోతాదీ usually ముహతాది or మహతాదుబంట్రోతు n. s. A village watchman who watches fields.

మోతాదు n. s. معتاد *Motād.* A charge: so much powder as is fired at once. ఒకవేటుకుకావలసిన మందు.

మోతుబరి usually ముతుబరి n. s. معتبری *Motubari.* Opulence, respectability, confidence. కలిమి, గొప్పతనము, నమ్మకము.

మోతుబరు usually ముతుబరు adj. معتبر *Motabar.* Respectable, substantial, rich, trustworthy. కలిగినవాడుగా వుండే, నమ్మదగిన.

మోద n. s. A pack of paun leaves. 20 కట్టలు (of 100 leaves each) are a మోద or pack.

మోది n. s. مودی *Mōdī.* A shopkeeper who supplies one with provisions. వెచ్చమిచ్చేవాడు.

మోమినువాండ్లు n. s. from مومن *Momin.* A sort of Musulman weavers. తురకలలో నేసేవాండ్లు.

మోయిను n. s. معین *Moaiyan.* Manner, mode, way. Rate, ration, mess of food for a day: batta. రీతి, వంతు, బత్తెము. మోయినుజాబితా a list of servants, showing the salaries they receive.

మోరచెంగు for మోర్చింగు n. s. منہ چنگ *Monhchang.* A jews-harp. ముఖవీణ.

మోరా n. s. مورہ *Mōrā.* A footstool. కాలికింది పీట.

మోరీ usually మోహిరీ n. s. مہر *Mohr.* The gold coin valued 15 rupees.

మోర్జా, మోర్జాలు n. s. for مورچه *Morcha.* A battery of guns. బత్తేరి.

మోళా n. s. Style, manner, sort?

మోల్దామిలింత n. s. అనగా ఆశ్లాయసి. Q?

మోసుబా n. s. for محاسبه *Muhasaba.* under some public charge or accusation. వానిమీద మోసూబాజరుగుతున్నది he is under trial.

మోసూలు, మోహసీలు n. s. محصل *Mohassal.* Restraint placed on a person to prevent his escape or to enforce the payment of a demand. Arrest, confinement.

మోస్తరు n. s. Muster, sample: this word is used even by farmers. మాదిరి.

మోహనరాయి n. s. The stone beam crossing the top of a pagoda gate. గోపురద్వారమునకువేసి యుండేరాతిదూలము.

మోహీము See మొహిం.

మోహీము for మోహిము n. s. Encampment. దండుదిగినస్థలము, మొకాము. మోహీముచేసుట to encamp.

మౌంటు n. s. (E) The "Amount." మొత్తము.

మౌకూపు n. s. See మౌఖూఫు.

మౌజె n. s. موضع *Mauza.* A town, a considerable village. వూరు, పల్లె.

మౌరూసి n. s. موروثی *Maurusī.* A heritor. A hereditary farmer, the original settlers in the township, (from *wāris*, heir.) అనాదికాపు.

మౌళా n. s. Style, manner, sort?

య

య Several words spelt with య belong correctly to ఎ and ఏ: but in the present Glossary words are given in the common spelling.

య॥ Contraction for యకరా an acre. య॥ ౧౫ fifteen acres.

యకాయకి adj. یکایکی *Yakayaki.* Sudden, speedy, solitary. ఆకస్మికమైన, త్వరితమైన.

యకాయకి or యకాయకిగా adv. (Mahr.) Straightway, suddenly, all at once, unawares, unexpectedly. దిగ్గున, అటక్కున.

యక్మాజ n. s. Stubbornness?

యక్రారు n. s. Probably an error for مقرر *Muqarrar.* Confession, admission, acknowledgment. యక్రారుచేయుట to confess.

యతిరాజి n. s. اعتراض *Etirāz.* Displeasure. కోపము.

యత్నీకృతము n. s. (Error for యత్నము) Effort, endeavour. ప్రయత్నము.

యత్నీకృతుడు n. s. He who tries, an essayist, he who makes an effort, a plotter. యత్నముచేసే వాడు.

యా (یا *Yā*) The Persian word meaning *or*— This conjunction is wanting in Telugu and Kannadi, but is thus supplied, (in official or vulgar letters) గాని.

యాగాత n. s. Saint '*Agatha*' a patron saint among Sudras in Madras.

యాగి n. s. یاغی *yāghī* A rebel తిరగబడ్డవాడు.

యాట n. s. (for వేట) Game killed for hunting. venison; a sheep, a goat. యాటమాంసము mutton.

యాతాం or యేతాము n. s. یاتم *Yatam.* The pump called a *picota.*

యాదాస్తు for యాద్దాస్తు n. s. یادداشت A memorandum, a rough note, a memorial. జ్ఞాపకార్థమువ్రాసుకొన్నది.

యాది for యాద్ n. s. یاد *Yād.* Memory, recollection. జ్ఞాపకము.

యాపారి, యాపారిబ్రాహ్మడు or వేపారి for వ్యాపారి n. s. A secular bramin. లౌకికములోఉండే బ్రాహ్మణుడు.

యారిదా n. s. A clerk? గుమాస్తా.

యాలం or యాలాం for ఏలాం (usually ఏలం వేలం or వేలాం.) n. s. An auction. In Bengali it is spelt *nilām* (Haughton, p. 1607,) and in Mahratta (MM. 910,) *nilāmb.* In Portugueze it is *Lielam* which apparently is from the Arabic الاعلام *Il i'lam*, notification, proclamation.

యాలంచీటి n. s. A lottery ticket? లాటరిచీటి.

యాలంవేయుట v. a. To sell by auction పాటపాడి వచ్చినవానికి అమ్మివేసుట.

యాళి n. s. (Tam) A dragon, such as is sculptured on pagodas. మృగవిశేషము.

యాదగా for ఈద్గా n. s. عیدگاه *Idgah.* The place where Musulmans hold a festival: a sort of chapel. ఒకతరహామసీదు.

యానరాసి n. s. (Perhaps for హీనరాసి) Grain thrashed but not cleared from the chaff. అరుపుకాకుండావుండే ధాన్యము.

యాసివి for ఈసివి adj. عیسوی *Isawi* Christian. క్రీస్తుసంబంధమైన. యాసివి ౧౮౪౬. i. e. ఆ న ౧౮౪౬ AD. 1846.

యెణలు n. s. (Canarese) "The first crop of rice" (Tulava language?)

యెత్తుబారి for ఎత్‍బార్ n. s. اعتبار *Etibār.* Confidence, trust. నమ్మకము usually, Influence. ప్రాబల్యము.

యుల్చ or యులిచె or యులిపి n. s. A snipe. ఉల్లంకిపిట్ట of which the బొగ్గలిపి and ముక్కలిపి are various species.

యేరువ n. s. A ship's keel. వాడపొడగుండాఅడుగునవెన్నుగువేసియుండేదూలక.

యేర్వాలుతిరిగినది A phrase which means The boat tacked about. ఓడమళ్ళితిరిగినది.

యేలం n. s. See యాలం An auction.

యేలపాటలు n. s. plu. The cry (*ēla'ēla*) *hollo, huzza'* used by boatmen or others while labouring.

యేళ్లు for ఏడు adj. Seven.

యోమయ for యామియా n. s. یومیه *Yaumiah.* Daily allowance, a sum granted to particular individuals in room of the ancient daily allowance. ఒకతరహాభరణము.

ర

ర‖ R. The hard R of Hindustani is often changed into D; thus پهڑانا phirāna becomes ఫిరాయించుట.

రంగు for రంగ్ n. s. رنگ *Rang.* Colour, paint. వర్ణము. A suit at cards. రంగువేయుట to paint. రంగుఖులాయించుట to turn up for trumps.

రంగుగా adv. Elegantly, finely. సొంపుగా, సొగసుగా.

రంగుచేప n. s. A certain fish. మత్స్యవిశేషము. Russell plate 91. A species of sparus, of a dark purple colour.

రంగుపాగలేర n. s. A certain kind of scarlet silk cloth. వస్త్రవిశేషము.

రంజకము for రంజక్ n. s. رنجک *Ranjak* The priming of a gun. పిరంగిచెవి, తుపాకిచెవి. వానిబుద్ధిరంజకమువంటిది he is very clever: or quick as fire.

రంబాల్లు n. s. A ship's shrouds. వాడస్తంభానికి కట్టేనూలునిచ్చెన.

రకం for రకాం n. s. رقم *Raqam.* Class, sort, set (of people or things.) మొత్తం, తరహా, జత.

రక్షిణిచెట్టు (or రక్షి?) n. s A certain tree called Cyperus Elatus. Rox. 1. 204.

రఖావలి n. s. رکهاولي *Rakhāwali.* Watching fields (Ganjam.) పొలమును కాయడము.

రజపుత్రులు or రజపుత్రవాండ్లు n. s. Rajpoots. జాతివిశేషసంబంధమైనవాండ్లు.

రజముచెట్టు n. s. A tree called *Celosia Corymbosa.* Rox. 1. 681.

రజా n. s. رضا *Razā* Leave of absence. శెలవు.

రజాయి n. s. رزائي *Razāi.* A quilt. నడుమదూదిపెట్టికుట్టినదుప్పటి.

రదాలము (రొదాలము?) n. s. Noise, sound, buzz?

రద్దు n. s. رد *Rad.* Rescission, rejection, repeal, abrogation. కొట్టివేయడము, తోసివేయడము.

రద్దుచేయుట or రద్దుపరచుట v. a. To annul, abrogate or revoke.

రద్దైన adj. Annulled, quashed, blotted, void, set aside. కొట్టివేయబడ్డ, తోసివేయబడ్డ.

రనాము (K) "A weapon" (Reeve) ఆయుధము. See రణము in TED.

రఫ్వ for రాఫ్ n. s. رفو *Rafu.* Darning, a darn. పోగుతీయడము. రఫ్వచేసుట to darn. రఫ్వచేసేవాడు a darner.

రఫ్వాగరు n. s. *Rafūgar* A darner. పోగుతీసేవాడు.

రఫ్లాసు n. s. "Ruffles," కుచ్చెకట్టినబట్ట?

రఫాకతు n. s. رفاقت *Rifāqat.* League. బందుకట్టు, సమయము, సమాఖ్య. రఫాకతుఅవుట To league together in roguery. To become friends.

రమారమీ adj رمارمي *Ramarami.* More or less about, on an average. సుమారు.

రమాసి *Ramāsī.* n. s. The cant dialect used by Thugs: it is apparently meant for సమస్య?

రయాని n. s. Farmers, the tribe of cultivators. Tenantry, peasantry. Petty retail salt dealers? కాపులు.

రయితాంగము n. s. The agricultural body: farmers, the peasantry, the country people or community. కాపులు.

రయితు or రయ్యతు for రయత్ n. s. رعيت *Raayat.* A "ryot" or subject. కాపు. Sir Thos. Munro spells this word "Rayat." A farmer or sub-renter. ఖూనిరయ్యతు the *man* charged with murder.

రవకారము n. s. Plastering a wall. గచ్చుపూయడము.

రవపాళీయం or రవశెల్లా n. s. Muslin. సన్నగానాణ్యముగాపుండేబట్ట.

రవానా n. s. روانه *Rawana.* Sending on: dispatch. Pass, permit, passport: పంపించడము, రహదారియున్నా. రవానాచేయుట To dispatch or transmit. రవానాచిట్టీ A port clearance.

రవాళము n. s. from రవళి Sound, note, voice, noise. ధ్వని.

రవీసు, రవేసు for రవిష్ n. s. رويش *Rawish.* Customary fees. రుసుము. రవేసు n. s. Pomp, grandeur, style. రవేసుఆకులు n. s. The best and most fashionable betel leaves. కేశాకులు.

రశీదు n. s. رسید *Rasīd.* A corruption for 'Receipt' or the Persian *rasida.* చెల్లుచీటి.

రశంగిధాన్యము or రసింగిధాన్యము n. s. A certain kind of rice: so named from a port so called. ఒకజాతిబియ్యము.

రసదు or రస్తు for రసద్ n. s. رسد *Rasad.* Food, provisions, commissariat supplies: (also explained as పైకం cash?) దండుకు కావలసినసామాను.

రశపుత్రుడు or రశపుత్రవాడు n. s. A Rajpoot. Bobb. 1. 158.

రస్తా for రాస్తా n. s. راستہ *Rāsta.* A road. బాట.

రస్తాళిఅరటిపండ్లు n. s. A certain fine sort of plantains. ఒకవిధమైనఅరటిపండ్లు.

రస్తు n. s. *rastu* for رسد *rasd.* See రసదు Commissariat store of grain &c. daily supplies collected for troops on a march. రస్తుకుప్ప A store of provisions. Suca. 1. 112. కస్తురిపేటక దారువన్నె బంగారమురస్తుకుప్పతెలిగంబుల వెన్నెలలోనితేట.

రస్మి n. s. رسمی *Rasmi.* Custom. Income. మామూలు, వచ్చుబడిన్ని.

రహటు or రాటు n. s. Plague, trouble, annoyance. ఉపద్రవము.

రహదారి or రాదారి n. s. رہداری *Rahdari.* A passport. A duty on roads: transit duty. a guard taken on a journey, a safe guard. పాదుషాసిపాయీలానిలుపకుండా పోనిచ్చేటందుకై యిచ్చేచీటి, తోడుగాతీసుకొనిపోబడ్డజనము. రహదారిపుల్లరి A tax levied on cattle that travel over grass lands.

రహితాంగము n. s. The peasantry. కాపులు.

రహితి A nominal money used in Canarese accounts. One gold *chacram* or *Rahti ruca* is four *chinna rucalu:* and four such *rucas* (40 fanams,) make one *rahiti* hoon. Rahti seems to mean *Kontaroy.* కంఠీరవవరహాలు. Local Rec. 1. 323. line 3. & x. 211. line 15.

రహితు or రయితు, రైయ్యతు n. s. رعیت *Raayat.* A farmer. కాపువాడు.

రక్షణ్యము or రక్షిణ్యము n. s. Patronage, protection. సంరక్షణ. A modern word used for "Salvation."

రాగడి or ర్యాగడి Error for రేగడ adj. Clayey. loamy. కృష్ణమృత్తిగాఉండే.

రాచూరిబాణము n. s. A rocket used in war. పెద్దఆకాశబాణము.

రాజపట్టము n. s. (Tamil இராஜபட்டம்) Public matters: politicks. రాచకార్యము. రాజపట్టము మాట్లాడుట to speak on political matters.

రాజశ్రీ or రాజేశ్రీ vulgar errors for రాజశ్రీ (a title) His highness.

రాజార్థం n. s. A plot, treason. కృత్రిమము, ద్రోహము, కుట్ర.

రాజీ adj. راضی *Rāzī.* (But used in Telugu as a noun.) Content, consent, will. ఇష్టము, సమ్మతి, సమాధానము. రాజీచేసుట to satisfy, appease. నాకురాజీగానున్నది it is agreeable to me, I consent to it.

రాజీనామా n. s. راضی نامہ *Rāzi nāmah.* An amicable agreement. A written testimony given by a plaintiff, (upon a cause being finally settled,) that he is satisfied, a deed of resignation, an acquittance, a release. వాదిప్రతివాదులుసమాధానమైవ్యాజ్యము తీసివేయవలెనని వ్రాసియిచ్చుకొన్నది, ఉద్యోగముఅక్కరలేదని వ్రాసియిచ్చుకొన్నది. రాజీనామాయిచ్చుట to relinquish a claim, to resign an office.

రాటు or రహటు n. s. Plague, trouble, annoyance, ravages. రాయిడి, ఉపద్రవము. దండురాటుచేత by reason of an invasion.

రాదారాదా or రాతారాతా forthwith.

రానువకట్టుబడి or రానువసిబ్బంది n. s. Yeomanry, militia.

రాతిపండు n. s. The rock apple: a certain drug?

రాతోరాత్ or రాతోరాత్రగా adv. راتے رات *Rāte Rāt.* At night రాతోరాత్రగావెళ్లినాడు he went at night.

రాదారి for రహదారి رہداری *Rahdārī.* A passport. సరకులను లేక మనుష్యులను అడ్డిలేకుండాపోనియ్యడమునకైఅధికారియిచ్చేచీటి.

రామంచాడిగా adv. Freely, without check. ఆతోటయెప్పుడురామంచాడిగాఉన్నది it is open to every body. అక్కడికిరామంచాడిగాపోతున్నారు every one that pleases goes there.

రామదాసు, అడవిరామదాసు n. s. A kind of hawk. (Jerdon's Catalogue No. 307.)

రామనామాలు n. s. Name of a certain ancient coin, inscribed with the 'name of Saint Rama.'

రామనీంగు n. s. Some sort of Artillery. Loc. Rec. 6. page 10. ఒకతరహఫిరంగి.

రామానుజకూటము n. s. A convent of Vaishnavas. వైష్ణవులకొందరికిన్నిపొత్తుగావుండేయిల్లు.

రాయసము n. s. (Tamil ராயசம்) The business of a secretary. రాయసగాడు a secretary. A secretary or amanuensis.

రాయితి, రాహితి for రియాయితి n. s. رعايت *Riāyat*. Remission, indulgence. తగ్గింపడము.

రాయితిగా for రియాయతిగా adv. As a remission or favour. i. e. తగ్గింపి.

రావు n. s. راو *Rao*. A Mahratta title added to the names of many bramins. In its meaning it is something like the American Hon'ble, which will include a stage coachman and an auctioneer.

రాస్తా or రస్తా n. s. راستا *Rāsta*. A road. బాట.

రాష్ట్రం or చిన్నరాష్ట్రం n. s. The drug called Galangal.

రిక్కపోయుట v. a. To level heaps of salt. (Vizag.)

రిజాల adj. رذاله *Rizālā*. Mean, vulgar, disreputable, bad, base. నీచమైన, అల్పమైన.

రియాయతి for రియాయత్ n. s. رعايت *Riāyat*. Remission, indulgence, favour, abatement in a demand. తగ్గింపడము, తోసియివ్వడము.

రివాజు for రివాజ్ n. s. رواج *Riwāj*. Currency, vent, usage, practice, custom. వాడుక, మామూలు.

రివాజుశాస్తి n. s. Excess (in taxation) above what is usual (Bellary) where lands have customarily been taxed too low, an additional sum is laid on, and this is called the excess tax.

రిశ్వత్తు for రిష్వత్తు n. s. رشوت *Rishwat*. A bribe. లంచము.

రీజన్ n. s. (E) "Reason." బేరీజన్గా unreasonably. (This is a blundering phrase) అక్కడనేను బేరీజన్గామాట్లాడినందున as! I spoke inexpertly, or, as I spoke in ignorance of the custom.

రీజనులు n. s. The clue lines of a sail ?

రుంజలు or రుంజాలు n. s. Drums.

రుక్క usually రొక్కా or రోకా n. s. رقعه *Ruqa*. A note or short letter. చీటి.

రుచికాయ n. s. A pickle. ఊరుగాయ.

రుజు or రుజువు n. s. رجوع *Rujū*. Signature, a confession, proof. (The word *Ruju, roozoo* is bad, and ought to be abolished; being a mere blunder.) చేవ్రాలు, నిరూపణ, దృష్టాంతము. రుజువువేసుట to sign. రుజువుచేసుట To prove. అతనిరుజువున in his presence. నేనురుజువుగాపోయి చూచినాను I went in person and saw it రుజువైన proved, established. రుజువాది n. s. Confession, proof, acknowledgment, admission.

రుద్రగడపచెట్టు n. s. A certain tree with whitish leaves ?

రుమాలు for రూమాల్ n. s. رمال *Rūmāl*. A handkerchief. Also a turban. చేతకట్టుకొనేగుడ్డ, తలగుడ్డయున్ను.

రువ్వ n. s. A farthing or pice. అరదుడ్డు, పైసా.

రుశ్వతు, రిష్వత్తు for రుష్వత్ n. s. رشوت *Rishwat*. Bribery. లంచము.

రుసుము or రుసూం n. s. رسوم *Rusum*. Fees, dues, custom, bribe, commission. స్వతంత్రము.

రూ॥ In accounts signifies a Rupee.

రూచికాయలు n. s. A sort of tight gold necklace ?

రూపాయ n. s. روپايا *Rupāyā* A rupee. plu. రూపాయీలు. In Hyderabad two coins are used called the ఓబ్బిరూపాయిand the గోవిందబక్షీలు.

రూపు (A nautical word) Reef lines.

రూపు n. s. روپ *Rūp*. Form. ఉరువు, ఆకారము. Thus వాండ్లుపల్లెరూపుచేసుకొనిరి they established or founded a hamlet. రూపురూపులో face to face, this is an error for *rū-ba-rū*.

రూబకారి usually రూపుకారి adv. روبكاري *Rūbakārī*. Face to face. By word of mouth. ఎదుట, వాచా. n. s. A written statement or deposition. వాఙ్మూలము.

రూబరు adv. روبرو *Rūbarū*. Face to face, before, over, against. ఎదుట, ముఖాముఖముందర. రూబరుచెప్పినాను I told him to his face.

రూబురూబులోఁ జెప్పుట v. n. To tell face to face. ముఖముఖముందర చెప్పుట.

రూమాలు usually రుమాలు n. s. رومال *Rūmal*. A handkerchief. A turban. చేతిగుడ్డ, తలగుడ్డ.

రూము n. s. (room ?) A point of the compass.

రూలుకఱ్ఱ n. s. A wooden 'ruler.'

రెంటాలకుపోవుట v. a. To go to the necessary. పెరటికిపోవుట.

రేఖలా n. s. ریکلا *Rekla*. A small gun. చిన్నఫిరంగి. Bobbili 3. 38. and Local Rec. VI. page 10.

రేజుదాను n. s. for ریگدان *Rēgdān*. A sand box used by a writer. (Reeve.)

రేణు n. s. Said to mean. దూదలపిడ ?

రేడకట్టు n. s. Raw silk ?

రేనాడు or రేనాటిసీమ n. s. The country on the banks of the Penna west to the Gandicota hill. గండికోటదుర్గానికి పడమటిపినాకినీనదీతీర మందుండేదేశము.

రేవల్చిన్ని, రేవాంచిని n. s. for ریوند چینی *Re-wand Chīnī*. Rhubarb (called in Russian, *revennaja*) It is properly *chīnī*, being brought from 'China.' Also used erroneously, for Gamboge. ఒకమందుదినుసు.

రేవుకారి n. s. The employment of a waterman or ferryman. చాకలపని, పడవలుతోసేపని.

రైతాంగము n. s. The peasantry, or farmer-class. కాపువాండ్లు.

రైతు n. s. for رعیت *Raiyat*. A cultivator, a farmer. కాపు. (Vulgarly written Ryot: but the old spelling, in Bengal was Rayat, or Reiat; which seems preferable.)

రైత్వారి n. s. (Vulgarly Ryotwarry, which should be رعیتواری *Rayatwari*.) An individual farmer's settlement of rent: or of the government demands.

రైయ్యతువారిలెక్కలు n. s. The accounts regarding each individual farmer. ప్రతికాపునుగురించినలెక్కలు.

రొక్కము, రొఖ్ఖము n. s. Coin, cash, money. నగదు.

రొఖ్ఖ usually రొక్కా n. s. رقعہ *Ruqqa*. A letter, a written note. చీటి.

రొఖ్ఖాదాయము n. s. Money rent: revenues paid in money, not in kind. నగదుగావచ్చేఆయము.

రోగను for రోఘను n. s. (روغن *Roghan.*) Melted butter n. s. Ghee. Grease, varnish. నెయ్యి, జిడ్డు, వానీసునున్ను.

రోటి n. s. روٹی *Rōtī*. Bread, a loaf. భక్ష్యవిశేషము.

రోణము n. s. Error for ఋణము which see.

రోదము n. s. The sheave of a pulley.

రోష్టు n. s. Confusion, disorder. Trouble, annoyance. Violence, outrage. తొందర.

రొక్కడా or రొఖ్కడా n. s. Cash, ready money, hard coin. రొక్కము.

రోకా for రొక్కా n. s. رقعہ *Ruqqā*. A letter epistle, a written note. చీటి.

రోజీనా n. s. روزینہ *Rozina*. Pension, daily allowance. భరణము, బత్తెము.

రోజు n. s. روز *Rōz*. A day. adv. Daily, every day. రోజుగుజస్తా (guzashta) the day before. రోజుమజుకూరు The said date, on the same day. On the abovementioned date.

రోజుమర్రా n. s. روزمرہ *Rōzmarrah*. Daily allowance, batta. బత్తెము.

రోజూకా n. s. Affair, matter. See రుజూ.

రోజువారు adj. روزوار *Rōzwār*. Daily. నానాటి.

రోషనాయి n. s. روشنائی *Roshnai*. Light. (Sums charged for lamps or oil ?)

రోసుబడి n. s. Drudge, slave, wretch, rascal. సిగ్గుమాలినవాడు. రోసుబడితనము Rascality, shamelessness, impudence. (from రోసుట v. a.)

రోసుబడి adj. Loathsome, disgusting, shameless. రోతైన, సిగ్గుమాలిన. రోసుబడివాడు a disgusting man. రోసుబడిముండ a shameless wretch.

రోసుబడితనము n. s. Loathsomeness, disgust, shamelessness, impudence. సిగ్గుమాలినతనము.

రౌతు n. s. A stone. (Ganjam.) రాయి.

రౌను, రవును n. s. from the English word "Round.") Round, circuit, journey. గుండ్రము, ప్రయాణము.

ర్పా॥ Contraction for రూపాయాలు 'Rupees.'

ర్యాయతి for రియాయతి n. s. رعايت *Riayat.* Remission, indulgence. Deduction, allowance, sum substracted. తోసియివ్వడము. ర్యాయతిచేసుట to deduct, refund, allow.

ల

లంకీని, లంకినీగుడ్డ or లంకినీలు n. s. Nankeen cloth. గోధుమలకు వేసేదళెము గావుండేగుడ్డ.

లంగరు n. s. لنگر *Langar.* An anchor. నంగూరము. లంగరువేసుట to cast anchor. లంగరుతీసుట to weigh anchor. లంగరువాడి or లంగరువాళి a sea-port.

లంగరుఖానా n. s. لنگرخانه *Langar khānā.* A poors house or hospital, where (langar) victuals are bestowed. అన్నసత్రము.

లంగు n. s. A bond or tie ? care, incumbrance.

లంగులుకాసు n. s. Loss, detriment (Herein *lang* is a mere *anuk:* devoid of meaning ?)

లంగోటి n. s. لنگوٹي *Langoti.* A modesty piece. గోచి.

లంటడు n. s. A sinewy man, a hulking boy. కుండువలెవుండేవాడు.

లండలకుక్క A fat gross wretch.

లంతర or లుతావాడు n. s. A slave, drudge, underling. This perhaps is Hindi : but is not in Shak. or M M nor Reeve.

లంబుమైన, లంబైన adj. Unwieldy, awkward. తులకనగావుండని.

లంబాడి or బంజారి لمباري *Lambāri* Lumbadees. A certain sort of gypsies, also called Brinjaries, who trade in bullocks, salt, grain, &c. లంబాడితండా a troop or camp of these vagrants.

లకిని or లఖిని n. s. A calam or reed pen.

లకురు n. s. అనగావాడకర్రబొంగులు.

లకోటా, లఖోటా n. s. The envelope of a letter; sealing; a parcel or post packet. జాబులోగా పెట్టుముద్రవేసేకాకితముసంచి.

లక్కి n. s. A prize. లాభము, అదాయము, as in lottery. వాడుమంచిలక్కికొట్టినాడు he has got a prize. This probably is the English word *lucky*.

లగాం n. s. لگام *Lagām.* A horse's bridle. కళ్లెము.

లగాయతు adv. لغايت *Lagāyat.* Since. For a long while, from the commencement, or beginning, ఆలగాయతు ever since, since. యీరోజులగాయతు beginning from to-day. ౧౧౩౨ ఫసిలిలగాయతు ౧౧౩౬ ఫసిలిఆఖరువరకుఆయనయేలెను beginning from fusly 1132 he ruled the land until the year 1136.

లగాయతు, లగాయతీ See లగాయతు.

లగాలగిచేసుట or లగాలగిచుసకూర్చుండుట v. a. from لگالگي *Lagālagī.* To insist on payment. తరుచుచేసుట.

లగించుట v. n. To apply, suit, fit. ఇముడుట, సరిపడుట.

లగితి n. s. Aid, supply, pecuniary assistance (Ganjam phrase.)

లగుడు n. s. The large hawk. Jerdon 28. పెద్దడేగ.

లగుబిగుగా adv. By some means or other; in any way. నయానభయాన.

లగ్గయెక్కడము n. s. Escalade. నిచ్చెనలువేసికోటగోడయెక్కిదూకడము.

లట్టుపైటుగావేసినజాబు or నట్టుఉట్టుగావేసినజాబు A "not (post) paid" letter. దూకలివ్వకతపాలులో వేసినజాబు.

లతాలున adv. Suddenly, all at once. దఢీలుమని.

లడాయి n. s. لڙائي *Larāi.* Battle, fight. యుద్ధము, జగడము.

లడాయించుట v. n. from *Larāi.* To fight, contend. పోట్లాడుట.

లడి n. s. لڙي *Larī.* A string of pearls, flowers, &c సరుట, సరము. A skein of gold thread or silver thread. సరిగెకండె.

లడ్డు n. s. لڙو *Laddoo.* Scrape, hobble, puzzle. లడ్డు, లడ్డువాలు or లడ్వాలు A kind of sweet meat. లడ్డువేసుకొన్నాడు he turned restiff. యిదివొకలడ్డువచ్చిపడ్డది there is a difficulty. This originates in a word belonging to dice play; when a "man is dead" or cannot be moved.

లతాడా, లత్తాడు n. s. لتاڑ *Latār.* Hobble, mess. Also, a deep boggy place in a road. A troublesome task. అడుసుబురద, పీకులాట.

లత్తాడి n. s. A bog, a plashy place. అడుసుబురద గావుండేచోటు.

లత్తుఖోరు, లత్ ఖోర్ n. s. لاتھی خور *Lāthī khor.* (cudgel-eater) A graceless rascal.

లధాపుకులం n. s. from لداف The caste of దూదేకులవాండ్లు cotton cleaners.

లద్దమనిషి n. s. A corpulent big man. నిండాదొంగ్లాను గావుండేవాడు.

లద్ది n. s. The dung of a horse &c. గుఱ్ఱముయేనుగ మొదలయినవాటిమలము.

లబటాయించుట or లబడాయించుట v. a. To heap up or gather, make money. To plunder. లంకొంచుకొనుట, వారివేసుకొనుట.

లబ్బున adv. Quickly, at once. (Cuddapa dialect.) దబ్బున.

లప్పము n. s. *Lappam.* Gum mastic, used in stopping the seams of ships. Cement: putty. వాతనందులుమొదలయినవాటికివేసేటిది.

లబ్బి, లబ్బిలు or లబ్బైవాండ్లు n. s. لبا *Labbā.* Labbi Lubbee. A caste of people who are also called Moplas (Mā-pilla) on the Malabar Coast. They originally were Arabs, but at present they speak a low dialect of Tamil, and have lost the appearance of Mahomedans.

లభిస్తు adj. Proved, verified. See లావిస్తు.

లమిడి n. s. Wretch, scamp, jade. (Perhaps corrupted from لومڑي *Lōmrī* a bitch-fox? or from لونڈی *lāundi* a slave girl. లమిడీముండ jade.

లయిలేహాయి n. s. لیہائی *Lihāia.* Paste (తెలు.) పిండి.

లరయి n. s. لڑائی *Larāi.* i. e. లడాయి A fight, battle. యుద్ధము.

లవణద్రావకము n. s. A certain extract from salt. See Ainslie. ఉప్పుధృతి.

లవాజిమ or లవాజుమా n. s. لوازمہ *Lawāzimā.* Establishment. (Domestics, retainers, horses &c The train generally of a great personage. MM.) Affairs (Details, particulars, record in a law-suit.) పరివారము, కమామీసు.

లష్కరు n. s. لشکر *Lashkar.* An army. దండు. Hence a Lascar.

లష్కరుకరకరాజి or లష్కరుకరకరా n. s. Purveying for troops. దండుకురస్తుజాగ్రతచేయడము.

లాంతరు n. s. A 'lantern' (Reeve) దీపముపెట్టడమునకుఅద్దములతోచేసినది.

లాఖి n. s. لاکھی *Lākhī.* Crimson. A red dye extracted from the shellac. ఒకయెఱ్ఱనిచాయ.

లాఖిరాజీభూమి n. s. لاخراجي *Lakhiraji.* Land that does not pay revenue to Government land held free of rent. The Lakhiraj land is of two classes. (See Reg. XXV. of 1802. Sect. 4.) 1. That which pays no rent, being corn fields, &c. 2. That which is laid out in houses or gardens. This latter is called నివేశనం *Nivesanam.*

లాగాయతు for లాగాయత్ n. s. لغايت *Lagayat.* Beginning, commencement. ఆరంభము, లాగాయతునుంచి from the beginning or from a long time.

లాగు n. s. Grain?

లాగుబడి, లాగువడు n. s. Cost, charge, expense. శలవు, వ్రయము. See లాగువడ.

లాగులుకొసులు n. s. Profit and loss. సుఖదుఃఖములు.

లాగువడ n. s. Expense, cost. శలవు, అనగా నేలను సాగుబడిచేసేటందుకు, పాడైనయిండ్లు పూళ్లుమొదలయ్నువాటిని బాగుచేయడమునకైన శ్రేష్టశలవు. లాగువడకట్టి or లాగువారుకట్టి A bill of charges incurred.

లాచారు adj. لاچار *Lachār.* Helpless, without remedy, forlorn, poor. నిరాధర్యగావుండే.

లాటసన్యాసి n. s. A sort of begging friar. ఒకరకమవిచ్చు మెత్తుకొనేసన్యాసివాడు.

లాటి لاٹھی *Lathi* A staff, club, stick. A pump handle. (Sea phrase.) Any lever; as a winch handle, the bar of a capstan or printing press.

లాటు n. s. A "lot" at an auction. వేలములోపెక్కుడు.

లాటుసాహేబు n. s. '*Lord Saheb*' The Governor.

లాడము n. s. (Corrupted from نعل *nal*) A horse shoe. లాడంకట్టుట to shoe a horse.

లాడులిగాడు n. s. Scrape, hobble. తొందర, తంటము. ఏదైనాలాడులిగాడువస్తేతదేవాండ్లెవరు if any thing goes wrong who is to bear the brunt?

లాడెజోగి, లాడెసన్యాసి n. s. A sort of begging friar. బిచ్చమెత్తుకొనేఒకతరహాసన్యాసివాడు.

లాడు n. s. لداو *Ladāo.* The temporary brick-work that sustains an arch while being built. Plaistering ; ceiling-work. వంపులకట్టేటప్పుడు దానికిఆధారముగాకట్టేటిది, గచ్చుపూయడము, క్రొతులువేసికలకలువేయకుండాయిటికలనుకంతనచేయడముదీన్నిపడుంగుఅంటారు.

లాడు n. s. Amble, trot. *lādū karna.* To mount a colt for the first time. (Shak.)

లాపోసు or లాపోసు n. s. Combination, scheme, plot, league. కుట్ర. ఫిర్యాదితోలాపోసుఅయినాడు he went over to the enemy.

లాపోసుచెక్క n. s. Sheathing planks. వాడఅడుగుకు వేసేసన్నపాటిపలకలు, వీటినిమూరబల్ల అంటారు.

లాబిస్తు for లాబిస్తా adj. لابستہ *Labista.* Laid, brought, filed (as a charge.) దాఖలుచేయబడ్డ.

లాము n. s. A hollow in a hill ? లోయ.

లాయము n. s. A horse stable. గుర్రపుశాల. Perhaps corrupted from cavalry " lines." (See Pal. 50.)

లాయఖు, లాయిఖ adj. لايق *Layaq.* Fit, proper. Suitable. తగిన.

లాయిలాజు adj. for لاعلاج *Lāilāj.* Cureless, remediless, helpless. తీరని, పరిహారములేని, ఉపాయములేని.

లాల n. s. A Toorkee or Paithāni phrase for *brother* (like అన్న in Telugu) and borne by certain Hindus.

లాలిచి for లాలచ్ لالچ *Lāluch.* Temptation, inducement. బులుపు.

లాలు (لال *lāl*) Red. లాలుకుంచెలు n. s. from لال *Lāl.* red short fringes. ఎరగాడుర్రపిచ్చిజల్లులు. OG.

లాలూచి n. s. لالچ *Lāluch.* Avarice, covetousness, cupidity. అత్యాశ.

లావణము n. s. A list of soldiers ; or, of servants. The profits of a custom-house. (Reeve) జీతగాండ్లపట్టి. లావణముబ్రాసుట to enlist. అతనిపేరులావణముఅయియున్నది his name has been entered on the list.

లావాటి adj. Large, big. స్థూలమైన.

లావాదేవి n. s. for ليوادیوی *Lēwā dēwī.* Traffic, mercantile transactions. ఇచ్చుకోళ్లుపుచ్చుకోళ్లు.

లాహిరి, for లహిరి n. s. لہر *Lahar.* Intoxication. మైకము. (Radha. 1. 109. N. 9. 326.)

లింగకట్టు n. s. (Tamil) A lump of vermilion. ఇంగిలీకపుగడ్డ.

లింగఘంటుడు n. s. One who wears the Lingam or *phallus*: chiefly among Sudras : but a few bramins are included. Lingavants. See Dictionary in జంగము.

లిగాడుగాపుండేవాడు n. s. A pauper, a destitute creature. బీదగాపుండేవాడు.

లిడితి for లిర్తి n. s. لرتی *Lirtī.* Neglect, disregard. వానిసంసారము లిడితికిందికివచ్చినది his affairs fell into confusion. The word is Dakhini. Shakesp. page 2043. *lirti mēn parna* to fall into error.

లిఫాఫా n. s. لفافہ *Lifafā.* Envelope. కాగితపుతిత్తి, జాబులువేసిలకోటాచేసేకాకితపుతిత్తి.

లిఖి error for లిపి n. s. Writing in general, hand writing.

లీస్టు or లీష్టు n. s. A 'List :' జాబితా.

లుంగి n. s. لنگی *Lungī.* A Musulman garment. తురకలుమొలకుచుట్టుకొనేబట్ట.

లుక్కు n. s. A crack or leak ? (Masulipatam.)

లుక్సాను, లుగసాను for నుక్సాను نقصان *Nuqsān.* Loss, detriment. Tare and tret. నష్టము.

లుచ్చా adj. لچّا *Luchcha.* Mean, base, low, worthless. అల్పమైన, తుచ్ఛమైన. లుచ్చామనిషి. a base fellow.

లుచ్చాతనము n. s. Meanness, baseness. అల్పత్వము, నీచత్వము.

లుగ Plumpness, good condition. పోలు. లుగచెడిన in bad circumstances. లుక్సానుఅయిపోయిన.

లుటాయించుట v. a. from لٹانا *Lutānā*. To plunder, rob. కొల్లబెట్టుట, దోచుకొనుట.

లుడుగు or లొడుగు n. s. A bell at an ox's neck. A fib, joke, ఎద్దుమెడనకట్టేపెకలరహాగంట.

లుల్లిగాడు, or లొల్లిగాడు n. s. A spendthrift, a bankrupt. దివాలుఖోరు.

లుకీకరించుట v. a. To deride, sneer at. వెక్కిరించుట.

లూటాడుట from لٹانا *Lutānā*. To plunder or *loot*. కొల్లబెట్టుట.

లూటి n. s. لوٹ *Lūt*. Plunder, sacking. కొల్ల, దోపిడి.

లూలి n. s. لولي *Lūly*. కుంటెనకత్తె.

లెఖ్ఖ, లెఖ్ఖ n. s. A mistake for లెక్క an account.

లెగుచుట v. n. The same as లేచుట to arise: for which this is a mispronunciation very common at Masulipatam and Rajahmandry.

లేఖరి * n. s. Writer, penman. వ్రాసేవాడు, వ్రాతకాడు.

లేజన్ for లేజం n. s. لیزم *Lēzam*. A sort of bow with an iron chain for a cord: used in feats of strength. సాముచేసేవాండ్లయినుపగొలుసుచేసినకర్ర.

లేటు adj. "Late." మునుపటి. (The English word) as లేటుమేనేజరు the "late" manager.

లెలుడి n. s. لیورِي Sending a criminal in procession round the town. దొంగనుకట్టిపీధివీధికితిప్పుట.

లేసన్ n. s. Meant for a "Licence." లేసను, శలవుచీటి. Reg. Act XIX. of 1852.

లైను n. s. A "line:" (the English word) వరుస.

లొటిపిటఅల్లి n. s. Scirpus articulatus, a species of rushes. Rox. 1. 214. ఒకతరహాఅల్లి.

లొటుకుపడుట for లోటుపడుట v. n. To be ruined or fall into difficulties. చెడిపోవుట.

లొడవిడరాలు n. s. A chatterbox, a tattler (Prit. in 1 Thes V. 13.) వదురుబోతు.

లొడవిడలు n. s. Nonsense, idle talk. కూతలు.

లొడబెట్టుట v. a. లొడివిడిచేసుట v. a. To rummage. గందరగోళముచేసుట.

లొల్లిగాడు n. s. A penniless wretch, a beggar. దులోవి.

లొల్లిచేయుట v. a. To strip, beggar, ruin. దులోవిగాచేసుట.

లోటు n. s. Loss. నష్టము.

లోడి, లోడు or ముగ్దు n. s. A club used in violent exercises. సాముచేసేవారిసాధనము.

లోపాయకారి or లోపాయికారి n. s. A subrenter: or tenant. లోగుత్తచేసుకొన్నవాడు, వాడువాండ్లకు లోపాయకారిగావున్నాడు he is secretly a confiderate of theirs.

లోలక for లూలక్ n. s. لولک *Lūlak*. A drop or pendant of an earring. A roll of paper. తొంగటము, కాకితచుట్ట.

లోలాయపడుట v. a. To be teazed or pestered (with frequent visits.) To be in trouble. లోలాయపడుచూవున్నాడు he is an idler or vagabond. He is in trouble.

లోవైనం adv. Formerly, heretofore, already. ముందర, లోగడ.

లోసబరు n. s. A ship's course for *out* at sea: literally the *inner* ocean. ఫైలిసబరు the *outer* voyage meaning a *coasting* trip.

లౌంసు or లౌన్సు n. s. Meant for "Allowance."

ల్యాక Disjunctive conj. Vulgar error for లేక Without. అథవా.

వ

వ Some words commonly written with an initial V will be found under ఒ the vowel O, and others under బ B, and others under వొ VO.

వ, *va* or *wa* The Persian conjunction "and." This occurs in some Telugu and in many Canarese papers written while the Musulmans were in power. Thus పాలించిన, వ, ధరించిన *pālinçina, wa, dharinçina* ruling and possessing.

వంచ n. s. A piece of గోనె (sacking) used for packing: or for baling a boat.

వంచాలించుట, వంచాయించుట or వంచాడించుట v. n. To hesitate, scruple. సంకోచించుట. వంచాలించక without hesitation.

వంటరి adj. Alone, single. ఏకాకియైన. ఒంటిగాడు గావుంటే.

వంద్ర, వందర n. s. A rent of which a part is remitted: a favourable lease. Quit-rent. వంద్రపొలము land granted on a light rent. వందరభూమి Land unfit for ploughing.

వందాలగ n. s. *Vandālaga*. A certain plant.

వకీలు n. s. وکیل, *Wukīl*. An attorney, a pleader. An agent ambassador, representative, official. లాయరు, గుమాస్తా.

వగ n. s. from (Tamil வகை) Part, portion, manner, kind. Goods, property, means. భాగము, రీతి, బంధవలము.

వగమానము n. s. (Tamil வகைமானம் Vagheiman) Contrivance, plan, for doing any thing. దోవ.

వగైర, వగైరా (postposition وغیره, *Wagairah.*) Etcetera; and so forth. గురించిన, చేరిన, మొదలయిన. (వగైరాగుత్త (Ganjam.) A rent taken by so and so *etcetera*, by several partners) రామయ్యవగైరాలు Ramaya and others.

వజను for వజన్ n. s. وزن *Wazn*. Weight. భారము, బరువు.

వజా n. s. وضع, *Wazā*. Deductions, substraction, a set off in an account. తోసివేత, తోసియివ్వడము. వజాచేయుట to deduct. కట్టుబడివజా the cattubadi fees being deducted.

వజారతు for విజారత్ n. s. وزارت *Wizārat*. The dignity of Wazīr, the office of prime minister, ministry. మంత్రిత్వము.

వజనె n. s. An unopened knot or bud of leaves. This is used in medicine.

వజీరు n. s. وزیر *Wazīr*. A vazeer or royal minister. In some poems it is used for మంత్రి; but usually it means a horseman. రౌతు or warrior. Suca 1. 302. రావిలుకవటాణినెక్కెడివజీరునిబోలినయాన్నపాలునిన్.

వజ్జిరం or వజ్రం n. s. Glue, used by carpenters. చెక్క అతకడమునకై వేసేజిగట.

వట్టం n. s. The loss sustained in exchanging money: agio: or premium granted or gained in pecuniary transactions. తరుగు. వట్టమిచ్చుట or వట్టముకట్టియిచ్చుట to pay a premium or agio in exchange.

వట్టాలకర్ర n. s. A pole on which a weight is carried by two men: also written వట్నాలకర్ర.

వట్టు for ఒట్టు adj. General. అందరికిసాధారణమైన. వట్టుహుకుం a general order. ఒట్టంచెకచ్చేరి the General Post *Ancheh* Office.

వట్రె n. s. (Tamil ஒட்டடை) A cobweb, soot: dirt made by an insect different from a spider. Regard, care. వాడునన్నువట్రెపెట్టలేదు he cares not for me.

వట్రం (Tamil வட்டேம்) A pouch. for betel. అడపం.

వడం n. s. (Tamil வடம்) A rope, a cable. మోకు. తేరువడము the cable with which a car is drawn. The white necked stork. కొంగ.

వడవారం n. s. (Tamil ஒடவாரம்) Both shares, gross produce: both the farmer's and government's share. ఉభయవాశి.

వడుచుట v. a. (Tamil வடிக்கிறது) To pour; draw in an alembic. ఆముదమువడిచినారు they boiled the oil.

వణ్ణము Error for అన్నము Food.

వతను for వతన్ n. s. وطن, *Watan*. (literally, native country, home) Office or means of subsistence. Patrimony. Hereditary duty with lands attached. Custom, usage. మిరాసినేల, మిరాసి, వాడుక, మామూలు.

వతనుగా adv. (From وطن, Watan.) As a subsistence. Publicly, openly, as usual. బాహిరంగముగా, మామూలుగా.

వత్తడి n. s. Plague, teasing. తొందరము, ఓకులాట.

వత్తాసి n. s. (Tamil ஒத்தாசை.) Help, assistance. సహాయము. వత్తాసిగా in an aid.

వద్దిచెట్టు n. s. (Tamil ஒதியமரம்) A certain tree.

వనభూషణము n. s. The bird called Mocking bird. ఒకపక్షి.

వన్నము or వణ్ణము n. s. Error for అన్నము food.

వయినమరం n. s. (Tamil ?) Satin wood ?

వయిరాను for వయిరాన్ adj. ویران, *Wairān*. Desolate, ruined, depopulated. పాడైన, మనుష్యసంచారములేని.

వరకం n. s. The multiplicator in arithmetic. A rut cut by water.

వరగారు n. s. The heavy crop; the great crop reaped after the rains. తొలికారు.

వరబడి n. s. Drought. కరువు. వరబడిసంవత్సర ము a year without rain.

వరబీజము or వరిబీజము n. s. The disease of swelled testicle. బుడ్డ.

వరభోకి n. s. A squanderer, a prodigal. దూబర బిండి.

వరవుకాలువలు n. s. (Tamil) Tributary streams, the feeders of a river. వాగులు.

వరాలు for వరహాలు n. s. Pagodas, gold coins. Jagann. 1. 35.

వరిది (Kan) *Varidi.* News, intelligence. Warning, orders. వరిది సేజరు the same as Subadār, Major. ఆయనవరిదిలోవుండేవాండ్లు those who are under his command.

వరుమానము n. s. (Tamil) Income, revenue, resources. వచ్చుబడి.

వర్గామతుజమీను n. s. (Marata) Land transferred from one farmer to another. ఒకరివకరా ళ్లువశముచేయబడ్డభూమి.

వర్గావర్గి n. s. (Marata) Exchange, transfer, transposition. బదలాబదలీ.

వర్గావర్గిచేయుట v. a. To exchange: countermarch; make two men change places. మార్చుట.

వర్గు n. s. (Marata) Change of appointment. Change or exchange of place. ఉద్యోగములను మార్చుడము.

వర్తంగిచెక్క n. s. "*Vartangi.*" "Sappan wood." (See the Tariff.)

వర్ది n. s. Report, notice. (see వరిది.) News, warning, Orders. ఆయనవర్దిలోవుండేవాండ్లు those who are under his orders.

వలందేజు adj. ولنديز (*Valandez. Hollandois.*) Dutch. ఒలాందా.

వలతాడు n. s. A noose or cord to catch cattle with. పసులనుపట్టేదారము.

వలదు n. s. ولد *Walad.* Son. Son of కొడుకు. నబీఖానువలదుహైదరుఖాను Nabi-khan, son of Haidar khan.

వలాగ్రం or వళాగ్రము n. s. A species of areca nut. వక్కలలోభేదము.

వలాయతు for విలాయత్తు n. s. ولايت *Valāyat.* Country, native land. England. దేశము, సీమ.

వలిచలు n. s. plu. (Tamil) Roof laths. పెండెలు.

వళువు n. s. (Tamil உளவு) *Treachery*: betrayal. Secret. Chicanery. Clique. Underhand plot. Secret alliance. కుట్రకురుకనియనుకూలము. వళువుయెరిగినవాడు he who knows the secret of the business.

వల్లడి n. s. (Tamil வல்லடி) Violence, oppression, mischief. దౌర్జన్యము, చేటు.

వల్లడికాడు n. s. (Tamil வல்லடிக்காரன்.) A powerful or violent man. దౌర్జన్యముచేసేవాడు.

వళ్లికె (usually తిరువళికె) n. s. A Tamil word for a lamp. నిలువులవళ్లికె a lamp on a stand. Charitr. 5. 2036. దీపము.

వశవర్తియైన adj. Affable, gracious, accessible: subordiate, obedient. విధేయుడైన. వాండ్లయింకావశవర్తికిరాలేదు they are not yet subjected.

వసంతగుండము n. s. A species of the కుంకచెట్టు.

వసతి n. s. Pension, allowance, living. భరణము.

వసతిదారు n. s. A proprietor or landholder. A pensioner.

వసవాసు n. s. وسواس *Waswās.* Awe, apprehension. భయము, అదరు. MM.

వసీలా n. s. وسيله *Wasīlah.* Support, intervention, patronage. ఆసరా, ఆధర్వు.

వసూలు n. s. وصول *Wasūl.* Payments, liquidation, collections. తండలు, తండితెచ్చినరూకలు. వసూలుచేసుట to collect, realize. See under జమ *Jumma.*

వస్తాదు for ఉస్తాదు n. s. استاد *Ustād.* A leader, a captain, a tutor or master. నేర్పేవాడు, చదువుచెప్పేవాడు (of fencing, singing or dancing) MM 933. He who "teaches" one, i. e. his rival or utter superior: his master.

వహీ n. s. (for بہی *Bahī.* An account book, a book in general. A *head* in accounts. In surgery, a sinus in a wound or ulcer. లెక్కపుస్తకము, పుంటినరము.

వహీలెక్క n. s. A booked account.

వాకఫు usually వాకూఫ adj. واقف, *Wāqif.* Skilled, versed in, knowing, acquainted. సమర్థుడైన, తెలిసిన. వాకఫులోకితెచ్చుకొనుట. to ascertain.

వాకబదారుడు or వాకిఫుదారుడు for వాకూబ్ దార్ n. s. (واقفدار, *Wacūf-dar.*) He who is skilled in, acquainted with, experienced, exercised, or versed in: a man of mature age: a man of sense. వయసువచ్చినవాడు, తెలివిగలరుడు, అనుబద్ధవాడు. వాకిఫుచేసుకొనుట. to procure information, ascertain, find out.

వాజిబీ adj. (واجبی, *Wājbi.*) Just, right, reasonable, proper, expedient. న్యాయమైన, సరియైన, తగిన.

వాటకద్యములు n. s. (Marata.) Verses culled out of different poems, to form a delectus or elegant extracts. ఆటవిడుపుపద్యములు.

వాటా n. s. باٹا *Bātā.* A division, share. Part, portion. తుక్కిడి, భాగము.

వాడగాలి n. s. (Tamil வாடைக்காற்று.) The north-wind. ఉత్తరపుగాలి.

వాణిద్యము n. s. A corruption of వాణిజ్యము Traffick. వర్తకము.

వాతగానివాడు for రాతవన్నెవాడు (perhaps error for ద్రాతకనిచేసేవాడు) A cloth dyer: a chintz maker.

వాదనము n. s. A sort of coarse cloth, like canvas, used in packing bales. మూటలుకట్టేముతకగుడ్డ.

వాదర n. s. The edge of a sword. కత్తియొక్క అంచు.

వాపసు n. s. واپس, *Wāpas.* Restitution, returning. మళ్లించడము. వాపసుచేసుట or వాపసు పంపుట to send back.

వాయిద n. s. (وعده, *Wāidah, Vaida.*) Period. Term fixed for payment. Pay day. Instalment, stated period. గడువు. వాయిదాబందిప్రకారము at the stipulated period. వాయిదాబందిరాజీనామా An agreement to pay a debt by certain instalments.

వారకము n. s. Money advanced for cultivation. సాగుబడిచేయడమునకు ముందుగాయిచ్చివెనకతీసుకొనేరూకలు.

వారపత్తునేల n. s. (Tamil வாரப்பத்துநிலம்) Land that pays revenue to Government. సర్కారుకుపన్నుయిచ్చేభూమి.

వారము n. s. (Tamil வாரம்) Share or part. భాగము, పాలు. కాపువారము inhabitant's share. మేలువారము the government share.

వారావధి n. s. (Tamil வாராவதி) A bridge. వంతెన.

వారి (واری, *Warī*) An affix, as, తారీఖువారి according to dates. మాహేవారి ماهواری monthly. ఆసామీవారి *āsāmī wār* man by man.

వారినామా n. s. A receipt by the captain for goods laden on a vessel: an inventory?

వారిసత్వము for వార్సుత్వము n. s. (from وارث *Waris.*) Heirship. The being his heir. కర్తృత్వము.

వారిసు for వారిస్ n. s. (وارث, *Waris*) An heir or lawful successor. కర్త.

వారువ n. s. A line or range (of pits in a salt work) A canal?

వాలా (والا, *Wala.*) An affix. "He who has" Thus *bacha-wāla,* one who has a child, ***ghora wala,*** a horsekeeper, one who has a horse *nao-wala* a boat man *garī wala* a coachman, a carter: *paisa wala* a monied man, one who is rich, *ghar-wala,* the landlord, the house holder. The feminine is wālī: thus, *bacha walī* she who has a child: and the plural wāleh, as *paisa walēh* those who are rich. Also of places, thus ఢిల్లీవాలా *Dillī wāla* he who lives in Delhi. *Kalcatta Walī,* the goddess who rules Calcutta.

వాలుగొమ్ము n. s. (Ganjam phrase.) A canal or sluice from a tank. అలుగులు.

వాలెకారు (K.) n. s. A peon, one who carries messages. See Reeve. బంట్రోతు.

వాసిరా n. s. (Kadapa.) Compensation. మొదటనష్టముకాచియిచ్చినది, చెల్లుగాయిచ్చినది.

వాహవా *interj.* (واه واه, *Wah Wah*! Bravo! well done! huzza! శభాషు.

విచారణయ్యము n. s. Vulgar for విచారణ Investigation, trial. విమర్శ.

విజారతు n. s. وزارت, *Wizārah.* The office, of Minister. మంత్రిత్వము.

విట్టలు n. s. *Vitthal Deo.* A certain god worshipped by the Madhvās. విష్ణుభక్తులుధూర్వులుచెప్పేపేరు.

విడిగోళ్లు or విడిగోళ్లయెద్దులు n. s. Spare bullocks. తాజాయెద్దులు.

విడుదుర n. s. (Tamil விடுமுறை.) Release, leave of absence.

విథివాసము, విత్యాసము Error for వ్యత్యాసము n. s. Which see.

విధాయకము n. s. Ordinance, order, decree. విధి, ఆజ్ఞ.

విరి n. s. Error for ఇరు. Thus విరిపార్శ్వంబుల on both sides.

విరివికట్టుట v. a. To pinion. పెడరెక్కలుకట్టుట.

విరిద్ధము Error for విరుద్ధము n. s. Difference, enmity.

విళంబరము n. s. (Tamil விளம்பரம்.) Publication, notification. ప్రసిద్ధము, ప్రకటన. విళంబరము ప్రాకికట్టుట to fix a notice in a conspicuous place. విళంబరపత్రిక notice.

విలాయతి, విలాతి, విలాయతు n. s. (for H. వలాయత్) Country, land, home. The common phrase for England: or for Persia. విలాయతిగ్రామము n. s. A hamlet or dependant village.

విలియ n. s. Arrangement, order, distribution. విలియవేయుట to compare. విలియపడలేదు This does not agree with it.

విలేవారి n. s. Arranging according to different heads, distribution, settlement. పరిష్కారముచేయడము, బాకీతువారిగాయేర్పరచడము.

విల్వ n. s. See విలియ.

విల్లంగము n. s. (Tamil விவகாரம்) A claim, or dispute. సర్వవిల్లంగశుద్ధిగా without any the smallest claim. This is a phrase in bills of sale, transferring property.

వివర్పు n. s. Error for విభేదము n. s. Difference. భేదము.

విశిరితి n. s. Leisure. సావకాశము, తీరుబాటు.

విషకంటకాలు n. s. A plant producing a black seed used as a plaister for boils.

విషముగోళము n. s. A certain drug?

విసిరుబాటు n. s. Means of success. గతి. ఈపూటకుఅన్నానికిచేతులోవిసిరుబాటులేక I cannot afford a meal.

విసిపలక n. s. A bench, seat. కూర్చుండేబల్ల.

విస్తుపోవుట v. n. To be astonished or amazed. ఆశ్చర్యపడుట.

విస్తువ for ఇస్తువ n. s. Estate, property. సొత్తు.

వీనాసు n. s. Some sort of cloth. ఒకరకపుగుడ్డ.

వీశ n. s. (Tamil வீசை.) A weight of 5 seers or 120 Rupees. అయిదుశేరులు.

వీసబడి or వీసుబడి n. s. Cess or tax levied on a town and then divided among several persons each of whom pays his share.

వీసుబడి n. s. See వీసబడి.

వుగ్గము n. s. See ఉగ్గము.

వురుఫు n. s. (H. عرف *Uruf.*) Alias, otherwise called.

వృధిపడియ n. s. (Ganjam) Land immemorially waste.

వెంకెన n. s. అనగాకడబర్త్రు. Q.?

వెంగరులు n. s. A sort of fish. Russell. No. 191.

వెంగ్యము n. s. An error for వ్యంగ్యము which see.

వెందుట Error for ఎందుట.

వెండ్రకాయ n. s. (Thus spelt in D.) A crab.

వెక్కపూరి n. s. అనగాపకాడికా. Q?

వెక్తి n. s. A corruption of వ్యక్తి.

వెగటించుట v. n. To be distasteful. అసహ్యపడుట. అదినీకువెగటించినదా did you dislike it?

వెట్ట n. s. (Tamil வெட்டை.) Toughness, excessive hardness. యీబంగారువెట్టగావున్నందువల్ల కమ్మిసాగదు this gold is too tough to draw into wire.

వెట్టు n. s. A stamp or tool for cutting coin?

వెట్టుపావడ n. s. (Tamil வெட்டு பாவாடை) A certain cloth, like fine handkerchief embroidered with gold or silver. కుచ్చుగాకట్టినగుడ్డ, రుమాలు.

వెత్యాసము n. s. వెత్యాసము n. s. Error for వ్యత్యాసము n. s. Difference.

వెన్నగరులు n. s. A sort of fish? see వెంగరులు. Russell No 191.

వెన్నోలపత్రము n. s. A note of hand. This is a corruption of the Tamil வெண்ணோலைபத்திரம் *Venn Olie pattiram.* తాకట్టుపెట్టకుండాపూరక ప్రాసియిచ్చినపత్రము.

వెలిగలిగెప్పు n. s. A plant called కటభి. Q.

వెలిమాడు n. s. Exports, as opposed to లోమాడు imports; goods received.

వెలివిడుపుధాన్యము n. s. Grain of a blackish colour.

వెల్లలి or వెల్లలినేల n. s. A plain, the low lands.

వెల్లాయి n. s. (Tamil வெள்ளாவி.) The steam of water used in bleaching cotton cloth.

వెల్లిగడ్డ n. s. (Tamil வெள்ளிக்கிழங்கு.) The sweet potatoe. చిలగడము.

వేజెము Error for వ్యాజ్యము n. s. Dispute.

వేటుబడిసొమ్ము n. s. Money advanced to weavers, &c. నేసేవారికిముందుగాయిచ్చినరూకలు.

వేనుగ్రాను, అనగాదీర్ఘవృంత. Q.

వేపిలిచేప or యాపిలిచేప n. s. A kind of fish.

వేరియు n. s. (in navigation.) A tack in sailing. వేరియుఫిరాయించుట To make a tack or turn.

వేరుమద్ది n. s. A certain tree. See మద్ది or అర్జునము.

వేరుమల్లె n. s. A certain medical herb.

వేలాం n. s. Auction. వేలాంపాట to sell by auction.

వేవిలి adj. Occasional, done at intervals.

వేశిలి or వేసిలి n. s. Disagreement, unhealthiness, contagion. ఉపద్రవము, తెవులు.

వేష్ట n. s. Mortification, annoyance. వేసట. (A low word.)

వేసాలు n. s. Dress, feigning. వేషము, వేడిజము. వేసాలమారి one who feigns.

వైకటికుడు n. s. A jeweller. రత్నములుసానబట్టే వాడు. D.

వైకుంఠము n. s. (Literally, *heaven*,) A taunting word for a dungeon. (See *Bykunta* in the Gloss. to 5th Report.)

వైరాను adj. ویران *Wairan*. Desolate, waste, depopulated, ruined. పాడుపడ్డ, నాశమైన.

వైరాను n. s. Desert. ఆపరగణాలురెండున్ను వైరానులోవున్నవి these lands are desolate.

వైశాఖడోలు n. s. See ఆయిందాజ్యాస్తి.

వొ Words beginning with Vo, Wo, will generally be found under ఒ the vowel O.

వ్యభజనము error for విభజన n. s. Allotment of shares or portions, dividing.

వ్యాపారి n. s. A class of secular bramins. గోలకొండవ్యాపారీలు another class of the same kind of bramins.

శ ష స

శ, ష, స S', SH, S. These three letters are so mingled in the spoken Telugu that in the colloquial and mixed language they are often used wrongly. And they will here be considered as one and the same initial.

సంకు n. s. (శంకు * a pin or stake) *Sankoo*. A cross, used in survey measurement. See Revenue Selections folio vol. 3 page 834.

సంగ n. s. A low hollow : a pool?

సంగుబందకట్టించుట v. a. (سنگ بند *Sang band*. Stone facing.) To have the banks of a pond faced with stone. కుంటకురాళ్లుకట్టుట.

శంగోలము n. s. (Tamil செங்கோல்.) A sceptre, a royal staff. Notes on A. 4. 37.

సంజరుఖానా n. s. (for سنجرخانی *Sanjar Khānī*.) A kind of cloth. Some sort of shawl presented as a gift in honour. వస్త్రవిశేషము.

సంజాయం n. s. The same as మాఫీ.

సంజాయించుకొనుట or సముదాయించుకొనుట v. a. (from سمجھانا *Samjānā*.) To beg off; to apologize for. To repair, to put in order, or in repair. To rest himself, recover himself. సమాళించుకొనుట.

సంజాయించుట or సముదాయించుట v. a. (from سمجھانا *Samjānā*.) To calm, comfort, pacify. To persuade, cajole, talk over. వోదార్చుట.

సంజాయిషి n. s. سمجھایش *Samjāish*. Peace, satisfaction. Explanation, persuasion. సమాధానము.

సంతతోద్ధారముగా for సంతతధారగా adv. Vastly, excessively. ఎడతెగకుండా.

సంతనచేసుట v. a. To collect money by subscription.

సంతనను n. s. (سلطنت *Sultanat*.) Pomp? display? Loc. VI. 58.

సంద n. s. A certain forest tree?

సందివాలము, సందివాళము n. s. (Tamil சந்திவாளம்.) Sandivālam. Loss in redeeming a pledged article. Agency, fees, commission or percentage paid to brokers. A penal sum, deposited and to be forfeited for the non-fulfilment of a purchase.

సందుకాపెట్టె for సందూక్ పెట్టె n. s. (صندوق *Sandūq*) A box.

సందుగాపెట్టె n. s. (صندوقچه *Sandukcha*) A small box or trunk.

సంధిరోగము n. s. Epilepsy. వాకిస్రోగాలు.

సంపాయించుట, సంపాదించుట for సంపాద్యము చేసుట v. a. To earn.

సంబరకాకి, సంబారిపిట్ట n. s. The bird called king crow?

సంబరాలు n. s. Sweet words: coaxing. సంబరాలుపెట్టుట to coax, fondle.

సంబళిచెట్టు n. s. The tree called Vitex Negundo.

సంబళులు or సంబాళు n. s. A superior kind of rice. కుసుమ ధాన్యము.

సంబాళించుట for సమాళించుట v. a. (from سنبهالنا *Sambhālnā*. Tamil சமாளித்திருக்க) To manage, to furnish, bring about, control, restrain.

సంభ్రవం for సంభ్రమము n. s. Joy, pleasure. సంతోషము.

సంమంధం for సంబంధము * n. s. Connection, relation. అనుబంధము.

సంయి for స్యాయి n. s. (سیاهی *Siyāhī*) Ink. సంయిబుడ్డి an inkstand. D. H. 1. 158.

సకటుసుమారుగా i. e. సక్రుత్తుగా adv. Here and there, scatteredly, moderately (for S సకృత్.)

సకలాతి or సుకలాతు n. s. سقلات *Saqlāt*. Woollen cloth: scarlet cloth. Broad cloth. In the Glossary to Chaucer's Poems, '*Chekelatoun*'. i. e. French. *Ciclaton* "cloth of gold." In the extreme north of India this signifies a *blanket*.

సకలాతిబొంతచేప n. s. A sort of perch fish. (Russel, No cxxx.)

సకాలి or సకాలిచెట్టు n. s. (Sukalee) A kind of tree. Rox. page 762.

సక్తుచేయుట v. a. (from سخت *Sakht*.) To use violence. నిర్బంధము చేసుట. సక్తుహుకుం positive orders.

సకీల్ n. s. سرخیل *Sarkhail*. The chief or General. (called Surkeel.)

సగటుసుమారు adv. سگت شمار *Sagat Shumar*. On an average. సరాసరి.

సగించుట for సహించుట v. a. from سہنا *Sahāna*. To suffer, forbear, sustain. తాళుట, తడుట.

సగిలి or సగిలె n. s. Toughness; as of wood: stubbornness; Strength, richness, as of corn land. compare జవురము.

సగిలిపారిన or సగిలెపారిన adj. Tough, stubborn, fat, as land. మొండిపారిన, గడుసుబారిన.

సగ్గుబియ్యము for సబ్బుబియ్యము n. s. The grain called sago.

సగ్గులిబి or సగ్గులిమి n. s. A mud nest like that of a wasp. కందిరీగగూటివంటి తొకమంటిగూడు.

సచోటా adj. (سچوٹا *Sachōta*.) Honest, upright, faithful, guileless. నిజమైన, సరసుడైన. Jagann. 3. 120; here it is 'sneaking, pitiful.'

సజావలు for సజావల్ n. s. سزاول *Sazāwal*. Violent measures to enforce payment. తరుభు.

సజావు adj. (*Sajāo* or rather سزاوار *Sazāwār*.) Clear, unobstructed, plain, as a road. సజావుగా honestly.

సజ్జగడ్డి n. s. A sort of root like seaweed: the alkali of which is called సజ్జాకారము or impure chlorate of Soda. Ainslie. 1. 395.

సజ్జనకోల n. s. (from سزا *Saza*, punishment.) A scourge or whip, a rod. చదివేదిన్నవాండ్లను శిక్షించకోల. H. 3. 180. రెట్టలగట్టిబట్టిందిరేఖ మారుకొట్టుచెట్టుగ సజ్జనకోలదెకను.

సతకోపము vulgarly శఠగోపము or శఠగోపుర ము n. s. A dish-cover, shaped like the cup of a hooka. On it are two marks like shoes, called Vishnu's sandals.

శఠన, సఠన n. s. Pride, insolence, deceit. Jealousy, envy. ADC. గర్వము, మోసము, కక.

సతకు n. s. Help? aid, convenience?

సడాయించుట or సదాయించుట v. a. To spur. కాలిముల్లుతో గుర్రమును ఢాడాయించుట.

సతిరి n. s. (corrupted from چھتری *Chhatrī*. ఛత్రి) An umbrella. గొడుగు.

సతాయించుట v. a. (ستانا *Satānā*.) To plague, tease, torment, persecute, vex. హింసించుట, బాధించుట.

సత్తిగెయినాము n. s. (from K. సత్తిగె an umbrella or parasol.) Field or land granted to an umbrella bearer. గొడుగుకట్టేవాడికియిచ్చినసేల.

సత్తిపార n. s. A sort of fish. Russel. No. 11.

సత్తుపమానా n. s. See కందుమానా.

సదనపువెదురు n. s. A kind of bamboo. ఒకతరహాముండికట్టెవెదురు, దీన్నియీటెకర్రలకువేస్తారు. Rox. 2. 193.

సదరహీ, సదరు, సదర్హి adj. (صدر Sadr.) Aforesaid, abovementioned. పైనచెప్పిన, పైనవుదాహరించబడ్డ. This word is often used for ఆ, meaning that, the aforesaid.

సదరున adv. from صدر Sadr. Above. పైన. సదరునచెప్పినప్రకారము as is abovestated.

సదర్హీలు n. s. plu. The abovesaid persons. పైనచెప్పబడ్డవాండ్లు.

సదాపు n. s. سداب Sadāb. A certain herb called "rue."

సదురుబోయులు n. s. A certain division or sect in the బోయ tribe. ఒకతరహాబోయవాండ్లు.

సద్దించుట v. a. To polish cloth by dry beating with mallets. బట్టలనుకట్టనవేసుట.

సద్రి for సదర్ صدر Sadr. i. e. Sadarhi. The abovesaid.

సధ్యా for సద్యః * adv. At present. తత్కాలమునకు.

సన్, సన or సన్న n. s. سن San. Year. సంవత్సరము ; this is generally written స్న thus స్న ౧౨౬౦.

సన్వారు adv. سن وار Sanwār. Yearly, annual.

సని plu. సనియనులు or సనీలు n. s. for سنين Sanīn. A bayonet (Shakesp.) సిపాయీలతుపాకీలకొనకుతగిలించేచేరియీటెలు.

సనికిపార n. s. A hoe or spade of a peculiar shape called *mamati*. ఒకతరహాపార.

సనుగులు n. s. A piece of stuff, containing several handkerchiefs woven in one web. తాను.

సన్న n. s. *Sanna*. A lever : a pole put under a weight to lift it. బరువుపైకిలేవడమునకైఅడుగునవేసితేపేకర్ర.

సన్నదు n. s. سند *Sanad*. A patent of office or nobility. An order. A written grant, instrument or diploma, charter or letters patent. తాకీదు, ఆజ్ఞాపత్రిక, యోగ్యతాపత్రిక.

సన్నరాష్ట్రము n. s. A medical root. Alpinia galanga minor. ఒకమందుదినుసు.

సన్నాయి n. s. شهنائي *Shah-nāī*. A clarionet. ఒకవూదువాద్యము.

సన్మాది n. s. (from سن ماضي *San-i-mazi*. The past year.) Old debts, balances of former years. గడిచినసంవత్సరపుబాకీ.

సన్మాని plu. సన్మానులు n. s. They who have much influence or honor. సన్మానముగలవారు.

సపము error for శవము n. s. A corpse. పీనుగ.

సపాసి adj. Empty, fasting. ఉత్తదిగావుండే, కడుపుగావుండే. వానికడుపుసపాసిగావున్నది he is fasting.

సప్రాణించుట v. n. To be well, abated. స్వస్థముగావుండుట.

సఫరు n. s. See సబరు. సఫరుసామాను sea stores.

సఫేది n. s. سفيدي *Sufaidī*. Ceruse, white lead used in painting. తెల్లవన్నము.

సబబు n. s. سبب *Sabab*. Reason, ground, cause. కారణము.

సబరు or సఫరు n. s. (سفر *Safr*.) A voyage. The season for voyaging out at sea. పైసబరు the season for coasting. The two monsoons. దరిసబరు sailing along the shore. లోసబరు putting out to sea. మేములోసబరుపోతూవుండగా while we were far out at sea.

సబరు n. s. صبر *Sabar*. A top-gallant mast. వాడస్తంభములోకొనది.

సబ్జ n. s. سبزه *Sabza*. Green leaf : the intoxicating drug called bang. బచ్చిగంజాయాకు.

సబ్నివీసు or సబ్నీసు n. s. صوبه‌نويس *Subāh nivees*. The District clerk or paymaster. నౌకరులకుజీతముయిచ్చేవొకఉద్యోగస్థుడు.

సబ్బువియ్యము n. s. (rather called సగ్గుబియ్యము) Sago.

సమత్తు or సముతు n. s. for سمت *Simt*. A subdivision, quarter. తాలూకాలోవొకభాగము.

సమత్దారి n. s. سمتداري *Simt darī*. The office of a సముతుదారు (سمتدار) *Samutdar* ; a clerk or accountant.

సముష్టి * adj. Assembled, collected. సముష్టిగా collectively, in general. వాండ్లుసముష్టిగావు న్నారు they live in one family.

సమస్థానము n. s. A mistake for సంస్థానము n. s. Any seat of Government.

సమానము n. s. A pair of tweezers?

సమాళించుట v. a. (error for *Samālnā.*) To manage, control. నిర్వహించుట. సమాళించిమాట్లాడుట to speak with good care.

సమారిరి adv. Error for సరాసరి.

సముఖా n. s. *Samakh.* A binnacle or compass stand. వాడలలోకుంబాసుఉంచేపెట్టె.

సముజాయించుట or సముదాయించుట v. a. (from سمجهانا *Samjāna*) To calm, comfort, pacify.

సముజాయిషి n. s. سمجهايش *Samjāish.* Peace, satisfaction. Explanation, conciliation, persuasion. సముదాయించబడము, తెలియచెప్పడము.

సముతు n. s. سمت *Simt.* A subdivision, a parish. తాలూకాలోవొకభాగము.

సముతుబంది, సముత్బంది or సముద్బంది n. s. (for سمت بندي *Simt bandi*) Arranging villages into a subdivision of a Taluk. యేర్పరచబడము.

సముత్తు n. s. (for سمت *Simt*) A subdivision of a Taluk. తాలూకాలోకవొభాగము.

సముద్దారుడు n. s. See సముద్దారుడు.

సముదాయించుట v. a. (from سمجهايش كرنا *Samjāish carna*) To comfort, persuade. To appease, lull. To supply. ఓదార్చుట, అమరజెప్పుట.

సముద్దారుడు n. s. for سمتدار *Simt dār.* He who manages a Samut or subdivision of a Taluk. ఒకసముతుయొక్క అధికారి.

సముద్రపండు n. s. Sea-apple. It is about the size of a large melon of a very dry texture and bitter taste. Literally, foreign apples.

సముద్రపచ్చ n. s. A plant called convolvulus speciosus. (Partington.)

సముస్థానం error for సంస్థానము n. s. Which see.

సమ్మంధం Error for సంబంధం used thus, సొమ్ముసమ్మంధం Odds and ends.

సమ్మతు n. s. See సముతు.

సమ్మాలు or శమ్మాలు n. s. A certain kind of cakes. భక్ష్యవిశేషము.

సయి or సహీ interj. صحيح *Sahīh.* Right! correct! Well said! This word is sometimes used *with* a signature, or *instead* of a name signed.

సరంగు for సరాంగు (سرهنگ *Sarhang.* A Serang, head lascar, or native boatswain.

సరంజాం n. s. سرانجام *Saranjām.* Apparatus, the needful, *set out* or *trim*; sundries. Things, articles, property. సామాను, వస్తువులు. రూపాయాలుసరంజాంచేశి he got the money ready. నావల్లసరంజాంకాదు It cannot be effected.

సరంబీ n. s. (A Malay word; see Marsden page 168) A porch, gallery, awning: a clinker-built house made of shingle or board. (Masulipatam) సరంబీకొట్టు n. s. Sarambi coṭṭu. A room with a cieling. బల్లకూర్పుచేసియుండేగది.

సరకారు or సర్కారు n. s. سركار *Sarcār.* The Government. దివాణము.

సరకులసామాను n. s. Goods, luggage?

శరతు, షరతు for శరత్ n. s. شرط *Shart.* Agreement, conditions agreed on. ఒడంబడిక.

సరదా n. s. The trigger of a gun. తుపాకిమద్రుముకదేటట్టుగాఅదిమీటుపాకిక్రిందివి.

సరపణి or సరపళి n. s. (సరిపెణ) A silver chain, a necklace. గొలుసు, ఒకకంఠాభరణము.

సరఫరాజి n. s. سرفرازي *Sarafrāzī.* Promotion, kindness or regard; exaltation; advancement: accomplishment of a work. అభివృద్ధి, అభిమానము, గౌరవము. లష్కరుసరఫరాజి purveying for a marching army or for troops passing. అందువల్లసరఫరాజుఅయినది I was much honoured. Lit: my head was exalted.

శరబడి n. s. Sarabadi (Tamil.) Tribe, caste, family. తెగ. Rottler, p. 243.

సరవడి n. s. A sledge, a kind of carriage. ఎద్దులుయీడ్చుకొనిపొయ్యేపైకిలొయ్యమొద్దు, దీనిమీదమనుష్యులుకూర్చుండిపోతారు.

సరసునీరసు *Saras nīras.* Good and bad, one with another?

శరా for షరా n. s. شرح *Sharah*. Remark. Postscript. Nota-benè. ఒకదాన్నిగురించిచెప్పేవిశేషము, దీన్నివిచారించవలసినది.

శరాకతు, శరాఖతు for షరాకత్ n. s. شراکت *Shirākat*) Partnership in business. పాలిభాగస్వత్వము.

సరాగంగా adv. Without any difficulty, ధారాళముగా, నిరాటంకముగా.

సరాజి meant for శిరాజి.

సరాదు n. s. The shaft of a well? or its foundation. గోడసరాదున At the foot of the wall.

శరానా or సురానా, శరాణా n. s. (from چرانا *Churana*, theft) A fine levied on those who steal (ears of corn.)

సరాపు, సరాబు n. s. for صراف *Sarrāf*. A banker, a money changer, a cashkeeper.

సరాయి for షరాయి n. s. شراعي *Sharāi* Tight trowsers. నిడుపుగావుండేచల్లడము.

శరారత్ n. s. شرارت *Shararat*. Wickedness, outrage, cruelty. దుర్మార్గము.

సరాసరి adv. More or less, about, on an average. సుమారు.

సరికొల్లచేప (*Sari kulla*) n. s. A sort of fish: "Perca" a perch. Russell No. 123.

సరికేలి n. s. سرخیل *Sar-i-khail*. i. e. a general or commander. The Major Domo. The king's favourite. This Title సరికేలి pronounced సర్కీలు Surkeel is in use at Tanjore and Vizianagram and Punganore.

సరిగిరో n. s. سرگرو *Sarigiro*. The prophet or head of a sect, an abbot. గురువు.

సరితట్టుట v. a. To make equal, to arrange differences, to make content or satisfied. సరిపుచ్చుట. ఆబియ్యముఆనెలకుసరితట్టిపోయినది the rice was all used up in the month.

సరితరం n. s. Classification of lands, an account wherein fields are rated according to the goodness of the soil. నేలలనుతరంవారిగా ఏర్పరచడము.

సరిష్ట n. s. for سررشته *Sarrishtah* The order, arrangement. క్రమము.

సరిష్టదారుడు usually శిరస్తేదారుడు n. s. for سررشته دار *Sarrishtah dār*. The head Native Accountant and manager. The head officer in a Court of Justice.

సరిహద్దు for సరహద్దు n. s. سرحد *Sarhad*. Boundary, land mark; a frontier. పొలిమేర.

సరీ interj. Aha! very fine! oh!

శరీకు, షరీక్ n. s. شریک *Sharik*. A friend or ally. సహాయుడు. శరీకతు friendship.

సరేసు n. s. سریش *Sarēsh*. Glue. జిగురుద్రవము.

సరుకు n. s. Goods, commodities. సరుకుగాచెల్లించుట to pay in kind not in money.

సరుచష్మా n. s. for سرچشمه *Sarchashmā*. A captain of a certain number of companies of peons each commanded by a Dafadar.

సరుజు n. s. سرج *Sarj*. A saddle.

శరుతియ్యానా for షరత్ యానాకౌల్ *Shartiyāna cawl*. A conditional agreement. ఒడంబడిక.

సరుదునీరు n. s. A land flood. సరుదుకట్ట a dam.

సరుపేచు for సర్ పేచ్ n. s. سرپیچ *Sarpēch*. A gold cloth lappet worn over the turban. పాగామీదకురకలుకట్టుకొనేసరిగకుట్టు.

సరువు n. s. سرو *Sarv*. A cypress tree. ఒకచెట్టు.

సర్కాయించుట v. n. from سرکانا *Sarcāna*. To move, put aside, shift. తొలుగుట.

సర్కారు n. s. سرکار *Sarcār*. The Government. A District. సర్కారుఉద్యోగము public employ, employ under Government.

సర్కీటు n. s. (English) 'Circuit.' జిల్లాకోర్టల్లాగావుండినకోర్టు.

శర్తియానా, శర్తియానాకౌలు n. s. *Shartiyāna kowl*. A conditional agreement. ఒడంబడిక.

శర్తు n. s. for شرط *Shart*. Agreement, conditions stipulated. ఒడంబడిక. శర్తుగల adj. Conditional. ఒడంబడికగల.

సర్దారుడు for సర్దార్ n. s. (سردار *Sardār*. Sardárudu Sirdar.) Chief, Captain, Leader, Ringleader, Ruler, Head, Gentleman, Lord. పెద్దగావుండేవాడు.

సర్దేశముఖి or సిరదేశముఖి n. s. سردیس مکهي *Sardes mukhi*. The head officer of a province.

Also the allowance granted him of ten percent on the collections. See Malcolm's Memoir. 1. 66.

శర్ధ n. s. *Sardha.* A mispronunciation for శ్రద్ధ Faith, confidence, wish, desire, strong inclination.

సర్నామా n. s. سرنامه *Sarnamah.* Superscription, direction. పైవిలాసము.

సర్పేసు or సర్పేశ for సర్ పేచ్ سرپیچ *Sarpēch.* A head tire or gold band over the turband. తురకలు పాగామీద కట్టుకొనే సరిగ కట్టు. Tara. 3. 16.

సర్బరాయి usually సర్బరా n. s. سربراهي *Sarbarāhī.* Furnishing supplies, preparation. సామానులు సమకూర్చుట. అశ్వదళసర్బరాయి Providing requisites for a regiment. Foraging.

సర్రె for దరియ n. s. A steep, a hollow between hills.

సర్లష్కరి, సర్లష్కరు or సల్లష్కరు n. s. سرلشکر *Sarlashkar.* General: chief, leader. సేనానాయకుడు.

సర్వమంచాలా n. s. Land granted on a light quit rent. సర్వమాన్యము.

సలగం n. s. Dung, ordure. పురీషము. సలగామాను to eat purisham.

సలక n. s. A crack. బీటిక. సలకతీసినది it is cracked.

శలవు n. s. for సెలవు Charges, cost, expense, expenditure. వ్యయము. See preamble to Reg. 1. of 1816. శలవు in this sense is a foreign word unknown in the northern circars. It is Tamil.

సలహా n. s. (for صلاح *Salāh*, and also used صلح *Sulh.*) Advice, counsel, peace, concord. బుద్ధి, సమ్మతి.

సలహాకారి usually సలహాకారి n. s. from صلاح *Salāh.* An accomplice, an adviser. సహాయుడు.

సలా n. s. for సలహా Persuasion, صلاح *Salāh.* Counsel, advice, temptation. బోధన.

సలాం n. s. سلام *Salām.* Salutation. దండము.

సలాకు n. s. سلاخ *Salakh.* The mark on coin. రూపాయీ అంచున వుండే టిది, యిదివుంటే రూపాయి సరిగ్గా మూరదు.

సలాటముగా adv. Freely. ధారాళముగా.

సలాబం or సలాబం n. s. (Tamil) A pearl fishery. ముత్యములెత్తడము.

సలాము n. s. سلام *Salām.* Salutation, a bow. (see దండము.)

సలీసు adj. سليس *Salīs.* Easy. సులభమైన. సలీసు తరం a favourable assessment.

శలువ usually శిలువ صليب *Salib.* The Christian Cross. క్రీస్తును వేసిన కొయ్య.

సల్తన for సంతన n. s. Joining, junction. ఇమిడిక.

సల్లష్కరు i. e. సరిలష్కరు n. s. سرلشکر *Sarlaskar.* General, Chief, Commander సేనానాయకుడు.

సల్లూకి or సలూకి for సల్లూక్ n. s. سلوک *Sulūk.* Good terms or understanding, kindness, benevolence. మంచితనము, మంచితనము.

సవరక్షారలవణము for సౌవర్చలవణము n. s. A sort of salt. ఒకతరహా ఉప్పు.

సవతు or సవుతు n. s. Kind or sort. A sort of cloth used for turbans. మాదిరి, ఒకతరహా పాగయున్ను.

సవద్రి n. s. A ship's bowsprit. వాడకు ముక్కుకట్టే సియుండేకొయ్య.

సవరవాండ్లు n. s. *Savara.* The name of a savage tribe in the Kimedy Hills in Vizagapatam. చెంచువాండ్లు, యానాదివాండ్లు. See account of the మాళయా సవరలు in Loc. Rec. VII. 136.

సవలచేప n. s. A fish. Russell, plate 41 says Sawala, and in plate 143. Sowarah.

సవాయి n. s. *Savāi.* The main-stay (sea term.)

సవాయిగావుండే adj. Scrofulous, tainted by old venereal complaints. సవాయిరోగము such taint.

సవారి n. s. سواري *Sawāri.* Riding: any mode of conveyance. సవారిపోవుట To take a ride. గాలిసవారి or కాలుసవారి walk, an airing, walking afoot.

సవాలు n. s. سوال *Sawāl.* A question, interrogation, inquiry, a proposal, or one bidding at an auction. ప్రశ్నఅడగడము.

సివాస్సి or సంబ్బాసి error for సగంబాసి adj. About half.

సిష్టకల్లి n. s. (see స్రి—) Craft, wicked device: Skill, cleverness (used in a contemptuous manner.) కుయుక్తి.

శహబాసు interj. شهباش *Shahbash.* Well done! Elphinstone in his Caubul 1. 374. observes that it is pronounced *ai shawasha* اي شواشا adding, "Oh well done; perhaps the original words are *ai-shah-bash.* Ah, be a king. "At pueri ludentes Rex eris, aiunt" an ingenious reference to Horace.

శహరు for షహర్ n. s. شهر *Shahr.* A city: the capital. పట్టణము.

శహరుగస్తు vulgarly సిరిగస్తు n. s. شهرگشت *Shahr gasht.* Parading or going in procession round the town. The name given to the final day of the హోళీపండుగ hoeli feast or మొహరం. గ్రామప్రదక్షిణము, ఊరేగింపు.

సహీ చేయుట or సయిసుచేసుట v. n. from صحيح *Sahīh.* To sign. చేవ్రాలుచేసుట.

సహీ adj. صحيح *Sahih.* Proper, correct, right, but this word is constantly attached to notes, bonds and deeds &c. or uttered at the close of declarations or statements of terms, conditions, proposals &c. implying approval and acquiescence: and is often used after the signature of one's own name. See a clear proof in Tod's Rajasthan 1. 202. where he misinterprets it (సహాయ) *Sahāya*; whereas it is *Sahīh.*

సా॥ a contraction for సాకిన్ also for సాహెబు and sometimes it means సాష్టాంగదండము.

సాంద్ర n. s. The name of a class of toddy sellers.

సాంబా سانبا *Sāmbā.* n. s. The large red stag (Malcolm) commonly called the Elk: but it is not the elk. The Samver of Bengal. See minute description in British Cyclopœdia, reprinted in Napier's scenes and sports. 1840 vol. 2. page 80. It is omitted in Shakesp. in Haughton in Molesworth in Reeve and in Wilson. పెద్దదుప్పి.

సాకతుంగ or సాఖతుంగ n. s. A weed called Cyperus rotundus; cattle eat it, hogs are fond of the roots, the roots dried and powdered are used as a perfume.

సాకిన్ or సాకిను ساكن *Sākin.* n. s. Residing: an inhabitant, tenant. సాకినుచెన్నపట్నం inhabitant of Madras. In such expressions Sākin-i-Chennapatnam, the order of the words is according to Persian syntax, the letter i being put between as representing "of." సా॥ మంగళగిరి inhabitant of Mangalagiri. కాపురస్థుడైన, కాపురముఉండేవాడైన.

సాఖ్తి adj. ساختہ *Sākhta.* Manufactured. చేసే as of salt. నమ్మకుసాఖ్తి (meant for *Sākht*) the manufacture of salt.

సాగపొలము n. s. Low lands: a dell; a low moist field.

సాగబడి, సాగబళి or సాగవళి for సాగుబడి n. s. (Tamil சாகுபடி.) Cultivation, tillage. కృషి. వ్యవసాయము.

సాగుమానం error for సమాగమనము* n. s. Which see.

సాచా adj. سانچا *Sāncha.* Honest, faithful, true, real, just. పెద్దమనిషియైన, న్యాయమైన, నిజమైన. సాచామనిషి an honest man. సాచాగా adv. Honestly, fairly, faithfully. By fair means, truly, really. పెద్దమనిషితనముగా, న్యాయముగా.

శాజీర, సాజీరా (شاجيرا *Shah-Jira.*) n. s. Cumminseed. A certain odoriferous seed used in cookery. జీలకర్ర.

సాజు ساز *Sāz.* n. s. Maker. చేసేవాడు. నమ్మక్ సాజు *nammak sāz* a salt manufacturer.

సాటా n. s. Barter, exchange. మార్పడము adj. Similar, equal. సమమైన. సాటాకోటిబేరము bartered merchandize. సాటాయిచ్చుట to give in exchange, to barter.

సాటాతెచ్చుట or సాటావేయుంచుట v. a. To compare. సాటువచేసుట.

సాటి or సాటు (Tamil சாட்டு.) Thus used లాభ సాటిబేరము a bargain, sale with profits.

శాడాయించుట v. a. چلانا *Chalāna.* To spur a horse. గుఱ్ఱముకాళ్లతోతట్టితోడాయించుట.

సాణితనము for శాణాతనము n. s. (*Shānī* for سيانا *Syāna.*) Cleverness, skill. చమత్కారము, నేర్పుతనము.

సాతు n. s. ساتھ *Sāth*. Company, escort. జోబు, తోడు, సహవాసము.

సాదరా n. s. Cloth of gold, or silver stuff. జలతారుబట్ట.

సాదరు, సాదిరు adj. صادر *Sādir*. Issued, given, proclaimed, enacted. సాదరుచేయుట صادرکرنا to issue, give (an order.)

సాదర్వారి, సాదల్వారి, సాదిర్వారిద్. n. s. صادروارد *Sāderwārid*. Expense and receipt. Out goings and incomings. Now used for petty charges for pens, ink, paper, lamp-oil &c.

సాదా adj. ساده *Sādah*. Plain, clear, downright, distinct, unmixed, unornamented. Blank, unwritten. సాఫుగానుండే, ఉత్త.

సాదిరుచేయుట v. a. See సాదరు.

శాదిలింగం n. s. (Tamil சாதிலிங்கம்.) Vermilion; red paint: factitious Cinnabar; made of mercury and brimstone. See Ainslie. 2. 253.

శానభోగు or శ్యానబోగు n. s. *Shanabhog*. (Kannadi.) A village clerk or accountant. గ్రామకరణము. Munro spells it *Shambogue*.

సాని adj (ثاني *Sānī*.) Second, second in rank. రెండో, నాయబ్. Thus; నాసానికరణములు my fellow-clerks.

సానిక n. s. An earthen bowl. పాత్రవిశేషము.

సానిచేప, సాని మొయ్య n. s. Shanee Moia, A species of Labrus. Russell's fishes. No. 119 and 120 మత్స్యవిశేషము.

శానితనము for జాణతనము n. s. Wickedness, cunning, trick, prank.

సాపడుట v. a. (Tamil.) To eat. భోజనముచేసుట. Bhanu. 4. 11.

సాపత్యం n. s. Error for సాపత్న్యము.

సాపాటు n. s. (Tamil) Food, eating. అన్నము, భోజనమున్ను. సాపాటుకాచేసుకొనివచ్చెను he dined and then came. సాపాటురాముడు A glutton.

సాఫు for సాఫ్ adj. صاف *Sāf*. Clean, clear, pure, fair. (see తేట, మడి, and శుభ్రమైన) *fair* as a copy. సాఫుబట్టలు clean clothes. Vulgarly *saf* also means straight, level, not crooked. సాఫుప్రతి a fair copy: (of a paper.) సాఫువ్రాయడము n. s. Copying out fair. తీర్పుగావ్రాయడము. సాఫుచేసుట to ruin, utterly destroy.

సాబకు for సాబిక్ adv. سابق *Sabac*. Formerly. సాబకుహుకుంచొప్పున in conformity to the former orders.

సాబత్ adj. ثابت *Sābit*. Proved. నిరూపింపబడ్డ.

శాబాసు or శాబాసు for శబాబాస్ شاباش *Shabāsh*. interj. Bravo, excellent. శాబాసుగిరి n. s. Triumph, exultation. జయము.

సాబితు for సాబత్ adj. ثابت *Sābit*. Proved, established, brought home, verified. సాబితుచేయుట to prove, establish.

సామాను n. s. (سامان *Sāmān*.) Things, baggage, luggage, goods, wares, tools, apparatus, stuff, substance. A service or set of things. అంగడిసామానులు marketing. వంటసామానులు cooking ingredients.

శామిలాతుబంజరు n. s. بنجر *Shāmilātbanjar*. Land mixed with waste. Land, part of which is waste. కొంతపాడుగానుండేభూమి.

శామిలు usually షామిలు or షామిలాత adj. (شامل *Shāmil*.) United, conspiring, leaguing. దుర్మార్గముగా చేరుకొన్న, కలుసుకొన్న, కూడుకొన్న. శామిలుగా adv. Unitedly, in league.

సాయబు, సాయిబు for సాహేబు n. s. (صاحب *Sāhib*.) Owner, master, possessor. పెద్దమనిషి, యజమానుడు a gentleman. Also an ordinary word for Musulman, just as a Frenchman is vulgarly called a Monsieur.

సాయరు n. s. from سایر *Sāyer*. (A journey.) The transit duty. Variable imposts, customs, duties, tolls. సుంకము.

సాయి, శాయి for శ్యాయి n. s. سياهي *Syahi*. Country Ink: this is made of lampblack and never turns rusty. English Ink is called ఇంకి and (if made with galls) soon loses its blackness.

శారం n. s. (Tamil சாரம்) *Shārām*. Scaffolding. పరంజు. (Madras) Tamil Dictionary page 275.

శారటు or సారట్టు n. s. (The English word) A "chariot:" used for gigs &c. కుర్రపుబండి.

శారదగాడు n. s. A masquer or buffoon, who in a farce plays the part of Siva.

సారవ n. s. *Sarva*. A bridge (Cud.) A scaffolding: rather పరంజు q. v. శారము.

సారసవేరు n. s. *Sārass root*. A medicinal drug ఒకమందుదినుసు.

సారా, సారాయ or సారాయి n. s. Spirituous liquor. Wine. Arrack. మద్యము. సారాయిఅంగడి an arrack shop, gin shop.

సారీ n. s. ساری *Sārī*. A petticoat. చీర.

సారువాపంట n. s. The crop raised on low lying land. (Raj. and Nellore.)

సారె n. s. A man (at chess.) సారెనుపడేయుట v. a. To place (a piece, or man) at dominos or drafts.

సార్జంటు, సార్జంటు or సార్జెంటుడు n. s. "Sergeant." జాతిబంట్రోతు. Bobbili. 3. 106.

శార్పనా, షార్పనా or శాహరుపనా n. s. شهر پناه *Shahr panāh*. A city wall. పట్టణముచుట్టూ వుండు ప్రహారిగోడ.

సార్థా n. s. Success, completion, achievement. అనుకూలము, సంపూర్తి, సాధ్యము.

సార్థాఅవుట v. n. To succeed: be finished. సఫలమవుట, అనుకూలమవుట.

సార్థాచేయుట v. a. To settle, prepare, get ready. పరిష్కారముచేసుట, సిద్ధముచేసుట.

సార్థాపడుట v. n. To prosper. పూరాపడుట.

సార్వ n. s. See. సారవ.

సార్వా n. s. Any grain that has a light coloured husk, as rice?

సాళవాదాళవాలెక్క n. s. The account regarding the white and black grain crops: i. e. For the whole year. This term is peculiar to the north.

సాలస్త్రీ or సాలిస్త్రీ n. s. سالستری *Sālastri*. A farrier, a horse doctor. గుర్రపువైద్యుడు.

సాలాబాదు سال آباد *Sāl-ābād*. adj. Annual.

సాలాబాదుఖర్చు or సాలాబాదఖరుచు The permanent charges of a village, as those for the Pagoda &c. దేవాలయముమొదలయినవాటికినిలకడగాగ్రామములోనుంచియిచ్చేశెలవుమొదలయినఖర్చులు.

సాలాబాదుగా adv. As usual. మామూలుగా. H. 4. 192. సాలాబాదుగనతండుసెలవుపుచ్చుకుండెన్.

సాలామిశ్రి usually సాలంమిశ్రి n. s. Salep. A nutritious nut which makes a glutinous kind of gruel. ఒకమందుదినుసు.

సాలీన n. s. i. e. سالیانه *Salyāna*. Yearly income. Annuity, yearly stipend. వర్షాశనము.

సాలీయానా or సాల్యానా adj. Annual, yearly. ఏట.

సాలు, సాల్, or సాలె n. s. سال *Sāl*. A year. సంవత్సరము. సాలుగుజస్తా last year. సాలేహాలు, సాలుమజాకూరు the present year. సాలాఖైరు the end of a year. సాలెఅయిందా the ensuing year.

శాలువ n. s. سال A shawl.

సాగువాపిట్ట n. s. The bird called a quail.

సాల్బసాల్ adv. سال بسال *Sāl-bā-sāl*. Annually. ఏటా, ప్రతిసంవత్సరము.

సాల్యాన adv. سالیانه *Salyāna*. Yearly. ఏటా (adj.) Annual. (ప్రతిసంవత్సరపు). సాల్యానలెక్క annual accounts.

సాల్యానా n. s. Annual income, annuity. వర్షాశనము.

సాళ్లు (for చాళ్లు plu. of చాలు) n. s. Furrows. లాంగలపద్ధతులు.

సావడచేప n. s. A kind of fish of the species called chimæra. మత్స్యవిశేషము.

సావధముచేయుట v. a. (error for సావధానముచేయుట.) To convince, bring him to his senses. స్మారకమువచ్చేటట్టుచేసుట.

సావరం n. s. *Sāvaram*. (Persian چاور *Chawar*.) A measure of land; *nominally* containing thirty *catties* (some contain only ten) each కత్తి being about 14 acres and 14 kuntas. i. e. acres $14\frac{7}{20}$. This mode of measurement is peculiar to zemindary land, in which *Sāvaram* signifies that part of the estate which the zemindar retains in his own hands; as discriminated from శేరి shēri q. v. which was land let out to tenants. Jaim. Bha. 6. 205.

శావి n. s. (Italian, and Portugueze, "chiavi") a key. తాళంచెవి.

సావిడాలు n. s. plu. A large kind of fish imported dry from Bombay. ఒకచేప.

శావిరం or షావిరం error for సౌవీరము n. s. which see. Ainslie. 2. 355.

సావిలివాండ్లు n. s. A sort of gypsies?

శావుకుడు or శావకుడు error for సేవకుడు * n. s. A servant.

సాహిత్యం n. s. (Error for సహాయము) Help.

శాహిది n. s. (for షాహిద్ شاهد *Shāhid.*) A witness. సాక్షి.

సాహుకారు n. s. ساهوكار *Sāhucār.* A banker or money broker.

సాహేబు n. s. صاحب *Saheb.* Master, owner. యజమానుడు.

సింగాడా for శృంగాటకా * n. s. An aquatic plant. (Trapa bispinosa) నీళ్లలోపెరిగే యొక్కచెట్టు. సింగాడికాయలు the nuts of this; which are like almonds.

సింగారి n. s. A sort of grain grown in Nagpoor. ధాన్యవిశేషము.

సింగోటి n. s. A pair of antelope's horns joined together, butt to butt, as one stick, pointed at each end. జింక కొమ్ములను రెండుకట్లా మొనలువుండేటట్టుగా చేర్చినఆయుధవిశేషము.

సింహాము or సింహాములక n. s. A timber. నరికి ఒక విధముగా చెక్కి తీర్చిన పేకుమాను.

శికస్తు or శికస్తుగావుండే adj. شکست Broken, ruined, burst. శిథిలమైన.

శికా or శిఖా n. s. سکه *Sicca.* A seal or impression, a die for coin, a stamped coin. ముద్ర. శిఖావుంగరము a ring with a seal.

సిఖాయించుట v. a. سکهانا *Sikhāna.* To teach, tutor, tamper with, to instigate. చదివించుట, నేర్పియుచ్చుట, దుర్బోధనచేసుట.

శికారా n. s. A hunting hawk. వేటాడేడేగ.

శికారి or సికారి n. s. شکاری *Sicāri.* Sporting, fowling, hunting: also an airing on foot, or horseback, a walk or ride. వేట, సవారి, కాలుసవారి. శికారిపోయినాడు he has gone out to walk or ride.

శికారి or శికారీ n. s. شکاری *Shicārī.* A huntsman, a fowler: a hunting hawk. వేటగాడు, వేటాడేవాడు, వేటాడేడేగ.

సికారు, or శిఖారు n. s. شکار (*Shikār.*) Game, hunting. An airing, a walk, drive, or stroll. వేట, కాలుసవారి, సవారి. శికారిపోవుట to go out for exercise, or to shoot.

శికిమీ or శిక్మీ adj. شکمی *Sicmi.* Subordinate; as a subdivision. శికిమీయిజారాదారుడు a sub-renter. లోగుత్తదారుడు. శికిమీ is equivalent to లో "in."

సిక్కా n. s. سکه *Sicca.* Seal, stamp, impression. This word is from the Italian or Turkish *Zecca.* i. e. the mint. ముద్ర. see శికా.

సిక్కువాడు n. s. A "Sikh" or Panjābī. శిఖదేశస్థుడు.

శిగ్రా or శిగ్రాపొడి n. s. A perfumed powder used in worship. ఒకతరహాగంధపొడి.

సిగనాలు or సిగనవక్కలు n. s. plu. Boiled betel nut. ఒకతరహావండినవక్కలు.

సిఢ్ఢాయము n. s. Savings in expenditure, embezzlement. అపహరించడము, అపహరించికూడబెట్టడము.

సిద్ది *Siddī* سیدی *Sīdī.* n. s. Abyssinian, negro. African, or black. The Siddees are a tribe of Mahomedans, inhabitants of Gogo in Guzerat.

సిపాయి or శిపాయి n. s. سپاهی *Sipāi.* A soldier usually Hindu or Musulman soldier. H. 5. 207.

సిఫారసు n. s. سفارش A recommendation.

సిబ్బంది n. s. سبندی *Sibbandi.* Rangers, militia. Armed peons, Irregular infantry. An establishment of clerks, peons &c. కట్టుబడివాండ్లు, బంట్రోతులు.

సిమ్మతు for సింత్ n. s. سمت *Simt* (vulgarly సమ్మతు *sammat.*) A quarter of the heaven. A hamlet.

సియ్యం adj. سیوم Third. మూడో.

సిరకా for సిర్కా n. s. سرکه *Sirca.* Vinegar. కాడి.

శిరస్తా n. s. سرشته *Sirasta.* Custom, usage. వాడుక.

శిరస్తా, శిరస్తాదారుడు or శిరస్తేదార్ n. s. سرشته دار *Serishtadār.* The head accountant or manager in a revenue office or Court. లెక్కలకుజవాబుదారుడుగావుండేపెద్దఉద్యోగస్థుడు.

శిరా n. s. شیره *Sirah.* Indian Ink; made of lampblack, gum, and sugar: as distinguished from (ఇంకి) English ink, made of galls and vinegar. The smell will always shew which is present: English ink which soon turns pale: but sira, made with lampblack never loses its colour. మషి.

శిరాజి n. s. and adj. شیرازی *Shirazi*. Brought from Shiraz. S. 1. 176. Swa. 4. 36. షీరాజనే దేశము, ఆదేశపుసొమ్ము.

శిరాన n. s. سرانا The tilt of a bed.

సిరిము n. s. See శిరము.

సిరు for సీర్ n. s. سر *Sir*. The head. Hence the words సిరుదేశముఖు *Sir-desmuk*, Sar-desmook, Sir-despondia and ser-canoongoi. Elph. p. 27.

సిర్క for సిర్ఖా n. s. *Sirca*. Vinegar. కాడి.

సిర్నామా n. s. سرنامه The direction or heading of a letter. వక్కణ.

సిలక n. s. A question. ప్రశ్న. Gordon, in Luke XX. 3. మీతో వొకసిలక అడుగుతున్నాను.

శిలభుచేప n. s. A kind of fish. మత్స్యవిశేషము. Russell. No. 100.

సిలసిల n. s. سلسله *Silsila*. Succession, series. వరంపర.

సిలసిల or సిలసిలగా adv. Successively, perpetually, in routine. క్రమముగా, వరంపరగా.

శిలుకు n. s. سلك *Silk*. Balance, outstanding money. సిలుకు or సిల్కు adj. Remaining. నిలవ. Reeve. సిలుకుబాకీ a remaining balance, sums yet unrealized.

శిలుము for చిలుం n. s. چلم A chillum for a hookah. హుక్కాలో నిప్పువేసేటిది.

సిలువ n. s. (from صلیب *Salīb*.) *Siluva*. The Cross. క్రీస్తునువేసినకొర్రు an expression which Pritchett uses in his Telugu Testament.

సిలేమానురాయి n. s. *Suleimānī*. Onyx. A stone used in burnishing.

సిలైసు n. s. (The English word) Slice తునక, తుండు, బద్ద.

శివకస్తిక, or శిందుగమాను n. s. See చిందుగచెట్టు.

సివాయి, or శివాయి adv. سوای *Siwāi*. Except, but, save, beyond. Extra, separately, besides. తప్ప.

శివాయి adv. سوای Besides, except. తప్ప. ఇది శివాయి besides this.

సివాయిజమ or శివాయిజమ n. s. سوای جمع Extra heads of Revenue. Extraordinaries (Malcolm.) more than the settled revenue.

శివారు or సివారు n. s. سوار *Siwār*. Fields and meadows lying around and appertaining to a village. గ్రామముచుట్టూవుండేపొలము, గ్రామముతో చేరినచేను.

శిసలు for సిసల్ adj. *Sisal*. Settled. నిర్ధారణమైన.

శిస్తు, or సిస్తు n. s. شست *Shist*. A land tax, assessment. కప్పము. రయాతుశిస్తు favourable assessment.

శిసాల adj. سه ساله *Sih sālah*. Triennial. మూడుయేండ్లకు వొకమాటువచ్చే.

శీకి or సీకి (for చివికి the participle of చివుకుట v. n.) Being rotten by water.

శీకు or సీకు n. s. (The English word.) "Sickness." అతనుశీకులో వున్నాడు he is unwell.

సీతదుక్కి n. s. Breaking up a field, ploughing it in winter against sowing next spring. ఎండకాలములో విత్తడమునకై వానకాలములో దున్నిపెట్టడము.

సీతభేది n. s. (Tamil சீதபேதி.) The disease Tenesmus. A slimy flux. చీముచీముగాఅయ్యే ప్రవర్తి.

సీదా adj. سیدها *Sīdha*. Right. న్యాయమైన, కుడి.

సీదా n. s. (i. e. సీదావృత్తి daily bread) Rice bestowed as alms in a raw uncooked state: provisions, undressed victuals: forage. See Kasiyātra page 119.

సీదాగా adv. Honestly, uprightly, rightly. న్యాయముగా, పెద్దమనిషితనముగా.

సీనె n. s. (سینا *Sīna*. Sewing.) The gore or lining at the girdle of a petticoat.

సీపి n. s. سیپی An oyster. గుల్ల.

సీరక or సీరుక n. s. A fabulous monster, or roc of vast size. Perhaps the same as సీరము a dragon.

సీరుక for సిర్కా n. s. Vinegar. కాడి.

సీరుకుడు n. s. A ploughman. కృషికుడు.

సీర్క n. s. سرکا Vinegar. కాడి.

సీసా n. s. شیشه Bottle, phial of glass. చిన్నబుడ్డి.

శీక్ష n. s. A wrong spelling for శిక్ష * punishment. దండన.

సుందులు n. s. A sort of grain. ధాన్యవిశేషము.

H. 4. 155. సన్నసుండులు another sort of this grain.

సుకాని for చుక్కాణి n. s. A rudder. వాడసుతిప్పేటిది.

సుకాలి or సుకాలివాండ్లు n. s. A sort of gypsies. ఒకతరహాలంబాడివాండ్లు.

సుక్తికటెలి n. s. (سکهی *Sukhti.*) A year without rain. వరపుగావుండేసంవత్సరము.

సుఖసంకథనవినోదంబునన్ or సుఖసంకథావినోదంబునన్ error for సుఖసత్కథావినోదంబునన్ When he was listening at ease to the sacred history.

సుగియలు n. s. A kind of cakes. భక్ష్యవిశేషము.

సుగ్గు or కడుపుసుగ్గు n. s. Bloody flux. నెత్తురుభేది.

సుజ్జి for సొజ్జి n. s. سوجی *Sūjī.* A mess or dish made of grits of roasted rice. See సొజ్జ.

సుఝుగు, జూఝుగు or జూదుగు n. s. Cheating. మోసము.

సుఝుగుట v. a. To cheat, over-reach. మోసపుచ్చుట. HK. 4. 184.

సుతరాం or సుతలాము adv. Totally, utterly. బొత్తుగా, ఒడసారము.

సుతారించుట v. a. To manage. To look after, take care of. నిర్వహించుట.

సుదామదు or శుదామద్ n. s. and adj. (perhaps from شد *Shud* it is; and آمد *āmad* it comes) Custom, usage, customary, usual. వాడుక, మామూలు, వాడుకైన, మామూలైన. సుదామదుప్రకారముగా according to custom.

సుదారించుట v. a. To manage. నిర్వహించుట.

సుద్ద for శుద్ధ adj. Utter, downright. వట్టి.

సుద్దా adv. Also, even. Likewise, too, including. కూడా.

సుధారించుట v. a. To manage. నిర్వహించుట.

సునామణి or సునావణి n. s. سنانا *Sunāna* Reading out or reciting. చదువుట. సునావణిచేయుట to read aloud. నాఅర్జిసునావణిఅయినదా has my petition been read out?

సునాసంగా error for సునాయాసముగా adv. Easily, lightly. సులభముగా, అవలీలగా.

సునుగుట v. a. See సుఝుగుట.

సున్నచేయబడ్డవాడు n. s. An insignificant fellow. a nobody. వ్యర్థుడు.

సున్నతి n. s. سنت Circumcision. తురకలుచుల్లికాయకొనతోలునుకోసుకోవడము.

సున్నాంగి n. s. The same as చున్నాంబి which see.

సుబరకేళి n. s. *Subar-kēli.* The kelson or plank lying on a vessel's keel.

సుబా n. s. صوبه *Subah.* A sooba or province. రాజ్యము.

సుబేదార్ or సుబేదారుడు n. s. A subadar. Governor of a province. In the modern army a sergeant or native captain. "Subadar Colonel Munro Saheb," Sir Thomas Munro.

సుబ్రహ్మణ్యము * n. s. The name of a certain river; a sort of bastard ruby found there?

శుమారు or సుమార్ شمار *Sumār.* prep. About. సు॥ రు॥ ౨౦౦ i. e. సుమారురూపాయలుఇన్నూరు About Rupees 200. సుమారుగావున్నాడు he is pretty well now, he is rather better to-day. శుమారుగారా come gently, fair and softly. సుమారుపదిరోజులు about ten days.

సురిపెట్టె or సురుగులపెట్టె properly సొరుగులపెట్టె n. s. A chest of drawers.

సురీ n. s. سوري Name of a country. Syria?

సురుగు or సురుగుచెట్టు A cypress tree?

సురుమాయి n. s. سرما *Surmā.* Collyrium. కాటుక, అంజనము. Bhanumati. 4. 21.

శురువు, సురు or సురువు n. s. شروع Commencement. ఆరంభము.

సులాకి, or సులాకు n. s. The dent in coin: the mint mark. రూపాయిమీదపడేపొకగురుతు. From سلاک *Sallāk.* an ingot.

సులువు, or సులూ adj. Corrupted from సులభము Easy.

సుల్తాను n. s. سلتان *Sultan.* A sultan or Musulman prince. తురకదొర. Vemana. 814.

సుసీలుచేయుట v. a. To rectify, to reform?

సుస్తి adj. and n. s. سست سستي Lazy, Laziness. సోమారి, సోమారితనము.

సూనరి n. s. A flower seller. పూలమ్మేవాడు. M. XII. 1. 357. సూనరియన్నంబుజూదరియన్నంబు.

సూరతు n. s. سورت Features. But in Bobbili 3. 66. సూరతుమందుగుండ్లు means brought from Surat. సూరతుముత్యాలు very fine pearls brought from the same country.

సూరతుకొడుకు or సూరత్ సంబంధమైనకొడుకు n. s. From *Sūrat zāda*. A natural son, one by a concubine. ఉంచుకొన్నదానికిపుట్టిన కొడుకు.

సూళె n. s. (Tamil சூளை.) A kiln (of bricks.) ఇటికెలఆవము.

సూళెచేకటులు or సూలచేకట్లు n. s. A sort of bracelet. కంకణవిశేషము. S. 1. 176. సూలచేకటులొకమూలలవైచి.

సూళెరాయి n. s. Jasper. ఒకతరహారత్నరాయి.

సూత్రం n. s. vulgar error for సూత్రము which see.

సెంగోలు n. s. See చెంగోలు or సింగోలము.

సెక్తి error for శక్తి * n. s. Power, ability. బలిమి.

సెమ్మె n. s. شمع *Shamma*. A candlestick. దీపస్తంభము.

సెలగ n. s. *Selaga*. A word used in measuring grain A double handful of grain, "One lot;" from which a new reckoning begins. The handful or pinch of grain put down as a mark of reckoning. కొలిచేటప్పుడు సేరలకొకటి అనిఅరిచి కొలుచునప్పుడు గుర్తుగానుంచే దోసెడుగింజలు. From the Arabic "Silqa" سلقہ See Burckhardt's Nubia, 4to. p. 234. q. v.

సెలగుల్లాడుట v. n. To play pranks or tricks.

సేంబా or సేంబారోగము n. s. *Sēmbā*. The glanders. గుర్రమునకువచ్చేఒకరోగము.

సేకరముచేసుట v. a. To collect, accumulate, usually, to earn, get. జాగ్రతచేసుట.

సేకాడా usually సేకడా adv. Per-centum (Mahr. in Bellari.)

సేటు n. s. Set. The title assumed by Guzrati bankers, saocars.

సేటుసంది n. s. "Landed militia." Elphinstone p. 11.

సేపించుట Vulgar for చేయించుట (causal of చేయుట) v. a. To make. A rustic ballad says కొత్తసింబాలంటనే, సేపించిందికత్తెరివాడంటనే.

సేబథళ్ళాయి n. s. (Perhaps for చెంబడితాయ?) A scate. మత్స్యవిశేషము. Russell on fishes. No. 5.

సేబాసు interj. شاباش *Shabash*. Well done! Bravo!

సేరి n. s. *Sherī*: or *Serī*; Free land: which though not Inaum pays no *direct* tax to Government. Land rented by a farmer from a Zemindar or possessor of a Manyam, and free of tax to government. "Land which pays no money rent, but a portion of the crop is taken as payment in kind." Vide Judicial Selections Vol. IV. 739-740, and also Elphinstone's Report on the Peishwa's Territories p. 41. also his appendix page XXIV. But in all these places the definitions are not quite exact. In the Rajahmandri district *Sheri* merely means land which is *not* Inaum. Land which is free of *direct* tax. See note on సొవరము.

సేరిమాను n. s. A certain tree. Rox. 2. 442.

సేరు n. s. *Sēr*. A *seer*; a weight of eight తులములు, or eight Indian ounces. పరిమాణం. పక్కాసేరు a large seer equal to 96 Rupees weight. కచ్చాసేరు or కచ్చాసేరు a seer of 30 Rupees weight.

సేవెలు n. s. *Sēvēl*. Vermicelli. A kind of grain. మణుగుపూలు, ధాన్యవిశేషమున్ను.

సేషి * n. s. *Sēshī*. (Vaishnava cant.) An epithet of God. దేవుడు. శేషితిరువళ్ళముఅట్లాయుండినది it was the will of providence.

సై n. s. *Sai*. A year. సంవత్సరము.

సైడు, or సైడ్డు n. s. (an English word) A "side" or page.

సైతాంగవాయి n. s. *Saitān gavai*. A mast made all of one piece; not the topmast separate.

సైను n. s. 'Sign'. i. e. Signature. సైనుచేయుట to sign.

సైరు usually సాయరు n. s. Seyr. The transit duty on goods. సుంకము.

సైలోను n. s. 'Ceylon.' సింహళద్వీపి.

సైసు interj. *Sais!* Stop! stay! నిలిచింటు.

సొంటి n. s. See సుంటి.

సొంటిముండ n. s. A scurvy wretch?

సొగసా or సొగుసా n. s. Pinchbeck: a composition of gold and copper called Tambāc. See Rottler page 384.

సొనాయి n. s. usually సన్నాయి A sort of clarinet.

సొనాయించుట v. a. سنانا *Sanāna*. To read or recite.

సొనారు for సోనార్ n. s. سنار A goldsmith. కంసాలవాడు.

సొన్నా n. s. سونا Gold. బంగారు.

సొన్నాయి n. s. سنائي A sort of clarinet or rather hautboy. See proofs in Buch. E. I. 601. plate and explanation.

సొన్నారి n. s. سوناري The trade of a goldsmith.

సొరంతలేదు (for స్మరంత) There is not the least bit.

సొసాయించుట v. a. سنانا To persuade, talk over, encourage. To cheer, welcome. మందలించుట.

సోంటా n. s. سونٹا *Sonta.* A mace or curved stick carried by palankeen bearers &c. సోంటా కఱ్ఱ.

సోజరు n. s. (The English word) a soldier.

సోణ n. s. The tip? ముక్కుసోణ The tip of the nose.

సోణంగినాయి n. s. (Tamil) An Arab greyhound. See జోనంగికుక్క.

సోదా or శోధా n. s. سودا Searching, overhauling. పరిశోధించడము.

సోదాచూచుట v. a. سوداديكهنا To overhaul or search. పరిశోధించుట.

శోధ for శోధన * n. s. Search, enquiry, trial. Refining, purifying. వెదకడము, విమర్శ, శుద్ధి చేయడము.

సోపుగావుంచుట v. a. To embalm. శవముకుల్లిపోకుండాపరిమళద్రవ్యములనుపుంచికాపాడుట.

సోబతు n. s (vulgarly సోబతి.) صحبت *Sohbat.* Accompanying, being a guard. Intimacy: keeping company. Escort, convoy. తోడు.

సోమారివాండ్లు n. s. A sort of vagrants in Madras who subsist on leavings. "Gentlemen; idlers."

సోమాసి n. s. (K.) A kind of sweetmeat. An instrument used in making this sweetmeat.

సోరంగచేప n. s. "*Soring.*" A certain fish. Russell No. CXIII. A species of Sparus?

సోరవా n. s. شوربا Broth, also called సూపు "soup."

సోల n. s. چولا A sort of waistcoat.

శోళకం or శోళగం n. s. *Sholagam.* A dry hot wind. The south wind which the English call the long shore wind. (Guntoor.)

సోలతు, సోల్తి or సోలత్తు n. s. *Sholti.* Agency in bribery: a go between: intervention.

సోల్జరువాండ్లు, or సోల్జరులు n. s. Soldiers. "soldats." Bobbili. 3. 107.

సౌఖండీసావడి n. s. چوکهنڈي A particular building. ఒకకట్టడము.

సౌతు or సవతు n. s. A match, a pattern, specimen, sample. మాదిరి.

సౌత్తు n. s. *Sautu.* Model, pattern, fashion. తురకసౌత్తు Musulman fashion. See సౌతు.

సౌదా n. s. سودا Traffic, trade. Goods, wares, commodities. వర్తకము, సరుకులున్ను.

సౌదాగరు n. s. سوداگر A merchant, a trader. Also a horse dealer. వర్తకుడు, గుర్రాలవర్తకుడు.

సౌరతుణ n. s. A mistake for సంరతుణ which see.

స్టాటువరహా or పరింగివరహా n. s. French coin valued at 36 fanams or 45 annas ఫ్రెంచినాణ్యము.

స్టాంపు n. s. (the English word stamp.) ముద్ర. స్టాంపులు stamped papers.

స్థానాపతి n. s. A mediator. మధ్యవర్తి.

స్థానాపత్యము n. s. Mediatorial functions. మధ్యస్థము, మధ్యస్థత.

స్థిరద్రవ్యము * n. s. Real property, land and house.

స్థోమతు n. s. A false spelling for తోమత్తు which see.

స్పృష్టి or స్రుష్టి n. s. Impurity occasioned by the decease of a relative. ఆశౌచము.

స్యాయి for శ్యాయి n. s. سياهي Ink made with lamp black. మసి.

స్రష్టి n. s. vulgar error for సృష్టి which see.

శ్రావించుట * v. a. To read to. వినిపించుట.

శ్రోత్రియము * n. s. A favourable assessement. స్వల్పముగాతీసుకొనేపన్ను.

స్వర్గ n. s. Error for సర్గ a chapter or canto.

స్వల్పించుట v. n. To draw to a close, decrease,

lighten, go off, as a fever. తేల్పుపడుట, తొలంచుట.

సాఫారం usually సరసాఫారము n. s. (a low bad word) The whole. యావత్తు.

స్వారి i. e. సవారి n. s. سواری Riding, going abroad, a drive, an airing. A conveyance. Utt. Haris. 4. 22. కాలుసవారి walking a foot. గుఱ్ఱపుసవారి riding.

స్వారు n. s. سوار *Sawār*. Riders, troopers, horsemen. సాదులు, అనగా తురుకువాండ్లు.

హ H. This letter is sometimes dropped as an initial as Ukum for حکم *Hukum* : it sometimes is transposed as hāshām for احشام *ahshām*. Ibrahim becomes ఇభ్రాం Ibhram.

హంకరింపు n. s. The act of drawing or pulling out. ఈడ్వడము, గుంజడము ? See అంకారించుట.

హంగామా n. s. ہنگام The working season, time, period.

హంగామి adj. ہنگامی Temporary, for the time being. తాత్కాలికమైన, సిద్ధ్యాపుండే. హంగామిసిబ్బంది a temporary establishment.

హండా n. s. ہنڈا A brass boiler or great kettle. చరువము.

హండి n. s. ہنڈی A small cooking pot. కుండ.

హంశం, హంశము Error for అంశము n. s. Share, portion.

హంసాయి n. s. ہمسایہ A neighbour. ఇరుగుపొరుగువాడు. హంసాయిదస్తుఖత్తులు the signatures of the neighbours, affixed to a statement made by all.

హంసాయిగ్రామం n. s. A neighbouring village. పొరుగూరు.

హాకామి n. s. حاکمی *Hākĭmĭ*. Authority. హాకామిచేసిపోయెను he took upon himself to go. స్వతంత్రించిపోయినాడు.

హాకీకతు or హాకీఖతు n. s. حقیقت Account, statement, representation of occurrences or affairs. Facts, matters. వృత్తాంతము, సంగతి.

హక్కయిన adj. حق Rightful, due. బాధ్యతగల.

హక్కస్సు n. s. عکس Spite, opposition. Hatred. పగ. హక్కస్సుతీర్చుకోవడము to revenge himself.

హక్కు n. s. حق Lawful right or title. బాధ్యత.

హక్కుదారుడు n. s. حقدار Owner, proprietor. బాధ్యుడు.

హక్కుదావా n. s. حق دعوا *Hak dawa*. A statement of rights, a bill of dues. A claim. బాధ్యతనుగురించినమనవి.

హక్కుశాయి or హక్కుహంసాయి n. s. A neighbour, coparcener.

హజరతు حضرت His honour, his reverence. హజరతుమన్రోసాహేబులవారు his honour Colonel Munro.

హజారము n. s. حضور A court, where persons of distinction sit. కొలువుకూటము. Radha. 2. 150.

హజీరా n. s. A certain pot-herb?

హజ్జుబజారిధరకాడికి adv. Error for *arz*, ارزبازاری At the market price. అంగడిధరప్రకారము.

హటకరి n. s. (*Hatakari.*) A certain subdivision of the weaver caste.

హడ్డి for అడ్డి n. s. Hindrance, check. ఆటంకము.

హత్యారు n. s. ہتھیار Instrument, tool.

హద్దు n. s. حد Boundary. Limit, term. హద్దుమహద్దులు from side to side.

హమాంబాబత్తు n. s. ہمہ بابت Grand total.

హమేషా adv. ہمیشہ Continually, always. ఎల్లప్పుడు.

హయ్యాం, హయ్యాను n. s. ایام *Ayyām*. Period, season, time, days, reign. కాలము..

హరకార n. s. ہرکارا A messenger or courier. సమాచారముతెచ్చేబంటు.

హరణఖరణశక్తిచొప్పున adv. By tooth and nail. యావచ్ఛక్తిని.

హరాంజాద adj. حرامزادہ Wicked, vicious దుష్ట. హరాంజాదగుర్రము n. s. A wicked horse. దుష్టగుర్రము.

హరామి adj. حرامی Wicked, vicious. దుష్ట.

హరిగోలు n. s. (K.) A small boat. Suca. 3. 288. హరిగోలుగుంపునావనజంబులలతిగాడ్పునదెలించు.

హరు adj. ہر *Har*. Each, every. ప్రతి.

హరుకు (K.) adj. Torn, rent ; n. s. A tear or rent. చింపి, తుంటు, తునక.

హరోల్ n. s. (*Harāval* هراول a Turkish word.) The van. సేనాముఖము, దండుయొక్క ముందరి భాగము.

హర్కతు for హరకతు n. s. حرکت Opposition, hindrance. ఆటంకము.

హర్కారా n. s. هرکاره Messenger, courier, spy. వార్తావహుడు, వేగువాడు.

హర్గిజ adv. هرگز Ever, at all, not by any means.

హర్జీ n. s. Error for అర్జీ. عرضي.

హర్దొహిస్సా n. s. هردوحصه *Har-do-hissa.* The whole, undivided gross produce. ఇరుగోరులు.

హర్రాస్తా adv. هرراستا Every way. ప్రతిదారి.

హర్ర adj. هر Every, each. ప్రతి.

హాళస్తి adj. Open, unconfined, roomy. విశాలమైన. ఈయిల్లుహాళస్తిగానున్నది this house is commodious or spacious.

హలాకు or అల్లాక్ adj. هلاک *Hallāk.* Ruined, destroyed, lost, slain. నాశముచేయబడ్డ, హతముచేయబడ్డ, చంపబడ్డ. హలాకౌట v. n. To be killed, perish, be fatigued. చంపబడుట, చచ్చుట, డయ్యుట.

హలేకార్లు n. s plu. اهل‌کار *Ahl-i-kar.* People, attendants, menials.

హల్కా adj. هلکا Mean, base, low, inferior. Light, trifling, vulgar. నీచమైన, అల్పమైన, క్షుద్రమైన. హల్కావాడు n. s. A mean, despicable man. అల్పుడు.

హల్లా n. s. هله *Halla.* Scaling a fort. Assault, escalade. (J. C. M.) హల్లాచేసుట to scale a fort. లగ్గయెక్కుట.

హల్లు adv. هلو *Hallu.* Gently, softly, slowly. తిన్నగా.

హవాయి for అవాయి n. s. (H.) هوای Alarm, consternation. దిగులు, తల్లడము. హవాయిదస్తు money collected by consternations.

హవాల్ error for అహ్వాలు n. s. احوال State, condition, circumstances. స్థితి.

హవాలా n. s. حواله Charge. అతనిహవాలాచేసినారు they committed it to him.

హవుజు or హౌదు n. s. حوض *Hawz.* A basin, tank, bath, fountain. A particular metal vessel for heating or holding water.

హవేలీ n. s. حویلی *Havēlī.* A mansion, a palace. నగరు. హవేలీతోట a royal garden. హవేలి గ్రామములు villages which were formerly kept in the hands of the Nabob or in his immediate management.

హాశ్శీలు for హాశీలు n. s. حاصل Duty payable: tax. పన్ను.

హషం n. s. حشم Train, equipage, suite. The plural is احشام *Ahsham.* Followers. హషాం బంట్రోతు a peon in attendance, a sort of militia man.

హషు adj. حشو Petty, trifling.

హషుంవజా n. s. "Deduction of a complete head or whole item. Bellary." A poor definition. It seems to be meant for హషొవజ حشووضع *Hash-vaza.* i. e. పైనవజాచేయబడ్డది (Cud.) A mode of keeping accounts: the net sum being entered in the books instead of the gross.

హాశిను n. s. حسن *Hasan?* "Black land in a state of cultivation." (Bellary.)

హాకిము n. s. حکیم (Dobbili.) Master, ruler. ధణి.

హాజరు or హాజర్ adj. حاضر Present, ready. హాజరుజామీను bail for producing a culprit.

హాజరుబాషి n. s. حاضرباشي Attendance. కనిపెట్టియుండడము.

హాజీలు or హాజీర్లై for హాజర్ adv. حاضر Ready, present. సిద్ధముగా. Satya. 2. 133. 186.

హాట్కరదా or హాటఖర్డ n. s. (Marata.) A rough account.

హాతూప్చిహిసాబు n. s. *Hath pūchi hisāb.* A rough account?

హామి n. s. حامي *Hāmī.* A protector or defender. Assurance, the confirmation or ratification (to an engagement :) afforded by a third person's pledging himself to the fulfilment of it. హామితక్కావి n. s. Advances for cultivation on the responsibility of the third person. జామీనుమీదయిచ్చేవారకము.

హామిషం n. s. Food, maintenance, means. అన్నము, జీవనాధారము, బండవలము.

హాలసాలు for హాల్సాల్ n. s. حال‌سال The current year. నడిచేసంవత్సరము.

హాలి or హాలీ adv. حالي At present. ప్రస్తుతమందు, ఇప్పట్లో.

హాలు adj. حال Current. నడిచే.

హాలున adv. At present. ఇప్పట్లో.

హాలికారు n. s. plu. *Ahlicār.* اهل کار Official servants. ఉద్యోగస్థులు, ఖంట్రోతులు.

హాశ్చర్యం, or ఆశ్చర్యం for ఆశ్చర్యము * n. s. Surprise, astonishment.

హాశ్శిలు, హాసీలు or హాసీల్ n. s. حاصل Customs, duty payable, tax.

హాస్పత్రి or ఆశుపత్రి n. s. A hospital. రోగులుండేయిల్లు.

హిక్మా n. s. اغماض *Hikma.* Error for Ighmaz.

హిక్మాయించుట (Hikmāinchi. error for ighmazi اغماضي Scornfulness.) v. a. To refuse, scorn, disobey.

హిజారు n. s. ازار *Izār.* అనగాగుడిక Short breeches. Suca. 1. 190. H. 4. 107.

హిజిరి n. s. هجري The Mohemedan æra. తురక సంవత్సరము.

హిమ్మత్తు n. s. همت Boldness, courage. Aid: instigation.

హిసాబు or హిస్సాబు n. s. حساب An account. లెక్క. హిసాబెనివాడా n. s. (Lit: an account of the settlement.) As (or on account of) the ryot's portion in the crops. See నివాడా.

హిసేబు n. s. See హిసాబు. حساب

హిస్సా n. s. حصه *Hissa.* A share or portion. భాగము.

హీనరాశి n. s. The lowest part of the rick or heap: where the grain is not clean (?)

హీర్ష n. s. Error for ఈర్ష్య.

హీలా for హిలా n. s. (*Hila.*) حيله Stratagem, trick, deceit, artifice. వంచన, మోసము.

హు॥ i. e. హుకుం Command, order.

హుండా n. s. "An estate." A canton? Thus వాల్తేరుహుండాప్రభువుటరు the Proprietor of the Waltair Estate.

హుండామునగా adv. In the lump or gross.

హుండావణి n. s. هنداوني The price paid upon a bill of exchange.

హుండి n. s. هندى A bill of exchange, a box for money received, (particularly in a pagoda,) like the poors' box. Or, at a custom house.

హుకుం n. s. حكم *Hukm.* An order. ఆజ్ఞ.

హుకుమత్ n. s. حكمت Orders. See Reg. V. of 1827 page 3, line 14.

హుజూరు n. s. حضور *Huzūr.* The presence. Court. Audience chamber. సముఖము, సముఖము.

హుజ్జత్ or, హుజితు حجت *Hujjat.* n. s. Perverse wrangling, objecting or making difficulties. Violent disputing, rebelling. హుజ్జతుచేయుటి to bully.

హుటావళీ for హుట్టువళి (K.) n. s. The produce of a field or of trade. The amount of an assessment. పుట్టుబడి

హుటాహుటిగా adv. Swiftly. త్వరగా.

హుటాహుటిప్రయాణము n. s. A forced march. From اٹهااٹهي ootha oothee.

హుట్టువళి n. s. (K.) Proceeds, collections. See హుటావళీ.

హుతాళి for ఉత్తాళము n. s. (K.) Haste, precipitancy. ఆతురము. పోయినశుక్రవారమునాడుసముద్రముహిండాహుతాళిగావుండినది last Friday the sea was boisterous.

హుత్తేరె or హుత్తేరి interj. *Hut Tère*: an indefinite imprecative exclamation.

హుమ్మస్సు n. s. (Error for *Himmat*?) Arrogance, self-conceit. గర్వము.

హురుమత్తు n. s. حرمت *Hurmat.* Honour, chastity, esteem. See ధూర్జటిచెప్పినకృష్ణరాయవిజయము. 1. 71.

హుశ్యారు for హుష్యార్ adj. هشيار Alert, active, watchful, careful.

హుషారు or హుష్యార్ n. s. هشياري Smartness attentiveness. Cleverness, readiness, wariness. జాగరూకత, జాగ్రత.

హెబ్బారు n. s. (K.) A chief or head man. హెబ్బారువరు a chief Vaishnavite bramin: a class of bramins so called.

హేజీబు n. s. (حجيب *Hejēb*?) A clerk? a writer? See Kirabahattari page 22. I suppose it comes from حجاب porter or chamberlain.

హోరియా or హోలీ حيله n. s. Trick, pretence. అక్కడయిక్కడ హోరియాలుచేసుకొంటూ idling away the time.

హోష్ఖరము or హోక్కరము n. s. Cause, ground, reason, sign. యిదివానకుహోష్కరముగావున్నది this is a symptom of rain.

హైబతు n. s. هيبت *Haibat.* Perturbation, distress. కొంచలము, వైకల్యము.

హైరాను adj. *Hairān.* حيران Bewildered, at a loss, deserted. At his wits end. In confusion. నన్నుతిట్టికొట్టిహైరానుచేసి they bullied and harried and worried me.

హొజీరు n. s. See వజీరు.

హొదా or హోదా n. s. عهده Employ, office, duty, rank. హోదాదారు an employé, an officer.

హోరుగాలి n. s. (K?) A tempest, a gale. బలమైనగాలి.

హోళిగ usually పోళి n. s. (K.) A broad round cake made of wheat flour, and filled with boiled pease, sugar &c.

హోళిపండుగ n. s. The HOELI feast, held at the beginning of the vernal equinox: in which the Hindus throw coloured powder over each other. Broughton describes it in his Mahratta Camp and writes it HOHLEE. It commences on the date వసంతపంచమి and lasts about six weeks. But it is held in the ten days preceding full moon in the month Phalguna, commencing on the eighth day of the bright fortnight and ending on the night of the full moon. See Memoir in Bengal Chronicle, republished by Pogson in his History of the Boondelas. Calcutta 1828, p. 72.

హోషు n. s. هوش *Hōsh.* Senses, consciousness, sprightliness. బేహోషు *behosh* بيهوش out of his senses. హోషుతప్పినతర్వాత after he became senseless.

హోష్యారు or, హుషారు هوشيار *Hoshyār.* adj. In his senses, alert.

హోహో interj. (Mahr.) Yes! Yes! for అవు, అవు.

హౌదా n. s. هودة *Hauda.* A seat on an elephant. Bunj. 1.123.

ఝరీ چهري A switch.

ఝేమించుట See ఝమించుట.

SUPPLEMENT.

చందు n. s. چند *A preposition used with dates* "On" Thus చందు ౨౬ మాహెఅక్టోబరు "On" the 26th of October.

బారబలావతీలు n. s. plu. باره بلوتي The twelve hereditary servants of a village. ఆయగాండ్లు Thus, నంబివాడు, రెడ్డి, కరణము, పారోహితుడు, తలారి, వడ్లవాడు, కమ్మరవాడు, కుమ్మరవాడు, చాకలవాడు, మంగలవాడు, మాలవాడు, మాదిగవాడు These twelve are, The officiating priest in a Vishnu temple, the head farmer, the town clerk, the village priest, the watchman, the carpenter, the blacksmith, the potmaker, whitster, barber, pariar, and cobbler.

THE END.